CLASSICAL COMEDY 1508–1786
A LEGACY FROM ITALY AND FRANCE

LEGENDA

LEGENDA is the Modern Humanities Research Association's book imprint for new research in the Humanities. Founded in 1995 by Malcolm Bowie and others within the University of Oxford, Legenda has always been a collaborative publishing enterprise, directly governed by scholars. The Modern Humanities Research Association (MHRA) joined this collaboration in 1998, became half-owner in 2004, in partnership with Maney Publishing and then Routledge, and has since 2016 been sole owner. Titles range from medieval texts to contemporary cinema and form a widely comparative view of the modern humanities, including works on Arabic, Catalan, English, French, German, Greek, Italian, Portuguese, Russian, Spanish, and Yiddish literature. Editorial boards and committees of more than 60 leading academic specialists work in collaboration with bodies such as the Society for French Studies, the British Comparative Literature Association and the Association of Hispanists of Great Britain & Ireland.

The MHRA encourages and promotes advanced study and research in the field of the modern humanities, especially modern European languages and literature, including English, and also cinema. It aims to break down the barriers between scholars working in different disciplines and to maintain the unity of humanistic scholarship. The Association fulfils this purpose through the publication of journals, bibliographies, monographs, critical editions, and the MHRA Style Guide, and by making grants in support of research. Membership is open to all who work in the Humanities, whether independent or in a University post, and the participation of younger colleagues entering the field is especially welcomed.

ALSO PUBLISHED BY THE ASSOCIATION

Critical Texts
Tudor and Stuart Translations • *New Translations* • *European Translations*
MHRA Library of Medieval Welsh Literature

MHRA Bibliographies
Publications of the Modern Humanities Research Association

The Annual Bibliography of English Language & Literature
Austrian Studies
Modern Language Review
Portuguese Studies
The Slavonic and East European Review
Working Papers in the Humanities
The Yearbook of English Studies

www.mhra.org.uk
www.legendabooks.com

ITALIAN PERSPECTIVES

Editorial Committee
Professor Simon Gilson, University of Oxford (General Editor)
Dr Francesca Billiani, University of Manchester
Professor Manuele Gragnolati, Université Paris-Sorbonne
Dr Catherine Keen, University College London
Professor Martin McLaughlin, Magdalen College, Oxford

Founding Editors
Professor Zygmunt Barański and Professor Anna Laura Lepschy

In the light of growing academic interest in Italy and the reorganization of many university courses in Italian along interdisciplinary lines, this book series, founded by Maney Publishing under the imprint of the Northern Universities Press and now continuing under the Legenda imprint, aims to bring together different scholarly perspectives on Italy and its culture. *Italian Perspectives* publishes books and collections of essays on any period of Italian literature, language, history, culture, politics, art, and media, as well as studies which take an interdisciplinary approach and are methodologically innovative.

APPEARING IN THIS SERIES

20. *Ugo Foscolo and English Culture*, by Sandra Parmegiani
21. *The Printed Media in Fin-de-siècle Italy: Publishers, Writers, and Readers*, ed. by Ann Hallamore Caesar, Gabriella Romani, and Jennifer Burns
22. *Giraffes in the Garden of Italian Literature: Modernist Embodiment in Italo Svevo, Federigo Tozzi and Carlo Emilio Gadda*, by Deborah Amberson
23. *Remembering Aldo Moro: The Cultural Legacy of the 1978 Kidnapping and Murder*, ed. by Ruth Glynn and Giancarlo Lombardi
24. *Disrupted Narratives: Illness, Silence and Identity in Svevo, Pressburger and Morandini*, by Emma Bond
25. *Dante and Epicurus: A Dualistic Vision of Secular and Spiritual Fulfilment*, by George Corbett
26. *Edoardo Sanguineti: Literature, Ideology and the Avant-Garde*, ed. by Paolo Chirumbolo and John Picchione
27. *The Tradition of the Actor-Author in Italian Theatre*, ed. by Donatella Fischer
28. *Leopardi's Nymphs: Grace, Melancholy, and the Uncanny*, by Fabio A. Camilletti
29. *Gadda and Beckett: Storytelling, Subjectivity and Fracture*, by Katrin Wehling-Giorgi
30. *Caravaggio in Film and Literature: Popular Culture's Appropriation of a Baroque Genius*, by Laura Rorato
31. *The Italian Academies 1525-1700: Networks of Culture, Innovation and Dissent*, ed. by Jane E. Everson, Denis V. Reidy and Lisa Sampson
32. *Rome Eternal: The City As Fatherland*, by Guy Lanoue
33. *The Somali Within: Language, Race and Belonging in 'Minor' Italian Literature*, by Simone Brioni
34. *Laughter from Realism to Modernism: Misfits and Humorists in Pirandello, Svevo, Palazzeschi, and Gadda*, by Alberto Godioli
35. *Pasolini after Dante: The 'Divine Mimesis' and the Politics of Representation*, by Emanuela Patti

Managing Editor
Dr Graham Nelson, 41 Wellington Square, Oxford OX1 2JF, UK
www.legendabooks.com

Antique bust of Menander (c. 342–290 BCE), arguably the father of classical comedy. Few of his works now survive; but the Latin plays of Plautus and Terence were known to be based on his Athenian 'New Comedy' genre. Italian Humanist comedies drew in their turn on Plautus and Terence.

Classical Comedy 1508-1786

A Legacy from Italy and France

RICHARD ANDREWS

Italian Perspectives 55
Modern Humanities Research Association
2022

*Published by Legenda
an imprint of the Modern Humanities Research Association
Salisbury House, Station Road, Cambridge CB1 2LA*

*ISBN 978-1-83954-097-4 (HB)
ISBN 978-1-83954-098-1 (PB)*

First published 2022

All rights reserved. No part of this publication may be reproduced or disseminated or transmitted in any form or by any means, electronic, mechanical, photocopying, recording or otherwise, or stored in any retrieval system, or otherwise used in any manner whatsoever without written permission of the copyright owner, except in accordance with the provisions of the Copyright, Designs and Patents Act 1988, or under the terms of a licence permitting restricted copying issued in the UK by the Copyright Licensing Agency Ltd, Saffron House, 6–10 Kirby Street, London EC1N 8TS, England, or in the USA by the Copyright Clearance Center, 222 Rosewood Drive, Danvers MA 01923. Application for the written permission of the copyright owner to reproduce any part of this publication must be made by email to legenda@mhra.org.uk.

Disclaimer: Statements of fact and opinion contained in this book are those of the author and not of the editors or the Modern Humanities Research Association. The publisher makes no representation, express or implied, in respect of the accuracy of the material in this book and cannot accept any legal responsibility or liability for any errors or omissions that may be made.

Trademark notice: Product or corporate names may be trademarks or registered trademarks, and are used only for identification and explanation without intent to infringe.

© Modern Humanities Research Association 2022

Copy-Editor: Charlotte Wathey

CONTENTS

	Acknowledgements	ix
	List of Illustrations	x
	Chronology	xi
	Introduction	1
	PART I: NARRATIVE	
1	Roman Models and Greek Precepts	13
2	Italian *commedia erudita*	16
3	Italian *commedia dell'arte*	23
4	Italy in France, 1540–1604	27
5	Comedy in Italy, 1600–1700	33
6	Comedy in Paris, 1600–60	38
7	French Classical Theory: Italy Plagiarized by France	43
8	Molière between 1660 and 1673	48
9	Comédie-Française and Théâtre-Italien, 1660–1760	53
10	'French' and 'Italian' Styles of Comedy	59
11	Marivaux and Eighteenth-Century France	67
12	Comic Opera: Italy into France?	73
13	France in Italy: Carlo Goldoni (1707–1793)	78
14	Figaro from Beaumarchais to Da Ponte	84
15	Alternatives to Classical Comedy	91
16	Break-up and Aftermath	96
	PART II: ANALYSES	
17	The Content and Function of Comedy	101
18	Component Parts, I: Roman Dramaturgy	117
19	Component Parts, II: Italian Improvisation	129
20	Observance of *classiciste* Rules	144
21	Comedies and their Societies: Satire?	159
22	Characters and Masks	177
23	Children and Parents	195
24	Women and Men	207
25	Servants and Masters	227
26	Disguise and Mistaken Identity	241
27	Erudite and Artisan Comedy	255
	Bibliography	271
	Index	283

For Gillie, Bridget and Greg
as always and for ever

ACKNOWLEDGEMENTS

All translations into English in this volume are mine, unless otherwise credited.

During more than four decades I have read early editions of plays and scenarios in academic libraries in London (British Library), Venice (Biblioteca Marciana and Biblioteca Correr), Oxford (Bodleian and Taylorian Libraries), Manchester (John Rylands Library), Dublin (Trinity College), Siena (Biblioteca Comunale degli Intronati), and Leeds (Brotherton Library). To all those institutions and their wonderful staff, I offer heartfelt thanks.

I must acknowledge the undergraduate students who patiently endured my attempts to teach courses on 'Classical European Comedy', in Canterbury around 1980 and then in Leeds in the 1990s. Their responses and suggestions helped me to construct a view of what can and cannot be said on this subject. I also have warm memories of colleagues and students who were involved in staging my translation of the Sienese comedy *Gl'ingannati* — in Leeds in 1987, and in Siena itself in 1991. Practical experience, and the directing skills of Martin Banham, provided insights into the play as well as huge creative enjoyment.

I am warmly grateful to the seminar group entitled 'Theater Without Borders', which has convened in every year of the current millennium. This happy energetic group of scholars from America, Europe, and Asia has been my academic family in retirement, providing comradeship and ratification.

In terms of individual colleagues, I have had help and support from Joseph Farrell, Peter Hainsworth, Serena Laiena, Jennifer Lorch, Lucy Rayfield, Brian Richardson, Corinna Salvadori Lonergan, Julian Rushton, and Lisa Sampson.

Rob Henke encouraged me to start the whole project — perhaps not realizing what he was letting both of us in for. For many years he and I have been ploughing parallel furrows in neighbouring fields of knowledge, exchanging advice, warnings, and jokes across a hedge which does not really divide us. He now appears in this book, as Fig. 22.2.

If I have unwisely rejected any suggestions I have received from all these friends, then the blame is mine alone.

At Legenda publishers, I have received a warm comradely welcome, and essential practical advice, from Simon Gilson and Graham Nelson. Charlotte Wathey has been a helpful and meticulous copy-editor.

My wife and children, to whom the book is dedicated with love, continue to be indispensable to my personal and intellectual survival. Sometimes knowingly, and sometimes not.

June 2022

LIST OF ILLUSTRATIONS

Frontispiece: antique bust of Menander. [Photo: Richard Andrews]

FIG. 1.1. St John's College, Oxford, MS 87 (15th century), title page. [By permission of the President and Fellows of St John's College, Oxford. Photo: Richard Andrews]

FIG. 2.1. Ludovico Ariosto, *La cassaria*, title page of the first printing (Florence: Zucchetta, c. 1510). [Permission of the British Library.]

FIG. 4.1. Page 6 of *Compositions de Rhetorique* (Lyons, 1601) by Tristano Martinelli. The artist is unknown. [Gallica/Bibliothèque Nationale]

FIG. 8.1. Frontispiece engraving by L. Weyen for the play *Élomire Hypocondre* (1670) by Boulanger de Chalussay. [Gallica/Bibliothèque Nationale]

FIG. 9.1. *Le Départ des comédiens italiens* (1729): engraving by Louis Jacob after an original painting by Watteau. [Gallica]

FIG. 9.2. First page of text from the play *Arlequin empereur dans la lune* (1684) by Fatouville, included in volume 1 of Évariste Gherardi's *Le Théâtre italien* (Amsterdam: Braakman, 1701). [Leeds University Library, Special Collections, Italian F-9 GHE. Photo: Richard Andrews]

FIG. 10.1. Frontispiece to Fatouville's *Arlequin empereur dans la lune* (1684) in volume 1 of Gherardi's *Le Théâtre italien* (Amsterdam: Braakman, 1701). [Leeds University Library, Special Collections, Italian F-9 GHE Photo: Richard Andrews]

FIG. 10.2. Frontispiece to Fatouville's *Arlequin Protée* (1683) in volume 1 of Gherardi's *Le Théâtre italien* (Amsterdam: Braakman,1701). [Leeds University Library, Special Collections, Italian F-9 GHE. Photo: Richard Andrews]

FIG. 18.1. St John's College, Oxford, MS 117 (dated 1477), fol. 51v-52r. [By permission of the President and Fellows of St John's College, Oxford. Photo: Richard Andrews.]

FIG. 20.1. Flaminio Scala, *Il teatro delle favole rappresentative* (1611), fol. 87r. [Reproduced by permission of the Board of Trinity College, Dublin. Photo: Richard Andrews.]

FIG. 20.2. Illustration of 'La Scena Comica', from Sebastiano Serlio's *Secondo libro d'architettura* (Venice, 1560). [Gallica]

FIG. 20.3. Frontispiece by Pierre Brissart to Molière's *Le Malade imaginaire*, from a 1682 anthology of his plays, copied into a volume printed in 1895. [Photo: Richard Andrews]

FIG. 20.4. Frontispiece by Pierre Brissart to Molière's *L'Avare*, from the 1682 anthology, copied into the 1895 album. [Photo: Richard Andrews]

FIG. 22.1. Ancient theatrical masks: carvings on the Roman theatre in Myra, Turkey. [Photo: Richard Andrews]

FIG. 22.2. Professor Robert Henke wearing a modern copy of a *commedia dell'arte* mask. [Photo: Suzanne Loui]

FIG. 22.3. Frontispiece to Goldoni's *L'amore paterno*, from Volume v of *Delle Commedie di Carlo Goldoni* (Venice: Pasquali, 1761). [Photo: Richard Andrews]

FIG. 24.1–2. Medallion created in 1604 by Guillaume Dupré, showing a portrait of Isabella Andreini backed by a figure of Fame. [(c) The Frick Collection]

FIG. 24.2. Frontispiece to Goldoni's *Il ritorno dalla villeggiatura*, from Volume xi of *Delle Commedie di Carlo Goldoni* (Venice: Pasquali, 1761). [Photo: Richard Andrews.]

FIG. 27.1–2. Details from pages 15–16 of the first printing of Molière's *L'Avare* (1669). [Gallica/Bibliothèque Nationale]

CHRONOLOGY

Throughout the period treated, France was recognizable in modern terms as a single nation state. Italy was divided into separate states and territories, large and small, including the States of the Church ruled by the Pope. They were subject to fluctuating levels of political dependence on outside powers.

1494	First invasion of French armies into Italy, under King Charles VIII. The 'Italian Wars', involving French and other foreign military presences, continue until 1559.
1508–09	The first full five-act comedies in imitation of Plautus and Terence are performed in prose at the ducal court of Ferrara: Ludovico Ariosto's *La cassaria* and *I suppositi*. They are printed soon afterwards, and signal the start of the genre now known as *commedia erudita*.
1513	Performance, in the ducal court of Urbino, of *Calandra* by Bernardo Dovizi da Bibbiena and *Eutychia* by Nicola Grasso. Both comedies are in prose, and printed in the 1520s.
c. 1518	Niccolò Machiavelli's prose comedy *La mandragola* is performed in a private house in Florence, and printed in 1521.
1520	Ariosto begins composing verse comedies, and re-writing his first two into verse. However, most Italian erudite comedies continue to be written in prose.
1527	The Sack of Rome by German and Spanish troops confirms the weakness of small Italian states in the face of larger foreign powers.
1532	In the republic of Siena, the Accademia degli Intronati collectively compose, and privately perform, the prose comedy *Gl'ingannati*. It is printed in 1537.
1535	Italian translation of Horace's *Ars poetica* by Lodovico Dolce, who then also wrote Italian comedies for performance in Venice.
1536	Bilingual Greek-Latin edition of Aristotle's *Poetics*: translation by Guglielmo de' Pazzi.
1540	First printing of *Les Abusez* by Charles Estienne, a French prose translation of *Gl'ingannati*.
1541	Sebastiano Serlio is invited to France by King François I. A bilingual edition of his work on architecture, including designs for stage scenery, is published in 1545 and often reprinted.
1541	Jacques Peletier du Mans translates Horace's *Ars poetica* into French.
1545	First surviving written contract of an Italian *commedia dell'arte* company: its signatory members do not yet include women.
1540s	Italian *arte* troupes sell their shows both to rich patrons and to the general public. They perform improvised versions of classical comedy plots, in hired rooms and open public spaces. Major patrons of companies and actors will be the rulers of Florence and of Mantua.
1545	Jacques Bourgeois translates Ariosto's *I suppositi* into French verse, but with no attribution to Ariosto.

1548	Royal performance of Bibbiena's *Calandra* in Lyon for Henri II and Caterina de' Medici. The professional troupe from Florence includes actresses: the first documented appearance of women on a public stage in either Italy or France.
1549	Italian translation of Aristotle's *Poetics*, by Bernardo Segni. (No French translation appears until 1671.)
1554	A volume entitled *Delle commedie elette* published in Venice: an attempt to identify and anthologize the best Italian erudite comedies so far produced.
1554–55	Two Italian comedies performed at the court of Henri II.
1555	Jacques Peletier du Mans produces his own *Art poétique français*.
1559	Caterina de' Medici becomes Regent of France, during successive reigns of three of her sons.
1560	Beginning of the French civil wars of religion.
1561	Julius Caesar Scaliger's *Poetices* printed in Lyon: written in Latin by an Italian, it will make a major contribution to French *classiciste* theory.
1564	First surviving contract of an Italian *commedia dell'arte* company that includes an actress.
1567	Two professional *arte* troupes compete in Mantua, both of them including star actresses.
1570	Lodovico Castelvetro's commented edition of Aristotle's *Poetics*: his interpretations will be accepted as authoritative by subsequent theorists and dramatists throughout Europe.
1572	St Bartholomew's Day Massacre in Paris: Protestants slaughtered by Catholics.
1572	*Erofilomachia*, by Sforza Oddi: the first '*commedia grave*', explicitly justifiying the inclusion of serious themes in a comedy.
1577	The Gelosi company, including Francesco and Isabella Andreini, perform in Blois for King Henri III and his Florentine mother. They then obtain a licence to perform in Paris.
1579	Pierre Larivey publishes *Six premières Comédies facécieuses*, each one a prose adaptation of an identifiable Italian erudite comedy. They act as models for future French dramatists.
1584–85	Two Italian *commedia dell'arte* companies compete in Paris. Tristano Martinelli invents and launches his stage persona of Arlecchino, based on a figure from French folklore.
1589	Death of Caterina de' Medici.
1589	Spectacular wedding in Florence of Grand Duke Ferdinando I and Christine of Lorraine (granddaughter of Caterina de' Medici). It involves performances of the Sienese erudite comedy *La pellegrina*, and of two *arte* scenarios improvised by the Gelosi.
1594	Henri IV (Bourbon dynasty, converted from Protestantism) consecrated as King of France.
1598	Edict of Nantes signals the end of French religious wars.
1600	In Florence, Maria de' Medici marries King Henri IV.
1600	Tristano Martinelli in Paris with the Accesi company, on licence from the duke of his native Mantua. He offers a book of comic poems and pictures to the king and queen.
1602–04	Last visit to France of the Gelosi company, including the Andreini couple.
1604	Isabella Andreini dies in Lyon, having established a star reputation in France as well as in Italy. The Gelosi company is dissolved.
c. 1605–c. 1630	'*Commedia ridicolosa*' plays are repeatedly printed in Italy: scripted imitations of professional *commedia dell'arte* shows, for recitation by amateur academics.

	Meanwhile Pier Maria Cecchini composes two short treatises on stage acting technique — only one of them is printed, in 1628.
1610	Louis XIII becomes King of France, aged nine: his mother Maria de' Medici acts as Regent until 1614.
1611	Flaminio Scala publishes *Il teatro delle favole rappresentative*, a collection of scenarios for improvisation offered to a reading public.
1611	Pierre Larivey publishes three more comedies based on Italian models.
1613–47	Giovan Battista Andreini, son of Francesco and Isabella, makes a series of attempts to establish himself in Paris. He publishes five comedies there in 1622.
1624	Cardinal Richelieu begins his dominance as King Louis XIII's first minister. He promotes the establishment of *classiciste* rules for French literature and drama. During his time in authority there are no Italian acting companies in Paris.
1629	Pierre Corneille's *Mélite* is staged in Paris, inaugurating a new style of classical comedy.
1630	In Mantua, war and plague bring an end to regular ducal patronage of Italian professional actors. End of the 'golden age' of *commedia dell'arte*.
1634	Niccolò Barbieri publishes *La supplica*, an Italian defence of professional actors: he dedicates it to King Louis XIII of France.
1637	The first fully public Italian commercial theatre opens in Venice. It serves the new vogue for opera, rather than spoken comedy or tragedy.
1642	Death of Richelieu. Cardinal Mazarin (Mazzarino) replaces him as chief minister.
1643	Louis XIV becomes King of France, aged four, ruling until 1715.
1644	Italian acting troupes recalled to Paris by Mazarin and the Queen Mother, Anne of Austria. Molière forms his theatre troupe, and starts touring the French provinces from 1645.
1658	Publication in Florence of *Didascalia, cioè dottrina comica* by Girolamo Bartolommei Smeducci. An Italian version of French *classiciste* precepts, it then influences Luigi Riccoboni.
1658	Molière's *Troupe de Monsieur* installed in the Petit-Bourbon theatre, Paris, sharing with an Italian troupe. His first successful comedy is *Les Précieuses ridicules* (1659).
1660	Molière's company moves to the Palais-Royal.
1662	A new Italian company, including Domenico Biancolelli as Arlequin, is established under royal patronage at the Palais-Royal, still sharing the theatre with Molière.
1665	Molière's troupe is re-designated as *Comédiens du Roi*.
1673	Death of Molière. His *Comédiens* continue without him.
1680	The two French troupes in Paris are merged into one by royal command, founding the Comédie-Française. The Théâtre-Italien is granted the use of the Hôtel de Bourgogne. French and Italian styles of comedy are both popular with Paris audiences.
1688	Death of Domenico Biancolelli. Evaristo Gherardi takes over as Arlequin.
1697	King Louis XIV expels the Italian actors from Paris, on the grounds that their plays are too scurrilous.
1697–1716	Some Italian actors and troupes still work in France, outside the city of Paris. Pierre-François Biancolelli continues to perform as Arlequin, and to publish plays and sketches. The Comédie-Française functions unimpeded, and develops the genre of *comédie de caractère*.
1701	Definitive edition (in Amsterdam) of Gherardi's *Théâtre italien*, a retrospective collection of plays previously mounted in Paris by the Italians.

1702–15	Luigi Riccoboni works in Venice as actor, troupe director, and dramatist.
1709	Dedicated seasons of *opera buffa* are mounted by the royal theatre in Naples.
1715	Louis XV becomes King of France, aged five: his Regent is Philippe, duc d'Orléans.
1716	The Regent re-establishes a Théâtre-Italien company in Paris, under the direction of Luigi Riccoboni. The new Arlequin is Tommaso Visentini.
1720	Marivaux's *Arlequin poli par l'amour* is premiered by the Italians. Over the next twenty years, Marivaux writes a significant majority of his French comedies for the Théâtre-Italien.
1729	Carlo Goldoni begins composing comic opera librettos, for Venice and elsewhere.
1733	Pergolesi's *La serva padrona*, a ground-breaking *opera buffa*, is premiered in Naples.
1735	Nivelle de la Chaussée's *Le Préjugé à la mode* is staged in Paris, initiating the genre of 'tearful comedy' (*comédie larmoyante*).
1738	Goldoni begins writing partly-scripted scenarios for Italian improvising companies.
1741	Carlo Bertinazzi takes over as Arlequin in Paris, after Visentini's death in 1739.
1743	Goldoni's first fully-scripted play, *La donna di garbo*, is premiered in Venice.
1746	*Le Préjugé vaincu*: the last play by Marivaux to be performed in a public Parisian theatre.
1750	Goldoni's manifesto-play, *Il teatro comico*, promotes scripted comedy of character against improvised *arte* farce.
1752	In Paris, the public controversy known as the *Querelle des Bouffons* (in which the king and queen take opposite sides) debates the acceptability of operas in Italian and in French.
1757	Denis Diderot's *Le Fils naturel* represents and promotes the non-comic genre of *drame bourgeois*, or *drame sérieux*.
1761	Goldoni's *Villeggiatura* trilogy of comedies is premiered in Venice.
1761–65	In Venice, Carlo Gozzi mounts a series of theatrical 'fables' in explicit opposition to Goldoni. They are staged by a company which still employs traditional *arte* masks.
1762	In Paris the Théâtre-Italien is formally merged with the Opéra-Comique, though the company retains a separate identity.
1762	Goldoni moves from Venice to Paris, and becomes in-house dramatist to the Théâtre-Italien.
1774	Louis XVI becomes King of France.
1775	Successful premiere in Paris of Beaumarchais's *Le Barbier de Séville* (revised four-act version).
1776	Goldoni's last comedy, *L'Avare fastueux/ L'avaro fastoso*, appears in both French and Italian.
1782	*Il barbiere di Siviglia*, with music by Paisiello, is premiered in St Petersburg.
1783	Final dissolution of the Théâtre-Italien. Goldoni remains in Paris until his death in 1793.
1784	Beaumarchais's *Le Mariage de Figaro* is finally performed at the Comédie-Française, after years of being blocked by state censors.
1786	*Le nozze di Figaro*, by Da Ponte and Mozart, is premiered at the imperial court in Vienna.
1789	The French Revolution: theatres in France are released from royal governance.
1797	Napoleon Bonaparte invades Italy with a French army, and brings an end to the

	Republic of Venice. Later, as Emperor, he takes over and transforms the other states of Italy.
1797	Premiere in Paris of Beaumarchais's *La Mère coupable*, the third play in the Figaro trilogy.
1815	Final defeat of Napoleon at Waterloo. The separate Italian states are restored. European culture generally starts to move from Classicism to Romanticism.
1816	Premiere in Rome of Rossini's *Il barbiere di Siviglia*.

Ever since writing was invented, men have exploited that kind of drama of which the three obvious marks have been the representation of ordinary life, the provoking of laughter and the happy ending.

W. G. Moore

INTRODUCTION

> When youth and love are working together to deceive an old man, then everything he does to thwart them can rightly be called *The Futile Precaution*.
>
> — BEAUMARCHAIS, the concluding words of *Le Barbier de Séville* (1775)

I

This book is a study of stage plays and scenarios which were prepared to call themselves comedies, and which were written and performed in Italy and France between 1500 and 1800. The notion that there was a genre of comedy which came to an end with the French Revolution and Romanticism will not in itself appear very radical to theatre historians — at least not in theory. In practice, however, this genre has rarely, if ever, been addressed as a single continuous tradition lasting nearly three centuries. Studies of eighteenth-century comedy, in any European language, do not often trace its elements back to sixteenth-century Italian *commedia erudita*.

I propose here to tell a single story, which starts with Ludovico Ariosto's *La cassaria* of 1508, and ends (notionally and symbolically, for reasons which will start emerging in Chapter 14) with the two versions of *The Marriage of Figaro* — the French one by Beaumarchais of 1784, and the Italian one by Lorenzo Da Ponte set to music two years later by Mozart. My contention is that this type of comedy maintained a degree of continuity for all that time, ending with some of its features (though certainly not all of them) largely unaltered. The term 'classical comedy' seems appropriate for two linked reasons. Firstly, it is an established critical convention (perhaps starting with Goethe) to contrast the Romanticism which radicalized European culture in the nineteenth century with a Classicism which it sought to replace; and the drama examined in this book belongs to the earlier category. Secondly, the comic playwrights with whom we are concerned based themselves on Roman models of the 'classical' world, and never lost awareness of them despite some significant changes and developments. (The same statement, substituting 'Greco-Roman' for 'Roman', is of course also true of stage tragedy, which is not discussed here.)

A more innovative proposal, not to my knowledge made by any previous scholar, is that an account of classical comedy involves narrating a back-and-forth interchange or dialogue between two vernacular linguistic cultures: the Italian and the French. (To speak of two 'national' cultures during this period would be anachronistic, since there was no Italian nation state until the mid-nineteenth century.) The emphasis here is on reciprocal influences, and this effectively excludes

English drama. English playwrights certainly developed their own versions of the classical comic genre, but their contributions to it were not fed back again into theatre on the European continent. During the time covered by this book, comic dramatists in Italy and France neither knew nor imitated Jonson, Wycherley, Congreve, Goldsmith, or Sheridan. (A relatively late exception was Voltaire, after his residence in England in the 1720s. His 1739 comedy *La Prude* was explicitly based on Wycherley's *The Plain Dealer*; but then Wycherley in his turn had been adapting Molière's *Le Misanthrope*.) The English influences which did affect French and Italian theatre (including, perhaps surprisingly, comic opera) were not examples of classical stage comedy. They came either from novelists such as Samuel Richardson (whose obstinately virtuous Pamela became a heroine of plays and operas); or from the new divergent theatrical genre labelled 'sentimental comedy', which in France became *comédie larmoyante* or *drame sérieux*. In this sense, English influence on continental dramaturgy contributed indirectly to the break-up of the classical comic genre, rather than to its further development.

Spanish playwrights, by contrast, did borrow some things initially from the Humanist classical format, and did then in their turn influence plays written in France and Italy. However, in my judgement, the Spanish contributions to other dramatic literatures were extraneous to the core elements of classical comedy which I shall list below; and indeed their more free-wheeling approach tended to disrupt that continuous tradition. (This is a view which some might want to contest; but it is a premise which explains the small weight I have given in this study to Spanish influences on the Italian and French stages after 1600, influences which in themselves are undeniable.)

The history of popular comic drama in northern and central Europe — where a major input was provided by English touring companies — is quite separate at this time from that of theatre in the Romance languages.

I have then adopted an extra parameter in this study, with regard to the choice of material to examine. I shall give greater weight to, and spend more time on, plays which are still recognized by the modern theatre repertoire, and are thus still familiar to some European (or 'western') audiences. There are episodes and components in this narrative which are not familiar to today's theatregoers. The most striking example is the contribution of Italian actors to the Parisian theatre scene between 1650 and 1750, in the form of the officially licensed Théâtre-Italien — the company for which Marivaux, who figures importantly in my story, wrote a majority of his plays. The lively chaotic shows mounted by the Italians were an important general influence on him and on others, but they are not revived on the modern stage. I shall treat that material in less detail than it may intrinsically deserve. With this conscious selectivity, I am suggesting that 'classical comedy' has produced some formats which are still understood, and some drama which is still enjoyed, in the modern or post-modern era. This study of a theatre genre of the past is therefore slanted towards the present in favouring the dramatic forms, and the play scripts, which are still a 'legacy' for modern audiences. And thus we have arrived at the book's title.

II

The decision to use the word 'classical', as a category or a description, obliges me to confront the fact that the word has long been associated with French literature, and particularly with French drama, in ways which have sometimes amounted to a proclamation of French cultural identity. Critics and historians have defined the literary and dramatic culture of seventeenth-century France as 'classical' on an assemblage of criteria, which go far beyond indicating merely that writers and playwrights looked to Greco-Roman antiquity for their examples and their rules. The concept of *classicisme* has been used to cover a range of features which those writers claimed, or hoped, to infuse into their creations. In a 1973 essay by W. D. Howarth, which appears in my Bibliography, they are summarized as follows: 'harmony and simplicity in terms of form; refinement of language, elevation of subject-matter; a search for psychological truth; and renunciation of local colour' — that last expression denoting a desire to deal with general truths rather than with a passing social or historical moment.[1] By contrast, I am using the term 'classical comedy' in a more limited and technical sense: it points to a set of narrative components which tend to recur in the plays studied in this book. It does not imply any stylistic or tonal qualities like the ones listed by Howarth. It still does imply a dramatist's awareness of the comedies of Plautus and Terence, though not necessarily a slavish imitation of those models. In addition, however, some original components of the Roman comedy template quickly acquired variants and additions from medieval novella and romance: these contributed regularly to the early modern genre and have to be included from the start.

I offer now a list of features which audiences expected to find, and usually did find, in comedies composed and performed between 1500 and 1800: they will define a play as 'classical' for the purposes of this study. They all relate to the events enacted in the fictional plot, and to its invented characters — that is to content, not to style or tone, and not to methods of performance.

a. The urban family

In the vast majority of cases, the cast of characters in a classical comedy will be focused around one or two families living in an urban environment, along with their friends and dependants. The vicissitudes of the plot will concern those families personally and privately, with no larger public resonance for the community which they inhabit. These purely private implications, and the concentration on a particular stratum of society, were initially seen as mandatory for the comic genre.

b. A happy ending

The denouement of the play, which the audience is invited to anticipate and to approve, involves a successful coupling between a male and a female character who

---

[1] 'Qui dit classicisme, dit harmonie et simplicité quant à la forme; raffinement du langage, élévation du sujet; recherche de la vérité psychologique; et renoncement à la couleur locale' (Howarth 1973: 523).

desire each other. (The 'Lover' was a formally recognized role category for an actor or actress.) In the ancient Roman sources, this coupling did not always involve marriage. In our early modern period, after the pervasive influence of medieval romance, it usually did; but there is an alternative minority genre of adultery comedies, where astute lovers triumph over an incompetent husband.

(The main element which defined these plays as comedies was that the contrasting 'unhappy endings', which heroes and heroines fought to avoid, were contained within limits. In most cases we see no threats of death and destruction, though there were exceptions, some of which were labelled 'tragicomedy'. The fate which young Lovers in comedy are usually trying to escape is either that of having their illicit relationship discovered, or, more often, that of ending up married to the wrong person.)

c. Obstacles defeated

The happy ending is achieved in the face of obstacles, and the action of the play shows how they are overcome. In the Roman models, obstacles were most often provided by blocking characters, against whom the protagonists had to struggle. In early modern plots the problem could equally be the resistance or confusion of one or both of the Lovers. Alternatively, characters may be ignorant of some important facts about each other, and discovering the truth provides a resolution.

d. Laughable characters

The behaviour of some characters in the play is presented as ridiculous, and laughter is generated at their expense. Such characters are often those who try to block the desired denouement; but they may alternatively be peripheral to the main story, or even in some cases be the Lovers themselves.

(Despite the central importance of derisive laughter, the element I have deliberately excluded from the list of essential criteria is that of satire. Many of the playwrights under consideration attacked or mocked the particular society for which they were writing; but others preferred to expose aspects of human behaviour which they saw as universal — opting for what Howarth called 'renunciation of local colour'. This subject is addressed in Chapter 21.)

e. Generational conflict

The story frequently depicts family generational tensions between fathers (male 'Elders' were another formally recognized role category) and their offspring. The centrality of such confrontations to events in the main story may vary. Parental opposition is often, but nevertheless not always, the major obstacle which might prevent the Lovers coming together.

f. Class conflict

Equally often, the plot makes use of tension or conflict between social classes. In ancient Rome masters were confronted by slaves; in early modern Europe they faced paid 'Servants' (a third fixed role category for actors), or dependants. As with generational conflict, the importance of this element varies from play to play in terms of how much it contributes to the main intrigue.

g. Deceit and misunderstanding

The happy ending is usually achieved via actions which involve either deliberate deceit or misunderstanding. The Lovers may initiate tricks and devices, or collude in those devised by others, especially by Servants. Deceit often involves disguise or false identity. Alternatively, confusions about identity may occur without being deliberately engineered.

Not all these characteristics will appear punctually in every classically comic play: we can expect most of them, but not all of them, at any one time. In particular the pre-existence of the genre in the audience's mind occasionally resulted in a play which deliberately recognized certain expectations and then flouted them. Even the happy ending could occasionally be subverted. In Molière's *Le Misanthrope* (1666), and Marivaux's *La Fausse Suivante* (1724), the Lovers end up by accepting their incompatibility and going their separate ways. Some comedies by Carlo Goldoni (1707–1793) end with the rejection of a marital union which was originally desired by a young couple. The effect of those denouements relies on the audience knowing that a comedy usually ends differently. Alluding to generic requirements, and then not entirely fulfilling them, is a possible reaction to the genre's existence in the first place, especially with comedy, whose essence is mockery, game-playing, and subversion of norms.

III

Further remarks are in order about the subversive aspects of the classical comic format, expressed above in criteria *e*, *f*, and *g*.

Attempts to block the happiness of Lovers very often come from their Elders, that is from people to whom their society normally grants a greater degree of power. Classical comedy is thus associated with a conflict between the generations, which the young people win (a fact which I address at more length in Chapter 23). There may be some variants on the obstacle courses laid down — it is not in every case a question of simple parental prohibition, and sometimes the Lovers themselves are their own worst enemies. Nevertheless, the original template for this comedy seems to preach the triumph of youth over old age, in a way which imaginative critics can then interpret as a perennial cycle of renewal, analogous to the way in which spring always takes the place of winter. (The extent to which these comedies subverted the domination of men over women is more debatable, see Chapter 24.) In addition, alongside an eternal clash of the generations, the classical comic tradition also regularly depicts a class struggle, a battle of wits between masters, both Elders and Lovers, and their Servants (for which see Chapter 25). In most societies, inequalities of wealth and social status create perennial tensions alongside inequalities of age. The conflicts produced are not trivial in our lives, but they can be made hilarious on stage.

Both sorts of confrontation are endemic to the classical comic genre: they sometimes overlap and contribute to the same story. The young are set up to triumph over the old, and the servant (however briefly) over the master: audiences know that the comic genre comes already laden with those expectations. The starting model was Roman comedy, whose defining spirit may have had links to the Saturnalia festival, when hierarchies were formally but temporarily reversed. Plautine plots in particular come across as playful formalized combats on stage between categories of character whom convention marks out from the start either as winners or as losers; and the winners are those who in real society were more likely to lose. This convention was accepted without argument in the very first Italian revivals of the genre, in the early sixteenth century. At the end of the eighteenth century it was still going strong, as my opening epigraph from Beaumarchais shows, though it was increasingly subject to questioning and variation. Classical comic drama thus plays fast and loose with hierarchies; and it also tends to celebrate actions which are not conventionally moral. In order to achieve their triumphs, its heroes and heroines make extensive use of lying, trickery, and deceit. In particular comic protagonists often make use of, or are perplexed by, various forms of disguise or mistaken identity (see Chapter 26). This trope was also copied from Roman comedy: it recurs to a remarkable degree, and with remarkable persistence, over three centuries. Its essential implausibility underlines the fact that the genre was always based on elements of stylized theatrical game-playing, and of wish-fulfilling fantasy. Comedy may make selective use of perceived realities, both social and psychological, but it always distorts them or decorates them in the cause of giving pleasure to its audience.

IV

We do not write plays quite like this any more, for stage or film or television (or not very often) because our society no longer functions in the same way. But we know that these plots exist and are traditional, and many of us still go to see them in the theatre. Some of us, therefore, are willing to sink our disbelief in a recognizable piece of festive fiction. Perhaps we are prepared to acknowledge that there are elements in the comic conflict which have a general resonance, beyond the individual historical moment. Winter remains winter, and spring remains desirable, in all temperate-zone societies. Subordinate groups in every social structure still seek to reverse their subordination, or to enjoy a story which reverses it for them. Theatre audiences in the twenty-first century still understand that the 'happy ending' of a comic play involves at least one pair of young people overcoming obstacles and getting married. So in which dramas do modern theatregoers find and accept the 'legacy' of classical comedy, even if we do not identify the genre with that label?

I shall not be studying English-language theatre in this volume; but it has produced many comedies in classical format which the anglophone public still goes to see. Not so very infrequently we revive Goldsmith's *She Stoops to Conquer*, or Sheridan's *The Rivals*. English Restoration comedy works for us too: it has a tendency to undermine the simpler formats of the tradition, offering a reduced emphasis on inter-generational conflict, but it still makes reference to those formats and still tends to end with a triumphant, sometimes subversive, coupling. From earlier, there are relevant plays in the Shakespeare repertoire. Orlando and Rosalind in *As You Like It*, Lorenzo and Jessica in *The Merchant of Venice*, are paired off despite the barriers raised against them by the usurping Duke and by Shylock. The four Lovers in *A Midsummer Night's Dream* flee to the forest to escape parental and legal oppression. A simpler version of the standard comic story is supplied by Fenton and Anne Page in *The Merry Wives of Windsor*. *A Comedy of Errors* exploits the fun that can be created by identical twins on stage — with almost explicit borrowings from Plautus's *Menaechmi*. Shakespeare's relationship to a classical form of theatre, to a set of rules or habits propounded in his time by Italian theorists and practitioners, is complex and selective, but still not deniable. The comedies of Ben Jonson, and the genre we now call 'Jacobean city comedy', are more firmly and openly based on Italian models.

In France, the classical comic formula was accepted without reservations, and even rigorously theorized (as I shall show from Chapter 7 onwards). Its masterpieces continue to figure in commercial theatre repertoires today. Molière and Marivaux have rarely been absent from French stages: they now also both receive penetrating re-interpretations from directors in other countries. Those two dramatists are felt to be as endemically French as Shakespeare is endemically English; but both of them take account, in different ways, of an Italian tradition alongside a French one. Molière's Lovers are not portrayed very romantically, compared with those we find in Shakespeare; but they do always get their way, in the face of preposterous objections from ridiculous (and heavily caricatured) Elders. Marivaux tends to shake off the conflict between generations in favour of more complex inner tensions suffered by his aspiring Lovers; but he retains and explores the traditional confrontation between master (or mistress) and servant, and in his plays the denouement is still a marriage achieved via trickery, deceit, or disguise. Also in France, there are regular revivals of the complex 'Figaro' comedies of Beaumarchais, which, as I shall note immediately below, are now more familiar internationally in their operatic adaptations.

In Italy the comedies of the sixteenth century, which begin our narrative and which I see as having created the whole genre, are now relatively unknown; but the eighteenth-century comedies of Goldoni, who knew Molière and other French dramatists well, are still being staged. In his mature compositions Goldoni offers sharp critical reflections on social behaviour, and he is sometimes less indulgent than his predecessors to the passions of stage Lovers; but his comic plots do still revolve around what is going to happen to such young people, in terms of matrimonial union.

Goldoni was also deeply aware — as were his audiences, and as audiences in Italy can still be today — of a long-standing unique aspect of the Italian performing tradition. Intrigues and happy endings had long been narrated through the antics of a set of brash cartoon-like figures, who circled round each other in repeated stereotyped plots. The clownish father-figure Pantalone would be skirmishing with younger Lovers who included his own offspring; but he also had subversive Servants such as Arlecchino to deal with, and Arlecchino himself might be pursuing Colombina in hope of a lower-class coupling. The Italian genre which is now called *commedia dell'arte* (a term first found in a Goldoni play of 1750) is a contribution to classical comedy of which we constantly have to take account, and which from time to time modern companies still try to revive. Its history starts in the mid-1500s, and we shall see that it also became routinely familiar to French audiences in the seventeenth and eighteenth centuries. It is relatively rare for modern playgoers to experience *commedia dell'arte* revivals, but some notions of the genre still survive, especially in the professional training which actors undergo.

In what Italians call 'prose theatre' — that is, theatre which is spoken rather than sung — some modern playgoers may feel that these stories are slowly losing their interest. But even if this is so, a different or overlapping audience constituency still affords them a secure place in the repertoire of 'lyric theatre', or opera. Pergolesi's ground-breaking and internationally successful *La serva padrona*, created in 1733, is still occasionally revived or recorded. Rossini's *La Cenerentola* reminds us that unhappy stepdaughters and oppressive step-parents belong to folklore as well as to a high tradition of comic drama. In *Il barbiere di Siviglia*, which the same Italian composer based on the French play by Beaumarchais, the heroine is potentially at the mercy of her lustful exploitative guardian. The generational conflict is resolved by Figaro, the tricky Servant who is so much cleverer than his master the Lover. Figaro features even more strongly in Beaumarchais's *Le Mariage de Figaro*; and this became *Le nozze di Figaro* by Da Ponte and Mozart, a masterpiece which never loses favour. I shall eventually argue that it was with the Figaro plots that the history of classical comedy reached a kind of climax, in the 1780s, but also then ran out of steam. Innovative creation for the stage moved then in different directions, but the classical legacy did not disappear from repertoires. Opera audiences throughout the industrial 'west' are still prepared to find classical comic plots familiar, and to swallow a set of conventions based on a society which they no longer inhabit.

V

The reference above to Italian masks invites a separate clarification: this is not a book about *commedia dell'arte*. It is a book about a genre of theatre in which the *arte* was one component, alongside others.

The contribution was of course important. From the mid-sixteenth century on, the performance methods, the recognizable figures, and the plot units and relationships, which we lump together and call *commedia dell'arte*, were a presence and a point of reference in Italian and French stage comedy. They created many long-standing expectations for theatre audiences. Wherever *commedia dell'arte* appears, or can be discerned, it has to be acknowledged in this study — even in some forms of theatre which were not strictly 'classical' or even strictly comic. Nevertheless, I shall argue in my conclusion that what eventually characterized classical comedies was a balance, even a creative tension, between 'erudite' and 'artisan' elements, in which neither side could do without the other. The artisan strain was rooted firmly in professional theatre practice, but not always, or not exclusively, in the *arte* as we now recognize it.

I noted above that my proposed criteria for labelling comedies as 'classical' relate to the stories enacted on stage, and to the characters depicted: they do not refer to performing or staging techniques, which were subject to variation. Throughout this book I have taken material indiscriminately from scripts which actors were expected to memorize, and from surviving scenarios for improvisation. Characters created by playwrights, and 'fixed types' created and perpetuated by generations of actors, have been approached as aspects of a single phenomenon (Chapter 22), rather than by emphasizing their differences. Dramaturgical habits which derived from improvisation techniques (Chapter 19) were melded with other features which came from elsewhere (Chapter 18).

VI

This book is conceived as two separate Parts, which complement each other but whose composition has been approached in different ways.

Part I is a Narrative of the chronological phases, as I see them, of classical stage comedy between 1508 and 1786, with interactions between Italy and France stressed at all points. The story aims to be told as swiftly as possible in short chapters, and does not make use of footnotes or endnotes: only a brief summary of the main sources used (or to be consulted by readers) is attached to each chapter.

Part II contains a series of Analyses: it surveys, under various headings, plays from stages summarized in Part I. Its principal aim is to note which aspects of the classical comic genre changed over the period, and by how much, and which did not change at all. Some Part II chapters investigate technical aspects of dramaturgy; others discuss themes and trends within the content of comedies. Part II is supported by conventional footnote references.

In both parts, as will be apparent, the book deals chiefly with what is contained in the surviving scripts, scenarios, and summaries of comic plays. That is to say, the majority of my evidence is textual. Some scholars in Theatre Studies may find this regrettable, but I find it unavoidable — especially when the plays offer (among other things) a legacy for modern theatre practitioners. It is play texts, and nothing else, which are re-read and then re-interpreted today. Physical staging practices of the past are important and engaging as history, but knowledge of them hardly ever contributes to a contemporary production. Attempts to understand older acting styles produce little that is concrete, and nothing in terms of voice or gesture which can be imitated or reproduced — at least, not when referring to any period which pre-dates recording and filming technology. (The steps and postures of formal dance are an exception to this: they have been successfully analysed and performed.) Theatre historians regularly examine the provenance and likely attitudes of identifiable past audiences, and there are some passages in this book which address such questions. For directors and actors, however, those audiences are long gone, and resurrecting them is neither possible nor desirable.

We all know that a full theatre experience does not just contain words from a page. It involves scenery, costumes, music, voices, movements, spectators, physical environment, political context, and much more. In practice, though, when we contemplate and re-stage plays from earlier than the twentieth century, those words on the page are the only 'legacy' which we can adopt and adapt. The fact that some of the comedies studied here are still revived shows that the process of textual transmission, which in shorthand I am classing as 'erudite', actually works as a central element of 'artisan' theatrical culture. In our early modern period, European dramatists studied, tried to adapt, and in fact substantially transformed, the scripts which had come down to them from Plautus and Terence. We in our turn are now reading, and trying to make sense of, the texts which those dramatists left behind.

PART I

Narrative

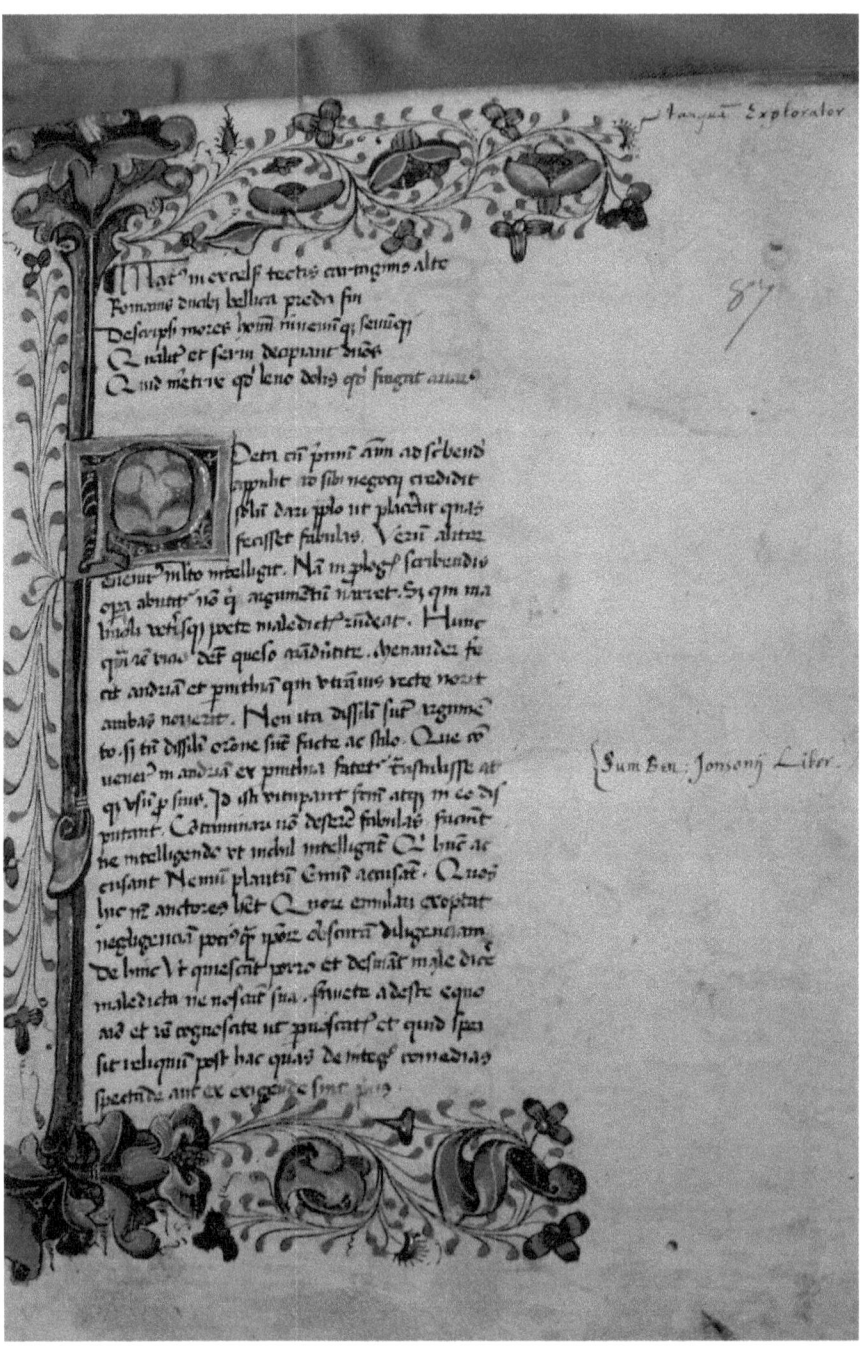

FIG. 1.1. Title page of a 15th-century manuscript of Terence's comedies. The marginal addition on the right shows that it came into the possession of the English Humanist playwright Ben Jonson (1572–1637).

CHAPTER 1

Roman Models and Greek Precepts

Theatre as an activity was condemned by the Church fathers during the first centuries of Christianity; so by around 1200 CE ancient Greek and Roman dramatic texts were largely unknown in western Europe, and certainly uncomprehended. The words 'tragedy' and 'comedy' had shifted to occupy areas of meaning which to us now seem confused, or at least confusing, and which were not associated with theatrical performance. Then the movement which we call 'humanism' motivated scholars and thinkers to search for and recirculate large numbers of surviving texts from classical antiquity and to reconsider them in a more objective light, often with attempts to place them in their historical or social context. Many of the works available for renewed study had been rescued from physical decay just in time, around the year 800 CE: they had been copied from older papyrus originals by monks during that Carolingian era, and then often left to slumber undisturbed in monastery libraries for several centuries. As interest in Roman comedies began to revive, those early medieval manuscripts began to be recopied, sometimes as carefully decorated luxury products (see Fig. 1.1). Various phases of this recapturing of Greco-Roman culture have since been designated as 'Renaissances', or 'proto-Renaissances', by modern historians. That word is now of course used most often to designate a period of cultural change which started in Italy in the fifteenth century. It is here that our story begins.

In the west European school curriculum, many works written in classical Latin had survived as objects of study, helped of course by the fact that medieval Latin was still the international language of religion and scholarship. The six comedies of Terence had been studied and appreciated for the moral aphorisms which could be extracted from them, and for the issues of ethics and behaviour which they were perceived as raising. The plays of Plautus — more clownish, more scurrilous, and less moralistic — were not so well known. For a long time any awareness that these texts were meant to be performed on stage had disappeared. But the Humanist trend towards a more scholarly approach to criticism began to make this fact comprehensible. The new enthusiasm for hunting down forgotten writings from the classical period led to the rediscovery of twelve whole comedies of Plautus in the year 1429. Then in 1435 the six comedies of Terence became associated with some commentaries on them written in later antiquity, also recently rediscovered. This helped scholars to understand some conventions which underlay this type of writing; and most of all to realize that these were scripts to be acted before an audience. Even before later attempts to tackle the Greek *Poetics* of Aristotle or the Latin *Ars poetica* of Horace, these commentaries — attributed at the time just to the fourth-century grammarian Aelius Donatus, now known to be partly by Evanthius — laid the ground for a theory and practice of stage comedy, based on the authority of classical antiquity. The fifteenth century was also when the new technology of printing was invented, enabling such discoveries to be circulated more rapidly. The first editions of Plautus and Terence appeared from the 1470s; and the 'Donatus' commentaries were first attached in print to Terentian editions in 1476. These plays and glosses, surviving just as Latin texts, became sources and inspirations for readings, and then for staged revivals, of theatrical genres which were simultaneously brand new (in contrast with immediately preceding practice) and ancient (in their derivation).

For scholars who spoke Latin-derived languages such as Italian and French, ancient Greek was notably harder to learn. Nevertheless, a more tentative acquaintance was also being made with surviving dramatic texts from classical Greece. For non-tragic plays, this effectively meant the Old Comedy of Aristophanes: the subsequent Athenian New Comedy was known only by repute, and from quoted fragments, until the rediscovery of some texts by Menander in the twentieth century. Neither the structure nor the content of Old Comedies found favour, even with those Humanists who learned to understand them. Aristophanes's humour was too raucous for their gentlemanly sense of decorum — though the professional Italian improvising players who came a little later might have had fewer problems with it. More importantly, scholars and then dramatists accepted the objections formulated in the 'Donatus' commentaries to any play which deployed its comic aggression against identifiable, even named, individuals in contemporary society. Comic satire was supposed to be general, not particular. This prohibition, or inhibition, remained in force for the whole three centuries of revived classical European comedy (see Chapter 21 below). Aristophanes never established a presence.

Plautus and Terence were known to have copied or adapted their plays from the Athenian New Comedy: therefore, even though none of his plays was yet available, Menander (see Frontispiece) can be seen as the symbolic founding father of the dramatic genre discussed in this book. His two Roman imitators offer alternative approaches to writing stage comedy, as regards content and tone: during the early modern period, examples taken from one or the other were often used as ammunition in theoretical debates. In very general terms, Plautus seemed to offer energetic and often vulgar entertainment with stylized theatricality and plenty of laughter; while Terence offered more realistic psychological analysis and moral reflection, sometimes without much laughter at all. Most early modern comic dramatists aimed for a blend of the two; and Chapter 18 will show how the structures and conventions used by both of them were adopted in early modern drama. However, there were repeated disagreements during our period, both in theory and in practice, on issues such as acceptable levels of vulgarity, and how much ridicule and humiliation could be deployed on stage against certain classes of character. We could say that Terence acted as a model for what we now call 'high' comedy, and Plautus for 'low' comedy or farce — I shall address this frequently perceived distinction in Chapter 17. Partly because of such arguments, the two ancient Roman authors could be challenged or reinterpreted between 1500 and 1800 by playwrights and performers, but they were never forgotten or fully rejected during those three centuries.

Increasingly important over the period studied was the influence of theoretical remarks about theatre and about comedy which had survived from the ancient world. Aristotle's Greek *Poetics* became seen as a set of rules for the composition of plays, in all genres including comedy — the notion that his comments were more descriptive than prescriptive, which might represent the opinion of more recent scholarship, was occasionally considered but not often accepted. The advice of Horace, in his Latin *Ars poetica*, was seen as compatible with that of Aristotle, and given equal weight. The effect on early modern European comedy of these alleged authorities is an inescapable running theme of this book, starting particularly with Chapter 7 and the formulation of French *classiciste* rules. 'Erudite' dramatic theory loomed constantly over 'artisan' dramatic practice: it was sometimes a hindrance and sometimes a help.

Bibliographical Note

There are facing-page English translations of all the Roman comedies in the Loeb Classical Library series. Earlier translations appearing in Penguin Books (by E. F. Watling, Plautus 1964–65; and by Betty Radice, Terence 1976) can sometimes be more convincingly amusing and colloquial.

The Donatus/Evanthius commentaries on Terence are edited in the original Latin by Wessner 1902–06. There are many paperback translated versions of Aristotle's *Poetics* and Horace's *Ars poetica*.

For the transmission of texts by the two Roman dramatists, see Reynolds 1986, and McLaughlin 2015.

Useful general surveys of Roman comedy are Duckworth 1952; Beacham 1991; McDonald & Walton 2007; and for Greek comedy, Revermann 2014.

CHAPTER 2

❖

Italian *commedia erudita*

It was on the strength of the new scholarly interest in the Latin texts that certain courts and patrons in fifteenth-century Italy sponsored attempts to perform some comedies of Plautus and Terence on stage. Surviving records of such activity begin around 1482: university students had probably been doing it for longer. Left in their original language, the plays would have a restricted audience (except at the papal court in Rome, where most clerics knew Latin). Overall, we know of a string of productions in Rome and in Florence. The Dukes of Ferrara, the Este dynasty, became especially enthusiastic; and from 1486 they made their courtiers attend stagings of Roman comedies translated into the vernacular, as part of a drive to interest the educated nobility in a new form of culture. Initially the Italian verse translations used were short of entertainment value: they were long-winded in a way which destroyed the quick-fire dialogue of the originals. Princess Isabella d'Este, who married the Marquis of Mantua in 1490, thought it would be better to use simple prose; and an experiment along those lines was offered at her Mantuan court in 1503, authored by a student or academic who still remains unidentified (he used the name 'Publio Philippo Mantovano'). But this play *Formicone* (named after its protagonist) was not simply a translation — it was a new comedy in Italian, which closely imitated the content and style of Plautus without actually being Plautus.

Back in Isabella's home court of Ferrara, one of her protégés was Ludovico Ariosto (1474–1533), eventually to be celebrated as the author of the chivalric epic poem *Orlando furioso*. In his youth Ariosto had taken part in productions of the translated Roman comedies, and he had developed a good sense of theatre. In 1508 and 1509 he wrote and staged for the Este court two successive new comedies in Plautine style entitled *La cassaria* [The Play of the Strong-box] and *I suppositi* [The Substitutes]. They were more substantial than the anonymous *Formicone*; and they were printed almost immediately, around 1510 (see Fig. 2.1), without the author's permission and indeed against his wishes. (*Formicone* was not printed until 1524.) Nevertheless the fact of such texts being published at all soon indicated that the humanist community wanted play scripts to possess a new cultural status. Rather than being pieces of occasional entertainment associated with religious or courtly festivities, a play was to rank as a full-scale literary product, to be read or performed at any time — as had been the case with the Greek and Latin plays which had been recorded on papyrus and bequeathed to posterity.

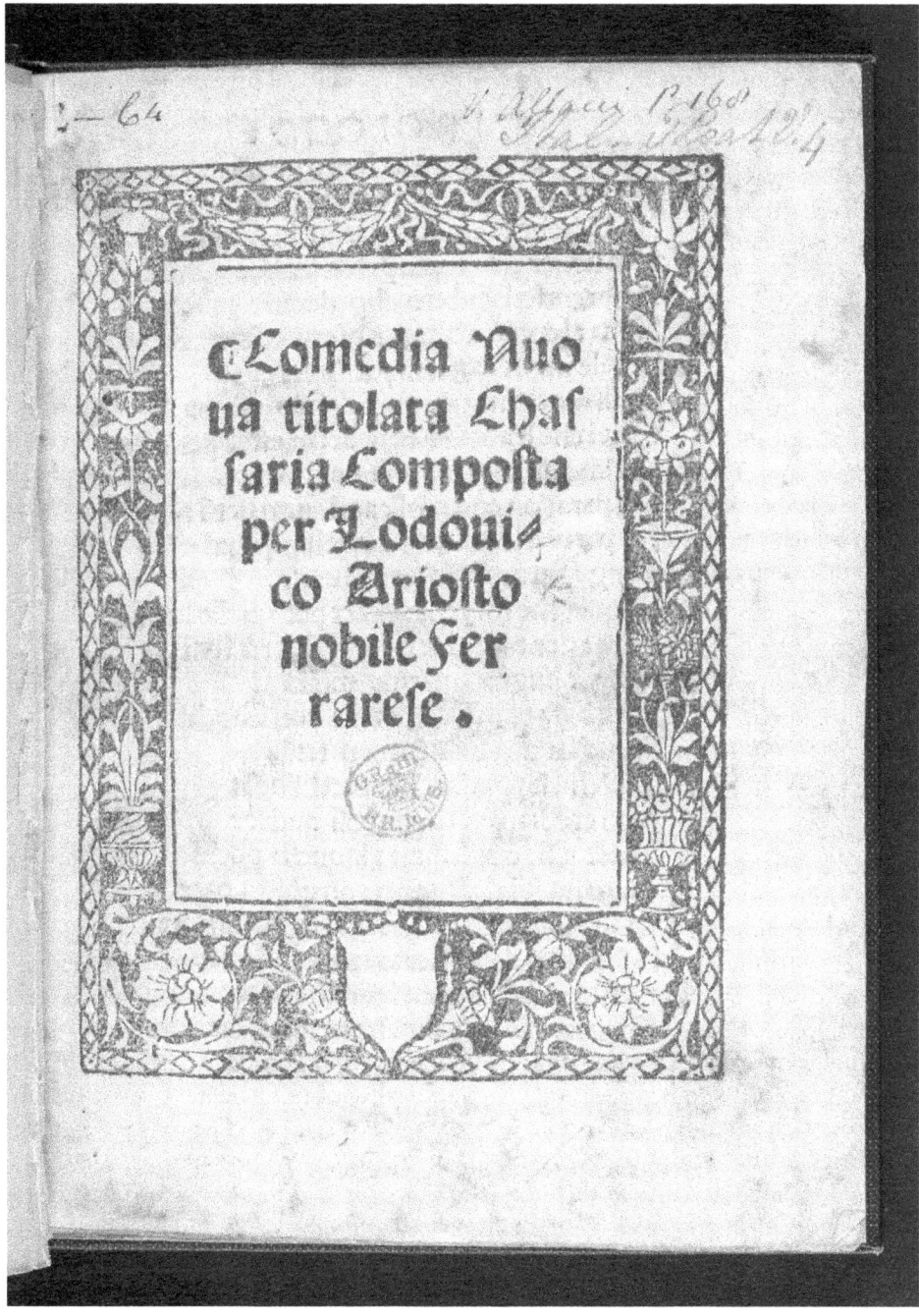

Fig. 2.1. *La cassaria*, by Ludovico Ariosto, the edition of c. 1510. The first printing ever of a new comedy in classical style.

It is this last point most of all which defines Italian humanist drama — which started with comedy, and then drew in other genres — as the beginning of European theatre as we now know it. Ariosto's first two plays marked the emergence of Italian vernacular comedies, closely based on Plautine and Terentian models but original compositions none the less. Historians now call the genre *commedia erudita*, 'erudite comedy': it was first written and performed in courts, clubs, or Academies by gentlemen amateurs educated in the humanist tradition. At least a hundred such scripts were composed between 1508 and 1550: by 1630 the number of published Italian five-act plays which described themselves as comedies had reached over three hundred.

There were several clear defining characteristics to mark the new brand of stage comedy. 'Regular' plays (the term *regolare* was used at the time) were divided into five acts. This followed a remark in Horace's *Ars poetica*, which was becoming a canonical critical text. (The five-act structure was not in fact adopted textually by Plautus and Terence themselves, but had been imposed on their comedies by editors in late antiquity: see also Chapter 18 below.) The space represented on stage, within which the fiction was acted out, settled very quickly as being a street or a square in a contemporary city. In this early phase there were no changes of physical scene, the action never took place indoors, and a rustic or extra-urban setting was very rare. Such practice seemed to reflect the Roman dramaturgical models. It was reinforced very quickly by a commonly adopted scenography which was not of classical derivation at all. Exploiting the new techniques of Renaissance painting, a combination of backcloth and wings represented the required urban space in three-dimensional perspective, with practicable houses in which some of the characters were deemed to live, and a city panorama behind. (Later in the sixteenth century, Italian scenographers became masters of more ambitious visual settings, and of spectacular changes of scene; but these were used for genres other than comedy.) The setting helped to underpin a dramaturgy which was relatively realistic, rather than poetic or symbolic. The characters in the comic story represented a limited range of society, mainly rich city families and their servants or hangers-on, as had also been the case in Plautus and Terence. The extent to which the protagonist families were noble, or merely bourgeois, can be blurred; but the rules of the comic genre were understood to preclude them from holding public office or responsibility. By classical precedent, comedy was reckoned to deal with its characters' private affairs: any story with a wider public resonance belonged to tragedy. The existence of legal authorities in the city portrayed — like the Prince of Verona in *Romeo and Juliet* — could be used as a threat to some characters, or as a resolution of conflicts for others; but princes and rulers were themselves marginal figures, rarely appearing on stage. In general, the genre designations of 'comedy' and 'tragedy' were regarded as defining and limiting the social class of a play's protagonists.

A feature which is sometimes overlooked with regard to *commedia erudita*, but which had a huge effect on the development of modern European theatre, was the tendency to write it in prose. Before this time, all scripts ever composed anywhere for recitation on stage had been in verse; with local and national traditions dictating which metres were to be used. However, the texts of Terence's comedies had been transmitted in a written form which made them appear to be prose rather than Latin iambic verse: the confusion was only resolved at the turn of the sixteenth century. This fact may have influenced writers of early *commedia erudita*; but it was the personal preferences of Ariosto's princely patrons, the Este and Gonzaga rulers of Ferrara and Mantua, which were crucial in launching the new habit. Isabella d'Este had preferred prose translations of Plautus to the plodding rhymed versions which she had first experienced. Ariosto's *Cassaria* and *Suppositi* of 1508 and 1509 had been drafted in prose to please these patrons. Their author was in fact more of a classical purist, and wanted to rewrite the plays for publication in his particular chosen unrhymed metre, which he (if no one else) thought was a proper reflection of Plautine metrics. He was forestalled by his two plays being rapidly published in pirated prose editions: his verse redraftings did not reach the press until after his death. The prose versions made such an impression, however, that the most significant classical-style comedies which appeared in Italy over the next two decades were also in prose — with the obstinate exception of Ariosto's own subsequent forays into the genre in the 1520s. We can list here Bibbiena's *La Calandra* [Calandro's Play] (1513); Machiavelli's *La mandragola* [The Mandrake] (*c.* 1518) and *Clizia* (1525); the comedies of Pietro Aretino; and plays collectively authored by the Sienese Intronati Academy, such as the influential *Gl'ingannati* [The Deceived] (1532). There were then some Italian comic dramatists who did prefer to use verse (though not the eccentric metre which Ariosto had invented); but throughout the sixteenth century they remained a minority, concentrated most of all in Florence where there was a more doctrinaire attitude to classical imitation. The earliest French translations and adaptations of Italian comedies then followed the same trend: the prose comedy *Les Abusez* (1540), by Charles Estienne, was a close version of *Gl'ingannati*. The first ever English prose play was George Gascoigne's *Supposes* (performed 1566, printed 1573), a direct translation of Ariosto's *Suppositi*. In the subsequent history of classical European comedy, there were then some fluctuations — Molière was capable of using either prose or verse — but the radical possibility that a play might be acted in prose dates from the very beginning of the genre.

Inevitably, many plots of early *commedia erudita* looked very much like those of Plautus or Terence. Young men plotted furiously to gain access to young women, helped by servants who were more shrewd and inventive than their masters. The fathers of the young men were tricked out of large sums of money. The trickery often involved characters disguising their identity. In 1508 Ariosto's *Cassaria* stuck very close to the Roman formula — even to the extent of making his 'heroines', the object of the young men's desires, slave girls and potential prostitutes under the control of a pimp, women whom the young men had no intention of marrying. Just a year later, with *I suppositi*, Ariosto had perceived that this format needed altering. The patterns set up by medieval romance and epic, and even perhaps to some extent by folklore, were now an essential part of the fictions to which a Renaissance public was accustomed. A happy ending for young people had to take the form of their getting married: the obstacles in their path could still come from parental obstinacy, but this should be presented in terms recognizable from contemporary society. A familiar setting, in a named Italian city, made audience empathy easier. Soon it became possible also to broaden the dramatic conflicts beyond a simple clash between parents and offspring. Young lovers could triumph over a wider range of difficulties, including family separations, long-distance travel, misunderstandings between the lovers themselves, even honest confusions of identity. Issues of sexual fidelity, happily resolved, could make those lovers more sympathetic and interesting; and this could apply also to female lovers, whose feelings had been ignored or mocked by the ancient Roman sources (see also Chapter 24). In the context of the present study it is worth remarking that medieval narrative — with its concentration on romantic love, and the complexities of female as well as male emotions — was mostly associated with, or derived from, works written in French.

The Sienese comedy *Gl'ingannati* was collectively composed and staged in 1532 by the Intronati Academy. It has a heroine who has been abandoned by her lover and has to work to get him back: in order to do so, she detaches herself from family constraints and disguises herself as a boy. This produces a combination of romance, trickery, cross-sexual titillation, and even some pathos. The play (a recognized antecedent of Shakespeare's *Twelfth Night*) was enormously influential, and along with some other plays composed in Siena it became an enabling model for a number of Italian comic plots. The plays continued to make audiences laugh by offering a good number of straightforwardly ridiculous characters: ignorant male servants; promiscuous female servants; pedants, parasites, and pimps; braggart soldiers; and also the family patriarchs whose function in the story was to be tricked and to lose the contest.

There was another type of entertaining story, also rooted in medieval literature, which transferred comfortably to the comic stage: the adultery tale. Here the victorious youngsters were a mis-married wife and her lover, and the defeated object of derision was a husband who was too stupid, or too old, to attract any sympathy. For Italians, this structure was associated with short stories, especially the well-known *Decameron* collection of Giovanni Boccaccio which dates from *c.* 1350. It informs two early plays which have been acclaimed in their own time and since: Bibbiena's *Calandra* (performed 1513, printed 1521), and Machiavelli's *Mandragola* (performed *c.* 1518, also printed 1521). However, as *commedia erudita* developed through the sixteenth century, adultery stories remained in a small minority compared with plots where the desired denouement was achieved by a marriage.

In the latter half of the century Italian dramatists and theorists were beginning to extend the boundaries of the inherited classical genres. The invention of 'regular' five-act pastoral plays was an innovation not really based on Greco-Roman precedents: it produced plot situations and structures which contained a mixture of emotional tones, and also allowed elements of fantasy, magic, and the supernatural. The term 'tragicomedy' (coined by Plautus almost as a joke for his *Amphitruo*) was increasingly widely used, and increasingly associated with the new pastoral genre. This decline in generic rigidity had an effect on erudite comedy. The dilemmas and predicaments faced by young lovers could be treated with more moral seriousness, in plays which were sometimes categorized as *commedia grave* [serious comedy]. These offered a duality of tone, in which stories of romantic anguish were performed alongside sub-plots whose characters were much more farcical. In the later sixteenth century, the most significant writer in this genre, with the largest body of surviving work, was the Neapolitan Giovanni Battista Della Porta (1535?–1615). A familiar parallel for anglophone readers would be Shakespeare's *Much Ado About Nothing*, which is based on Italian narrative sources and offers characters and tones ranging from pathetic Hero to ludicrous Dogberry. The Italian versions continued to pursue stories of family separation which produced confusion about people's real identity.

The choice to compose *commedia grave* (or indeed pastoral, or tragicomedy) was made in a context of increasing theoretical debate about the parameters, or 'rules', within which classical-style drama should operate. In comedy in particular, pioneering practice had preceded theory; though attention had been paid from the start to prescriptions and norms found in the 'Donatus' commentaries to Terence. From the 1540s on, however, dramatists in all genres needed to take account of studies by Italian humanist scholars of precepts which they derived from Aristotle and from Horace. Classical forms of drama took their justification from the authority of the ancients; and that authority was sought from theoretical pronouncements as well as from practical example. Aristotle's *Poetics* in particular were taken firmly to be prescriptive rather than just descriptive; and it was a series of Italian commentators on that text who deduced from it a set of dramaturgical rules which would eventually be formalized as the 'three Unities' of time, place, and action. This started with the Latin *Poetices* of Iulius Caesar Scaliger published posthumously in 1561 in Lyon. (Scaliger was originally Italian, but resident in France.) The doctrine was reinforced above all by Lodovico Castelvetro's commented edition of Aristotle. Published first in Vienna in 1570, then in Basel in 1576, this volume had a pan-European resonance from the start: its author was originally from Modena. We shall see in Chapter 7 the notorious importance which principles formulated by Scaliger and Castelvetro were to acquire in seventeenth-century France. Comic dramatists were perhaps under less pressure from normalizing theorists than tragedians were. But they did have to deal with, or to avoid, attacks from moralists — about dramatizing scurrilous behaviour in their plots, about less respectable registers of language (including the question of whether local dialects were admissible on stage), and about mockery of figures of patriarchal authority. They always fell back, plausibly or not, on the notion that comic drama was a tool for deriding bad behaviour and encouraging spectators to avoid it (see Chapter 17.)

In addition, as Counter-Reformation values took control of the Catholic church, and imposed an increasing level of cultural censorship, the very existence of performed drama became questioned all over again, with reference to those same Church fathers whose revered texts had for a long time effectively suppressed theatre as a cultural activity. Attacks on theatre as such, which in England are associated loosely with Puritan sects, were in no way limited at this time to Protestant societies. When theatre became a full-time profession, in Italy and then in France, its practitioners were often on the defensive.

Bibliographical Note

In English, for the first half of the sixteenth century, see Andrews 1993. There is then succinct coverage of the second half, in the essay by Clubb 2019. For the question of composing comedies in prose or verse, see Brown 1973.

For introductory surveys in Italian, one could single out Pieri 1989, Padoan 1996, and Attolini 1997. Important ground-breaking anthologies continue to be those edited by Borsellino 1962–67 and Davico Bonino 1977–78; but since then there have been far more editions, and a few English translations, of individual comedies. The compendium of play summaries by Mango 1966 is still useful.

For Italian humanist critical theory, see relevant sections of Weinberg 1961.

CHAPTER 3

Italian *commedia dell'arte*

The new theatre professionalism developed from around the 1540s. Italian actors and mountebanks, who had previously existed at a marginalized vagabond level largely undetected by history, saw in the plot formulae of classical comedy both commercial potential and a route to greater social recognition. Thus the *commedia erudita* of courts and academies began to exist alongside what historians now call *commedia dell'arte*. That term is accurate in indicating the professionalism of the new troupes: *arte* was the Italian word for a craft skill, and also designated a trade guild. However, the expression itself dates only from the eighteenth century. The 'artisan' approach to classical comedy soon became intertwined with 'erudite' assumptions, and the interplay between them will be a theme of this book. From the start one has to emphasize the similarities between the two strains, as well as their obvious differences. The professional companies offered a major revolution in the performing process, but hardly any change in the comic product. Without the earlier establishment of *commedia erudita* — its stereotypes, and its range of typical or preferred plots — *commedia dell'arte* would not have appeared with the characteristics which we now recognize.

We are dealing here with a firmly Italian phenomenon, pioneered in the northern half of the peninsula and most of all in the Republic of Venice. Its practitioners banded together in troupes which were legal entities, bound by notarial contracts. Since nineteenth-century French scholars first made the term *commedia dell'arte* current, the genre has been historically renowned for its masked stereotyped characters, and for the practice of performing plays by improvisation on a scenario rather than by memorizing a written script. In addition it deserves more credit than it has received until recently for the revolutionary introduction onto European stages of female performers (see also Chapter 24), who quickly attracted fan bases among their spectators. The social origins of the first Italian actresses were probably far from respectable: they are likely to have been high-class courtesans, trained to entertain educated clients by improvising both verse and music. Nevertheless it was the presence of women on stage which raised the tone of what otherwise might have remained at the level of scurrilous clowning. Actresses appeared in roles which rose above sexual titillation, and helped to develop a higher rhetorical and emotional register of language: this fitted well with the romantic tendencies pursued by the Sienese comedies of the Intronati Academy and then by *commedia grave*. The presence of actresses also encouraged a greater mixture of genres, since their language borrowed heavily from the tragic and pastoral dramas in which they also starred. In a second generation of female performers, Isabella Andreini (1562–1604) made systematic efforts to break the association between actress and whore, and to present herself as a cultured literate woman (author of lyric poems and the pastoral play *Mirtilla*, elected member of a literary Academy), and as a respectable wife (to another actor, Francesco Andreini). Her example helped to set a model for whole families in which both men and women pursued acting simply as an inherited craft (indeed, an *arte*). Although the Catholic church retained serious doubts about admitting such families into its communion, by the mid-seventeenth century they had become a fixed part of the cultural landscape, in France and Spain as well as in Italy.

In comedy as such, the new female stars were accompanied on stage by a range of grotesque masked characters — the term 'mask' is appropriate for such a fixed role whether a facial mask was worn or not. These figures, instantly recognizable from their costumes, became as well known in early modern European popular culture, and as widely exploited and marketed, as characters from cartoon film in twentieth-century America and beyond. In Italy itself, the visual badges provided by masks and costume were accompanied by the vocal badges of fixed regional speech — comic accents from Venice, Bergamo, Bologna, Naples, even Spain — which passed less easily into other languages and cultures when the material was exported or translated. So in France and elsewhere, the old fathers Pantalone and the Doctor performed without their Venetian and Bolognese dialects; and servant characters such as Zani, Brighella, Scaramouche, and Arlecchino began to lose their specific association with the rustic regions around Bergamo. The braggart Capitano, based partly on Plautine models but partly also on resentful caricature of contemporary occupying troops, could retain a Spanish identity, or not, according to constraints of diplomatic prudence. When he was not from Spain, he was often from Naples. With or without their accents, these masks endured in recognizable form for centuries, on a transnational European level. As will appear in the next chapter, Harlequin himself was less Italian than Italians themselves now like to believe: the mask was inspired by a demonic figure from French folklore.

Italian professional companies needed a full-time cast covering three basic categories of mask: Lovers (*Innamorati*), Elders (*Vecchi*), and Servants (*Servi*). These categories were dictated in their turn by the standard comic plot formats of *commedia erudita* — based, as we have seen, on Roman comedy with a crucial infusion of medieval *novella* and romance. Elders (always male) existed on stage to be deceived and mocked by Lovers and Servants, with the lower-class characters often taking more initiative than their young masters and mistresses. Elders and Servants were explicitly classed as *parti ridicole* [funny roles]. Lovers, who did not wear facial masks, fluctuated between provoking laughter and inspiring romantic sympathy: they operated as the aristocrats in a theatrical class structure, and expressed themselves in a register of language which was educated and literary rather than colloquial. In comedy, which made up the majority of their output, the professionals continued to concentrate on the same kinds of plot as *commedia erudita*: some adultery stories (perhaps more of these than were attempted by the gentlemen amateurs), and the usual farcical or sentimental tales in which the young Lovers triumphed over the Elders, over Fortune, or over each other. Servants and even Lovers disguised themselves in order to trick adversaries; the discovery of long-lost family relationships made difficult marriages easier. It is not clear that this would have been the material chosen by indigenous popular comic drama, if the classical models had not been resurrected first by the courts and academies. The example of medieval French farce, and the content of a separate Italian genre of comedies about rustic peasants, suggest that stories of a slightly different kind might have been more spontaneously popular. Without the 'erudite' model, professionals might have preferred plebeian tales of straightforward trickery, including indeed adultery, but with more local satire, and more treatment of tensions and resentments between husband and wife, which is a theme largely ignored by plots with a classical or romance background. The limited range of fixed roles offered by *arte* troupes helped to build assumptions about which characters normally appeared in a comic plot: in particular, the absence from the standard cast list of a stereotypical older woman was of some significance in the later development of authored literary comedies (see also Chapters 23 and 24).

More generally, though, the initial impact on the classical comic genre of these Italian artisan improvisors was limited to technical aspects of dramaturgy and performance. Scenarios (*canovacci, soggetti*) tended when written down to be divided into three acts rather than five, perhaps reflecting a more convenient performing format involving just two intervals. Playing in masks underlined a tendency for the more ridiculous characters to become frozen and puppet-like, a set of fixed stereotypes with fixed attitudes. Performing methods based on improvisation — which, as we shall see in Chapter 19, required each actor to create a personal repertoire of recyclable material — influenced the structure of scenes and the composition of comic dialogue. These matters are of course not negligible, and the theatre of masks had a rapid impact on the practicalities of comic performance. It encouraged a confidential relationship between audiences and star performers, and as a result gave notable importance to monologues addressed to spectators, across the 'fourth wall'. However, in terms of the stories narrated on stage the *commedia dell'arte* was entirely derivative: in this sense it could be said that written erudite scripts influenced and even dictated improvised artisan scenarios, rather than vice-versa.

Although a majority of the stories performed by the professional companies consisted of comedies in more or less classical style, these actors were also capable of performing in other genres. Surviving collections of *canovacci* from the early seventeenth century show retrospectively the range of different scenarios which had been tackled during the decades before and after 1600: they include a tendency to combine comedy with pastoral, and there are a few complex mixed shows which include a musical element. In particular, the clownish masks which had been created for classical comic plots were sometimes made to migrate into fantastical or fairy-tale settings; so we may find Pantalone, Zani, and the Dottore figuring as servants or ministers in a royal palace, in contexts which may be pseudo-historical or even have magical overtones. This was a precedent for later developments, in particular for the roles given to such masked characters by the dramatist Carlo Gozzi, in Venice in the 1760s.

Bibliographical Note

The accounts in English of *commedia dell'arte* which have long been relied on (Duchartre 1929 and Nicoll 1963) are now out of date in their overall approach, though they still contain important facts. The chief Italian scholars who have radically revised our knowledge since are (in alphabetical order) Siro Ferrone, Delia Gambelli, Ferruccio Marotti with Giovanna Romei, Cesare Molinari, Ferdinando Taviani (also with Mirella Schino), and Roberto Tessari. Their major works appear in the Bibliography.

The 1611 scenarios of Flaminio Scala (see also Chapter 5) were edited by Ferruccio Marotti in Scala 1976; and a full anastatic reprint of the original volume is Scala 2018. Selected items from other seventeenth-century scenario collections, which remained in manuscript, are in Testaverde 2007. An important anthology of *commedia dell'arte* material is found in the six volumes of Pandolfi 1957–61.

The most accessible short English account of the genre is the 'Introduction' by R. Andrews in Scala 2008: ix–lvi; that volume then offers translations and close analyses of thirty Scala scenarios. Important longer studies in English are Richards & Richards 1990, Fitzpatrick 1995, Henke 2002, and Katritzky 2006. A work which rightly continues to be referred to in detail by scholars is Lea 1934. The essays in Balme, Vescovo & Vianello 2018 concentrate mainly on the subsequent influence and reputation of *commedia dell'arte*.

For the influence of women on stage, see Henke 2002 and Ferrone 2014; for Isabella Andreini in particular, Andrews 2000 and 2013.

CHAPTER 4

❖

Italy in France, 1540–1604

Humanist scholarship began to take root in France as well as in Italy during the sixteenth century: it was a trend encouraged by King François I, who came to the throne in 1515. As regards attention paid to classical theatre, the decade of crucial initiatives was the 1540s. In 1541, there appeared a French translation of Horace's *Ars poetica* by Jacques Peletier du Mans; and the following year Charles Estienne offered a French version of Terence's *Andria*. Estienne in particular was impressed explicitly by Italian *commedia erudita*: as early as 1540 he published a ground-breaking prose translation (with a few cuts and alterations) of the Intronati comedy *Gl'ingannati*, giving it in subsequent editions the title of *Les Abusez*. (The reputation and influence of this single Sienese play is ubiquitous in the sixteenth century, abroad as well as in Italy.) Estienne was transparent, and indeed enthusiastic, about the fact that he was inspired by Italians, but others working in the same vein were more grudging. In 1545 a verse adaptation of Ariosto's prose *I suppositi* was published by Jacques Bourgeois. He gave it a long roundabout title (*Comédie très elegante* [etc.]) which made its source unrecognisable; and he avoided mentioning Ariosto at all in his introductory 'Argument', where he claimed just to be imitating Plautus and Terence.

In 1548 Bibbiena's *Calandra* was performed in Italian in Lyon, for a visit by the new King Henri II and his Florentine Queen — with actresses taking at least some of the female roles. This meant that the French elite's first live experience of an Italian classical comedy involved the inclusion of women performers. It is in fact the first documented appearance of actresses in a high-status public theatre show, pre-dating any such evidence from Italy (see also Chapter 24). In 1554 and 1555, the royal court then hosted performances of two more comedies in Italian: Angelo Firenzuola's *I Lucidi* (effectively a translation of Plautus's *Menaechmi*), and Luigi Alamanni's *La Flora*.

'Arts of Poetry' in French, based on ancient models, were produced by Thomas Sébillet in 1548, and by Peletier in 1555: they dealt with literature generally and not just drama. But there also appeared some new plays in French, tragic and comic, composed along classical lines and following Italian examples. Chronologically the first such comic script was *Eugène* by Étienne Jodelle (composed and performed 1552, printed 1574): its plot was less obviously classical, but rather an attempt to fit native farce material into the new canonical five-act structure. It was followed however by other comedies which were closer in content to the ancient models, some closely inspired by Italian sources and others more original: pioneering authors included Jacques Grévin, Jean de la Taille, Jean-Antoine de Baïf, and Odet de Turnèbe. There was an initial reluctance to adopt the medium of prose — though it had been championed from the start by Estienne, who thought that it liberated comedy from what he saw as the unnatural constraints of verse.

All these developments took place in the context of a wholesale Italian invasion into French cultural consciousness, starting with artists and architects — including Leonardo da Vinci, in 1516 — who had been brought back by François I after his Italian military campaigns. The subsequent dependence on Italian cultural models then involved some paradoxes which the French found difficult to swallow. France was a large kingdom with ambitions to become (in modern terms) both a nation state and a Great Power. Italy, by contrast, had never in history been a single political unit. Viewed in terms of realpolitik, the peninsula was a miscellaneous gaggle of small disorganized cities, which tended to give themselves more importance than they could militarily sustain. In a way which was probably mysterious to an outside viewer, these communities had nevertheless developed a more sophisticated economy, and a more enviable standard of living, than existed in northern Europe. On the strength of that wealth, Italians were producing the cultural revolution which we now call the Renaissance. However, around the year 1500 the French monarchy realized, and the Italian cities were shocked to discover, that these fractious little states were never going to unite or acquire a critical mass, and were open to being walked over by stronger nations with bigger armies. The first half of the sixteenth century was thus characterized by the 'Italian wars', during which France, Spain, and the Holy Roman Empire (the latter two eventually combining under Habsburg rule) could flex their muscles against each other, fighting for influence and control precisely over these rich but impotent Italian territories. The metaphorical 'invasion' of France by Italian artists and writers was the by-product of a literal invasion of Italy by French soldiers. From the start one can detect an ambivalent, even evasive attitude among French intellectuals, as they worked to produce a French Renaissance; and it was sometimes expressed as outright hostility to Italy. They wanted to absorb the classics, and to increase national prestige by excelling in the new European styles and practices dictated by humanist culture. Italy, however, was on the one hand seen as subject territory in military terms, and on the other hand resented for its commercial and financial power. French writers did not want to acquire their knowledge of the ancient world from Italians, or did not want to admit that they had done so. And so Jacques Bourgeois published his version of an Ariosto comedy with no mention of Ariosto.

During the later sixteenth century, French life was heavily disrupted by disastrous civil conflict between Catholics and Protestants, culminating in the St Bartholomew's Day Massacre of 1572. This inevitably had a curtailing effect on high aristocratic culture. The total number of known *comédies érudites* (as we might choose to call them) composed before 1600 is around thirty. Of these, the most notable body of work, certainly the most influential on subsequent French dramatists, came from Pierre Larivey (1549–1619), who published anthologies in 1579 and 1611: each of his nine prose comedies was an adaptation of a single identifiable Italian original. Larivey acknowledged his dependency on Italian culture, but he also tried to underplay it, over-stating his own originality. The small overall number of French comedy scripts is explained by their appealing to a limited audience, in courts and colleges. As we have seen, some Italian or Italianate plays were staged at the royal court: they were not all comedies, since elite scholars were also taking an interest in reviving classical-style tragedy and in pursuing the Italian invention of pastoral drama. But there is no firm evidence as to whether the plays of Larivey, or the equally striking *Les Contens* by Odet de Turnèbe (composed 1580, printed 1584) were ever performed.

In fact, fully scripted five-act Italianate comedies soon became rivalled by Italian theatrical 'texts' which could not be recorded on paper — that is, by the unscripted performances of visiting professional companies. If *commedia erudita* and *commedia dell'arte* were competing for the attention of French audiences, it was the artisans who won the contest. After the pioneering visit to Lyon in 1548, Italian actors are known to have been invited frequently to France by royalty, starting in 1571 with the company of Zan Ganassa who then established himself permanently in Spain. Even during the decades of crisis provoked by the religious wars, those troupes of which records survive were welcomed at the highest level. The Queen of France from 1547, and then effectively Regent for her three young sons until around 1588, was the Florentine princess Caterina de' Medici ('Catherine de Médicis', 1519–1589). The 1548 Lyon performance by a Florentine troupe had been organized in her honour. She continued to support Italian influence on French culture, and the most prestigious professional actors were among those who benefited, most of all the Gelosi company under Francesco and Isabella Andreini, and the Accesi who often included Tristano Martinelli. Other groups regularly toured the French provinces, but we do not know their names and they have disappeared from history. However, surviving documents about theatre performed in provincial towns suggest that, as far as comic drama was concerned, the native French farce tradition also still had a hold on public taste: there are references to plays about marital cuckoldry, and grotesque scenes satirizing the legal system, neither of which themes derive from the classical tradition. The Italians themselves often concentrated on 'Zani and Pantalone' sketches promoting the sale of medicines and remedies (thus stressing the 'mountebank' character associated with lower grades of the profession), rather than on adaptations of classical-style comic narratives. It is recorded that the sexual favours of some of the travelling actresses might be sold to the highest bidder, along with the patent medicines.

More extensive surviving records, about visiting Italian troupes who were less scurrilous on all fronts, deal with the city of Paris and with the royal court. Those two entities were not identical: the court moved between different locations, and there were sometimes clashes between royal and civic authorities over granting or refusing permissions to travelling players. The more puritanical elements in the Paris municipality were not in favour of 'lewd' public performances; and there were other powers that wanted to retain their monopoly of, and control over, performance venues. However, in the years 1584–85 there were at least two separate Italian companies acting regularly in Paris, competing or collaborating or both. They are tentatively now identified as the Uniti and the Confidenti. This was the moment at which the Mantuan actor Tristano Martinelli (c. 1555–1630) took over the personality of a subversive demonic figure from French folklore named Hellekin, and adopted it with Italian modifications as his own stage persona. The figure of Arlecchino (Arlequin, Harlequin) lasted long beyond Martinelli's lifetime and became legendary. As we shall see, the mask's development was driven most of all by later Italian actors who also performed it in Paris: the history and the mere existence of Harlequin provide one of the major areas in which Italian and French comic theatre traditions became inseparable.

Meanwhile we can also note that the brief Italian theatre ascendancy in Paris in the 1580s coincided, in that same city, with a burst of publications which had connections both with Italy and with theatre. The list includes: two original French *comédies érudites* (*Les Contens* and *Les Néapolitains*); two new comedies written in Italian but nevertheless published in Paris (*Fiammella* and *Angelica*); a French pastoral drama (*L'Athlette*) explicitly 'imitated from the Italians', and a French tragedy (*Orbecc Oronte*) which would merit the same label; a reprinted translation of Ariosto's *Suppositi* from 1552 (not the first unattributed one by Jacques Bourgeois); a facing-page translation of Torquato Tasso's renowned pastoral *Aminta*; and a collection of Italian letters by Alvise Pasqualigo who was also a comic dramatist. All these appeared in 1584 and 1585, many of them issued by the printer Abel l'Angelier who was clearly an Italophile.

The civil wars which resumed in 1585 eventually made Paris a less desirable destination, even perhaps sometimes a prohibited venue, for Italian actors. But the Bourbon monarch Henri IV, who took the throne in 1594, eventually invited Martinelli and his Accesi company back to the capital in 1599. The ageing star stayed for two or three years, and in 1601 he underlined his Harlequinesque persona with a volume (*Compositions de rhétorique de M. Don Arlequin*) dedicated to the king and queen. The queen was France's second Florentine consort, Maria de' Medici, whose dominant presence in the first two decades of the seventeenth century encouraged further Italian cultural influences in court. Martinelli's book may have been printed only in one copy, and as befits a joke composition by an anarchic clown it consists mainly, though not entirely, of blank pages. What it does offer is woodcut pictures of *commedia dell'arte* figures, concentrating predictably on Martinelli himself (see Fig. 4.1); and some pieces of multilingual verse which underline Arlecchino's liminal status, poised between Italy and France.

In those early years of the century, the Gelosi company, directed by the glamorous Andreini couple, were also in Paris. On her way home to Italy in 1604, Isabella Andreini died in Lyon of a miscarriage: her reputation was by now so great in France that she was given a civic funeral and a medal was struck in her honour

FIG. 4.1. Anonymous engraving of Tristano Martinelli as Arlecchino, from the printed *Compositions de Rhetorique* which Martinelli presented in 1601 to Henri IV and Maria de' Medici.

(see Fig. 24.1 below). Her widower dissolved the Gelosi, clearly feeling that neither he nor the troupe as a whole could function on stage without her.

Bibliographical Note

In characterizing French views of Italy in this period I have relied, alongside my own observations, on Balsamo 1992, Heller 2003, and Rayfield 2021a and 2021b.

Previously French Renaissance comedy had been relatively rarely treated: basic sources are, in English, Jeffery 1969; in French, Lazard 1960, and Mazouer 2002b. An important collection of chronicle and archive extracts is Howarth 1997, which includes information about early tours by *arte* troupes.

Relevant plays are collected in the series of volumes edited by Balmas, Bassonville & Zilli 1986–97.

The creation and development of the Harlequin mask in Paris is exhaustively researched in Gambelli (1993–97); Ferrone 2006 is a full biography of Tristano Martinelli. The *Compositions de rhétorique de M. Don Arlequin* (Martinelli 1601) are discussed in Henke 2002: 160–67, and reproduced in many other studies of *commedia dell'arte*.

CHAPTER 5

Comedy in Italy, 1600–1700

Giovan Battista Andreini (c. 1578–1654), eldest son of Francesco and Isabella, was an actor, director of his own Fedeli troupe, and the most original Italian dramatist of the seventeenth century. The plays which he published between 1606 and 1639 do not often fit strictly into the classical comedy genre; though one of them, *Li duo Leli simili* [The Two Identical Lelios], is a fully scripted version of a standard improvised scenario involving twins, originally composed by his father Francesco. He can also be credited with the first attempt at a comic opera libretto, *La Ferinda* (1622), though he failed to find a composer for it. Most often he tended to mix genres, with elements of both pastoral and tragicomedy, and to be deliberately experimental. Many of his scripts were printed with a technical commentary explaining aspects of their staging, including how some special scenic effects were obtained. He also wrote theoretical works in defence of professional theatre as an activity, countering the aggressive stand taken by many churchmen. A number of these, as well as some of his plays, were published in France.

Andreini's attempts to break down barriers between improvised artisan performance and scripted erudite drama were mirrored by some practitioners, but resisted by others. Much dramatic activity was sponsored by aristocratic academies which wanted to distance themselves, socially and culturally, from low-class mountebank touring troupes: they saw their printed plays (in all genres, particularly pastoral and tragedy) as proper, respectable alternatives. They would also avoid temporary bans against professional theatre, which were proclaimed from time to time in various Italian cities. On the other side, professional actors had themselves been breaking into print from as early as the 1580s. In addition to Andreini we should highlight Flaminio Scala (1547–1624) who, as well as one five-act comedy in 1618, published in 1611 a collection of fifty scenarios for improvisation, *Il teatro delle favole rappresentative* [The Theatre of Tales for Performance]. This was the only such material which reached a printer, the scenarios being drafted in a form which could be followed by a reading public. They now constitute especially clear evidence about the sort of plot which the more up-market professionals liked to perform, and about how improvised *canovacci* [canvases] overlapped with what we find in published Italian playscripts. Another actor-manager, Pier Maria Cecchini (1563–1645), also had two comedies printed: he wrote two treatises on improvising practice, only one of which was printed. The Capuan actor Silvio Fiorillo (fl. 1570–1632) helped to introduce a southern Italian presence into the mainly northern touring circuits. As well as publishing six plays, Fiorillo regularly performed the figure of Pulcinella (a clown from Neapolitan folklore, who developed into Polichinelle in France and Mr Punch in England), and a braggart Capitano Mattamoros who was also from Naples. His family relationship to Tiberio Fiorilli (1608–1694) — the 'Scaramouche' actor who became famous in both France and Italy, and who was seen as influencing Molière — remains a matter of dispute.

By far the most informative published texts from this period in Italy are a group of prose comedies, in either five acts or three, printed mainly in or near Rome between 1605 and 1630. Out of half a dozen authors the most prolific, and most frequently reprinted, were Giovanni Briccio (1579–1645) and Virgilio Verucci (c. 1585–c. 1650). Italian critics have given this material the collective label of *commedia ridicolosa*. In many practical respects, the plays closely reflect professional *arte* practice. Their cast lists consist of figures such as Pantalone, Zanni (but not Arlecchino), Dottor Graziano, Franceschina, various Capitani and young lovers, plus other stereotypes of more local interest. These characters speak in a sometimes bewildering range of different Italian dialects or foreign accents — one of Verucci's plays is actually entitled *Li diversi linguaggi* [Various Languages], and it includes a comic Frenchman. The plots are mostly standard tales of lovers getting their way against parental resistance, sometimes helped and sometimes hindered by their clownish servants. In particular, and more prominently than in other theatre scripts of the time, *commedie ridicolose* contain many sequences which are structured in a repetitive, modular, 'elastic' fashion which can be seen as copied from improvising practice, a feature which I shall discuss more fully in Chapter 19. However, the authors' relationship to professional theatre was reluctant or ambiguous. Scholars see these scripts as having been composed for recitation by amateur academicians who loved the experience provided by the *arte* troupes, but for whom improvisation, as opposed to memorizing scripts, was either too difficult or contaminated by its commercial artisan associations. In fact, the scenario collection of Basilio Locatelli — two manuscript volumes dated 1618 and 1622 — is offered explicitly for amateur performance, with a contemptuous rejection of anyone who gets paid for acting. The decision to leave the material in manuscript, in contrast to the scenarios which Flaminio Scala had printed for sale, may be part of the message being conveyed. Nevertheless, *ridicolosa* plays are full of individual jokes, confrontations, and *lazzi* which are likely to have been filched from an unwritten professional repertoire. Scenarios and plays from this period show us that by now there existed a common stock of individual gags, and of stories for recycling, which audiences enjoyed and of which no one could claim ownership. The academic dramatists of *commedia ridicolosa* were closely imitating the despised professionals, reversing the process whereby those theatrical artisans had started by imitating scripted *commedia erudita*. The material on which they drew, and which was constantly exploited and repeated, was now available to theatre practitioners of every style and status, diffused both on paper and by informal oral transmission, in France as well as in Italy. Some of Molière's plays contain strong undeniable repetitions of plots and scenes from Briccio and Verucci. Molière may or may not have read those texts directly; though in fact many of the plays were reprinted throughout the seventeenth century and so were possible textual sources.

After around 1630, the history of comic drama in Italy becomes more obscure. The devastating War of the Mantuan Succession (1628–31) removed the Gonzaga dynasty which had been one of the most enthusiastic protectors of professional actors. A plague which coincided with the war probably took the life of Tristano Martinelli, the first Arlecchino. *Arte* troupes did not cease operating during the remainder of the century: many actors made their reputation in Italy before being head-hunted to go to Paris. But correspondence about acting companies, which is so plentiful in princely archives from earlier decades, either diminishes in the mid-1600s or (more probably) has not yet been systematically studied. By the end of the century, we see a new trend in professional comedy which could only operate within Italy: a tendency towards regionalism. The fact that individual comic masks were identified with single local accents encouraged the cities which spoke in those accents to adopt, or to create, theatre personalities with whom to identify. The first notable example of this comes from the work of Carlo Maria Maggi (1630–1699). Maggi started his career as an academic, a teacher of Latin and Greek in the Spanish-ruled state of Milan. He ended it as being most noted for writing in Milanese dialect, to the disapproval of his superiors. He created for the stage the comic mask of Meneghino, with whom some Milanese may identify to this day: a person who combines comic brio with salty folk wisdom. Meneghino was played by a series of actors, but also became a popular puppet figure — like Mr Punch in England, though with less subversive violence attached. Some other Italian cities also adopted, or created, such local comic figureheads, each one assigning cultural value to its own vernacular speech. Developments like this could not be exported abroad, and are not part of a European legacy; but the overall history of *commedia dell'arte* within Italy cannot be written without referring both to this regionalistic tendency and to the rise of puppet theatre. In a mainly oral tradition, figures such as Meneghino from Milan and Stenterello from Florence were still known to local popular audiences in the mid-twentieth century.

With regard to more literary comedy, it is also the case that 1630 marks a publishing watershed in respect of 'regular' comic scripts: there are fewer new ones issued after that date, and comedies from the sixteenth century cease to be reprinted. We have to conclude that Italian theatrical tastes were changing in this period, especially the preferences of wealthier literate audiences who might be interested in reading plays. Permanent commercial theatres had begun to be built in the 1580s in Venice, and then elsewhere in the peninsula. The works which were then performed in them tended increasingly to be pastorals and tragedies, and also the new genre of opera. Secular drama which was fully sung rather than spoken was launched in Italian courts around the year 1600. Eventually, especially in Venice after 1637, some public theatres effectively became public opera houses. The plots of the earliest court operas had related most clearly to the pastoral genre. In public theatres, their subject-matter then moved in the direction either of mythological fantasy, or of highly coloured stories allegedly taken from history, both kinds of tale being also used in spoken tragedy. Librettos also included some lower-class characters who provided moments of comic relief: the late operas of Monteverdi, with their plebeian page-boys and nurses, are now the best-known examples of this. Mythological subjects could be treated in a light-hearted or ironic vein, as in the case of Cavalli's *Calisto* (1651). The fact that some laughter was being provided by the new musical drama, alongside everything else it had to offer, may in itself have reduced people's interest in classical five-act comedy. But comic opera as such took a surprisingly long time to emerge (see Chapter 12).

The most prolific and successful Italian dramatist of the seventeenth century, Giacinto Andrea Cicognini (1606–1651), composed a number of opera librettos; but he also wrote a range of spoken dramas which largely ignored the classical distinctions separating comedy from other genres. He was heavily influenced by Spanish plays, which also paid little attention to those definitions. His father Jacopo (1577–1631), also a dramatist, had argued in favour of the looser non-Aristotelian models of Spanish drama, in prefaces such as the one to *Il trionfo di David* (published 1633). Giacinto Andrea's subject matter ranged from Hispanic-style 'honour' plays, through various tragicomic and tragic plots, to stories with serious religious content. He inserted masks from improvised comedy into plots which had a very different overall tone, as in his version of the Don Juan story *Il convitato di pietra* [The Stone Guest], printed posthumously in 1691. In general, audiences of this period wanted as many different emotions and sensations as possible to be offered by a single play or opera, including high technical levels of scenic spectacle irrelevant to the strict comic genre. Cicognini's Spanish-derived play *Le gelosie fortunate del principe Rodrigo* [The Lucky Jealousies of Prince Rodrigo] (published in 1654) was used as a source by Molière for a 'heroic comedy', *Dom Garcie de Navarre*, which failed in its own time and is rarely revived.

Luigi Riccoboni (1676–1753) began his career as a very young actor-manager in Venice in 1690: we shall see that he moved to Paris in 1716. Writing in French in 1728, and looking back on his attempts to reform dramatic writing, he complains about a 'decadence of taste' in Italian audiences, particularly about the prevalence in the repertoire of 'Spanish tragi-comedies'. He also reports a sudden decline, around 1680, in the abilities of his fellow-actors: 'no more Lovers with any education or taste [...] no more Harlequins who could combine cultural knowledge ('des connoissances') with natural talent'. This may be the biased view of a single man failing to push his own agenda, and his experience may have been less typical than he thought; but he was reacting to something which he perceived as being true. Some scenarios which he composed before and after 1700, in Italy and then in France, are available in a modern edition together with their introductory *proemi*. Left at the time in manuscript, and therefore not widely diffused, they now provide important evidence regarding what was permissible in comic theatre, or at least what eighteenth-century reformers wanted to permit, during a period when tastes were changing: they will be points of reference in Part II of this book.

Riccoboni failed to get his Italian audiences interested in revivals of tragedy, or of written comedies in verse: in particular, he tells us, his attempt to adapt and stage a verse comedy by Ariosto (at the Teatro San Luca in Venice, in 1715) was a failure. *Commedia erudita* composed according to the rules may at this time have been seen by Italian audiences as running out of steam: it had explored all the possibilities which its still limited framework could provide. The more facile and less 'regular' performances of the *arte* professionals were more familiar and more appreciated. We might judge that the erudite genre had failed to widen its horizons in terms of content, flexibility, and social reference. This would have been difficult for those writing and performing in the Italian peninsula, where the diverse urban centres were becoming provincial and culturally exhausted. Italian theatre practitioners — actors who were also their own dramatists, and who were constantly on tour — had to provide material which was suitable for all those communities, and so specific to none of them. Meanwhile, during this same century, and as my next chapter will show, the city of Paris had been able to break some of the previous moulds of classical comedy, to move the genre forward, to keep it still recognizable, but also to locate it in a world inhabited by its local audience. As will be explained in Chapter 7, it had also been formulating theoretical guidelines for dramatists in all genres, allegedly basing them on ancient precept, rules of which at least some Italians had been taking note.

Paris was in fact becoming a magnet for Italian theatre practitioners. During the 1690s Riccoboni was aware of, and even involved in, some translated performances in Bologna and Venice of French tragedies composed in previous decades. By 1700 France was dictating fashions and styles to much of Europe; but to start with French comedy had been heavily indebted to Italy.

Bibliographical Note

For Giovan Battista Andreini (also discussed in Chapter 6), I rely mainly on his plays themselves (many of them still without modern editions). See also studies by Rebaudengo 1994 and Fiaschini 2007.

'*Commedia ridicolosa*' is studied in Mariti 1978. The derivation of some Molière tropes from these Italian plays is noted more than once by Bourqui 1999; but see also Andrews 1989, 1998 and 2005.

For Luigi Riccoboni (also discussed in Chapter 9), see Riccoboni 1973 and 1979; and the original eighteenth-century printings of his other works. The quotation above beginning 'no more Lovers with any education or taste [...]' is translated from Riccoboni 1728, Chapter VII, p. 73.

CHAPTER 6

Comedy in Paris, 1600–60

French theatre activity was not of course limited to Paris, but it was in the capital that all significant developments occurred. The city tended to sweep up the best talents — sometimes helped by royal intervention, in that star actors might be commanded by the king to come and perform there. It was an attraction also felt outside France. For Italian troupes and actors, from the 1570s on, the chance of working in Paris signified fame and fortune: the city functioned as the Hollywood of early modern Europe. Underlying the whole of Parisian theatre production was the existence, for much of the time, of just two professional companies in the city, both of them licensed and regulated by the king or his ministers. The initial competing venues were the Hôtel de Bourgogne and the Théâtre du Marais: they were succeeded at intervals by the Petit-Bourbon, the Palais-Royal and the Théâtre de Guénégaud. From the early 1600s all troupes included female actors: as also in Spain, this Italian practice was adopted much earlier here than in England.

There is one fact which requires notice in this context, however, and it carries a certain irony. In France, and in Paris in particular, the authorities of the Catholic Church were still interpreting literally a decree dating back to the fourth century which excommunicated all actors. The Church as a whole was not enthusiastic about secular theatrical performance, and inside Italy the Papal States, unlike any other state in the peninsula, maintained a ban on actresses until the late eighteenth century. But it was only the 'Gallican' Church in France which exercised a formal prohibition, including excommunication, against the whole acting profession. It is well known that Molière was refused a proper burial service in 1673. In practice the question was bedevilled by fluctuating tides of opinion, by legalistic quibbles, and by clashes of jurisdiction. King Louis XIII — along with his first minister Cardinal Richelieu, about whom more below — was keen on theatre, and instrumental in establishing stable companies in Paris, both French and Italian. His mother, after all, was Maria de' Medici: she acted as his regent when he was a minor, and then maintained an interfering presence in the kingdom until 1630. In April 1641 Louis issued a royal edict declaring that the acting profession should not be associated with any form of blame or bad reputation, provided that the material they performed was not an offence to decency (there is an explicit prohibition of scurrilous *double-entendres*). His successor the 'Sun King', Louis XIV, was equally supportive during the early part of his life. Later in the century, the climate changed. The king's second wife Madame de Maintenon was a leading figure in a pious faction, the *dévots*; and in his older age the monarch became worried about the state of his immortal soul, repenting of the splendid performance spectacles which had glorified his earlier reign. Meanwhile, Church rules themselves were inconsistent. Italian actors, or actors in Italian companies, were regarded as coming under the Roman, rather than Gallican, religious jurisdiction. Unlike their French counterparts they were not banned from the sacraments, even within France — though, as we shall see, this did not save them in 1697 from being expelled from Paris, when *dévots* persuaded the ageing king that their material had become too scandalous.

Much earlier, a particularly determined effort to break into the Parisian market was made by Giovan Battista Andreini, whose five visits to the city with his Fedeli company stretch from 1613 to 1647. In 1622 the local printer Delavigne published five of his Italian plays. All but one are labelled as 'comedies' (including the comic opera libretto *La Ferinda*), though their tone and style is varied so as to represent a wide range of dramaturgies. Only one of these works, the generic hybrid entitled *La centaura*, was reprinted later in Italy. In 1624–25, during Andreini's fourth stay in Paris, there appeared from the printer Callemont, still in Italian, five of his theoretical writings in defence of the theatrical profession. During his final trip, in 1644, he brought out six publications which were not theatrical at all, but works with either a religious or an encomiastic content. This time the pieces were published without any printer's name attached, possibly indicating a privately funded last-ditch attempt to gain the attention of Parisian readers. Andreini's career was by then seriously on the wane. In 1647 he offered a dedicated manuscript of *La Ferinda* to Cardinal Mazarin, the king's first minister who was really an Italian named Mazzarino; but neither this nor other similar efforts to gain patronage obtained any response. It appears that cultural circles in Paris chose to ignore Andreini's presence for most of the time (as modern French critics have also tended to do). Nevertheless, some French dramatists may have been influenced by his innovative variety, without being prepared to acknowledge the fact.

Andreini's fourth and fifth visits to Paris (1623–24 and 1643–47) occurred on either side of a twenty-year period during which no Italian acting troupes performed in Paris. Various practical reasons have been proposed for their absence, and they have some plausibility. However, it is hard not to note also that these years coincide almost exactly with the period during which the chief minister of Louis XIII was Cardinal Richelieu; and that Richelieu was succeeded in 1642 by the Italian Mazarin. Italian actors were invited back almost immediately, in 1644, and remained a presence in Paris until the end of the century: I shall look in Chapters 9 and 10 at the history of the Comédie-Italienne. Meanwhile it was Richelieu's period of dominance which saw the launch of French classical rules for literary and dramatic composition, addressed below in Chapter 7. In 1643 Louis XIV came to the throne, aged less than five and destined to reign for seventy-two years.

In terms of published drama in French, the first thirty years of the seventeenth century offered little in the way of regular five-act comedy, Italianate or not. The native style of farce still had considerable popularity: five collections of farces were printed between 1612 and 1632. In the twenty years after Isabella Andreini's death in 1604, there were more visits by Italian improvising troupes: their shows, by definition, do not survive in written or printed form. Nevertheless they fed a steady influence into the material which French professional actors chose to perform; and those native comedians too made use of unscripted improvisation. Apart from that, Parisian audiences in those three decades were interested in mixed theatrical genres: in pastoral, in tragi-comedy with a large dose of fantasy and romance, in stories which could be explored with the help of stage spectacle. This period in which classical genre divisions were ignored coincided with an interest in adapting plots imported from Spain, where a rich national dramatic tradition explicitly kept Aristotelian restrictions at arm's length. Spanish *comedia* was described and defended by Lope de Vega in his *Arte nuevo de hacer comedias* of 1609, which received wide diffusion. Plays whose plots were based on Spanish sources — which might or might not call themselves comedies, might or might not adapt themselves to classical models — continued to have a presence on the Parisian stage for a number of decades.

During the 1630s there began an important innovative contribution to native French comedy, provided by a young playwright who arrived in Paris from Normandy: Pierre Corneille (1606–1684). (He needs always to be distinguished from his brother Thomas, who was also a dramatist.) Corneille's later exploits as a tragic dramatist, with all the theoretical controversy which he provoked, tend now to define his place in theatre history; but his comedies — from *Mélite* in 1629 to *La Suite du Menteur* ('The Sequel to *The Liar*') in 1644–45 — are in some ways even more of a watershed. They shifted the attention of the public back towards the comic genre; and they introduced to that genre new character types, and a new verbal style, none of which related to any Italian model.

Corneille's plots were partly taken from Spanish plays, but their stories were then adapted to an individual comic vision. From the outset, with *Mélite*, we see a new focus on what is happening in the minds of the young protagonists, the characters whose eventual pairings are to produce a (mostly) happy denouement. The obstacles to their marriages tend not to come from the stereotyped resistance of their parents: the older generation is marginalized in Corneille's comedies, sometimes not appearing at all. Servants also take a back seat in the drama. They are supportive confidants rather than the authors of complex tricks; and any subversion is limited to ironic commentary on their employers' behaviour. An Italian *arte* company would struggle to adapt its fixed roles to these plays — in a later assessment of *Mélite*, Corneille himself noted that the cast is lacking in overtly comic characters, 'personnages ridicules', or what Italian professionals called 'parti ridicole'. (The braggart Captain Matamore appears in an interesting maverick play, *L'Illusion comique* (1636), which does not fit the classical comedy format.) Corneille's stage is held by a set of young people who pursue their own projects and make their own mistakes. They skirmish and negotiate with each other, sometimes deliberately deceive each other, trying to balance the demands of a civilized code of behaviour against the selfish choices dictated by individual temperament. Those choices may lack conviction, be uncertain or ambiguous, or even show outright perversity. The lovers in Spanish drama operated against a fixed set of rigid rules concerning family honour. Corneille's characters are doing something similar: they are trying to discover how to behave well, like 'honnêtes gens' in the social and moral parlance of the time. But they are also trying to work out what their real feelings are in relation to courtship and marriage, and to the individuals whom they might court or marry. Corneille seems to have believed that his audience might still find their behaviour, particularly their errors, amusing; but the knowing sophisticated smile which he seeks is very different from the laughter provoked by a grotesque Pantalone or Harlequin mask. That difference is accentuated by the fact that the plays are in verse. Rhymed Alexandrine couplets, which were becoming a vehicle for much French drama in all genres, are a discouragement to vulgarity. They also keep spectators at a critical distance, inviting us to reflect on the implications of what the characters are doing and on the words they use to express themselves.

Corneille introduced two principal innovations which constituted a firmly French contribution to the genre of stage comedy: neither had been found in Italian precedents. Firstly, there is a desire to explore and analyse the more complex and ambivalent feelings which can be involved in relationships of romantic or sexual love. By comparison, the emotions conveyed by Italian stars such as Isabella Andreini had been shaped by virtuoso verbal rhetoric and external codes of obligation, more than by deep-level psychology (see Chapter 24).

Corneille's second innovation was to place his central characters explicitly in the audience's own world. His stories are set in seventeenth-century Paris, sometimes in named locations depicted by the stage set — two of his comedies are entitled *La Galerie du Palais* and *La Place Royale*. The main characters belong to a recognizable Parisian upper bourgeoisie which tries to take its standards from the aristocracy. In Italy it had been difficult for playwrights, or for troupe directors composing scenarios, to place characters in an identifiable location and social environment, in a community which could then be assessed or mocked on stage. If they were *arte* professionals, they had to appeal to audiences in all the different cities to which they toured. If they were erudite amateurs, they were wary of engaging with the specific rather than the general: one has to go back to Ariosto, between 1508 and 1530, to find a comic dramatist prepared to allude (very carefully) to social and political realities of his own Ferrara. (I shall explore this topic in Chapter 21.)

Neither of these innovations, once introduced by Corneille, would be dropped from future comedies written in France: between them, in different ways, they foreshadowed and enabled the successive achievements of Molière, Marivaux, and Beaumarchais.

In the late 1640s and early 1650s, new comedies were composed in Paris in a range of different styles. Some were modernized versions of Plautus, or close copies of Italian plays from the previous century. Others continued to draw on Spanish sources, though not always with Corneille's sophisticated and localized parameters. Now that they were writing for stable identifiable companies, dramatists were also influenced by the actors they wanted to recruit. In comedies, even from the 1640s on, they had to take account of the lingering reputations of some acclaimed performers, who had created equivalents of Italian *arte* masks but in a French tradition. Gros-Guillaume (Robert Guérin, d. 1634), Gaultier-Gargouille (Huges Guéru, d. 1633) and Turlupin (Belleville, whose dates are uncertain) were remembered for strong comic personalities, and characteristic material which was not written or recorded in detail but known in essence to a wide public. In the next generation there was Jodelet (Julien Bedeau, 1591–1660), who drew on Italian and Spanish models to create the mask of a derisive tricky servant who could be co-opted into either high comedy or farce. He patented a grotesque nasal tone of voice which then influenced stage clowns generally, including French incarnations of Harlequin. In England, even now, it is associated with the Mr Punch puppet. Jodelet starred in comedies written specially for him by Paul Scarron (1610–1660), including *Jodelet, ou Le Maître valet* (1643) where (as the title indicates) the servant and his employer exchange roles to further the young master's intrigue. (This plot device originated with Plautus's *Captivi*, had been taken up by Ariosto and other Italian playwrights, and would appear later in Marivaux.) Shortly before his death, Jodelet moved to join the recently formed troupe of Molière, who in 1659 wrote a part for him in the early controversial success, half farce and half topical satire, which was *Les Précieuses ridicules*.

Alongside these developments in French dramatic practice, there took place a significant cultural and intellectual campaign to regulate French dramatic theory. This is the subject of my next chapter.

Bibliographical Note

Bibliography on drama of this era, both in French and in English, is substantial. Howarth 1997 is of documentary relevance, here as for Chapter 4. A massive study in English which has stood the test of time, and is regularly still referred to, is Lancaster 1929–42.

For useful brief overviews, see Brereton 1977, Lough 1979, and Adam 1997.

For Giovanni Battista Andreini, see the Bibliographical Note to Chapter 5. Corneille's complete works are found in the collection of 1980–87: observations here on those plays are largely my own, but see also Mallinson 1984. A useful selection of summaries and analyses of seventeenth-century French plays in all genres is Vuillermoz 1998.

CHAPTER 7

French Classical Theory: Italy Plagiarized by France

During the seventeenth century all dramatic and literary activity in France had to take account of a strong campaign to impose a set of rules on artistic creation — rules alleged to be based on ancient authorities, and proposed during the previous century by Italian commentators. An attempt to trace the history of a genre of drama which I have chosen to call 'classical' must perforce consider the phenomenon of French *classicisme*. This was a movement which sought to impose what it saw as order and reason on all forms of French literature. It was particularly forceful in dictating rules for playwrights in all genres. Some of these detailed prescriptions initially provoked controversy, starting in 1637 with a public debate about Pierre Corneille's tragedy *Le Cid*. However, by the 1660s the 'rules' of *classicisme* (and the word *règles* was routinely used to refer to them) were largely accepted. Accepted in theory, at least; and accepted in practice by all those who wanted their plays to contribute to a high national culture. Since tragedy in the theatre, and the epic poem in non-dramatic literature, were seen as higher forms than comedy, more ink was expended by the theorists on dictating and discussing laws for those two more serious genres. However, the rules for tragedy included precepts about how theatre in general should and should not function; so although comedy was supervised less incessantly, it was not exempt from scrutiny.

The logical starting-points for classical theory (though its precepts emerged piecemeal, and not always in logical order) related to the overall function imposed on works of art, which was to instruct as well as to give pleasure (*prodesse* as well as *delectare*, in Horace's frequently quoted Latin). Artistic creations should support social and religious orthodoxy. If they involved fictional narrative — as was of course generally the case for a stage play — then the lessons taught or implied about how we should behave would only work if the story was believable. This was the basis of the general requirement that plots should be based on 'reason'; and of the more specific need for verisimilitude, *vraisemblance* in French. If the audience could not believe that real human beings would behave (or speak, or feel) as the characters on stage did, then the relevance of fiction to reality would be lost, and so would the moral of the tale. Most comedies of the sixteenth and seventeenth centuries may not strike a modern reader as preaching, or even implying, lessons about ethical conduct; but lip service had always been paid to this requirement, both in Italy and in France, whenever comic playwrights and actors felt under pressure to justify their craft. (I shall explore this more in Chapter 17.) Then in France in particular, the demand for *vraisemblance* was coupled with a requirement for *bienséance* — a word that had first been used in this context by Jacques Peletier's *Art poétique* of 1555. The two French words overlapped in a single concept, based on the broad Latin term *decorum* which had been explored by Italian theorists. At one end of its semantic spectrum, *decorum* involved notions of plausibility — of what characters on stage should be made to do, or not to do, granted their social background and personality type. At the other end it dictated what a cultivated French audience might, or should, find acceptable to watch or to listen to. Vulgarity was disallowed, as shown by Louis XIII's support for actors only if they avoided *double-entendres*; but it was also judged, following the example of Greek and Roman tragedy, that deaths and other violence should always occur off stage, and be narrated afterwards. (Whether the slapstick beating of a comic victim was or was not acceptable remained less clear: we shall see in Chapter 17 that it was disliked by the theoretician Nicolas Boileau.)

It was views about *vraisemblance*, however, which underpinned the more obvious restrictions which were placed on dramatic composition. We refer here to the 'three unities', which characterize drama which we still call 'classical', and which both English and Spanish playwrights remained more likely to ignore. (Once again we should note that the terminology used here, however summary and simplistic it may appear, was also used at the time: the phrase 'les trois Unités' was as current in seventeenth-century France as was reference to 'les règles'.) The unities were an attempt to impose criteria which were felt to be rational on the fundamentally irrational business of enacting a fiction on stage. They were indeed based on what could be observed as ancient Greek or Roman practice; though whether relevant remarks by Aristotle or Horace should be read as descriptive or prescriptive is seen nowadays as a more open question. To us, in retrospect, they show an unnecessary level of distrust in the ability of an audience to use its imagination or to suspend disbelief. It was stated that 'rational' spectators would be confused, or derisive, if faced with long time-lapses in a dramatic story (like the sixteen years which elapse between Acts III and IV of Shakespeare's *Winter's Tale*); and equally disturbed by constant shifts of place (as in many medieval or even later plays which moved characters between France, Spain, Jerusalem, and other locations). The fact that such breaches of the unity of time and the unity of place had often been used in earlier European drama, and that audiences had accepted them at the time, seemed to cut no ice. According to classical theorists, the action of a play should be limited to what could plausibly happen in a single day (though there were disagreements about whether that meant twelve hours or twenty-four); and it should occur in just one place (though some accepted that this might mean 'locations within a single city', or 'rooms within a single palace', rather than always one immovable urban space or a single room). Then there was the third unity, that of action: plays were supposed to concentrate on just one story involving a limited number of protagonists, without digressions or sub-plots. It was another aspect of 'rationality' that the audience's attention should be undivided.

The men who formulated and imposed these rules were literary intellectuals, some of them also authors or dramatists. Crucially enlisted to their cause, and then an active proponent of the doctrine, was Louis XIII's first minister Cardinal Richelieu (who, as previously noted, wielded power between 1624 and 1642). Richelieu's ambitions to make the kingdom of France an ordered, efficient, and prestigious state included raising the country's cultural profile. It was he who in 1635 founded the Académie Française, which was invested with the authority to draft and then impose the rules of *classicisme* (as well as its notorious power to dictate which words and structures were and were not acceptable in French written language). Moreover, Richelieu was particularly interested in the theatre, to the extent of becoming a kind of surrogate dramatist: he recruited a group of authors to compose collectively a couple of comedies to which he is likely to have made anonymous but authoritative contributions of his own. To start with, Richelieu had needed to be told by potential Academicians what the classical dramatic rules ought to be; but once he had understood them, he made them his own.

A crucial observation, in the light of our present study, is the relationship — and then also the divergence — between French erudite classical rules and Italian artisan theatre culture. Almost everything which the French pundits derived, or thought they were deriving, from the ancient models and authorities came initially from commentaries and treatises written in the sixteenth century by Italian humanists. It was noticed by René Bray that in a century when France was appealing constantly to the authority of Aristotle and Horace, no new editions or direct studies of those Latin authors were produced by French scholars: work on the primary sources was seen as having been satisfactorily done by Italian predecessors. The interpretations of Scaliger and Castelvetro, and then of their Dutch disciples, were taken as the starting-point for the work of Jean-Louis Guez de Balzac, Jean Chapelain, Père René Rapin, and Hippolyte-Jules de la Mesnadière. Precepts first formulated by Italians were debated, codified, made more coherent, and imposed with a new authoritarian rigour; but no Frenchman ever questioned the basic assumption made by those Italians, namely that the rules had been established in antiquity and were therefore valid for all time. Nevertheless, *classicisme* insisted on its own French identity, as we would expect granted that Richelieu was one of its prime movers. The cardinal and his team wanted to by-pass the Italians and claim as much as possible that they were learning directly from the ancient authorities. France, and not Italy, was to be the new Greece or the new Rome, in European culture. The fact that the French had initially learned about the antique world from Italian humanists was played down. We are reminded once again of the moment in 1545 when Jacques Bourgeois published his version of a comedy by Ariosto with no acknowledgement or mention of Ariosto, claiming that the work was a direct imitation of Plautus and Terence.

There was, then, a relationship with Italy here, however disowned; but there was also a divergence. The presentation of *classicisme* as a purely French initiative was helped by the fact that by the 1630s Italian artisan theatre practice, as opposed to Italian erudite theory, seemed to be obeying few classical rules at all — and this was the sector of Italian performance which the French knew at first hand. What audiences identified as 'Italian theatre', in Paris and in the French provinces, was what was sold to them by touring professional troupes. Improvised scripts delivered to foreign ears had to be kept on a simple non-literary level. The product which worked best in France was episodic farce, oriented to a more physical style of theatre, and with a level of graphic vulgarity which could cross the language barrier but had little to do with any notion of *bienséance*. Alternatively, Italian actors were associated with larger-scale spectacles which often involved both music and impressive changes of scene, using a high level of imported transalpine technology — all of which violated the unity of place, and probably other principles as well. However, this kind of blockbuster show, pointing in the direction of opera, was not seen in Paris until 1645. During the period of Richelieu's dominance in the 1620s no Italian theatre companies were invited to Paris, a fact which is unlikely to be mere coincidence. By the time they returned, the Parisian public had come to perceive a straightforward distinction between French styles of theatre which were subject to the classical rules, and Italian styles of theatre which were not. This is something which I shall explore further, as our narrative continues.

Meanwhile the implications of classical doctrine for comedy in particular were less radical than for other genres of theatre. The prohibition of vulgar language and obscene jokes was largely obeyed; scenes of slapstick violence were less easily abandoned. The unities of time and place (as we shall see in Chapter 20) were not difficult to observe in plots which focused on domestic family issues; though a significant change, which we might see as long overdue, moved the addressing of those issues away from the fixed setting of a public street to a more plausible indoor location. Observing the unity of action did enforce some changes. One could no longer have a serious romantic plot running alongside a separate farcical story, as in Italian *commedia grave*. Plays containing two pairs of lovers whose destiny needed to be resolved, rather than just one pair, also became problematic. It was easier to aim for couples of servants to get married at the end along with their masters and mistresses; and this encouraged the emergence of a new type of role, the sparky young female servant or *soubrette*, which had had no regular equivalent in Italian comedy.

In retrospect, for the theatre historian, the adoption of these rules complicates even further the relationship now existing between the new French and the older Italian brands of classical comedy. The rules broadcast in France were derived and adapted from Italian theorists. Meanwhile, improvising troupes from across the Alps were offering to French audiences forms of 'Italian comedy' which did not obey the rules. But if a French comic playwright accepted the precepts of *classicisme*, then he would go in search of examples to follow, plays which would show him how to produce successful modern adaptations of the now canonical Roman models. Those resources were to be found in published Italian comedies of the sixteenth century, and in the narrative and scenic repertoire units which those plays had fed into later dramaturgy, both scripted and improvised. Such stock material might be vaguely familiar to Parisian spectators: they would know it belonged to the comic genre, but they would not know where it came from. They would certainly not identify it as 'Italian comedy', in the terms which they now understood. Centuries later, surveying the whole story, we can see that it may not have been 'Italian comedy', but it was still comedy derived from Italy. Many French dramatists would know, privately, where they were finding help and inspiration in order to conform more closely to Plautine and Terentian models. It is of passing interest that two theorists of *classicisme*, Guez de Balzac and Chapelain, drew favourable critical attention to the century-old comedies of Ariosto, one of the more meticulous Italian imitators of Roman comedy, who had preferred to write plays in verse.

We can say now, therefore, that an effect of the new classical rules was to help switch the attention of comic dramatists and actors from Spanish models, which did not obey them, back to more 'regular' scripted Italian ones which did. How clear this was at the time to Parisian audiences is perhaps more doubtful: they may have been paying more attention to the new style of comedy which had been launched by Pierre Corneille. Grafted with Cornelian features, roots which were largely Italian could be made to produce plants which looked essentially French. The person who did this first and most successfully was classical comedy's first playwright of enduring genius, the first to contribute to a European repertoire legacy: Molière.

Bibliographical Note

The existence of *classiciste* theory is an unavoidable context for the study of seventeenth-century French theatre: no edition of a play from the period, can avoid giving an account of it. However my major source is Bray 1931. A good summary in English of the issues is found in Chapter 8 of Carlson 1993; see also Moore 1971.

For the dramaturgical interventions of Cardinal Richelieu, see Couton 1986.

CHAPTER 8

Molière between 1660 and 1673

Of the major dramatists treated in this study, Molière (Jean-Baptiste Poquelin, 1622–1673) is the only one who possessed all-round professional theatre talents: he made his living as actor, playwright, and director of a successful company. It is clear, though, that his supreme artisan skills were accompanied by a full erudite acquaintance with Roman comic texts: works by Plautus and Terence can be seen to lie behind some of his masterpieces. The quality and the complexity of his plays have of course provoked many volumes of analysis: I shall be addressing some individual aspects of his writing in later chapters. Here I shall simply identify the place held in my Italo-French narrative by this supreme comic playwright.

That Molière was familiar with the repertoire and the performance style of Italian actors is not disputed. During his early touring career in the French provinces, he certainly encountered Italian competitors on the same circuits. When he moved back to Paris in 1658, and his troupe received the patronage first of 'Monsieur' the king's brother and then of Louis XIV himself, he shared the Petit-Bourbon theatre, and later the Palais-Royal, with an Italian company. For much of the time, the two troupes performed on alternate days in the same space. When Molière's talent and success provoked envious resentment, he was lampooned as being a copycat pupil of the equally well-known actor Tiberio Fiorilli, who spent periods in Paris playing his *arte* mask of Scaramouche, or Scaramuccia: there is a much-reproduced caricature image of Molière standing in front of Fiorilli, holding a mirror and imitating the Italian's posture and facial expression (see Fig. 8.1, and cover illustration). Molière's Italianate credentials were thus held against him in his own time, before being recognized more positively since.

Molière's first surviving scripts, undated but deriving from his time outside Paris, are the two one-act farces *La Jalousie du Barbouillé* [Doughface's Jealousy] and *Le Médecin volant* [The Flying Doctor]. Both of them show firmly Italian features, and the latter bears a documented relationship to Italian scenarios. *La Jalousie du Barbouillé* contains the best surviving evidence in any play script of what an Italian Dottore mask was like, and of how the role was used to exasperate other characters and hold up the action. The central story features the hopeless jealous husband Barbouillé being defeated by his tricky wife Angélique, whose quick table-turning ruse — locking her husband out of the house, after first being locked out herself — derives from a fourteenth-century *novella* by Boccaccio (*Decameron*, VII, 4). Molière might not have known of this original source; but the story had been dramatized

FIG. 8.1. Molière is lampooned in 1670 for allegedly copying the performance gestures of 'Scaramouche' (Tiberio Fiorilli), in the satirical play *Élomire Hypocondre* by Boulanger de Chalussay. ('Élomire' is an anagram of 'Molière'.)

by the Venetian Andrea Calmo in *La Rhodiana* (IV.6–10), published in 1540, and the trope would have been absorbed into the common recyclable repertoire of Italian professionals. Molière himself used it again in his *George Dandin* (1668). He also re-adapted the plot of *Le Médecin volant*, repeating some of its jokes, into *Le Médecin malgré lui* [The Unwilling Doctor] (1666): both plays involve the illiterate servant Sganarelle, played by Molière himself, posing as a qualified medical practitioner. In the earlier farce, Sganarelle becomes a 'flying' doctor in a sequence involving frantic physical virtuosity, a *lazzo* in Italian jargon. By a series of rapid physical tricks which include 'flying' back and forth through a window, he manages to convince his duped victim that he is a pair of twins rather than a single person. Sganarelle was an *arte*-style stereotyped servant figure (though not using a facial mask) which Molière adopted again in some later plays: his name derives from the invented Italian verb *sgannare*, which (if it existed, and it might exist in Neapolitan dialect) would express the opposite of *ingannare*, to deceive. The surviving texts of both *La Jalousie du Barbouillé* and *Le Médecin volant* contain some scenes which are so brief and schematic that they rank as scenario rather than as script: they identify the most important things which characters need to say, and leave the conversational or comic details to be fleshed out by improvising actors. They also show a use of elastically repetitive dialogue structures which hark back to Italian improvisation, and which Molière was later able to adapt to a comic dramaturgy which was psychologically penetrating and not simply farcical (see Chapter 19).

The support and protection given to Molière by Louis XIV committed him in return to writing for a range of spectacular court performances and pageants. Some of his pieces were thus brief and occasional; some of them involved symbolic pastoral or even mythological figures rather than comic bourgeois families; some collaborations with the court composers Lully and Charpentier created the new genre of *comédie-ballet*, taking steps towards the creation of French opera. Nevertheless, despite his excursions to Versailles and Saint-Germain, Molière's most characteristic comedies were nourished by his regular Parisian public in the Palais-Royal. He wrote some popular farces around themes of jealousy and adultery; but the plays which have retained the most secure place in later repertoire are nearly all classical family comedies, where the central conflict is resolved by young sons, daughters, or wards marrying the partners they desire, in the face of resistance from their parents or guardians. However, the comic energy is focused less on the tricks or devices played by the Lovers or their Servants, and more on the ridicule directed at the blocking characters. In Molière's most typical comedies, the father (or in one case the mother) of a frustrated lover is possessed by an element of monomania, which makes their behaviour unreasonable and ridiculous. The deluded parent attempts to marry his or her offspring to someone who will satisfy, or measure up to, the overriding obsession which is the target of the comedy. Sometimes the tunnel vision satirized relates to an aspect of contemporary Parisian society which an audience could be persuaded to mock — a topical brand of gullible religiosity in *Le Tartuffe*, a fashionable version of cultural snobbery in *Les Femmes savantes* [The Learned Ladies], the play where the mother is the obsessive who henpecks the father. In such cases Molière may have sailed close to the prevailing wind and alluded to real recognizable individuals, rather than directing his ridicule at universal anonymous failings as was preferred by humanist and *classiciste* theory. (As is outlined also in Chapter 21, he was sometimes defended by Louis XIV himself against the anger of possible victims.) In other plays the targets are indeed perennial human faults such as extreme marital jealousy, avarice, ambition based on social snobbery, and hypochondria. To many readers and spectators, then and now, these comedies seem most of all to be dramatic portraits of the obsession, neurosis, or weakness of the principal character — who, when male, was played by Molière himself, in performances which also exploited his innate irascibility. This was the beginning of the term 'comedy of character', which soon became current in both France and Italy.

Then, in his most original drama *Le Misanthrope* (1666), Molière moved a step further: there are no obstructive parents in this story, and the personal monomania of the protagonist leads him to act as a blocking character against himself. Alceste's dogmatic insistence on frankness rather than social convention — a principle which he then finds it hard to maintain in practice — sets him at odds with the rest of society. His relationship with his fiancée Célimène, whose errors tend in the opposite direction, fails to attain a conventional denouement, and they end by going their separate ways. This pushing at the boundaries of the classical comic form achieves an unheard-of ambivalence which we could see as French rather than Italian: its structural precedents are the experimental comedies of Pierre Corneille, not anything derived from across the Alps. Nevertheless, Molière's plots are more often Italianate than anything else. *L'Avare* [The Miser] (1668) in particular is a kaleidoscopic recombination of scenes taken from scripted and improvised Italian sources, assembled with the same insouciant bravura as was adopted by the *capocomico* of a professional Italian troupe when he recombined well-used bits of material into a new scenario. It is also the only Molière comedy which uses the very Italian trope of a father discovering his long-lost children — their new identity, and their enhanced income, make them more palatable to their prospective father-in-law.

As has been remarked, Molière showed a close acquaintance with the ancient Roman plays which had launched the whole classical tradition. *Amphitryon* (1668) is a rewrite, even a completion, of Plautus's unfinished *Amphitruo*, with its adulterous interaction between humans and classical gods: as in Plautus, two of the main characters are Jupiter and Mercury. *L'Avare* can be related directly to Plautus's *Aulularia*, as well as to sixteenth-century Italian and French adaptations. And *Les Fourberies de Scapin* [Scapin's Tricks] (1671) is a joyous riff on Terence's *Phormio*.

While maintaining a professional eye on what his audiences actually enjoyed watching, as well as on the theories of the Académie Française, Molière maintained a respectful relationship (in his five-act comedies, at least) with the rules of Italian-derived French *classicisme*. Interestingly, he maintained an almost equal balance between prose comedies and those composed in Alexandrine couplets. The formal preference of French theorists tended to be for verse; but the Comédie-Française, which succeeded Molière and attempted to build on his achievements, continued to accept and produce plays written in either medium.

Bibliographical Note

Molière's *Œuvres complètes* are edited by Jouanny (1962); by Couton (1971); and by Forestier and Bourqui (2010). There are many editions of individual plays, and numbers of English translations.

Critical bibliography in French on Molière is of course extensive. In English, I would single out Moore 1964, Howarth 1982, the biography by Scott 2000, and the *Cambridge Companion* by Bradby & Calder 2006, which includes further bibliography.

For relations between Molière and improvised Italian theatre, see Andrews 1989, 1998, and 2005; and Bourqui 1999.

CHAPTER 9

Comédie-Française and Théâtre-Italien, 1660–1760

A major phase in our Italo-French narrative was the wooing of Parisian audiences by two rival theatre companies openly labelled as 'Italian' and 'French'. This chapter traces a factual outline of this story; then Chapter 10 summarizes the types of theatre which the two troupes offered.

We have noted that Molière's company, once they were back in Paris, shared their acting space with troupes of Italian actors. This arrangement lasted from 1661 until after Molière's death in 1673. Italian performers had been recalled to Paris in 1644, by Cardinal Richelieu's Italian successor Mazarin, and by Anne of Austria who was queen mother and regent for the infant Louis XIV. They left again during the turbulent period of the Fronde, the aristocratic uprising which challenged French royal power; but they were back by 1653. Established first in the Grande Salle of the Petit-Bourbon, then along with Molière in the Palais-Royal, they became a fixed element in Parisian theatre, enjoying a high level of audience popularity. The city's appetite for Italian performers became focused most of all on the Bolognese actor who played Arlequin — Domenico Biancolelli (1636–1688), known to the French just as 'Dominique'. Biancolelli has left us a unique testimony of Italian working methods, in the form of a personal notebook summarizing his contributions to more than eighty plays or scenarios, though its content is limited firmly to the episodes which involved his presence, and sometimes leaves us ignorant of the overall plot. The original Italian notes have been lost: we are left with a French translation from the eighteenth century, which may not be complete or fully accurate, but which is informative none the less. The shows recorded were mounted by the Italian company mostly between 1667 and 1672 (and so covering the second half of Molière's career in Paris), with a final one datable at 1680.

It was in 1680 that 'Dominique' became a naturalized French citizen, as did a number of his colleagues in the troupe over the years. In that same year, a royal decision was taken to concentrate all the French actors in Paris into a single company: it was soon entitled the Comédie-Française, and it survives to the present day. The name stands in explicit opposition to the rival Théâtre-Italien, which at the same time was granted full use of the Hôtel de Bourgogne. (The names of these companies are always hyphenated in French usage.) The Italian troupe had a constitution imposed on it in 1684, by the so-called *Règlement de la Dauphine*. Thus, according to royal cultural policy and also to public perception, there were two distinct styles of theatre which should be licensed in Paris, and what distinguished them was their nationality. The formalized confrontation, or market choice, between the two was a characteristic of Paris theatre for nearly a century, though with one major hiatus as we shall shortly see. In practice it related to performances which were comic, in the broadest sense, rather than tragic. I shall reflect in Chapter 10 on what material features of content and performance were attached to concepts of 'French' and 'Italian' theatre.

The death of 'Dominique' Biancolelli in 1688 caused so much shock both to his colleagues and his fans that the Italian theatre closed in mourning for a whole month. The Arlequin role was taken over by Evaristo ('Évariste') Gherardi (1663–1700). The public continued to flock to see the Italians, but the cultural attitudes of the French king, and therefore of his court, were changing. Italian actors had always been more scurrilous than the French ones, perhaps on the pretext that if they were rude in Italian then a polite audience could pretend not to understand. They were also becoming more sharply satirical of social practices, potentially of living individuals. (I shall relate some examples of this in Chapter 21.) The liberties they took began to try the patience of Louis XIV, as he became more pious and puritanical under the influence of his morganatic wife Madame de Maintenon. In 1697 a pretext was found for closing the Théâtre-Italien and sending its actors away. Scholars are divided about exactly what that pretext was — reputedly, a play was seen as a mockery of Madame de Maintenon herself — but the principle behind the expulsion is unambiguous. The dismissal of the Italians was an event sufficiently memorable to have been recorded in a picture by Watteau, which was frequently copied in later decades (see Fig. 9.1).

Three years earlier, in 1694, Évariste Gherardi had published a selection of fragmentary texts which aimed to record for posterity, but also to capitalize on, the types of spectacle which Italian actors had been offering to Parisian audiences — within the limits of what was reproduceable on paper. In practice the collection included only scripted scenes in French: material performed in Italian was seen as having been improvised, and in theory not transcribable, though in fact there are Italian insertions in the French dialogue (see Fig. 9.2). The later the show had been produced, the more 'Scènes Françaises' it included; and so for the more recent plays the reader gets a substantial impression of the play and its overall plot. The first edition of Le Théâtre italien was blocked by Gherardi's own colleagues, who claimed it had been produced without their permission. Later editions and supplements, some pirated and printed in Amsterdam, continued after the 1697 closure: a 'definitive' revised edition of 1700 (the year of Gherardi's death) was reprinted the following year in Amsterdam, then five more times down to 1741, and for a while the anthology offered nostalgic reminders of what the Paris public was no longer allowed to see.

Italian actors and companies were in fact excluded from the capital for nearly twenty years. Some left France altogether; some found employment in the provinces; others, with more obstinacy, crept back and infiltrated the 'unofficial' theatre mounted on trestle stages at the Paris Fairs, in the suburbs — a popular form

Fig. 9.1. 1729 engraving from a painting by Watteau, depicting the departure from Paris in 1697 of the banished Italian actors. Thirteen years after the Théâtre-Italien had been restored, this event was still seen as worth remembering.

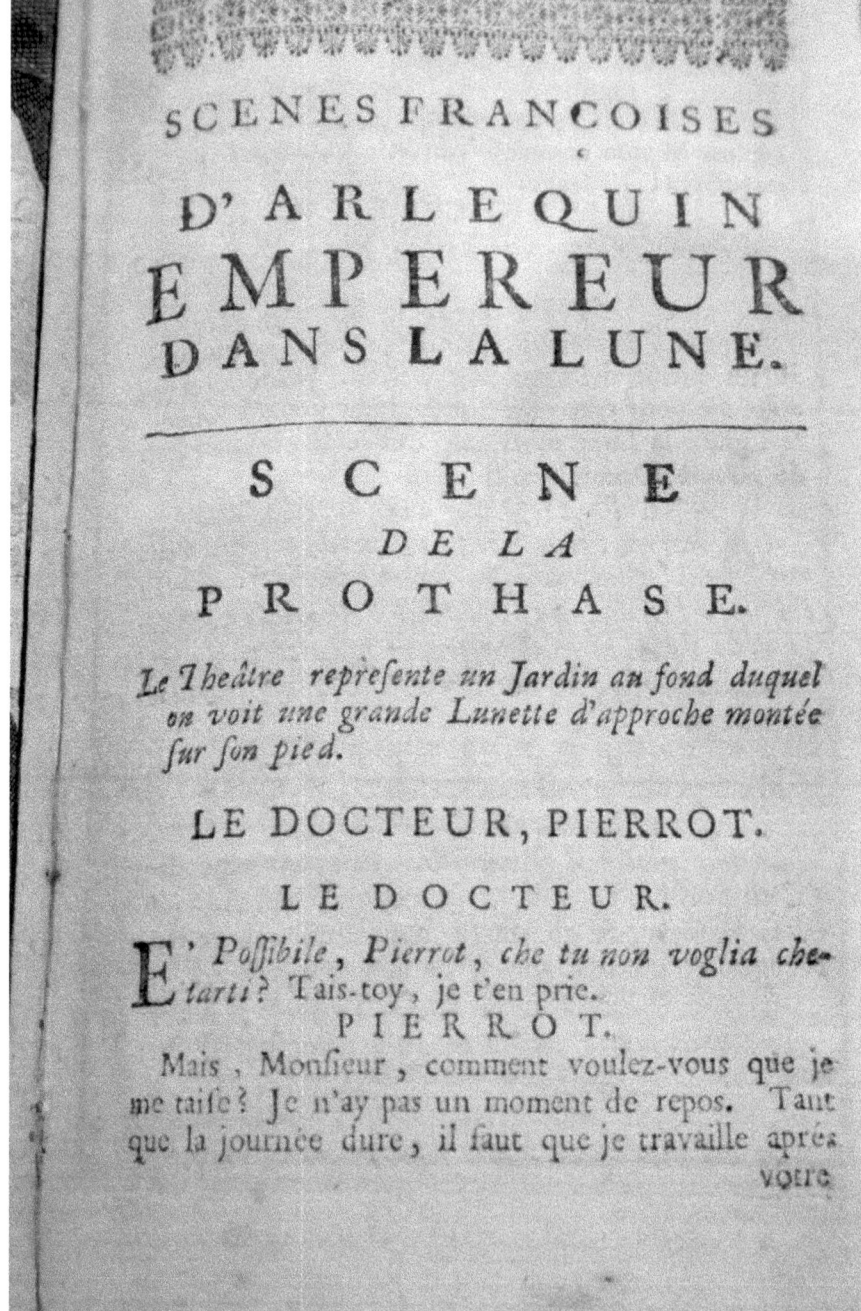

FIG. 9.2. The first page of text from Fatouville's *Arlequin Empereur dans la Lune*, included in volume I of Gherardi's *Théâtre Italien* anthology. A sentence of Italian dialogue can be seen intruding (printed in italics) into the 'Scènes Françaises'.

of apparently ad hoc performance which could circumvent many of the restrictions imposed within the city limits. A key figure in maintaining the tradition of Italian theatre, and passing it on to a subsequent generation, was Pierre-François Biancolelli (1680–1734), youngest son of 'Dominique' and sometimes referred to as 'Dominique fils'. He continued to perform the Arlequin mask, in the French provinces and then at the Fairs. His name is attached to more than eighty printed short play titles 'in the Italian style'; and in 1712 he edited a new anthology of plays and sketches entitled *Le Nouveau Théâtre italien*, no doubt aiming to replace that of Gherardi. Pierre-François is currently still under-researched, and his pivotal role perhaps underrated, by French scholars.

Louis XIV died in 1715, and his five-year-old great-grandson Louis XV had a Regent ruling France during his infancy: Philippe of Orléans, who was a liberal prince, especially in his artistic policy. It took only a year for him to reconstruct a new Théâtre-Italien in Paris, under the direction of Luigi ('Louis') Riccoboni, invited in after a career as actor-manager and dramatist in northern Italy. This was clearly a response to popular demand, a recognition that the public's taste for a perceivedly Italian style of theatre was not going to fade away. A new Arlequin was recruited, also from Italy: Tommaso Visentini (1682–1739), known as 'Thomassin'. Riccoboni (already discussed in Chapter 5) may have been chosen because he favoured a reform of Italian comic dramaturgy. He had a mission to raise the cultural profile of his native theatre, reviving the best elements of earlier Italian comic scripts and purging them of what was now felt to be too vulgar or immoral. His introductions to a set of scenarios (intended for publication but left in manuscript) show that he was influenced by, or attempting to stimulate, changing tastes and sensitivities in polite theatre spectators of the new eighteenth century. He was also explicitly inspired by an Italian presentation of French *classiciste* doctrine: the *Didascalia* or *Dottrina comica* published in 1658 by Girolamo Bartolommei Smeducci (1584?–1662). His campaign could not be fully successful — in Paris, any more than previously in Italy — because of the resistance of Italian actors themselves: they were attached to their own improvisational methods, to their fixed masked roles, and to the somewhat inflexible range of material to which those methods and roles could be applied. Parisian audiences too wanted their Italian theatre to be recognizably 'Italian': perhaps, paradoxically, Riccoboni's true spiritual home was the Comédie-Française. In the minds of the public, the new Italian company was both led and typified by star actors, such as Arlequin 'Thomassin' and the *soubrette* 'Silvia' (Zanetta Balletti, 1701–1758). Their style of theatre continued to function in Paris for two more generations until 1762: in that year the Théâtre-Italien was merged with the Opéra-Comique, which moved in on the Italians and took over their theatre at the Hôtel de Bourgogne. By then the 'Italian' genre had arguably begun to lose its creativity: Carlo Goldoni, arriving from Venice in the 1760s, certainly perceived a lack of innovative energy in the company, which was finally closed down in 1779.

During all this time, the Comédie-Française had continued to exist, and to commission and perform new comedies and tragedies, which were printed and which therefore survive. The company also regularly revived and celebrated the works of major seventeenth-century dramatists including Molière. Meanwhile their Italian competitors were increasingly both writing and performing in the French language. According to a report of 1684, the French actors had complained to Louis XIV that the Italians had started speaking French. The king was unmoved, at that time, and said 'well, so you can speak Italian' — showing a jocular indulgence towards the immigrant performers which he would not maintain thirteen years later.

The two companies were supported in Paris with equal enthusiasm. As far as we can tell, they were patronized by the same audiences, who wanted to enjoy them both and to savour the contrast between them.

Bibliographical Note

Much of this narrative is summarized in Mazouer 2002a. The notebooks of Domenico Biancolelli are edited and discussed in Gambelli 1993–97. For accounts in English, see Scott 1990, who also surveys the content of Gherardi's *Théâtre italien*. Extracts from that collection are edited by Spaziani (Gherardi 1966) and Mazouer and Guichemerre (Gherardi 1994–96); but one has to consult the original 1700 volumes for a full impression of what they contain. There are also manuscript scenarios edited by Colajanni 1970.

It is in a play included in the first volume of Gherardi 1701 — *Arlequin Jason, ou la Toison d'Or comique* (1684) — that we find the story of the unsuccessful complaint to the king, about the Italians performing in French.

For Pierre-François Biancolelli, crucial sources are the doctoral thesis of Margherita Orsino 1993 and her published article of 1998. The thesis includes a full list of titles attributed to Biancolelli.

For Luigi Riccoboni, see the Bibliographical Note to Chapter 5.

CHAPTER 10

'French' and 'Italian' Styles of Comedy

During the years in which the Comédie-Française and the Théâtre-Italien confronted each other, the Parisian public came to conceive a clear-cut distinction between the styles and atmospheres of French and Italian theatre, and to absorb that contrast into a wider set of artistic categories. The two worlds were frozen into visual images by Jean-Antoine Watteau, who produced a pair of paintings entitled *L'Amour au théâtre français* and *L'Amour au théâtre italien*. In 1734 these pictures were turned into purchasable engravings by Charles-Nicolas Cochin *fils*, and therefore widely diffused. Both of them depict groups of figures who do not appear to be in a theatre, but are gathered out of doors to serenade and woo each other in an informal evening context. In fact the costumes of theatrical characters, especially those representing the Italian masks, were taking on a life of their own, not always linked to any dramatic action. They were used as fancy dress, to create a pastoral or fairy-tale atmosphere in social pageants — the phenomenon known as 'Fêtes Galantes' — overlapping to some degree with Carnival. It was these airy manifestations, more than plots performed on stage, which eventually came to feed the imagination of artists, writers, composers, and choreographers in the nineteenth and early twentieth centuries, when they worked their own variations on resurrected images of what by that time was generally known as *commedia dell'arte*. (For more on this, see Chapter 22.)

Our attention here must be focused on the live comic theatre which was staged in Paris before and after 1700, and on the experiences which were offered by French and Italian actors respectively. The question of what features were seen as marking the two nationally labelled theatrical genres is a matter which requires some attempt at definition, and which is central to our current narrative. The two dramatic genres or modes were after all performed for most of a whole century, between 1660 and 1760, in the same capital city and for the same theatre-going public.

The material which survives, on the one side and on the other, is not identical in its nature or in its evidential value. A substantial number of plays which were mounted by the Comédie-Française, in the decades before and after 1700, have survived in print: they can be read and interpreted in the same way as other play scripts from the past. By contrast, in the various published *Théâtre italien* collections, especially the selection by Gherardi from the earlier decades, many of the French-language scripts leave large gaps for actors to improvise in Italian, so it is harder to re-imagine the printed texts as a full theatrical experience. In compensation, those texts contain more extensive stage directions than do the 'literary' French scripts, including some descriptions of elaborate scenic effects and pageants. Comparisons may or may not be made easier by the fact that there were some French dramatists who wrote material for both companies, altering their content and style to fit two different types of theatre. The principal authors who did this were Anne Maudit de Fatouville (d. 1715), Jean de Palaprat (1650–1721), Jean-François Regnard (1655–1709), and Charles Dufresny (1648?–1724); and then Marivaux, who is discussed in Chapter 11. In 1709, Alain-René Lesage (1668–1747) gave the French company his hard-hitting satirical comedy *Turcaret*, which is still well regarded and still survives in the repertory; but the *Comédiens* treated it with such resistance and suspicion that he spent the rest of his career as dramatist writing plays for the Paris Fairs, in a style which resembles that of the Théâtre-Italien.

The Comédie-Française was predictably entrusted with maintaining as far as possible the serious rules of French *classicisme* even in the less serious genre of comedy. Its comic plots aimed to be 'rational' and plausible, to reflect — with however much satirical exaggeration — the possible behaviour of real people in a recognizable society. The example of Molière loomed large, and his models inspired the format called 'comedy of character'. Here a particular psychological trait or failing was assigned to a central figure, and often reflected in the play's title. It provided scenes of entertaining misbehaviour, but was supposed also to lead to moral reflection; and it functioned as the pivot around which the various contests and intrigues revolved. It was normal for a marriage to provide the denouement of the story, the couple concerned having surmounted obstacles which might involve either generational conflict or barriers thrown up by their own temperaments (because the 'character' explored in the play's title might be one of the lovers themselves). Pairs of servants might also get married, after having helped or hindered in solving the problems of their employers. The investigation of 'character' involved a challenge for the dramatist, who would want to find a particular aspect of humanity, and a particular set of personal quirks, which were comically exploitable but had not been treated before. The actors of the Comédie-Française each played roles which were designated in their contracts under certain broad headings called *emplois*: Lovers, 'Noble Fathers', Servants, and so forth. In comedy in particular, the same names may recur in different plots, indicating a level of character repetition influenced by the Italian tradition, though they never wore masks. A few roles became recognizable and named — a notable example being the comic valet Crispin, who was played over two generations by father and son, Raymond and Paul Poisson. Nevertheless, actors in the French tradition prided themselves on flexibility, and on not simply playing the same part every time. They had to memorize a complete new script for each production, rather than ever having to improvise. (I shall reflect further on character types, and on masks, in Chapter 22.)

However, French classical rules set some boundaries to novelty and invention, and also limits to subversion and scurrility (a subject perused further in Chapter 17). It is probably unfair to claim, along with a French critic of the 1960s, that the Comédie-Française 'was afraid to make people laugh'. Nevertheless the company was seen as belonging to polite society, as well as pursuing cultural orthodoxy, and there were levels both of impoliteness and of perceived 'irrationality' which it had to avoid. Expectations are summarized in the Prologue to Dufresny's *Le Double Veuvage* [The Double Widowhood] (1702) in which a theatre-going marquis tries to explain to a less informed acquaintance the virtues which an educated public saw itself as seeking in a French comedy: 'One likes to see consistently expressed characters [caractères soutenus], a clear well-developed plot, some situations which are unexpected but also plausibly prepared, and occasional verbal jokes [plaisanteries] which are not vulgar'. We perceive here the continuing dominance of *classicisme*, which demands reason, *vraisemblance*, and *bienséance*. The marquis then says that *plaisanteries* should arise clearly out of the dramatic situation.

The Italian artisan actors in Paris, especially in their earlier period before 1697, were rarely concerned with such erudite standards. On the contrary, they offered their audiences a brief holiday from polite society, and also from rationality. The move to France, and the need to communicate across a language barrier, had significantly shifted the balance and importance of roles within an Italian *arte* company. The high rhetoric of romantic lovers, as created and delivered to great acclaim by Isabella Andreini and her male colleagues, could not easily survive the transition. Nor could the serious moralistic stories which those earlier actors were able to perform. At the Théâtre-Italien, before the 1697 banishment, it was the clowns who drew in the crowds. It was the Elder masks Pantalone and the Dottore (to some extent), and Servants such as Mezzettino, Scaramuccia, and Arlecchino (to a greater extent), who gripped the attention of French theatregoers by being subversive, anarchic, scurrilous and childish, and by accentuating the actors' skills in bodily expression to support what was being conveyed in words. We hear rather less, to begin with, about the appeal of actors playing Lovers in Italian style. Eventually the fact that the troupe was performing increasingly in French enabled the rise of female stars such as 'Isabelle' and 'Colombine' (Françoise and Catherine Biancolelli, daughters of 'Dominique') before 1697, and then 'Silvia' (Zanetta Balletti) after 1716. The stage personalities of these women now appear quintessentially French — 'unmasked masks' who combined personal attractiveness and flirtatiousness with a sharp derisive verbal wit. Like their clownish colleagues who did wear masks these leading ladies had fixed, recognizable stage personae, which showed through the roles they were playing, or the disguises they were adopting, in the plot.

Théâtre-Italien plots themselves (to judge by the contents of the 1700 anthology) paid little attention to being 'clear and well-developed', and were pretexts for a series of separate scenes which were almost cabaret numbers. Lip-service might be paid to the idea that the denouement of a comedy should involve a marriage, but this convention was not taken very seriously, and it might be mocked via couplings which were clearly unsuitable or mercenary. The fact that in 1688 Regnard offered the Italians a play entitled *Le Divorce* speaks for itself. Coherence and plausibility were thrown to the winds: the action might involve Arlequin and his colleagues appearing as classical deities, or as other kinds of supernatural spirit. Especially striking was the vogue for theatrical parody. Tragedies and pastorals offered by the

Comédie-Française, music dramas mounted by the recently established Opéra, were seized on by the Italians within a very short time, and their scenes and speeches were distorted for public amusement. The plethora of titles such as *Arlequin Jason, ou La Toison d'Or comique* [Harlequin as Jason, or The Comic Golden Fleece] (1684) is explained by the fact that they were mockeries of existing plays or operas. This can only have worked because the public had been to see the original shows and had a good memory for their details, even for individual lines of verse. The whole phenomenon confirms that Parisian audiences regularly frequented, and felt a need for, both polite or approved French culture and its impolite Italian alternative. That is why the Prince Regent acted so rapidly to reconstitute an Italian troupe in 1716, once Louis XIV's prejudices were safely out of the way.

The use of improvised scenes in Italian (whose content was recorded, if at all, in a brief summary) must regularly have led to speeches, as well as characters, re-appearing from one play to another (a strategy I shall investigate in Chapter 19). It also increased the element of risk-taking which live theatre always involves, and implied a level of knowing collusion between actors and audience which in the Comédie-Française was less apparent. In fact the most striking characteristic of the first Théâtre-Italien was its playfulness, based precisely on such cross-footlights collusion. The Italians played overt theatrical games with theatre itself and its conventions, effectively inviting the audience to join in. Actors broke character to address the spectators; stories were concocted which blatantly made no sense, but which still offered fragmentary satirical comments on contemporary life. A world of classical deities, or of fairy-tale fantasy, alternated or merged with allusions to real society. Most of all, both the masked actors themselves and the characters whom they impersonated in the plot were constantly adopting disguises which in common-sense terms could never work. These multiple levels of role-playing often involved cross-dressing: Colombine masquerading as the god Apollo, or as a lawyer; Pierrot as a naïve young girl; Arlequin as the female Muse of Comedy, or as a ridiculous old woman on the hunt for lovers. The short-statured Mezzetin (Angelo Costantini) once appeared as a parrot. The trademark stage masks and multi-coloured uniforms of Arlequin, Mezzetin, and Pierrot showed through to cancel out the disguise: perhaps the same was also true of Colombine's costume.

The Parisian spectator was obviously enchanted by this opportunity to drop common sense altogether, and (in modern jargon) to indulge his or her inner child. The desire for a temporary rest from adulthood is easy enough to explain, and is still regularly catered for in entertainment of many kinds. What distinguished this particular example was that two alternative types of spectacle were labelled by their nationality. It was the Italians who were allowed to be playful and childish; the French companies produced culture for grown-ups. The theatre-goers who exploited this situation were of course French; so they could distance the childishness from their self-image, see the playfulness as essentially 'other', and conceive a patronizing view of Italian culture as something quaint which they could enjoy but claim not to identify with. They could then revisit the Comédie-Française and the Opéra to reassure themselves that they were really French and really adult; and also to absorb the new shows which the Italians would allude to or parody. It is noteworthy that although the Théâtre-Italien moved steadily and predictably towards performing entirely in French, its Italian identity had to be preserved. The transalpine theatre dynasties who settled permanently in France kept their Italian family surnames after taking French citizenship. But when the company was recreated in 1716, its new director and its new Arlequin were not recruited from one of those resident families — they were brought in fresh from Italy. The artisan skills of Italian comedy had to be perceived as native and authentic. Maintaining a level of exoticism was part of the appeal.

The figure of Arlequin had in fact become crucial and inescapable, in Italian comedy as performed in France. 'Thomassin' Visentini was employed to continue a tradition laid down by Biancolelli senior and junior, and by Gherardi. Those beloved clowns had made the mask ever more indispensable. In a list of plays or sketches from Domenico Biancolelli's notebooks, from Gherardi's *Théâtre italien* anthology of 1701, and from Pierre-François Biancolelli's scattered compositions, Arlequin's name appears in the title of roughly one in four; and he figures as protagonist in many more. During the decades preceding 1697, the mask as played in Paris had undergone many changes. One of the most significant was that Arlequin was not always laughed at for being simply stupid (as when Biancolelli records himself as eating a bar of soap, taking it for a piece of cheese). Increasingly, in a process which applies to many clowns in many different cultures, he entered into collusion with his audience, using sharp, witty one-line jokes and ridiculing the pretensions of various figures who claimed social or intellectual authority. This transformation was openly recognized, even on stage. We shall see (in Chapter 17) how in an anthologized play of 1692 (Palaprat's *La Fille de bon sens*), Colombine addresses Arlequin (who was then played by Gherardi) about whether he is stupid ('sot') or clever ('habile'). She concludes that he now has two different souls in his body ('deux âmes dans le corps').

The mask had also become detached from its original identity and function in comic plots. No longer simply a naïve and scurrilous peasant from Bergamo, Arlequin took on ever more roles and disguises — a prince, a judge, a doctor, a palace washerwoman, a figure from classical mythology (parodying something recently performed in a rival theatre), an Emperor in the Moon (see Fig. 10.1). Arlequin took control of the stage; Arlequin was the star; Arlequin was the master of ceremonies. Parallels were explicitly made between this residually Italian figure and two minor classical deities: Momus, the god of mockery and satire; and Proteus, the watery sea-god who is a perpetual shape-changer. The title *Arlequin Protée* appears in Gherardi's first volume (see Fig. 10.2). In verses composed by Pierre-François Biancolelli for a sketch in 1713, we read that Arlequin 'is a Compendium of every character' ('est un Compendium de chaque caractère') from emperor to thief, with another mention of Proteus. (The significant title of that sketch was *Le Procès des comédiens Français et Italiens* [The Trial of French and Italian Actors].) Assuming a mask which was now potentially all things to all men, Tommaso Visentini had a hard series of acts to follow when he arrived in Paris in 1716 with only a limited

FIG. 10.1. Frontispiece to Fatouville's *Arlequin Empereur dans la Lune* in volume I of Gherardi's *Théâtre Italien*. Arlequin appears (taking his bow?) with Scaramouche, Isabelle, Colombine, and Le Docteur.

Fig. 10.2. Frontispiece to Fatouville's *Arlequin Protée* in volume I of Gherardi's *Théâtre Italien*. Arlequin appears as Proteus (with a fishtail addition to his normal costume), together with the god Glaucus (portrayed according to the script by the Italian mask Mezzetin). Neptune, here appearing as a statue, is also a character in the play.

knowledge of French. He had to establish a stage personality of his own, but he might also need to be the blank page on which all kinds of assumed characteristics could be satirically written.

In Paris, Italian comedy had thus indeed become 'the world of Harlequin', as it has been labelled by twentieth-century historians. In Italy, meanwhile, there is no evidence that the mask had acquired a similar profile or resonance. An Italian Arlecchino in Riccoboni's and then Goldoni's time was still just a 'second Zani' — fulfilling a lovably ignorant servant's function in the plot, and making lovably ignorant servant's jokes in a stage version of Bergamask dialect. In eighteenth-century Venice, the name attached to such a role seems to have been Truffaldino as often as Arlecchino.

The classical comic format had been created in Italy, and then both modified and codified in France. By 1716, in Paris, the genre had on the face of things become a largely French possession: Italian immigrant performers had wandered away from it, and were entertaining audiences (and perhaps entertaining themselves) in a more fantastical and undisciplined manner. The new century was to bring innovations into French drama which in the long term would transcend and exhaust classical comedy and bring it to an end. However, the story prolonged itself for more decades than might have been predicted: the dialogue between Italian and French contributions to comedy still had creative variations to deploy, in both countries or cultures. Significant developments would be provided by three dramatists of durable talent — two French, and one Italian — and by the long-delayed appearance on stage of comic material set to music.

Bibliographical Note

My judgements on these two styles come largely from direct observations of the material. They are supported by the studies of Mazouer 2002a.

Plays written for the Comédie-Française are found in subsequent editions of works by Dancourt 1985–89, Dufresny 1882, Regnard 1875 and 1920–29, and Lesage 1948 and 2000.

For the Théâtre-Italien before 1697, see the Bibliographical Note to Chapter 9; successive different collections entitled *Nouveau Théâtre italien* remain in their original printings. All Regnard's *Comédies du Théâtre italien* are edited by Alexandre Calame (Regnard 1981).

The central role of theatrical parody in the scripts of the Théâtre-Italien is highlighted in Orsino 1993 (see the Bibliographical Note to Chapter 9). The remark that the Comédie-Française was 'afraid to make people laugh' ('Les auteurs comiques craignaient de faire rire') comes from René Pomeau's 'Introduction' in Beaumarchais 1965.

CHAPTER 11

Marivaux and Eighteenth-Century France

Successive eighteenth-century French gatherings of scripts designated as 'Italian' can be compared with the contents of the earlier *Théâtre italien* volumes initiated by Gherardi: they allow us to follow changes in the material performed by the new Paris company after 1716. Allusions to improvised Italian-language scenes quickly decrease. Rather than offering just 'Scènes Françaises', most items are full-length structured plays in French, often by dramatists aiming to build a serious career. These include Luigi Riccoboni himself, four of whose plays (in bilingual presentation) fill a volume published in 1717. Various competing anthologies were produced with apparently the same title, and they have to be distinguished with some care: we have already mentioned the 1712 volume edited by Pierre-François Biancolelli. The weightiest collection bearing the title *Nouveau Théâtre italien* was a multi-volume compendium printed by Briasson, in editions stretching from 1718 to 1737. It includes eight plays by a French dramatist who occupies a permanent place in literary and dramatic history: Pierre Carlet de Chamblain (1688–1763), known by his nom de plume of Marivaux. Marivaux's first offering to the new Théâtre-Italien appears in Briasson printings from 1729. It is a one-act comedy entitled *Arlequin poli par l'amour* [Harlequin Civilized by Love], and was first performed by the Italians, including Tommaso Visentini as Arlequin, in 1720.

Arlequin poli par l'amour has features which place it well within the Théâtre-Italien tradition. Its action takes place in a fantasy rural kingdom ruled by a queenly Fairy. She has been struck by an irrational passion for Arlequin and will use her magic powers, cruelly and tyrannically, to force him to be her lover. She is served by the Italian mask Trivelin, played by the veteran Pierre-François Biancolelli, who had surrendered his Arlequin role to the newly arrived Thomassin. Arlequin himself starts as the childlike 'blank page' which I have suggested might now constitute the Parisian mask. He is woken to the power of love by Silvia the shepherdess rather than by the Fairy, and this starts a process by which he grows up, acquiring emotional self-knowledge and traditional Harlequinesque cunning. By the end, with the help of Trivelin who has changed sides, he has defeated the Fairy by capturing her magic wand, so that he and Silvia can embark on their private idyll.

Although this debut comedy by Marivaux remains celebrated and is sometimes still revived, it is untypical of his subsequent drama in many ways. Fairies and magic do not appear much again in his work; though his interest in philosophical and social debate produced some more abstract symbolic dramas (see Chapter 21) which set the action in fictional realms, in order to analyse contemporary society from the outside. Those plays have attracted the interest of modern directors, but they cannot play much part in an account of classical comedy. The majority of Marivaux's dramatic compositions are comedies which do belong to that genre: they aim to make audiences laugh, and most of their plots resolve themselves in matrimonial couplings which are achieved via disguise or deceit. In an interesting exception, *La Fausse Suivante* [The Pretended Serving Maid] (1724), the couple under scrutiny end by going their different ways through moral incompatibility, as in Molière's *Misanthrope*. The play also involves a heroine disguising herself as a man in order to spy on her potential husband, a trope which originates with the Sienese *Gl'ingannati* of 1532.

Marivaux usually follows the French or Cornelian pattern of comedy, in that the majority of his plays (again there are exceptions) do not involve confrontation between young Lovers and controlling Elders. As in Pierre Corneille, obstacles to the denouement arise mostly from the hesitations, doubts, even the self-defeating perversities, of the wooing protagonists. Marivaux's reputation with posterity rests largely with his ingenious but utterly plausible analyses of the fine tuning of amorous emotion, and of the skirmishing which can take place before a couple are persuaded to accept one another. In his novels as well as his plays, we see him mercilessly unpicking the different layers of his characters' feelings, most of all the ones which they themselves do not recognize. The term *marivaudage*, coined to describe his subtle and precise verbal style, has been through a series of definitions which have shifted over time, and has been used either positively or negatively according to the taste of different cultural periods. It is notable that Marivaux, unlike Corneille, always wrote comedies in prose: his emotional accuracy and reflective penetration were achieved without the formal support of Alexandrine verse.

In play scripts, this approach leads Marivaux's characters not only to fail initially to recognize their true feelings, but even to say the opposite of what they really mean — always in ways which the audience can see through, appreciate, and laugh at. The laughter thus inspired is of a complex kind, involving some rueful sympathy rather than simple derision. As a technique for writing dialogue, it introduces a new dimension into eighteenth-century drama, one which is hard to detect before 1700 even in the most brilliant stage comedies. Marivaux did not invent it from scratch. There are some earlier plays, written for the Comédie-Française around the turn of the century, in which one can see traces of a new subtlety. A character may make it clear that he or she is responding not just to the words spoken by his or her interlocutor, but to the way in which those words were spoken, and even sometimes to what was not said at all. This suggests that actors were more able than before to attach nuances of psychology and behaviour to their delivery of lines, and that dramatists could trust them to do so. It is a development which is easier for us now to associate with cultural styles and ambitions identified as 'French', in terms explained above. By contrast, the Théâtre-Italien deployed fixed stereotyped roles and superficial one-off gags; moreover its actors, accustomed to improvising dialogue, were likely to have a more slapdash attitude to the exact wording of their lines. This would seem to militate against the verbal precision demanded by *marivaudage*. It must give us pause for thought, therefore, that Marivaux not only began his career as a comic dramatist with *Arlequin poli par l'amour*, but that his full list of comedies which were professionally performed is weighted in a proportion of two to one in favour of items composed for the Théâtre-Italien, rather than for the Comédie-Française. A dramatist now seen as quintessentially French preferred on the whole to conceive and write for the Italian company, always knowing in advance which male and female actors would be creating his roles.

To underline the implications of this, I refer to a specific example. Marivaux's most celebrated comedy is *Le Jeu de l'amour et du hasard* [The Game of Love and Chance] (1730). Two young people are to meet for the first time, in the context of an engagement proposed, but not necessarily enforced, by their parents. Each of them independently conceives the idea of exchanging identities with their valet or *suivante*, so as to observe their proposed partner from an incognito vantage point. (On the male side, an exchange of identities between master and servant was an Italian device traceable back to Ariosto's *Suppositi* of 1509; and we can think back further to Plautus's *Captivi*.) The fact that both partners do this cancels and confuses the stratagem: the master and mistress encounter each other both pretending to be servants, and the servants meet up pretending to be their employers. The resulting confrontations and misunderstandings are entertaining and eventually heart-warming, still capable of working with a modern audience. They also raise questions about the behaviour and prejudices of different levels within the eighteenth-century class system: it is clear from Marivaux's prolific journalism, as well as from his more 'philosophical' plays, that he was an Enlightenment thinker interested in reforming class attitudes and relationships. Therefore, when reading the text of *Le Jeu de l'amour et du hasard*, we would imagine that the language and costume of all the characters would observe a level of realism, within the limits allowed by current theatre convention. But the comedy was written for the Théâtre-Italien, and the male valet who has to swap roles with his master Dorante is Arlequin, played by Tommaso Visentini. Scholars agree that Arlequin, however carefully disguised as a gentleman with a powdered wig, would never abandon his black leather mask; and it is possible that his trademark costume, patched with coloured lozenges, would also be detectable. Visually, therefore, his disguise was implausible: the audience knew who he really was, and they had to exercise a big suspension of disbelief over the fact that the other characters in the play behaved as though they could not see the mask and the patches. Alongside questions of costume, there would be characteristics of behaviour and verbal delivery that were also inseparable from Visentini's version of the mask. On the face of it, then, 'Italian' theatrical game-playing undercut or contradicted the 'French' realism of the script. Marivaux wrote his play for the Italians, and so knew what would happen. Similar observations apply to all those of his comedies whose cast list included Arlequin. (See Chapter 22 for a discussion of *La Double Inconstance*, 1723.)

We can only cautiously speculate about the practical effect of this, moment by theatrical moment, and about what the dramatist wanted that effect to be. Frédéric Deloffre, editor of Marivaux's *Théâtre complet*, suggests that in *Le Jeu de l'amour et du hasard* the audience's social sensitivities were protected by seeing Dorante's valet played by an Italian clown, who could not really be confused with the gentleman he was impersonating: 'Italian fantasy is used to serve a concern for decency and good taste'. Whether or not this is right, 'Italian fantasy' was certainly used by Marivaux for something; and we are left with a continuing conscious dialogue between French and Italian styles of comic theatre.

This is all the more significant in that during the relevant decades French dramatists were exploring new types of writing which were firmly removed from Italian style, and which pointed towards the eventual dissolution of classical comedy. Marivaux was aware of, and influenced by, the category called *comédie larmoyante* [tearful comedy] and later *drame bourgeois* [middle-class drama]. *Comédies larmoyantes* were launched in the 1730s, while Marivaux was still writing, starting with plays by Pierre-Claude Nivelle de la Chaussée. The word *drame* came to denote something which was neither comedy nor tragedy: the first time it was used as the formal definition of a French play was for Beaumarchais's *Eugénie* of 1767. However, the Italian word *dramma* had already been used for opera librettos of the previous century, to denote a blurring, or indeed an absence, of proper theatrical genre. These new tendencies were inspired at least partly by English models: the label 'sentimental comedy' is attached to plays composed from as early as 1696 (by Colley Cibber and then Richard Steele), which reacted against the hard-edged cynicism of Restoration comedy. In France they responded to the vogue for *sensibilité* — for sympathetic participation in other people's feelings, and especially for the sharing of other people's pain. Another adjective frequently applied to the *drame* was *sérieux*. The plays dramatized the lives of 'ordinary' (that is, middle-class) people, treating their sufferings and moral dilemmas with the same seriousness as was applied by tragedies to those of princes and princesses. In this respect the new genre opposed itself most consciously to classical tragedy, which continued obstinately to deal with remote royal and aristocratic figures from history or legend, people with whom the general theatre public could not identify. But there were disruptive implications for comic dramatists as well. So-called *comédie larmoyante* was rarely funny: it was 'comedy' only in the sense of concluding the tribulations of its characters with a happy, or at least morally uplifting, outcome.

Classical comedy had derived most of its laughter and its energy from a removal of sympathy, enabling the audience to enjoy deriding the behaviour of figures dramatized on stage. The cult of *sensibilité*, with its insistence on seeing things from other people's point of view, made that kind of mockery more difficult and sometimes impossible. It also signalled a move away from the conscious theatrical game-playing which was ultimately inseparable from classical comedy. *Drame sérieux* suggested new ways of reproducing feelings, behaviour, and dialogue on stage. What was sought at the time was a greater degree of realism; though it may now read more like an alternative theatrical code, establishing a new set of stereotypical patterns and audience reactions.

The new approaches to drama did not appeal immediately either to audiences or to actors: it takes time, in theatre, for people to accept major adjustments to their expectations. In so far as Marivaux was incorporating 'tearful' or 'sensitive' insights into his comedies, he may have been taking a more pragmatic approach, exposing the public to new ways of representing emotional life on stage without breaking the comfortably established mould of classical comic structure. Voltaire, the supreme Enlightenment *philosophe*, did not appreciate Marivaux's plays. He tried to resist the new genres in his own way, insisting that comedies which never made people laugh were unacceptable. He composed plays which have not gained repertoire status, and which fit uneasily, if at all, into the category of classical comedy.

Marivaux's career as playwright for public theatres lasted for a quarter of a century, from 1720 to 1746. One can see him retreating slowly from his attachment to 'Italian fantasy'. His last comedy to include Arlequin was *Les Fausses Confidences* [Deceptive Intimacies] of 1737, two years before the death of Tommaso Visentini; in that play Arlequin has a function secondary to that of a French valet named Dubois. In later decades, the Comédie-Française found it easy to take over Marivaux's major scripts, and to adapt the parts played by Arlequin for a renamed 'Pasquin' or 'François'. Nevertheless, for much of his career Marivaux chose to incorporate Italian elements into his plots and his presentation of them. He also chose to write comedy exclusively in prose. Moreover, for whichever company he was writing, he clung to some essential features of classical comedy. His comic denouements are procured, or at least preceded, by disguise, mistaken identity, or various forms of deceit such as characters lying about their feelings and intentions. These were no longer uniquely Italian devices — plays for the Comédie-Française used them just as often — but they belonged to a transnational comic tradition which was now two centuries old.

On the margins of all this Parisian theatrical activity — French comedy, Italian comedy, Marivaux's hybrids, and the new sentimental genres — different forms of comic drama were mounted out of town, banished either to the Paris Fairs or to private performances because they were not acceptable to the licensed theatres. Some of them were brief one-act *parades*, in a verbal style sometimes called *poissade*, the word used to describe the vulgar proletarian dialect found in fish-markets. They aimed to deploy that sort of language in an entertaining way, sometimes entirely scurrilous but sometimes claiming to be realistic. They were read later in Venice by Carlo Goldoni, who knew the work of one of its pioneering authors, Jean-Joseph Vadé (1720–1757). In a preface to the reader, Goldoni claimed that Vadé's *poissades* were a model for one of his late masterpieces, *Le baruffe chiozzotte* [Brawling in Chioggia] (1762). In Paris itself, Beaumarchais wrote some *parades* before embarking on his more famous Figaro plays.

Meanwhile, in more respectable theatres throughout Europe, the panorama of dramatic practices which aimed to inspire laughter was becoming even wider. In France and Italy, but also elsewhere, audiences were taking an increasing interest in what we can broadly call 'comic opera'.

Bibliographical Note

The *Théâtre complet* of Marivaux is edited with a thorough commentary in Marivaux 1968. There are also many editions of single plays. Larger-scale French critical studies are less numerous than those on Molière, and many of them deal with issues relating also to Marivaux's non-dramatic writing.

English-language studies of Marivaux's full dramatic production (as opposed to commented editions of individual plays) are relatively sparse, but see McKee 1958.

For Voltaire's comedies, see Goulbourne 2006.

CHAPTER 12

Comic Opera: Italy into France?

I am using the term 'comic opera' to denote 'musical drama with an entirely comic content'. In the context of the time, 'comic' has to imply plots involving mainly middle-class and lower-class characters. In acknowledging the rise of the phenomenon during the eighteenth century, I am passing over the various differentiating terms which were applied to such shows. Theoretical distinctions were sometimes made in Italy between *intermezzo*, *opera buffa*, and *dramma giocoso*; and in France between *opéra comique*, *comédie lyrique*, *comédie mêlée d'ariettes*, and terms involving the word *vaudeville*. The separateness of these categories can be unconvincing in retrospect, and it would be a distraction here to attempt to unscramble them. The essential fact to note from the start is that in Italy the tuneful musical arias and ensembles of comic opera were always linked by sung recitative; whereas in France spoken dialogue was used. (The use of speech alongside song defined the term *opéra comique*, which explains why in 1875 Bizet's *Carmen*, which is not noted for its laughs, was still classed in that category.) There were other distinctions, in terms of musical style and structure, between Italian and French opera traditions; but these apply mostly to 'serious' opera, *opera seria*, and need not be pursued here.

Music crept onto the comic stage in various ways and at various times. The scripts in Gherardi's *Théâtre italien* reprinted volumes of 1701 show an increasing tendency to insert songs into spoken plays, and many of their tunes are reproduced in appendices. In fact musical numbers became very popular in Parisian theatre, to the extent of spreading also into comedies written for the Comédie-Française, where a concluding *divertissement* sung by the play's characters would seem to threaten the 'rationality' imposed by *classiciste* rules. Meanwhile the trestle theatres of the Paris Fairs were making frequent use of music and dance, in order to circumvent bureaucratic rules about what they were permitted to do on stage. There was a special vogue for *vaudevilles*, a term which originally designated new words set to comfortably well-known tunes (*timbres*) — along the lines of what was provided in 1728 for London audiences by John Gay's *Beggar's Opera*. A *vaudeville*, implicitly or explicitly, invited the audience to join in with a tune they recognized. This may be linked to a surprising fact: audiences in the seventeenth-century Paris Opéra are documented as preferring simple melodies in 'airs' by composers such as Lully, which they could learn quickly and sing along with during the performance. In introducing music into spoken comedy, French and Italian companies in Paris may thus have been maintaining competition with the Opéra. However, it was not in France that opera composers were first persuaded to write music for whole librettos which belonged to the genre of comedy. Comic opera, like opera as such, began as a firmly Italian invention, and one which came surprisingly late.

It is hard to explain, but it is a fact none the less, that during the period when opera was first created in Italy around 1600, no music theatre genre based on an exclusively comic text ever got off the ground. Seventeenth-century librettos were a mixture of pastoral and tragedy, with a few more light-hearted scenes involving characters of lower social status inserted as momentary relief. There was a brief early vogue for 'madrigal operas', perhaps more accurately called 'madrigal comedies'. These sometimes narrated farcical encounters between masked figures from *commedia dell'arte*; but rather than being dramas for solo singers in individual roles, they involved all the lines for all the characters being sung in harmony by a single multi-voice ensemble. Sometimes the action may have been performed in dumb show or ballet at the same time. The best-known surviving example is Orazio Vecchi's *Anfiparnaso* [Amphiparnassus], printed in 1597. Then in 1622 Giovan Battista Andreini published a text which he explicitly presented as a comic opera, *La Ferinda*. This plot also used the professional stereotypes: Magnifico, Pedrolino, some Lovers, a Capitano, and a gang of minor caricatures using dialects and foreign accents. We have noted that he had it printed in Paris, but never persuaded a composer or a patron to mount it as a music drama either in France or in Italy.

The kind of comic opera which eventually became popular after 1700 is not often found in the previous century. Again we have to stress that what was missing was not simply operas which might sometimes make people laugh, but rather librettos which made exclusive use of the lower-status characters who defined the genre of comedy. Some Italian operas of the seventeenth century are seen as parodies, which mock the pretensions of their aristocratic heroes and heroines, and also of classical deities (as in Cavalli's *Calisto* of 1651). Monteverdi's last opera *L'Incoronazione di Poppea* [The Coronation of Poppea] (1643), with its self-regarding but ultimately immoral princely characters, hovers perhaps on the edge of this category. In operas which were more serious, lower-class figures might still provide some comic relief: much use was made in particular of impudent page boys and mercenary, parasitical nurses, both of which feature in *Poppea*. However the true 'comic opera' which we are searching for and failing to find would be one in which all the fictional participants either resembled the masks of *commedia dell'arte*, or were bourgeois targets of penetrating mockery such as is found in Molière. Historians list a small number of such properly 'comic' operas produced in Italy in the later seventeenth century, but they appeared in isolation and did not launch a trend.

There then occurred a major reform in the texts of Italian *opera seria*, associated with the librettists Apostolo Zeno (1669–1750) and Pietro Metastasio (1698–1782). Its principles can be traced back to an 'Arcadian' movement founded in Rome 1656. The reformists demanded a purity of genre associated with, and indeed openly influenced by, French *classicisme*: high-flown tragic stories had to be moralistic and taken seriously, and they were no longer permitted to include scenes of comic relief.

This led librettists and composers with comic talent to follow a separate path, and create short works of their own: first of all in brief *intermezzi* (interludes) which were inserted into serious operas. The fashion for such pieces, and the impetus to turn them into a separate genre, was associated most of all with the royal opera house in Naples. Here the shows became longer and more independent from other works, and were eventually designated as *opera buffa*: historians see this named genre as having started in 1706, with regular seasons of such works beginning in 1709. A major influential composition, still relatively short and still designated as an *intermezzo*, was *La serva padrona* [The Serving Maid as Mistress], first produced in 1733, with libretto by Gennaro Antonio Federico and music by Giovanni Battista Pergolesi. The work was repeatedly revived all over Europe long after Pergolesi's death in 1736, and indeed it is still performed today.

The second time *La serva padrona* was performed in Paris in 1752 (after a first visit in 1746), it gave rise to a controversy or debate referred to as the 'Querelle des bouffons' [Debate of the Clowns], the name 'bouffons' designating the visiting Italian troupe who were allowed to perform Pergolesi's work at the Opéra. The philosopher Jean-Jacques Rousseau was moved to compose a *Lettre sur la musique française*, in which he argued that music sung in French had always been inferior to that sung in Italian, partly because the Italian language was phonetically more suitable; and that French opera was largely incomprehensible to the average listener. In contrast he was full of praise for Italian comic opera, impressed particularly by the ensemble numbers in *La serva padrona*. This view was predictably unpopular with many French cultural pundits, and must have given some disquiet to contemporary French composers, though some of them took the point. It launched a public clash of opinions, in which members of the royal family took sides: the Queen (plus Rousseau) against King Louis XV (plus the composer Rameau, and Madame de Pompadour). The *Querelle* did not last for long; and Rousseau himself later softened his views about operas with French texts, when he heard Gluck's *Iphigénie en Aulide* which cannot be categorized as comic by any criteria.

In terms of what was subsequently performed in Paris theatres, the Italian *bouffons* seemed to lose the battle: it was French-style music drama (both comic and non-comic) which was licensed and received royal approval. It is suggested that from the mid-1750s *opéra comique* 'rapidly became the most creative form of French opera'. Nevertheless the *Querelle* did have the effect of making French audiences more aware of comic opera imported from Italy. The patronizing Parisian view of Italian non-musical drama, as attached to the Théâtre-Italien itself, could now be contrasted with a more thoughtful recognition of something which Italians might (at least in some people's opinion) be doing better on stage than the French. This was happening in a context which otherwise might have pushed the content and style of non-musical drama in a different direction. The introduction of *drame sérieux* and *comédie larmoyante* — even though these innovations were being accepted with reluctance — was offering a challenge to the conventions and the plots of recognizably classical comedy. Comic opera, on the other hand, tended to adhere more closely to that genre by reinforcing the theatricality associated with farce.

Musical structures made dialogue more stylised: they encouraged back-and-forth confrontations and quarrels, and also virtuoso verbal patter. Most notably, it was possible in sung ensembles to have different characters expressing different things simultaneously, often to revealing as well as amusing effect. On the other side, it was harder in opera than in spoken drama (*pace* Mozart, eventually) to present emotions in a subtle or fine-tuned manner. The brio and the rhythmic energy which was provided by music on stage kept any truly realistic depiction of social behaviour at arm's length, and evoked more traditional styles of stage caricature. Theatregoers were no doubt being made to reflect, and to adjust their expectations, by the tone of the new sentimental dramatic genres; but they were still at the same time being happily entertained, in the decades leading up to the Revolution, by the more festive freewheeling experience which comic opera, in its increasingly multiple forms, could provide.

In Italy itself, *opera buffa* (or *dramma comico per musica*, or whatever else one chose to call it) made steady advances in places other than Naples. By the middle of the century it had won a following in most cities which had the facilities to stage it. Those centres included Venice, one of Italy's most theatre-oriented states and the one most associated with hedonistic social activities and masked Carnival disguise. It was here, perhaps, that comic opera plots showed the greatest amount of invention. They used numerous conventional classical intrigues leading to the union of a young couple (and sometimes also of their respective servants); but these alternated with other stories which had little intrigue at all, and merely paraded tableaux of sarcastically stylized social types, lampooning aspects of contemporary behaviour. There were texts which managed to do both those things at once. In some librettos, an explicit distinction was made in the cast list between serious and comic roles (*parti serie* and *parti buffe*), as an invitation to greater variety of tone within the same story. However, most comic operas — of all types, and in France as well as in Italy — sooner or later involved at least one character adopting an implausible disguise, still pursuing comedy as a theatrical game. The writer who showed most facility and inclination to create comic librettos was the Venetian Carlo Goldoni (1707–1793). His texts were freely adapted by others, and taken up successively by more than one composer (including eventually Haydn and Mozart), giving him a status in *opera buffa* similar to that achieved by Metastasio in *opera seria*. He is now seen as the most prolific and influential comic librettist of the period. However Goldoni did not just write scripts for music: he will be treated separately in Chapter 13 as a major contributor to the story of classical Italo-French comedy.

Across much of Europe it was already normal for the librettos of *opera seria* to be written in Italian, whatever the nationality of the composer, and wherever they were going to be performed. A well-known example would be the operas which Handel wrote for London between 1711 and 1741; but Italian operas were also finding their way to courts in Russia, Scandinavia, Spain, and the German principalities. It was only in France itself that firm attempts were made to pursue a separate native genre described as *tragédie lyrique*. This insistence on a separate French style of (non-comic) opera dated back to Jean-Baptiste Lully, who had collaborated briefly with Molière.

Another aspect of the continued stand-off between the two traditions was a refusal by French audiences to accept castrato singers; though in fact these were rarely used in comedy. In most of Europe, an Italianizing trend overtook comic opera as well as *opera seria* during the second half of the eighteenth century. The situation remained more mixed in France, where consciously native approaches still competed with *opera buffa*. To complicate matters for historians, the expression *opéra comique* is first found attached to the undisciplined multi-media shows mounted at the Paris Fairs, creations which were frowned on by the controlling French authorities, but popular with the uncontrollable French public.

In Europe at large, an increasingly important centre of performance and patronage was the multilingual Austro-Hungarian empire, where composers of different nationalities — Spanish and German, as well as Italian — set texts in the Italian language. The Habsburg Emperor's court poet in Vienna, employed to write opera librettos in all styles as well as encomiastic verse, was an Italian, sometimes from Habsburg-ruled territories around Milan or Mantua. This 'Imperial Poet' was formally designated with the Italian title of 'Poeta Cesareo'. This narrative thus starts to widen, as it nears its conclusion, beyond a purely Italo-French cultural dialogue. The ground was being laid for the collaboration between Da Ponte and Mozart.

Bibliographical Note

This chapter has been rescued from factual inaccuracy by Julian Rushton, who also offered the judgement about the creative qualities of *opéra comique* after the 1750s. I am very grateful to Professor Rushton, who is then not responsible for my own interpretations or omissions.

The edition of Alain-René Lesage's *Théâtre de la Foire* by Isabelle and Jean-Louis Vissière (Lesage 2000) includes a succinct account of the theatre of the Paris Fairs, its legal battles, and the beginnings of *opéra comique*.

Monograph studies of comic opera in particular are hard to find: one has to make use of accounts which deal also with *opera seria*. In addition to the obvious general reference sources, such as *The New Grove* (Sadie 2001), I have consulted Smith 1971 and Robinson 1978. It is Robinson and his sources (pp. 95–96) who document the desire of early French audiences to sing along with the tunes of arias. For Goldoni, see the Bibliographical Note to Chapter 13.

CHAPTER 13

France in Italy: Carlo Goldoni (1707–1793)

Like some other dramatists in this three-century history, Carlo Goldoni wriggled out of the career as a lawyer to which his family were directing him, in favour of writing for the theatre. He was not an actor or troupe director like Molière; but (against the odds, granted the economic structures of his time) he came to earn his living as a writer for the stage, often holding formal contracts with theatres or companies as their recognized in-house dramatist. He supplied librettos for comic opera between 1729 and 1761, and was writing non-musical dramas by the late 1730s: only his comedies are now still revived, although he did attempt other genres. He is hailed by Italians as their greatest dramatist before the twentieth century, and indeed that is what he was; but his 'reform' of Italian comedy (he himself regularly used the word *riforma*) was based in no small measure on French models. In 1762, with most of his surviving *œuvre* completed, he left Venice for France, where he spent the last thirty years of his life.

Goldoni was a copious, even garrulous, composer of prefaces to his published plays, and then of personal memoirs composed both in French and in Italian. He also wrote an important manifesto play, *Il teatro comico*, to introduce the season of comedies he launched in Venice in 1750. The work shows a company of actors rehearsing a script, and debating — that is, broadcasting Goldoni's opinions — about what should and should not characterize a reformed version of stage comedy. He is thus the first major dramatist in this story who has told us at length and in detail what he thought he was doing, and why. (We can read considered theoretical opinions from Luigi Riccoboni, but they are not then attached to play scripts which have endured. Other playwrights, including Molière, justified themselves more briefly through prefaces.) Goldoni's comments on the merits and defects of his own plays, and on their success or failure with the public, are measured and often critically perceptive.

In the modern international theatre repertoire, Goldoni is perhaps best known for *Il servitore di due padroni* [The Servant of Two Masters]. (We can note in passing that this plot involves a heroine travelling in male disguise, in order to seek out her lover — a trope traceable back, via Marivaux among others, to the Sienese *Gl'ingannati* of 1532.) *Il servitore di due padroni* is now the most famous surviving text of Italian masked comedy: it has been translated and adapted with great success in a number of versions and languages, and its skill in the craft of farce has stood the test of time. Its author is therefore often identified retrospectively with the whole romanticized genre of *commedia dell'arte*. Goldoni would have found that disappointing. An important part of his *riforma* involved rescuing Italian theatre from fixed masks and from improvisation on scenarios, and moving to *commedia di carattere* (a term obviously taken over from the French) in fully written scripts. *Il servitore di due padroni* was composed in 1745, early in Goldoni's career, for an *arte* company for which he was working and to whose preferences and talents he had to defer. He drafted full dialogue for a few scenes, but most of the show was left in scenario form. Later in 1753, in what was already a second printed anthology of his comedies, he issued a version with every scene written out in full. The work was already popular and often revived, so it made no commercial sense to omit it from the collection. Goldoni said in his preface that actors other than those for whom it was first written needed a full text in order to perform it properly. The 1753 text is the one we now know: no version has survived of the original scenario.

In essence — though he never put it in exactly these terms — Goldoni perceived that if Italian stage comedy was to make any progress, control of the genre needed to be shifted from actors to dramatists. It was 'the Poet' who could give purpose to a script, by supplying psychological interest, social realism, even a moral message. The traditional masks were trapped into endlessly repeating material from their existing repertoire: isolated speeches (see Chapter 19), incapable of being organised into a coherent dramatic vision. In *Il teatro comico*, the leading lady of the fictional company is made to say: 'If we just do professional comedies (*commedie dell'arte*), then we're stuck. People are fed up with always seeing the same things; and the audience knows what Arlecchino is going to say before he opens his mouth'. This may be the first time the expression *commedie dell'arte* (in the plural) appeared in print: it was adopted and adapted as *commedia dell'arte*, in the singular, by nineteenth-century French critics and has become current since.

What proportion of the Italian public in 1750 was really 'fed up' ('annoiato') with the familiar masks and their repeated gags is hard for us to judge; but Goldoni felt that there were enough people in his audience who were ready for a change. The play which his company are rehearsing in *Il teatro comico* is a standard *commedia dell'arte* tale of rivalry between Pantalone and his son Florindo for the hand of Rosaura, daughter of the Dottore, with Arlecchino, Brighella, and Colombina in attendance. Predictably, Rosaura marries Florindo; but the disappointed Pantalone, instead of simply being mocked for his inappropriate lust, is given a concluding speech in which he tries to accept the situation with dignity, and which even contains some pathos (see Chapter 22.). Traditional farce is suddenly replaced by something more like the new French *comédie larmoyante*; a grotesque mask usually brought on stage to be humiliated becomes a human being whose fallible emotions demand respect. In a series of comedies up to 1754, Goldoni in fact embarked on a campaign to humanize Pantalone, even to recast him as a respectable, moderate model of the best traits of the Venetian bourgeoisie. But he was also trying —

carefully, slowly — to wean his public away from masks altogether. This involved persuading professional actors to accept a broader range of comic characters, and to work with memorized ('premeditated') scripts. After 1754, and until his departure for France in 1762, Goldoni's comedies abandoned the *arte* masks. His stage fathers continued, from time to time, to oppose the marital preferences of their daughters or sons; but they were no longer two-dimensional *Vecchi* wearing puppet masks. In one of his late masterpieces, *I rusteghi* [The Yokels] (1760), he gives us no fewer than four irresistible caricatures of patriarchal behaviour, men who pursue a somewhat bewildered family tyranny which refuses to move with progressive times — except that one of them turns out to be under the thumb of his sharp manipulative wife. Then the eponymous protagonist of *Sior Todero brontolon* (1762) enacts an old-style Pantalone role in blocking his granddaughter's marriage; but Todero's 'grouching' (which is the meaning of *brontolare*) is that of a nuanced character, whose unpleasant behaviour is that of a plausible miser and control freak.

The traditional *arte* Pantalone spoke Venetian dialect, alongside the different vernaculars used by the male servants and Dottore, and the literary 'Tuscan' spoken by the lovers. Goldoni was raised in, and was often writing for, the city in which Venetian was not an amusing exotic dialect but simply the language which everyone spoke, whatever their social class, though the parallel existence of an 'Italian' language which was becoming standard for cultural purposes was something of which educated Venetians were aware. Some of his greatest comedies, including *I rusteghi*, *Sior Todero brontolon*, and *La casa nova* [The New House] (1760), are all the more convincing because they reflect that fact: the only characters who do not speak Venetian are visiting foreigners who are gently caricatured. *Le baruffe chiozzotte* [Brawling in Chioggia] (1762) is a lively tour de force whose characters are all working fishermen and their families in the small town at the bottom of the Venetian lagoon; and their dialect, distinct even from that of Venice itself, is faithfully reproduced. However, Goldoni also wanted his status as a dramatist to equal that of his French equivalents; and he knew that in terms of international cultural perception he had to represent Italy (whatever that currently was) rather than simply Venice. Not all his plays were premiered in Venice, and he wanted to build a reputation, and earn fees, across the Italian peninsula. He therefore composed many of his important comedies in Italian, and set them in cities other than Venice: the well-known *La locandiera* [The Mistress of the Inn] (1753) is set in Florence, *Gli innamorati* [The Lovers] (1759) in Milan, and so forth. The 1753 anthology of his plays was published in Florence.

Even when satirizing habits and attitudes which he observed originally in Venice, Goldoni might set the action elsewhere to give his social criticism a wider Italian resonance. In 1761 he went as far as creating a set of three linked comedies which pursue a single continuous narrative about the same group of characters, while still managing to function as three autonomous plays. (This is the most ambitious project ever achieved in classical comedy: Beaumarchais's later Figaro plays also retain the same central characters, but they tell three different stories firmly separated in time). It is referred to as the '*Villeggiatura* trilogy', and is now highly regarded by Italians, though for practical reasons it has struggled to be performed and appreciated elsewhere. *Villeggiatura* was the practice whereby Venetian citizens who could afford it — and, crucially, many who could not afford it — spent certain seasons of the year partying in their country villas on the mainland, shifting the focus of social life away from their main residences on the lagoon. Goldoni's plays are scathing about the economic damage which this practice inflicted on aspirant but under-funded Venetians; but he chose to set the trilogy in the Tuscan port city of Livorno, with the wooded locality of Montenero standing in for the equivalent Venetian leisure zone along the Brenta river. All the characters, including the servants, speak an Italian acceptable in literary composition.

Goldoni's impatience with the old *commedia dell'arte* formats stemmed from two main objections: they were implausible, he felt, and often immoral. Arlecchino and other servants used language which was too vulgar, even obscene; and scenes where they derided their masters and sometimes contrived to give them a beating were unacceptable also on grounds of verisimilitude (*vraisemblance*, as he knew it was called in French). *Arte* farce was too full of events which never happened, or ought not to happen, in real life. At the same time, though, he knew that the artisan professionals had established ways of organizing dialogue, and structuring scenes, which provided an efficient level of entertainment and kept an audience's attention: he wanted to use that skill while conveying on stage his own observations of real psychology and social behaviour. He proclaimed that his dramaturgical practice was based on an equal balance between 'World and Theatre' ('Mondo e Teatro'): a statement which has inevitably been quoted by everyone who has studied him since. 'Theatre' stood for all the devices which helped a script to be functional and enjoyable; 'World' was the subject-matter which a dramatist found around him, and about which he had something to say. In the last resort, at least theoretically, it was 'World' which mattered most. Goldoni was repetitively insistent, in all his prefaces and memoirs, on the absolute necessity of 'Truth' (*Verità*, capitalized) in theatre; and it is in this connection that he wanted comedies to portray (and to criticize) plausible observable 'characters' in the French tradition. In addition, underneath the impressive skill and brio which his best comedies display, he wanted to promote social morality — to observe *bienséance*, as well as *vraisemblance*. Not infrequently this intention prevails over the more subversive traditions of classical comedy which require young couples to triumph over authority figures. Goldoni's happy endings never involve a marriage which cuts across the requirements of society. If chance, or the dramatist, arranges things so that love corresponds with propriety and convenience, then well and good; but there are plays in which a union which is socially acceptable takes priority over amorous feelings, or where (as in the denouement of *La locandiera*) such feelings do not come into the matter at all. When tyrannical parents do lose the battle (*I rusteghi*, *Sior Todero brontolon*), a formula or a fiction is found which allows them not to lose face, so that social decencies are maintained. The *Villeggiatura* trilogy dramatizes a long battle in the mind of its heroine Giacinta, in which she resists her desire for Guglielmo, and accepts the marriage with Leonardo which makes practical sense for her and her family. The conclusion of the final play, *Il ritorno dalla villeggiatura*, is full of resignation and even of tears, as the demands of the 'World' override those of theatrical convention. Previously, though, the 'Theatre' of this same trilogy has involved mercilessly funny confrontations and skirmishings in which antagonisms and rivalries — some frivolous, some more serious — are constrained and twisted by the language of good manners. Goldoni's single most frequently used 'Theatre' device is that of the frustrated aside, expressing for the audience what a character is really thinking or feeling but cannot say out loud.

Even just in the comic genre, Goldoni's production (well over one hundred titles in all) was uneven and over-prolific. He has been described with justice by Maggie Günsberg as 'overtly moralistic', and many of his plays proclaim restrictive doctrines about respectable family structures and behaviour. He had to earn his living by responding to the demands of a fickle Venetian public, whose tastes swung wildly between a succession of fads and preferences. These were sometimes stimulated by the alternative approaches of rival dramatists (Chapter 15 will say more about the competition offered by Carlo Gozzi). When he was moved to write comedies in verse, the results were mixed to say the least; and his tragicomedies, though popular at the time, satisfied a taste which was short-lived. He pulled himself together around the year 1759 to produce some of his best and most durable work; but one can deduce that he ran out of energy. Like many talented Italians before him (though most of those had been actors rather than writers), he accepted a lucrative contract from the Théatre-Italien in Paris. When he got there, he found that the Italian *comédiens* were stuck in a rut which he had long broken out of, but he had to conform to their expectations and those of their audience until the company finally dissolved in 1783. He wrote comedies — even another trilogy — in the old style for the old masks; and also sent back a few new plays to Venice without ever returning there. His last two comedies were written in French: *Le Bourru bienfaisant* [The Gruff Do-gooder] (1771) and *L'Avare fastueux* [The Ostentatious Miser] (1776), both then translated into Italian: the titles show him taking an interest in protagonists with contradictory traits in their characters. He spent a long semi-retirement in Paris and Versailles, earning money partly as a teacher of Italian to the royal family. His books of *Mémoires* are a monument to his relaxed good humour and quiet observational skills: they also provide interesting information about Parisian cultural life and politics. His state pension was revoked in 1792 by the new revolutionary regime, and then restored in June the following year on what turned out to be the day after his death. He died just in time to avoid the revolutionary Terror.

Bibliographical Note

Goldoni 1935–56 contains his complete works edited by Giuseppe Ortolani in fourteen volumes. The French *Mémoires* are in volume I, and the librettos for *intermezzi* and *opera buffa* in volumes X–XI. There are then numerous more recent editions of his individual plays. Goldoni 1983 contains the manifesto play *Il teatro comico*, together with the autobiographical prefaces he wrote to published editions of his comedies, edited by Guido Davico Bonino.

In English, biographies are Holme 1976 and Steele 1981; an important critical study, Günsberg 2001; essays edited by Farrell 1997; and Piermario Vescovo in Farrell & Puppa 2006. In Italian, among many others, Angelini 1993 and Fido 1997.

For Goldoni as a librettist, see Savoia & Emery 1993.

There are relatively few English translations of Goldoni plays. *Il servitore di due padroni* has been the subject of successful adaptations into chosen British idioms: notable recently were *The Man with Two Gaffers* (Blake Morrison for Northern Broadsides, 2006) and *One Man, Two Guv'nors* (Richard Bean for the National Theatre, 2011). The *Villeggiatura* trilogy was produced by the National Theatre in 1987–88, as a single five-hour production with the title *Countrymania*: the adaptation was attributed to the director Mike Alfreds, but was based on an unpublished translation by Peter Rink.

CHAPTER 14

Figaro from Beaumarchais to Da Ponte

In his *Mémoires* (III.36), Goldoni describes the phenomenal success of a new play called *Le Mariage de Figaro*: the premiere took place at the Comédie-Française on 27 April 1784. Goldoni was not sure that this comedy observed 'the rules of the art', but he acknowledged that it seized attention to a remarkable degree, and kept its audience in the theatre 'three quarters of an hour later than usual, without boring it' ('trois quarts-d'heure plus tard qu'à l'ordinaire, sans l'ennuyer'). He observed that those who continually criticized *Le Mariage de Figaro* kept going back nevertheless to see it again. He recalled the earlier Figaro play, *Le Barbier de Séville* (1775), noting that the dramatist Beaumarchais had previously become famous by defending himself in public pamphlets against a lawsuit (which we can date to 1773–74). The audience, he said, had interpreted certain passages in *Le Barbier de Séville* as replaying some of the personal issues raised at that time. Goldoni thus pin-pointed many basic facts about the two Figaro comedies. The thing he did not mention, surprisingly, is that earlier scripts of *Le Mariage de Figaro* had been banned by Louis XVI for being politically and socially subversive, and the work had been subjected to years of censorship before it was finally allowed on stage. This well-known fact had naturally contributed to its box-office takings. As one dependent on royal patronage, Goldoni may have thought it would be more prudent for him not to mention the controversy.

Pierre-Augustin Caron de Beaumarchais (1732–1799) is now best remembered in history precisely for the two comedies about Figaro, the barber of Seville who becomes a domestic servant. During his time, these plays might have appeared as a mere side-line to a remarkably varied and even perilous life as a watchmaker, inventor, musician, financier, litigant, entrepreneur, political journalist, and government agent. (To call this a 'career' would imply a calculated strategy which was entirely lacking.) In fact he took his activity as a playwright seriously, alongside all the rest. His first full-length play, *Eugénie*, appeared in 1767; his last one, *La Mère coupable* [The Guilty Mother], the third of a Figaro trilogy, in 1797. He was also the prime mover in another legal campaign (not the one that had made him notorious), in which dramatists secured intellectual property rights over their scripts against resistance from the Comédie-Française. In 1777 he founded the Société d'Auteurs et Compositeurs Dramatiques (SACD), which still represents French theatre authors.

Seen at a distance (and setting aside judgements about their respective artistic quality) the three Figaro plays seem to chart a simple progression from classical, even farcical comedy (*Le Barbier de Séville*) to the new genre of *drame sérieux* (*La Mère coupable*), with *Le Mariage de Figaro* poised between the two styles. *La Mère coupable* is not funny at all, despite the desperate (even melodramatic) intriguing which its plot contains, and it has no place in a history of classical comedy. It pursues a mood of anguish and remorse in the Comtesse Almaviva to whom its title refers, and what it demands most of its audience is sympathy and tears of compassion. Beaumarchais's first two plays, *Eugénie* (1767) and *Les Deux Amis* [The Two Friends] (1770), were both also *drames*; and he accompanied the 1768 publication of the first one with an *Essai sur le drame sérieux*, which states that that making spectators weep in a theatre is a more respectable goal for a dramatist than making them laugh. Despite this stated preference, he also had a clear grasp of comedy and its formats. *Le Barbier de Séville* was first drafted as a comic opera, and *Le Mariage de Figaro* concludes with a string of *vaudeville* stanzas to be sung in turn by its various characters. Before *Eugénie*, Beaumarchais had composed a series of short sketches or *parades* for private performance in the country house of a patron: six of them have survived in manuscript. They make use of cartoon-like Italianate masked characters (though using names which are partly French, almost bilingual); they are playful and farcical, full of systematically distorted language and sexual double entendres. Their author never intended them to reach the public domain, but they show that his dramatic talents and tastes were more complex than he wanted people to believe. In fact the two Figaro plays which now survive in the repertoire retain a high level of caricatural attack: what he himself in his *Essai*, quoting Latin authorities, called *vis comica* (comic force).

The concluding words of *Le Barbier de Séville*, spoken by Figaro himself, supply a jocular 'moral' to the conflicts and cavortings which the audience have just seen: 'When youth and love are working together to deceive an old man, then everything he does to thwart them can rightly be called *The Futile Precaution*' ('Quand la jeunesse et l'amour sont d'accord pour tromper un vieillard, tout ce qu'il fait pour l'empêcher peut bien s'appeler à bon droit la *Précaution inutile*'). As we have seen, this conclusion could be attached retrospectively to a long succession of Italian and French comedies over the previous two and a half centuries. The play tells a very familiar tale. Young Rosine, courted by a young suitor, wants to extricate herself from the clutches of her guardian, who wants to marry her for a mixture of lustful and mercenary motives. Her lover Comte Almaviva and his cunning sidekick Figaro battle through to procure the happy ending; and no sympathy is offered to Doctor Bartholo when he loses the game. *La Précaution inutile* is the play's sub-title, and also the name of a fictitious comic opera which is referred to during the action. As a form of words it can be traced back to the title of a scurrilous short story published by Paul Scarron in 1655. As the sub-title of a play it reached the theatre in a one-act farce published in 1661 by the actor-manager Nicolas Drouin, who used the stage name 'Dorimond'; it then became the full title of a play published in Gherardi's *Théâtre italien* collection. The plot intrigue of *Le Barbier de Séville* can be related easily to a number of precedents, either Italian or French — not least to Molière's *L'École des femmes* [The School for Wives] (1662), which also has an older man, Arnolphe, wanting to marry his ward. Another possible source, not often invoked, is a three-act play in verse called *Les Folies amoureuses* [Amorous Follies], written by Jean-François Regnard for the Comédie-Française and staged in 1704. Regnard's cast list includes the wicked guardian Albert, the resentful 'imprisoned' ward Agathe, and her lover Éraste. It also has a tricky supportive valet named Crispin who, in 1.5, gives a résumé of his past career as a jack of all trades or *homme universel*, rather like Figaro, though Beaumarchais's Spanish barber speaks mostly of his efforts to become a writer, in terms which allude to the dramatist's own past. (The word 'factotum' was brought in later, in Sterbini's libretto for Rossini's opera of 1816.) Though both plays involve large doses of disguise and deception, the tricks played in *Le Barbier de Séville* do not then derive from Regnard. Comte Almaviva, who is already operating incognito, invades Bartholo's house as a drunken soldier and then as a music teacher. Alongside the main plot, the audience is casually diverted by two grotesque servants: they are not imitations of existing Italian masks, but they operate in a similar theatrical dimension. The role taken by Figaro himself, as servant and master of deceitful ceremonies, can be traced comfortably back to insubordinate slaves in Plautus.

With its history of starting as a comic opera, and the blatant implausibility of its disguises, *Le Barbier de Séville* fits comfortably into an established pattern of classical comedy, showing the older generation being vanquished by the new. The contest is made more exciting because Dr Bartholo is not a complete fool, but a shrewd if somewhat desperate adversary: it is the elaborate twists and skirmishes between the contending parties which supply much of the entertainment, and the audience is challenged to keep abreast of who knows or believes what, and what lies are being told to whom. What makes the comedy stand out is its sharp allusive prose dialogue, which in itself also keeps the spectators on their toes. In 1775 much of its sarcastic satire was interpreted as direct address from its author, whose personal legal battles had been placed in the public domain over the previous two years. It was the presence of Beaumarchais himself, speaking through the persona of Figaro, which gave the play an unusual dimension. Figaro's complaints located the failings of real French society in a more or less fictitious Spain — much as Goldoni had moved his imprudent Venetians to Tuscany in the *Villeggiatura* trilogy. These subversive barbs, however, appear in a series of asides which run parallel to the plot: the intrigue itself is still comic fantasy, and Dr Bartholo is more of a standard Pantalone-style comic victim than a serious piece of satire in himself. Moreover, Rosine's eventual discovery that her suitor is indeed a great nobleman, rather than an impoverished student, is presented as a relief to her and the guarantee of a happy ending. It does not convey any scepticism about what aristocrats might represent in real society, and indeed Rosine herself is of higher social rank than Bartholo.

In the next Figaro play, however, the acceptability of aristocratic behaviour was perceived as being seriously questioned, even undermined. Having married his Rosine, the Comte begins to tire of her and becomes a philanderer. Figaro has become the valet in the Almaviva palace; and his prospective bride, the Comtesse's maid Suzanne, is the latest object of their master's attentions. First Figaro and then the two women work to restore order and harmony, still using the traditional comic resources of deceit and disguise. In the end it is the women who are made to succeed.

In later years, it is reported, the revolutionary politician Danton remarked that '*Figaro* has killed the nobility'; and Napoleon is said to have characterized *Le Mariage de Figaro* as 'already the Revolution in action'. What is certain is that after consultation with the state censors, Louis XVI banned an early version of the script in 1780, commenting prophetically that in order for it to be acceptable the Bastille would need to have been destroyed. After undergoing many cuts and amendments, the play was reluctantly licensed after all, and so Goldoni saw it at the Comédie-Française in 1784. From the start, however, public royal disapproval was mixed with some covert fascination. Private performances were mounted in court venues, and on one occasion Queen Marie Antoinette played the part of the Comtesse.

Critics have debated since about exactly how revolutionary *Le Mariage de Figaro* is, and in particular about which classes in *ancien régime* society it supports. From the separate perspective of classical comedy structures, at least two things are clear. Firstly, generational conflict is replaced entirely by class conflict. The person who needs to be defeated by intrigue is now Comte Almaviva; the authority which he tries to impose comes from his social status; and the couple who hope to become happy are his employees, not his children. Secondly, the Comte is thoroughly in the wrong, and his servants Figaro and Suzanne (along with his wife the Comtesse) in the right. In this play — as also in many of Goldoni's comedies — what triumphs is simple virtue, however much momentary subversion is used to procure its victory. The two servant protagonists are not scurrilous clowns, but attractive sympathetic people defending themselves against sexual exploitation. In the denouement the marriage between Figaro and Suzanne takes place, and that between the Comte and the Comtesse is rescued. (Rescued at least for the moment: the audience of 1784 could not know, and neither do most modern audiences, that *La Mère coupable* was going to tell a more sombre story in which both spouses had produced illegitimate children.) On that level *Le Mariage de Figaro* conforms to the moralistic tone and objectives of a *drame sérieux*, and the concluding mood (like that of much *opera seria* in the eighteenth century) is one of forgiveness and reconciliation. Beaumarchais managed to fulfil those objectives while maintaining a comic tone almost throughout. The play's initial title was in fact *La Folle Journée* [The Day of Madness] and its notional twenty-four hours are packed with a bewildering number of fast-moving events. The conspiracies are just as convoluted as those of *Le Barbier de Séville*, and the skirmishing dialogues between adversaries need to be followed with just as much care. There are moments of outright mechanical farce — such as Chérubin hiding in and then behind the chair, in 1.8 — which are handled so well that they manage to contribute to, rather than clash with, more emotional confrontations. Most of all, although Marceline and the Comtesse express some real distress at their mistreatment by the male sex, such moments of pathos do not dominate the play: the prevailing mood is one of self-control, enterprise, and energy. The critic René Pomeau was moved to class *Le Mariage de Figaro* as one of the most truly comic of all comedies ('entre toutes les comédies l'une des plus comiques qui soit').

It is well known that both the Figaro comedies were soon turned into operas with Italian texts. The first Italian opera entitled *Il barbiere di Siviglia* had music by Giovanni Paisiello and was premiered in St Petersburg in 1782, before Beaumarchais's *Mariage de Figaro* had reached the public stage. Paisiello's text swept across Europe during the subsequent decade, and was acclaimed as far away as New Orleans in 1801: it took some time, after 1816, for Rossini's version to supplant it in the repertoire. The reputation of *Le Mariage de Figaro* spread even faster after 1784, and it gained the same notoriety in Europe generally as in France. The Habsburg Emperor Joseph II, who saw himself with some justice as one of the most liberal rulers then imaginable (and who was Marie Antoinette's brother), nevertheless thought that Beaumarchais's play had gone too far, and banned it from stages in Vienna. The opera which we now know, *Le nozze di Figaro*, came into being as a result of an outstanding campaign of diplomacy by its composer Mozart, and perhaps most of all by its Venetian librettist Lorenzo da Ponte (1749–1838), who was working in Vienna for the opera house though never accepted as official Poeta Cesareo. Between them they persuaded the emperor that after judicious cuts in its content *Le Mariage* was capable after all of being turned into an opera which would work in its own terms, and which would fall short of being politically offensive. *Le nozze* was premiered in 1786, only two years after Beaumarchais's play. 'The most comic of all comedies' became what some music critics are still prepared to call the best opera ever written, in any tone or genre, in terms of its successful marriage of words and music.

Mozart's music is of course frequently sublime: the concluding scene where his Contessa bestows her forgiveness transcends anything which Beaumarchais achieves, and probably anything which anyone could achieve in mere prose. There are also individual numbers which correspond to nothing in *Le Mariage de Figaro*, and which are a testament to the dramatic creativity of Mozart himself — notably the deliciously ambivalent aria 'Deh vieni, non tardar', which Susanna sings in the final act to tease and bamboozle Figaro, whom she knows to be hiding within earshot. Elsewhere, the words which Da Ponte drafted for his collaborator are themselves a tour de force, in terms of how closely they often reflect the French source while still providing the pared-down text which is necessary for a libretto. They also reflect a high level of craftsmanship in composing succinct and suitable Italian verse, which must have been learned partly from studying comic librettos by Goldoni. Da Ponte shows the same verbal facility as his Venetian compatriot predecessor, the same ability to encapsulate predictable statements in lines which make way for the music but might still remain memorable. The comic drama which he produced on the page is a cleverly streamlined version of what happens in *Le Mariage de Figaro*, omitting side-lines and longueurs as well as the political satire which was unacceptable to the emperor. It also omits some of the complexities which Beaumarchais had created in the characters of his Comte and Comtesse. Their relationship is less shaded, and less probingly analysed, in the opera; and the Contessa is more unambiguously virtuous, less tempted by Cherubino, than is the case for Beaumarchais's Comtesse and Chérubin. This may have been a conscious decision; or it may be a form of moral simplification imposed by musical theatre, where verbal subtleties are harder to develop.

One of the many events comfortably shared by both play and opera is a moment which we can read now as truly significant in the long history of classical comedy. After various attempts by Figaro to deceive and entrap the Count through invented stories and false letters, the Countess and her maid Suzanne/ Susanna fall back on a standard theatrical (or metatheatrical) trick: they will exchange clothes and apparent identities, so when the Count thinks he is seducing the serving maid he is really addressing his wife. They do this without informing Figaro, who as a result gets left behind by the plot. The Count is duly deceived, and makes a fool of himself as was intended. Figaro is also deceived for a while, overhearing the encounter between the Count and the supposed 'Suzanne'. But then when he comes across the woman in the Countess's costume, he immediately recognizes the voice of his own beloved, and sees through the whole trick. The same things happen in the opera, even with the addition of Mozart's extra aria. When Figaro believes that Susanna is singing to and for the Conte in 'Deh, vieni, non tardar', it is her voice he is listening to: in the dark he cannot see that she is already wearing the Contessa's clothes. His conviction of her infidelity is maintained as he eavesdrops on the Contessa impersonating Susanna. But, as in the play, Susanna's vocal mimicry of the Contessa does not fool him for a second.

Recognizing a disguised lover's voice may have been permissible in tragedy and *opera seria* — there is an occurrence of it in Handel's *Radamisto* as early as 1720 — but in comedy and *opera buffa* it would have tended to spoil the fun. In *Figaro* it is as if Beaumarchais could not believe, or could no longer ask his audience to believe, that the venerable comic devices of disguise and impersonation can really work in the face of close familiarity between two human beings — especially if they are sincerely in love. The Comte may not recognize his wife's voice, but Figaro knows that of Suzanne. Judging also by his earlier *Essai*, Beaumarchais saw himself as moving steadily towards a new theatrical genre, towards what he saw as greater emotional truth, even if that would involve less fun and laughter. Festive play-acting and identity-shifting had characterized comedy for nearly three centuries, but we can deduce that Beaumarchais saw their potential as exhausted. In his view, theatre needed to move on.

Bibliographical Note

The standard edition of Beaumarchais's works is that of 1988; it includes the *Essai sur le drame sérieux* (pp. 119–40). See also Beaumarchais 1965, edited by René Pomeau. The *Parades* are edited by Larthomas in Beaumarchais 1977.

For critical studies, see in particular Howarth 1995 and Scherer 1954.

Beaumarchais 2003 contains *The Figaro Trilogy* translated by David Coward, as well as a succinct biography of Beaumarchais. Frédéric Grendel's 1973 biography has been translated by R. Greaves (Grendel 1977).

Regnard's *Les Folies amoureuses* is included in the 1920–29 edition of his plays.

Da Ponte 1956 is the standard edition of the three Mozart librettos. For bibliography on *Le nozze di Figaro*, a starting point is Carter 1987. For significant differences between the play script and the libretto, see Andrews 2001.

CHAPTER 15

Alternatives to Classical Comedy

Da Ponte wrote two more librettos for Mozart before the composer died in 1791. *Don Giovanni* (1787) was their addition to a long sequence of redramatizations of the Don Juan story which had first appeared in the Spanish play *El Burlador de Sevilla* [The Trickster of Seville], attributed to Tirso de Molina and published around 1630. The morality tale of the obstinate sinner brought to divine justice by his stone dinner guest is not classically comic in its content, or even in its underlying tone. It had dodged in and out of the comic theatre tradition for more than a century because of Don Juan's confrontations with his argumentative servant, whose name is different in every incarnation (Catalinón, Passarino, Sganarelle, Coviello, Leporello) and who was sometimes assimilated to a *commedia dell'arte* mask.

Then in 1790 the same two collaborators presented the Viennese court with *Così fan tutte*, subtitled *La scuola degli amanti* [The School for Lovers]. When Da Ponte first drafted it for Antonio Salieri, this libretto must have belonged firmly to the playful tradition of comic opera. Its basic situation, of lovers returning in disguise to test the fidelity of their betrothed ladies and never being detected in the process, is deeply implausible, the very opposite of Figaro's recognition of his fiancée's voice. A situation so unreal that it seems more appropriate for puppets than for human actors is set up to 'prove' the title's mockingly derogatory thesis about female behaviour: 'all women are unfaithful'. This quintessentially *opera buffa* world is reinforced by the even less convincing disguises of the serving maid Despina, as a male quack doctor and then as a male notary. The concept was thus a dramatic regression: it ignored all the new tendencies towards emotional truth and serious moral reflection which Beaumarchais had taken from the *drame*, which he had grafted on to the comic template of *Le Mariage de Figaro*, and which had been triumphantly transferred to Mozart's *Nozze di Figaro*. Equally, in an Italian context, it ignored the similar path being trodden by Goldoni's comedies, as opposed to his more clownish comic opera libretti. We do not know how many changes were made to the text of *Così fan tutte* when it was offered to Mozart instead of Salieri. We do know that the composer injected into his music so much beauty, and so much humanity, as to leave us with a deeply ambiguous range of possible experiences, which are now endlessly varied and experimented on by modern directors and singers.

Così fan tutte thus has a permanent problem status in terms of theatre history: it is a clash between two genres which is apparently irresolvable, however many resolutions have since been found via the greater subtleties of more recent theatre practice. The opera faces in two opposite directions at once, and its very existence can be seen as one of many indications that by the end of the eighteenth century the writing was finally on the wall for classical comic drama. Under a series of intense cultural changes and pressures, dramaturgy and performance were indeed feeling the need to move on. 'Serious drama', under a succession of different labels, had been creating a theatrical experience which claimed to poise itself between tragedy and comedy: it justified itself at the time by claiming to offer the best features of both genres, but viewed from a greater distance it now seems to ignore them both. Its driving force was a desire for realism, a wish to reflect (however sentimentally and formulaically, as it may appear to us now) the lives and the language of a middle-class theatre audience. On the side of tragedy, as well as avoiding endings which involved death and destruction, it threw out aristocratic protagonists with their high-flown moral dilemmas and their highly coloured, versified language. On the side of comedy, it effectively rejected laughter, both as a tool of condemnation and as a source of enjoyment; and some pioneers in the genre such as Denis Diderot (1713–1784) actually discouraged the inclusion of servant characters, who might distract from moral purpose by being amusing. (He refers to 'the Davus character', naming the cunning slave from Terence's *Andria* and confirming that Roman comedies were still a point of reference, though no longer models to be blindly followed.) Beaumarchais's progress from *Le Barbier de Séville* to *La Mère coupable* sums up a journey which was being undertaken by dramatic writing generally during the course of the eighteenth century, especially in France. Earlier, the *philosophe* Voltaire had engaged with the new genres, even fought against them, in plays written between 1725 and 1769: his comedies and near-comedies make fascinating reading, but have failed so far to gain much presence in modern stage repertoires.

In Italy, or specifically in Goldoni's Venice, an attack on classical comedy came from an unpredictable source — from a writer who objected to French-style *drame sérieux* as much as he opposed Goldoni's 'comedy of character' (which can be seen as combining some *sérieux* qualities with the continued pursuit of laughter). The aristocrat Carlo Gozzi (1720–1806) allied himself in the early 1760s with a troupe of *commedia dell'arte* actors directed in Venice by Antonio Sacchi. He made it clear that unlike the mercenary tradesman Goldoni he was donating his services as dramatist without payment. Between 1761 and 1765 he offered Sacchi a series of ten 'theatrical fables' (*fiabe teatrali*), which gained enthusiastic audiences probably because of their utter novelty: nothing comparable had been seen on stage before. Unlike most other innovative trends in eighteenth-century theatre, Gozzi's *fiabe* rejected social realism completely. They were stagings of fairy-tales, whose plots revolved largely around magical transformations and magically-imposed arbitrary rules: they had some basis in stories told to Gozzi in his own childhood, but were reworked with great theatrical skill. Some remarkable physical changes were effected on stage — for example human beings turning into statues or into animals, and vice versa. Gozzi's ideological programme was fiercely and even pathologically conservative: he was terrified of any ideas which might disturb a rigidly hierarchical social order. (It has been speculated that he foresaw, and feared, the imminent collapse of the Venetian Republic.) Paradoxically he then produced a theatre which was revolutionary in its style and its imaginative content. It was also entertaining: its level of physical spectacle, and the enjoyably escapist worlds which it created, probably accounted much more for its success with the public than did any reactionary ideas which it claimed (sometimes obscurely) to propound. Moreover, writing for Sacchi's troupe of *arte* performers, Gozzi incorporated a set of traditional masks into his plots: his *fiabe* contain Pantalone, Tartaglia, Brighella, Truffaldino (not Arlecchino), and the serving maid Smeraldina. These figures attend as servants, or at best as court officials, on the leading characters in the plot, who (as in most fairy-tales) are princes, princesses, and rulers of fantastical realms. In one play, *Il corvo* [The Crow], the stuttering Tartaglia, presented as despicably selfish, is turned into the chief villain of the story. In Gozzi's view of what he was doing, the *arte* masks on the one hand reinforced and maintained a truly Italian form of theatre from the past. On the other hand, since they represented lower classes of society, they could be kept firmly in their place. The male servant masks are ridiculous and cowardly; Smeraldina is vulgar but always dutiful to her mistress; while Pantalone is seen with condescension as representing the positive aspects of the Venetian populace: full of practical common sense, firmly patriotic, and always subordinately loyal. (Gozzi failed to notice that in this respect he was influenced by transformations imposed on the Pantalone mask by his despised rival Goldoni.) The masks are detached from the roles which they had traditionally played in farcical plots. They rarely manage to contribute to any happy ending, and are far removed from the brash family conflicts over courtship or adultery for which they had first been conceived. However, there did exist earlier precedents for transporting Pantalone and the others into royal palaces or fairy-tale worlds: I noted in Chapter 3 that it was done in a few of the scenarios published by Flaminio Scala in 1611. Later, the unregulated antics of Arlequin and his companions in Paris, described in Chapter 10, had unhooked the masks even more from any obligation to fulfil their original functions; though in Italy itself they had so far tended to be what they had always been, and to perform within the plots which we are still defining as 'classical comedy'. The use which Gozzi made of them is now seen as manipulative rather than theatrically conservative: his scripts exercise firm control over the masked actors, and give them less room for real improvisation than he might have wanted to claim.

Gozzi's *fiabe* were later taken up and reworked in Romantic and post-Romantic drama and opera: we are familiar in particular with the titles *Turandot* (the only original *fiaba* which does not involve magical transformations) and *The Love of Three Oranges* (in which such fantasies are central to the story). They seem to belong to a new artistic world, which was about to replace theatrical classicism and would bear little relationship to it: an interesting fate for an author who saw himself as firmly traditionalist. In terms of threats to classical comedy, they were a different kind of writing on a different wall from what was being provided by the *drame sérieux*, but in their way equally prophetic. In Venice for a brief period they deliberately and successfully challenged Goldoni and his careful reforms of the classical comic format. There were probably multiple reasons for Goldoni's definitive departure for France in 1762, but it is generally thought that one of them was the sudden success of Gozzi's *fiabe*, which he may have found inexplicable. He had already experienced many shifting allegiances of the Venetian public in its constant appetite for novelty, and perhaps had grown weary of trying to follow them.

Classical comedy in the eighteenth century was thus being eroded in Italy and in France by at least two identifiable competitors: fantasy theatre on the one hand, and 'serious drama' on the other. At the same time, literary and dramatic cultures in these two Romance languages were being asked to address new influences from northern nations. From England there came the rising popularity of a new style of novel associated initially with Samuel Richardson, which began to feed stories, characters, and concepts not only (as was predictable) into the *drame sérieux* but (less predictably) even into comic opera. From Germany there came movements such as *Sturm und Drang*, and the integration of popular and folkloric models into 'higher' forms of art — all driven by figures such as Goethe and Schiller, whose talents southern Europe could not dismiss. In theatre in particular, both English and German theorists were urging the Latin nations to take a serious look at Shakespeare, whose example if followed could only lead to abandoning classical rules completely. (Voltaire described Shakespeare as 'a barbarian not without genius', 'un barbare non sans génie'.) In the seventeenth century, neither English nor German had been languages which French and Italian producers of culture, or gentlemanly consumers of it, saw any need to learn. By around 1780 English and German works were being translated, and their original tongues were acquiring more status.

Despite all these alternatives, the structures of classical comedy were hard to shake off in pre-Revolutionary France and Italy: they still provided the climate in which dramatists had to operate. Relatively modest innovations often aroused heated resistance in an intellectual and cultural public which assumed without question that the rules derived, or thought to be derived, from the classical world were sacrosanct. Those rules were also used as a knee-jerk excuse for rejecting anything unfamiliar, whether or not they had in fact been broken. Goldoni tells us that people who wanted to attack his comedies fell back explicitly on the authority of ancient writers and their early modern commentators: 'My compatriots [...] suddenly became harsh censors of my productions; they sent echoing round their social circles the names of Aristotle, Horace and Castelvetro' (*Mémoires*, II.3). In his *Essai sur le drame sérieux*, Beaumarchais sarcastically characterized those who disapproved of the new genre as being outraged because it might be necessary to create a new Muse of *drame* to add to the classical nine: he too was addressing an entrenched conviction that even purely symbolic parameters laid down by antiquity could not be challenged.

In Italy there was also a lingering recognition that the history of comic drama had begun in the early sixteenth century with *commedia erudita*. Luigi Riccoboni, pursuing his attempts to reform Italian comedy, tried in 1715 to adapt and complete Ariosto's unfinished *Scolastica* or *Studenti* (versions with either title were available), removing or rewriting passages which he thought were too scurrilous for the taste of his age. His revised script has not survived. Decades later Goldoni, in his attempts to woo the Venetian public with novelty, tried writing a comedy — *La pupilla* [The Ward] (1757) — in the eccentric metre of *endecasillabi sdruccioli*, which Ariosto had invented and proposed as the best Italian equivalent of Latin iambics. Neither Riccoboni's nor Goldoni's venture was a success with the public. But both playwrights thought that Ariosto had inaugurated a continuous tradition of comic dramaturgy, and that they themselves still belonged to it. The narrative which we are about to conclude is based on that premise.

Bibliographical Note

For a close analysis of Mozart's *Così fan tutte*, with bibliography, see Carter 2004.

Diderot's reluctance to use servant characters in comedy is expressed in the first of his *Entretiens sur le 'Fils naturel'* (1757): the passage, including the reference to Terence's Davus, is translated in Sidnell 1994: 38–39.

The comedies of Voltaire are masterfully analysed in Goulbourne 2006.

Carlo Gozzi's *Fiabe teatrali* are edited by Paolo Bosisio (Gozzi 1984) and by Alberto Beniscelli (Gozzi 1994): there have also been English translations. The title now often rendered as *The Love of Three Oranges* originally involved three pomegranates: *L'amore delle tre melarance* was the first theatrical *fiaba*, staged in 1761.

CHAPTER 16

Break-up and Aftermath

In the end it was France that launched the series of shattering events after which European culture could never be the same again. Between 1789 and 1815, with first the Revolution and then Napoleon's expansive empire, existing patterns and certainties were swept away. During that period, theatre in France became on the one hand liberated from its royally imposed organizational structures, but on the other hand censored for a while and made to toe the revolutionary party line. The resulting seriousness of tone which was now demanded helped to change the public mood: spectators were now prepared to appreciate new forms of drama to which many had been resistant, and to accept a parallel revolution against *classiciste* dictates. Beaumarchais's *La Mère coupable* achieved a resounding if belated success in 1797. Meanwhile Italy was invaded by revolutionary France, and briefly colonized: the most dramatic intrusion was when young General Bonaparte marched unopposed into Venetian territory in 1797, and sold the thousand-year-old Republic to the Habsburgs.

After Waterloo in 1815, there was an attempt to reconstitute a version of pre-Revolutionary Europe, but the political world had permanently changed. Italians embarked on the creation of a nation state for the whole peninsula, something which had never previously existed. That goal was approximately achieved in 1861, when Venice became part of the new Italy. In the sphere of artistic culture too, the nineteenth century became utterly different from the eighteenth: the Romantic movement soon eliminated all adherence to artistic rules derived from Greco-Roman models. With regard to theatre, this post-Revolutionary cultural upheaval was centred principally in France, led by the vigorous theories and campaigns of Victor Hugo. In fact many of Hugo's challenges to the dominance of *classiciste* rules had been anticipated before the watershed in the treatises of Louis-Sébastien Mercier (1740–1814): *Du théâtre* (1773) and *De la littérature et des littératures* (1778). The dramatic theory of Romanticism was literary, aimed at the author rather than the actor: in the terms proposed by this present study it was firmly erudite rather than artisan.

In the midst of these transformations, classical stage comedy quietly disappeared from the front line of creativity and innovation. It was not so much that new dramatists sought deliberately to abolish it: rather, they seemed to ignore it. The Romantic barricades were being raised most of all against classical tragedy, and against the very existence of strictly defined and separated genres of theatre. In a deeply serious age full of revolutionary aspiration and a search for heroism, playwrights were seeking new forms of drama. Making an audience laugh was not a high priority. Following the example of Shakespeare, they wanted to allow comic and tragic material to be used in the same play; but in practice the comic was being swamped by the serious, the sentimental, and the heroic. Victor Hugo and Alfred de Musset in France wrote historical dramas, in which a frequent theme was the painful emotions — as opposed to the entertaining confusion — caused by sexual betrayal. In Italy meanwhile, Alessandro Manzoni composed plays with a strong choral element intended to inspire nationalist fervour: they belonged very much to their time, and have since been assigned to the history of literature rather than of theatre.

True creativity on the Italian stage, in the nineteenth century, came in the area of opera, and indeed Manzoni's dramas read like operas without music. The composing career of Gioachino Rossini between 1810 and 1829 offers an instructive insight into how the cultural climate was changing. Between 1810 and 1817, twelve out of nineteen of his operas were labelled as belonging to 'comic' categories (*farsa, dramma giocoso*, etc.) — they included *Il barbiere di Siviglia* (1816), based on the Beaumarchais comedy, and *La Cenerentola* (1817). Some plots which he used were of the classical comedy type. Others pursued a vogue for 'rescue' stories involving lovers being saved, or saving themselves, from Turkish slavery — the model for this which we now know best is Mozart's *Die Entführung aus dem Serail* [The Abduction from the Harem]. After *La Cenerentola* Rossini then produced twenty more operas, the last one being *Guillaume Tell* in 1829; but only two of them were comic. As a professional composer who responded to what the public wanted, Rossini thus enacts the transition between what had once been enjoyed in eighteenth-century theatres and what was preferred in the Romantic and post-Romantic age. The nineteenth-century version of *opera seria*, which Rossini was helping to create, featured dramas set in earlier historical periods, offering intense romantic passions combined with demonstrations of heroism. Operas composed by Bellini, Donizetti, and Verdi were Italy's main contribution to European cultural life in the 1800s. Their endings were often tragic: recent critics have had to mull over the tendency for librettists to make so many young heroines accompany their own deaths on stage with pathetic farewell arias. Female tragedy often involved an element of virtuous fortitude, in the form of unswerving fidelity to a husband or lover. In Paris the genre of *grand opéra* used plots of similar emotional voltage and similar exoticism, supported by an even more determined use of visual spectacle as provided by ballet and lavish scenography.

Altogether in nineteenth-century Europe, neither spoken nor sung drama were much focused on comedy — at least if we consider creations which offer real originality, and which have since been seen as worthy of revival. Nevertheless, away from the zone of high-minded (and expensive) innovation, various forms of popular and street theatre, in both France and Italy, continued to offer versions of classical comic stories, often pursuing stylized plot formats and traditional stereotyped figures derived from, or related to, *commedia dell'arte*. The Florentine 'unmasked mask' named Stenterello was created for the stage by Luigi Del Buono (1751–1832) as late as 1793, and was adopted as a symbol or figurehead for the city in many forms of commercial and popular drama. He was revived in a local village theatre tradition as recently as the 1980s, as a comic intrusion into plays whose genre and tone was very mixed. Ruggiero Leoncavallo's well-known opera *I pagliacci*, which lays claim to a level of contemporary realism, depicts a small company of actors touring round Italian villages, playing a standard adultery story in which the lovers are Arlecchino and Colombina. Leoncavallo wrote his own libretto for the work, which was premiered in 1892. The main message of its tale is that farcical humiliation is not very amusing for its victim, if played out in life rather than on stage. The famous aria 'Vesti la giubba' (sometimes translated as 'On with the Motley') makes precisely this point. Such an attitude recalls Hugo and Musset, or even Diderot's *drames*, rather than the mockery of cuckolds which often characterized classical comedy or farce. In his Prologue, Leoncavallo contrasts the flimsy costumes ('gabbane') of masked *arte* figures with the suffering souls of their flesh and blood performers. Stage comedy is trivial and ephemeral, we are told; its actors' real lives are starkly painful. The image of the unhappy clown, now very familiar, is Romantic rather than classical, and has no place in this present study.

In Paris, in a similar vein, one thinks in particular of the Théâtre des Funambules, where a version of the pantomimic Pierrot was created and performed by Jean-Gaspard Deburau (1796–1846). Deburau was immortalized by the actor Jean-Louis Barrault in Marcel Carné's film *Les Enfants du paradis* (1945). It is notable here too that this nineteenth-century Pierrot — as well as being mimed rather than spoken — was increasingly less funny, and more sentimental or even tragic, than the mask as it had originally been played. Meanwhile the Comédie-Française did not stop performing revivals of Molière, Marivaux, and Beaumarchais; but for a number of decades classical comedy, even comedy as such, played little part in the creation of a new dramatic literature. A hard-edged derisive style returned to Paris stages in the *opérettes* and *opéras-bouffes* of Offenbach during the 1860s and 1870s, and then in the farces of Georges Feydeau between 1873 and 1916; but in neither case are the rules of *classicisme* anywhere to be seen.

Bibliographical Note

The 1980s revival of the Stenterello mask occurred in the small village of Chiesanuova, near San Casciano Val di Pesa, in the province of Florence. Texts of the plays were printed by the village itself, for local consumption: see Lotti 1982.

PART II

Analyses

CHAPTER 17

The Content and Function of Comedy

I begin the analytic part of this study by attempting an overview of what people thought stage comedy was — or what they thought it should be — between 1500 and 1800. In every generation during this period, comic drama came under theoretical scrutiny. The seventeenth-century campaign to enforce the rules of French *classicisme* was the most obvious example of this; but before and after that period, in Italy as well as in France (and also in England and Spain), the content and function of the genre were repeatedly debated.

What, we can ask, was seen as the purpose of performed comedy, even the justification for its existence? What was permissible on stage, and what was not? and why? The theoretical issues addressed were in fact largely unaltered over three centuries: the same questions recurred, along with approximately the same answers. On the matter of what was allowed in practice, however, sensibilities became steadily more delicate from the sixteenth to the eighteenth centuries. We are pursuing here a story which involves continuity in theory but also changes in practice.

High and Low Comedy

> Good taste consists of saying and listening to the sort of things that befit a liberal and reasonable man. There are in fact certain things which are fitting for such a man to say and hear in jest, and the jokes of a liberal man will be different from those of a slavish one, and those of the educated from the uneducated. One can observe this difference in past comedy and contemporary: the old considered obscene talk to be funny, whereas the contemporary merely hints at such things for humor. They are very different in their respectability. — ARISTOTLE[1]

In the fourth century BCE, Aristotle was articulating a distinction, even an anxiety, which besets discussions about stage comedy, and about humour in general, in many human societies. It was certainly a regular preoccupation in early modern Europe. It could express itself as a contrast between 'comedy' and 'farce'; though the word 'farce' has a complicated ancestry, with different meanings initially in French and Italian.[2] Aristotle's distinction between 'past' and 'contemporary' comedy was

---

1 Aristotle: *Nichomachean Ethics* IV, trans. by Jeffrey Rusten (Rusten 2011: 579). It is worth noting that the Greek word translated here as 'good taste', επιδεξιοτη, is rendered by other translators as 'tact', 'cleverness', or even 'dexterity'.
2 It was some time before *farsa*, and the associated adjective *farsesco*, came to be used in Italian with what we see as its modern connotations. The more complicated meanings of *farsa* in fifteenth-

interpreted later as a choice between the Greek Old Comedy of Aristophanes (which he certainly knew) and the New Comedy of dramatists such as Menander (which he did not in fact live to see). It was the latter genre which was imitated by Plautus and Terence; and the Terentian commentaries attributed to Donatus did make such comparisons between Old and New Comedy. They were then picked up by Humanists who wanted to propose a similar hierarchy of taste — even though they had no direct knowledge of plays by Menander and his contemporaries.

In fact throughout our period we find references to higher and lower brands of comedy; and there is almost always an assumption, as in Aristotle, that good taste in such matters is associated with higher social class and better education. Comic dramatists themselves contributed to the debate. In his one-act *Critique de l'École des femmes* (1663), Molière put on stage some caricatures of members of his audience who argue precisely about what sorts of comedy they regard as being beneath them. In Scene 6 he gave one of them a remark which has become proverbial in French literary criticism:

> To sum up, in serious plays it's enough, to avoid criticism, to say things which are sensible and well written. But that's not enough in other plays; you have to make jokes; *and it's a strange business, making decent people laugh.*[3] (my emphasis)

Here Molière was engaging with current French debates on comedy and social propriety. In the following century Carlo Goldoni composed a successful comic opera libretto called *L'Arcadia in Brenta* [Arcadia on the River Brenta] (1749), in which a group of socialites in a country villa mount a brief *commedia dell'arte* sketch for their own amateur amusement. The host and protagonist Fabrizio, in a verse recitative, is concerned about just what sort of comedy he should present, or indeed is capable of presenting, to his peers:

> Will I have to play the fool? That's a job
> which is rather difficult.
> To make idiots laugh
> one doesn't need much talent.
> But to make wise people laugh is really demanding. (II.8)[4]

In translating the Molière quotation, I have imposed the modern English expression 'decent people' on the term 'honnêtes gens', which in a seventeenth-century French context demands more precise analysis.[5] However, in general terms, and

---

century Italy are succinctly surveyed by Pieri 1989: 25–30. In the English language, John Dryden distinguished farce from comedy (even from 'low comedy') in *Dramatick Poesy: An Essay* of 1668 (partially reproduced in Romanska and Ackerman 2017: 120–24). Dryden had condemned 'Nauseous Harlequins in Farce' in his verse Epilogue to George Etherege's comedy *The Man of Mode* (1676).

3   'En un mot, dans les pièces sérieuses, il suffit, pour n'être point blâmé, de dire des choses qui soient de bon sens, et bien écrites: mais ce n'est pas assez dans les autres; il y faut plaisanter; *et c'est une étrange entreprise que celle de faire rire les honnêtes gens*' (my emphasis).

4   'Il buffo io dovrò far? Quest'è un mestiere | ch'è difficile assai; | per far ridere i pazzi | non vi vuol grand'ingegno, | ma far rider i savi è grand'impegno.'

5   A penetrating study of attitudes in seventeenth-century France about whether it was proper for *honnêtes gens* to laugh comes in Howarth 1973, an article which addresses a number of issues treated in this present chapter.

addressing a succession of different times and places, the words 'decent people' express a concept which we still recognize. We know that not all tastes in laughter are shared; and each one of us, usually without formulating a theory about it, is likely to draw a line below which something that claims to be comic is felt to be boring, or not funny, or distasteful. Between 1500 and 1800 such prejudices were regularly expressed; and there were no inhibitions about associating them with class and education, or about proclaiming the superiority of one's own preferences and thus of one's own social identity.[6]

Dramatists in the seventeenth and eighteenth centuries were responding to, or in dialogue with, influential theoreticians. Nicolas Boileau tried to sum up all the *classiciste* rules in a single verse treatise, the *Art poétique* of 1674. He approved generally of the work of Molière, but nevertheless found that in some of his plays the master dramatist was too much 'a friend of the people' ('ami du peuple'), too inclined to combine the high-class model of Terence with the low-class buffoonery of the street charlatan. In a much-quoted couplet, he contrasted Molière's best work, as he saw it, with the more farcical *Les Fourberies de Scapin* (1671): 'In that ridiculous sack in which Scapin wraps himself | I can no longer recognize the author of *Le Misanthrope*'.[7] (I shall reconsider the contrast between these two plays in Chapter 27.)

In my epigraph from Aristotle's *Ethics*, the main criterion for distinguishing high comedy from low seems to be obscenity or vulgarity — most of all in words, given the emphasis on what we 'say or hear in jest'. Whether or not to include certain types of language in public performances is an issue which we can recognize as perennial. Boileau, in addition, was suggesting that violence on stage, what we now call physical or slapstick comedy, is also too vulgar. In his view it falls into a category of taste which we should see as too plebeian ('du peuple'), and it should not be used in high comedy. This too is an attitude which we know to exist, whether or not we share it.

The reduced tolerance of rude words marks one of the major shifts in the content of approved comic plays from the sixteenth to the eighteenth century. There was a similar change in the treatment of love affairs in comic plots — in the earliest period love was acknowledged as involving physical coupling, but by the mid-seventeenth century direct references to sex had been purged by Counter-Reformation moralism and the rules of *bienséance*. I shall investigate those narrative changes in Chapter 24, and stick for the moment to verbal scurrility.

---

6   At the time of writing this book, British theatregoers are unlikely to attribute their tastes and standards openly to their social class; but comedy faces new thresholds of acceptance and rejection, based on perceived political correctness. A case in point would be the growing disapproval of racist and misogynist jokes.

7   'Dans ce sac ridicule où Scapin s'enveloppe | Je ne reconnais plus l'auteur du *Misanthrope*' (Boileau, *L'Art poétique*, III, 399–400: the words 'ami du peuple' are from the immediately preceding lines). It is often noted that Boileau's memory of *Les Fourberies* is inaccurate: the person who gets enclosed in a sack and beaten (in III.2) is not the trickster Scapin, but the elderly Pantalone-style victim Géronte.

Vulgarity on Stage

Italian *commedie erudite* were performed in princely courts and scholarly academies. Perhaps because this involved gentlefolk performing to their own class, and not risking a loss of dignity in front of their inferiors, playwrights were often prepared to include sexual and scatological allusions in their scripts. A level of verbal elegance was maintained, however: we rarely see the equivalents of what in English we now call 'four-letter words'. Bibbiena's *La Calandra* of 1513 (for the ducal court in Urbino) contains an extended double entendre dialogue between a male and a female servant about the difficulty of getting a lock to open, at a moment when it has been made clear that the female servant Samia, unseen by the audience, is coupling with her lover behind the door. The key is stuck in its hole, we hear, and Samia is 'wiggling it about as hard as she can'.[8] In the influential *Gl'ingannati* (Intronati Academy of Siena, 1532), the serving maid Pasquella comments directly to the audience on the sexual frustration regularly displayed by her young mistress Isabella: 'She's always scratching her pin-cushion, always rubbing her thighs'.[9] Many more examples could be quoted from those early decades. It may be relevant that the lines have been given to lower-class characters; but we should also note that at that time the actors, as well as the spectators, were courtiers and academicians (with the female roles played by men or boys). Although all-male audiences were not unknown, women were present on most occasions.

With the rise of improvising *arte* troupes, who performed to a wider public, we can detect a greater unease about such language, at least from one side of the class divide. Many Italian writers, including some dramatists, disapproved openly of professional theatre and used its lower-class status as a stick to beat it with. The actors themselves were mercenary and plebeian, and so what they performed was to be condemned too. The improvisers themselves, inevitably, have left little record of the words they used on stage, and so it is hard to confirm or refute accusations; but well-known visual representations of *commedia dell'arte* scenes suggest that they could include moments of outright obscenity. In fact a 1598 treatise by Angelo Ingegneri suggests that 'mercenary actors' had identified 'the ridiculous' with 'obscenità' (modern Italian spelling would be *oscenità*), to the extent that it had become impossible to raise a laugh in an audience without it.[10] Members of *arte* troupes who ventured into print, trying to raise their cultural status, had to insist that not all professionals were the same: they distanced themselves from actors who presented scurrilous plots ('adulteries and rapes') in scurrilous language.[11] Niccolò Barbieri, who performed the Milanese mask Beltrame, published in 1634 a 'Familiar Discourse' on acting entitled *La supplica*, and dedicated it in suppliant fashion to the

---

8 'Scuoto quant'io posso!' (*La Calandra*, III.10). I have translated this conversation in full in Andrews 1993: 61.
9 'Sempre si gratta il petinicchio, sempre si stropiccia le cosce' (*Gl'ingannati*, II.2).
10 Ingegneri 1989: 6: 'gl'istrioni mercenari [...] hanno ridotto il ridicolo a segno che indarno può venire in lor paragone chi massimamente aborrisce l'obscenità ch'essi alle volte studiosamente vanno cercando'.
11 'Adulterii e stupri' are mentioned more than once in the treatises and prefaces by Giovan Battista Andreini which are discussed below.

French King Louis XIII who had treated him well.[12] It contains chapters which distinguish carefully between respectable *comici* and unrespectable *buffoni*. A class division was opening up within the theatre profession itself.

The genre called *commedia ridicolosa* by modern critics (see Chapter 5) reproduced the *commedia dell'arte* experience in fully written scripts, for performance by respectable amateurs. In the comedy *Li diversi linguaggi* (1609) by Virgilio Verucci, there is a playful dialogue between the young lady Lavinia and her servant Zanni: the allegedly illiterate servant offers what is almost a literary exercise in his stage Bergamo dialect, comparing his mistress in an extended flattering metaphor to a splendid tower or fortress. His anatomical details amuse Lavinia to start with — her eyes shoot fearsome cannon balls, her teeth are sentries against unwelcome invasions of sub-standard food. In the end, though, Zanni goes too far:

> But then, when I think about it, there's just one thing missing to make you absolutely like a fine castle. In all the best castles, like in the Sant'Angelo one here in Rome, the thing that really makes it fine and beautiful is if you plant right there in the middle the biggest and straightest tree trunk you can find...[13]

Lavinia is outraged by the crude innuendo, and chases him out with blows from her slipper in a piece of slapstick which concludes Act 1. In the early 1600s, it seems, comedies for an academic audience were still prepared to include sexually explicit references, provided that they were delivered by lower-class *arte* masks. Lavinia would be approved for defending her maidenly modesty; but meanwhile Zanni's graphic image would have raised a collusive laugh of its own. This last fact, as I shall shortly argue, tended to make moralistic commentators uncomfortable.

In France too, in the sixteenth and early seventeenth centuries, we can assume that scurrility quotients (in the stories performed, as well as in the language used) increased when actors and audiences were less educated and less inhibited. The native tradition of farce had not been known for its delicacy. When Italian improvising troupes then toured the streets and squares of French provinces, they included similar levels of scabrosity in their own material. Meanwhile companies such as the Gelosi certainly aimed higher than this when performing for the royal court; but we know less about how low they might have sunk before a more general public. City authorities in Paris, and monopolistic owners of performance spaces, tended to categorize all Italian actors as 'licentious', so as to have an excuse for banning them.[14] Different levels of refinement or rudeness were certainly attached to different social classes. The 'Italian comedy' which French audiences knew, and which they therefore associated with Italy as such, tended to have a lower place on this spectrum than French plays which observed respectable standards.

---

12 Barbieri 1971.
13 *Li diversi linguaggi*, 1.8: 'Ma quand che ghe pensi un po' mei, a trovi che, per far de vu in tutt e per tutt assomeiassev un bel castell, ghe manca solament una cosa e questa sì l'è che, sì com se ved daspertutt e anca in Castel Sant'Anzel chilò de Roma, se ghe pianta sempre int'el mezz un alber più gross e più dritt che sia possibbil...'. The full text of the later 1627 printing of this play is reproduced in Mariti 1978: 107–206; the scene quoted is on pp. 121–23.
14 'Documents of Control' relating to the earliest visits of Italian troupes are translated in Howarth 1978: 11–22.

In his royal edict of 1641 (see Chapter 6), Louis XIII tried to control the acting profession by discriminating between approved and non-approved performers: actors were socially and legally acceptable, provided they avoided double entendres. Under his chief minister Richelieu, the new precepts of *classicisme* included the demand for *bienséance*. These were rules made by scholars and gentlemen for their social and intellectual peers. Dramatists and actors who wanted to engage with respectable French society had to take account of them. Non-respectable comic theatre, including the Théâtre-Italien, continued to exist, but the aesthetic hierarchy now established had a social dimension which (as I noted in Chapters 9 and 10) also involved distinguishing comic styles by nationality. The French comedies of Pierre Corneille in the 1630s and 1640s are entirely free of vulgar language and allusions: his search for literary refinement was supported by their being written in verse. By comparison Molière included more slapstick and more linguistic vigour in his comedies, but moments which could provoke prudish disapproval are counted on the fingers of one hand. In *L'École des femmes* (II.5), the innocent Agnès repeatedly fails to complete her sentence 'Il a pris le …' [He took my….] when recounting her meeting with young Horace, and polite society made an attempt to be scandalized at the possible innuendo. Molière could respond that if a spectator filled the lacuna with a rude word, then that was the spectator's fault and not that of the dramatist; and he did indeed argue that, in Scene 3 of *La Critique de l'École des femmes*. Very few other moments of smuttiness can be listed in Molière's surviving scripts.[15] *Bienséance* in language was taken for granted by the Comédie-Française after its foundation in 1680, and the competing Italians had to be careful in wording their more scurrilous jokes. In the manuscript index to the eighteenth-century French version of Domenico Biancolelli's scenarios — a translation which may already have been bowdlerized — a warning is included that some of them contain 'indecent expressions', to which we could also add indecent gestures and actions.

Secular academic pleas for *bienséance* corresponded with a sustained campaign by religious writers and authorities to ban obscenity from the stage.[16] As a result, by the year 1700, overt vulgarity was no longer heard in plays performed to a respectable public. Marivaux raised the language of comedy to a new level of refinement and emotional precision, even when it was to be delivered by plebeian Arlequin or Trivelin. Beaumarchais's compositions operated a double standard. On the one hand he wrote unpublished *parades* for a closet audience which are full of blatant double entendres in quirkily distorted language; on the other hand his Figaro comedies for the public theatre maintain impeccable verbal propriety. In Italy, both Luigi Riccoboni and Carlo Goldoni looked back with a critical eye at *commedie erudite* of the sixteenth century. They knew that such plays had launched the tradition to which they both belonged, and they wanted to celebrate their national heritage; but both playwrights were worried by the language and plot details which they found there, and both wanted to purge such elements to make the texts acceptable to contemporary readers and spectators. The prefaces to Riccoboni's scenarios, which

---

15   Just two more are listed in Parish 2006.
16   For a succinct account of this religious propaganda, see Majorana 2018.

he had intended to publish, betray anxiety about the fact that comic plots have to centre around love — that is, around sexual attraction and the social misbehaviour to which it can lead. He recognized (or claimed, or hoped) that eighteenth-century audiences, as well as moralist critics, demanded a new level of decency in the theatre: 'these days, the properly instructed auditorium has made Comedy more circumspect'.[17] Polite society was becoming (or was being urged to become) politer. Riccoboni felt that in this respect professional *commedia dell'arte* troupes needed to be called to order, and that control of dramatic scripts should be passed from untrustworthy actors to responsible playwrights. Similar opinions were voiced later by Carlo Goldoni, for example in his preface to the printed version of *Il servitore di due padroni* (1753). Explaining that this play was originally drafted as a scenario, and that the role of the masked servant Truffaldino had been improvised, he invited future performers to replace his scripted words with their own, if they could think of something better. At the same time he begged them 'to refrain from smutty language and from lewd actions; in the knowledge that such things are laughed at only by the lower classes, and that respectable people are offended by them'.[18] Neither Goldoni's plays nor his comic opera librettos contain explicit sexual or scatological words or references.

Comedy and Morality

However, the criteria by which comedies might be approved or disapproved did not stem purely from aesthetic preferences associated with social class. At the centre of the distinction between high and low comedy were questions regarding the moral purpose of comic drama — questions which were raised throughout the history of the classical genre, and which repeated themselves over three centuries. What was socially and artistically proper depended on what was ethically correct. When we analyse what was said on this subject, we might now want to separate those two issues; but in an age when what was 'better' socially was automatically assumed to be 'better' also morally, it is not clear that such a distinction would be understood at the time.

The phenomenon of laughter in human beings gave food for thought to philosophers and moralists of the ancient world, and therefore also to our early modern period which depended so much on the ancients for its own culture. The writings of comic dramatists and actors sometimes show that they had to confront theorists who expressed a deep distrust of laughter as such. For example, Giovan Battista Andreini was one of the practitioners who had to resist attempts on the part of the Counter-Reformation Church to ban comic theatre altogether. In his *Prologo in Dialogo fra Momo e la Verità* [Prologue in Dialogue between Momus and Truth] (1612), he makes Momus, 'the god of contradiction and discord', challenge personified Truth

---

17 'In oggi l'uditorio corretto ha resa la Comedia piú circospetta' (Riccoboni 1973: 84).
18 'Prego però que' tali, che la Parte del Truffaldino rappresenteranno, qualunque volta aggiungere del suo vi volessero, astenersi dalle parole sconce, da' lazzi sporchi; sicuri che di tali cose ridono soltanto quelli della vil plebe, e se ne offendono le gentili persone' (Goldoni 1976: I, 3).

with an attempted Aristotelian syllogism: 'Making people laugh is an immoral thing [cosa viziosa]; the aim of comedy is to make people laugh and therefore to bring about something immoral; and so comedy should be condemned'.[19] To counter this, Monna Verità has to distinguish between proper and improper types of laughter — for example she condemns it when it is uncontrolled or excessive, which is an attitude expressed by a number of well-bred sources particularly in the eighteenth century.[20] Most of all, Lady Truth insists that laughter fulfils a legitimate social function only if it is used to ridicule bad or inappropriate behaviour. In early modern European culture this was the premise which was always used to justify comedy in drama (and indeed in non-dramatic literature), and to defend it against attacks both moralistic and snobbish. The Latin tag which eventually summarized this principle was *castigat ridendo mores*: 'it punishes behaviour by laughing at it'. The word *mores* implies behaviour which is habitual, or practised by whole social groups as well as individuals. Often attributed to Cicero or Horace, this phrase in fact has a more obscure origin: it is now ascribed to a French poet named Jean-Baptiste de Santeul (1630–1697), in which case it would not have been available to Andreini for his 1612 *Dialogo*. It was appropriated particularly by the Théâtre-Italien in Paris, perhaps on the suggestion of their Arlequin, 'Dominique' Biancolelli: the words were inscibed on various parts of their theatre building, and eventually on a bust of Biancolelli himself. Whether those freewheeling anarchic performers are the ones we should most associate with a stern moral purpose is open to doubt, but they must have thought that they would fend off some criticism by adopting the motto.

Andreini had often been explicitly defensive on this subject. Still in the year 1612, when his morally orthodox *Dialogo* appeared, he published a comedy called *Lo Schiavetto* [The Little Slave], which is an interesting mix of very diverse tones and influences.[21] The 'Little Slave' himself turns out to be a young girl in male disguise, pursuing an unfaithful lover in a narreme which dates back to the Sienese *Gl'ingannati* of 1532. But alongside this central romantic role is a more subversive one: a wandering male rogue called Nottola, who takes command of a village inn (and therefore of the whole stage) with a rabble of impudent criminal followers. It has been argued persuasively by Siro Ferrone that Andreini wrote this part as a vehicle for Tristano Martinelli, the creator of the role of Arlecchino.[22] Nottola/Martinelli is given some scenes of extreme vulgarity, including a gag involving uncontrollable laughter and some openly scatological moments, which would have been exploited and expanded by this uninhibited improvising actor. The kind of audience enjoyment invited by such clownish virtuoso displays would not

---

19 'Ecco l'argomento: il mover riso è cosa viziosa, il fine della comedia è mover riso, adunque procura cosa viziosa e per ciò merita d'esser biasmata'. The work is reproduced in Marotti & Romei 1991: 473–88, with this passage on p. 476.

20 In England, Lord Chesterfield notoriously advised his (illegitimate) son that 'I would heartily wish that you may often be seen to smile, but never heard to laugh, while you live [...] there is nothing so illiberal, and so ill bred, as audible laughter' (Lord Chesterfield to his son, 9 March 1748) (Chesterfield 1890: 68). Earlier, in *The Spectator*, no. 47 (1711), Sir Richard Steele had praised Terence's *Heautontimorumenos* for containing 'in the Whole not one Passage that could raise a Laugh'.

21 The full text, including the dedicatory preface, appears in Falavolti 1982: 57–213.

22 Ferrone 1993: Chapter 5 (on Martinelli), esp. 206–11.

belong to anyone's definition of 'high comedy', and we would struggle to see them as contributing to a moral purpose. Nevertheless, in Andreini's preface 'to the Benevolent Readers' which he printed with the script, he bends over backwards to find ways in which all the stories and most of the roles in his play can claim to possess an improving didactic function, if only as solemn warnings to those readers or spectators who might be inclined to imitate the failings of various characters. A later comedy by Andreini, *Le due comedie in comedia* [The Two Comedies in a Comedy] (1623) contains a Prologue in the same vein written by one of his actors, Giovan Paolo Fabri.[23] Here readers are exhorted not be misled by the fact that some bad behaviour in comedies gets pardoned at the end of the play: the comic genre, says Fabri, demands forgiveness and happy endings, but the misdeeds are still reprehensible and to be avoided. This reads like a hasty and slightly unconvincing attempt to paste over a crack in the moralistic logic to which theatre practitioners felt they had to adhere.

Thus the function which early modern Europe formally attached to comedy (and which I address further in Chapter 21) is summarized in down-to-earth English by the Restoration dramatist John Vanbrugh in his *Short Vindication of 'The Relapse' and 'The Provok'd Wife' from Immorality and Prophaneness by the Author* of 1698: 'The Business of Comedy is to shew people what they should do, by representing them upon the Stage, doing what they should not do'.[24] At the same time, throughout this whole period, it was feared by some that the real dynamics of comedy in a theatre were more complex than their comfortable theories wanted to claim. Observation of how audiences actually behaved, in response to manifestations of vulgarity or trickery or immoral behaviour, led some theorists to the appalled recognition that such things could be enjoyed in a spirit of collusion. They saw spectators laughing because they were on the side of the clown or the deceitful lovers; they saw rude words and vulgar actions being enjoyed because such transgression is fun. Immoral characters in comedy might actually — heaven forbid! — act as examples for the audience, might give them ideas rather than putting them off. Especially, as Fabri was one of the earliest to note, when those characters were not punished at the end of the play. One early commentator who worried about this was an Italian playwright who was also a cleric: Bernardino Pino da Cagli (c. 1525–1601), who in 1578 published *Breve considerazione intorno al componimento de la comedia de' nostril tempi* [Brief Consideration on the Composition of Comedy in our Times], in which he wrote:

> It is not enough to say that seeing a vice in someone else makes us learn to avoid it in ourselves, because that perverse judgement which comes from our ill-regulated desires does not regard as a vice anything which might satisfy those desires.[25]

---

23 Full text of the play in Ferrone 1986: II, 17–105.
24 Vanbrugh 1927: I, 206.
25 'Né basta il dire che nel vedere un vizio in persona altrui è cagione che impariamo di fugirlo nella nostra, perché il perverso giudizio, il quale viene dalle mal regolate voglie nostre, non istima essere vizio quel che par sotisfarle'. The full text of Pino's treatise is reproduced in Weinberg 1970–74: II, 629–49, with the words quoted appearing on pp. 633–34.

Here a Socratic view of man's natural taste for virtue, such as might be suggested by ancient Greco-Roman authorities, is replaced by a Christian concept of original sin. Pino thus argued that the stories and characters of comic drama had to be carefully engineered so that spectators could not possibly want to identify with incorrect behaviour, but only with characters whose actions and words were virtuous.[26]

If we leap forward two centuries to 1768, we find that not much had changed: Beaumarchais expressed the same doubts in his *Essai sur le drame sérieux*. Still addressing the theory that comic mockery induces us to deride and reject bad behaviour, he observes, as Pino had observed, that in practice it does not always work out that way: 'in despite of morality, the spectator too often finds to his surprise that he is more on the side of the rascal against the honest man, because the latter is always the less amusing of the two'.[27] The classically-derived theory of how laughter ought to function in a theatre was always open to being challenged, during the period of classically-derived comedy, by an awareness of the ambiguities which operate in practice. Laughter is irredeemably slippery. One of the things which comedy did, and still does, is to offer spectators a momentary release from normal social constraints, by getting them to enjoy participating vicariously in something which is amusingly immoral or vulgar. Today we might propose notions of a harmless, even therapeutic release of antisocial instincts; but theories about laughter which were available between 1500 and 1800 were unable to articulate such concepts, let alone to indulge or approve them.

Notions of high and low comedy were thus driven by moral considerations as well as by social self-imaging. It was hoped that properly educated gentlemen and gentlewomen would distance themselves comfortably from the behaviour and language of a clown, or a miser, or a ridiculous pedant, or a cunning servant — or even from a pair of lovers who shamelessly prioritize their passion over social propriety and family obedience. For a well-brought-up person, it should go without saying that such actions were unthinkable. Many of them were also reprehensible in a more absolute sense, according to tenets of morality backed by religion. The best comedy (surely?) should encourage spectators to behave rightly rather than wrongly. Vulgar humour and subversive stories should only appeal to vulgar people who were already subversive. At the same time there was occasional recognition, throughout the period we are studying, that the process was not really so simple.

---

26 For a more extended appraisal of how views regarding laughter and propriety affected Italian *commedia erudita*, see Andrews 1993: 204–26.

27 'À la honte de la Morale, le Spectateur se surprend trop souvent à s'intéresser pour le fripon contre l'honnête homme, parce que celui-ci est toujours le moins plaisant des deux' (Beaumarchais 1988: 127).

Derision and Collusion

> For the ridiculous consists in some form of error or ugliness that is not painful or injurious; the comic mask, for example, is distorted and ugly, but causes no pain. — ARISTOTLE[28]

At the root of the theoretical dilemma lay the one-sided descriptions, inherited from ancient writers, about how laughter works in practice. It was known that if Aristotle had ever completed a full-scale study of comedy, to set alongside what he had proposed about tragedy in the *Poetics*, then that text had not survived. For definitions of comedy and of its effect on an audience, his disciples had to make do with brief remarks highlighting how the genre contrasted with tragedy. The definition of the ridiculous in *Poetics*, v, was then a starting point for early modern discussions of laughter. Some similar passages in Cicero and Horace were seen as carrying equal authority.[29] We should note in passing that any theory of laughter in general will cover a wider range of phenomena than just theatre, but in the *Poetics* Aristotle was dealing most obviously with reactions provoked by dramatic literature and performance.[30] Inevitably, his definitions were influential on early modern writers of comic theory, and of comedy. Out of Aristotle and then Cicero a consensus view arose that we laugh at things because they are beneath us, because they are silly and wrong, because we feel superior to them: the essential Greek adjective which gets translated into English as 'base' or 'shameful', and which is associated with harmless 'error', was *aiskhrós* (αἰσχρός). In the Latin writers the concept was expressed in abstract nouns such as *turpitudo* or *deformitas* — the words used in Cicero's *De oratore* — which have equivalents in English and other modern European languages. In Aristotle, the defining weakness of a comic character was compared with the more serious flaw or *hamartía* (ἁμαρτία) displayed by a protagonist of tragedy: the distinction between the two genres was that tragic faults or failures inspire 'pity and terror' in the spectator, whereas comic ones inspire pleasing amusement. The idea that the single purpose of stage comedy should be to 'correct vices through laughing at them' (which I shall treat at more length in Chapter 21) arose seamlessly from the assumption that laughter is caused by derision, pure derision, and nothing but derision.[31]

If we detach ourselves for a moment from the moral argument, and simply peruse the reasons why comic scripts made audiences laugh, then it is undeniable that derision did play an indispensable part in classical stage comedy. The characters who

---

28 Aristotle, *Poetics*, v (Aristotle 1965: 37).
29 Horace's *Ars poetica* and Cicero's *De oratore*. Cicero's description of what makes us laugh (*De oratore*, II, 58; Cicero 2014: 373–75) echoes the words of Aristotle quoted above. It informs in turn the discussion of laughter and humour (in social conversation rather than in the theatre) which appears in Baldassarre Castiglione's *Libro del Cortegiano* ('Book of the Courtier') of 1525 (II, 45–94). That work was of course influential throughout Europe in the sixteenth century.
30 This point is made abundantly clear in Mary Beard's monograph on ancient Roman laughter (Beard 2014). For an exploration of how laughter was used in early modern society, see Thomas 1977.
31 In England Sir Philip Sidney, in his *Defense of Poesy* (1595), described laughter as 'a scornful tickling', and distinguished it from feelings of 'delight' (Sidney 2002: 112). The definition of laughter provided by Thomas Hobbes, in Part I, Chapter 6 of his *Leviathan* (1651), is often paraphrased as 'a sudden glory felt at the sight of an inferior' (cf. Hobbes 1998: 38).

are derided range from those who simply show themselves as foolish or despicable, via those who are pretentious and self-deluding — in Greek such a character was called an *alazōn* (ἀλαζών) — to those who are tricked and defeated in the contests of deceit which make up the majority of comic plots. Roman comedies had always been about winners and losers, and spectators laughed at those who lost: the pattern was taken up and continued in the early modern theatre. To borrow the words of W. G. Moore, the losers were necessarily depicted 'without emotion', and with a strong dose of the insulating fantasy which is endemic to all comedy. Moore suggests that Molière's Italian predecessors 'portrayed fools for whom we feel no pity, and knaves who inspire no fear'.[32]

Early modern classical comedy, like its ancient models, could not exist without victims. To begin with they were largely restricted to the categories which *commedia dell'arte* troupes called *parti ridicole*: miserly or lustful Elders, ignorant Servants, and braggart Capitani. A similar unthinking scorn had been aimed in Plautus and Terence at the mercenary pimp. (In the earliest Italian comedies there were also greedy parasites in the ancient Roman mode, but these figures no longer reflected a recognizable social category: their obsessive gluttony was soon transferred to servants of peasant stock, including Harlequin.) As the genre developed and became more sophisticated, so did the use of derision and its targets: Lovers themselves were mocked as victims of deceit, and of emotional excess. The fact that they were eventually saved from disaster led to more nuanced outcomes, in which superior laughter could be mixed with rueful sympathy. But in the majority of cases laughter was still provoked by feelings of superiority: the audience knew more, or knew better, than the fictional people on stage, and could see when they were being tricked or getting things wrong. They could see also how the characters' failures arose from the personalities assigned to them, from the blinkered obsessions and lusts which made them laughable in the first place. To explain the normal dynamics of such comedy, concepts expressed by the Greek *aiskhrós* or the Latin *turpitudo* are mostly sufficient.

All the same, worried moralists from Bernardino Pino to Beaumarchais were right to perceive that apparently turpitudinous characters were not simply banished from audience sympathy, not always swept away in a dust of derision. In a theatre we are easily tempted to collude for a while with an entertaining trickster, however much we may fear his equivalent in real life, especially if at the same time we are happily despising the gullibility of his victim. In their comments on how laughter works, ancient writers had not recognized this. They did not formulate, in their ethical world or in their psychology, any notion of comedy providing a therapeutic holiday from normal inhibitions — and this despite the separate existence of approved rituals like Saturnalia, which reversed normal hierarchies. They did not note either that a theatre audience constructs a dual relationship with the figure who appears on stage. We have one set of reactions to the character depicted, but a parallel and often contrasting opinion about the performer. We salute an actor's

---

32 Moore 1969: 19: the observations are applied to the seventeenth century, but are equally valid for Roman comedy.

skill, even when he or she is playing the part of a fool or a villain; and this fact can modify our feelings of distance from the character concerned. The tendency is nourished and expanded by the emergence of star actors in professional theatre, most of all when the same actors regularly play for the same spectators and have become well known to their fans.

By chance, the earliest salute to virtuosity which is recorded in a classical comic script comes from the very beginning of the genre, when the performers were not yet professionals. In Ariosto's first comedy *La cassaria* (1508), the servant Trappola, in a desperate attempt to get out of trouble, pretends for a while to be unable to speak. The physical clowning with which the amateur actor accompanied this charade must have memorably amused the court audience in Ferrara because the following year, in *I suppositi*, another servant character, this time unnamed, was made by Ariosto to suggest: 'Do you want me to pretend to be dumb, like I did that other time?'.[33] Clearly the same actor was appealing to his friends and fans, who may even have answered from their seats with a resounding 'Yes, go on!'.

This interactive element in comic theatre became reinforced and institutionalized with the rise of professional *arte* troupes. Famous leading performers accumulated their own bands of admirers, who hoped and even demanded that particular virtuosic routines would be regularly repeated in any show that could accommodate them. This applied to more 'serious' stars such as Isabella Andreini (who, as we shall see in Chapter 19, was famous for her 'mad scenes'); but it was particularly true for actors who played subversive roles, all the Zanni and the Pedrolini, and the Arlecchini. It is such popular clowns who regularly explode, or at least complicate, the Aristotelian notion that we always and exclusively laugh out of superior contempt: we can simultaneously deride (laugh *at*) the incompetence of the fictional character and applaud (laugh *with*) the live performer who is so competent at playing him. Molière made his reputation by creating in his scripts, and then brilliantly performing on stage, a series of choleric inadequates who were deluded, obsessional, and fatally prone to lose both the plot and their tempers. The more ludicrous his creations were, the more Molière himself was admired.[34]

Molière's protagonists do not encourage us to imitate or collude with them; but during the same period, characters or masks who were foolish were, paradoxically, also becoming popular heroes. This phenomenon, also rooted in our dual response to a clever performer playing an idiot, is seen most clearly and economically in what happened to the mask of Arlequin as seen on the Parisian stage. In the surviving notebooks of Domenico Biancolelli — where the actor summarizes all his own jokes and routines, and where the shows are collected in chronological

---

33   Ariosto, *La cassaria* (both prose and verse versions), IV.7, *passim*; and then *I suppositi*, II.2: 'SERVO: Vuoi tu ch'io mi finga mutolo, come io feci un'altra volta?' (prose version); 'FAMIGLIO: Che vi parria, s'io mi fingesse mutolo, | come feci anco in casa di Crisobolo?' (verse version). Crisobolo is the name of the old father who is duped in *La cassaria*. We cannot exclude the possibility that the relevant servant roles were assigned to a court fool, or to someone else of relatively low status who was known to have comic performing skills.

34   This, it seems to me, is a less problematic way (at least in the context of theatre) of expressing what Mary Beard (2014: 184) calls the 'fine line between the person who makes you laugh and the one you laugh at'.

order of their staging — Arlequin can be seen making a complex transition from simply portraying a stupid character to taking control of the whole play and of the audience's sympathy (see also Chapters 10 and 21). In the early *I morti vivi/ Les Morts vivants* [The Living Dead], he is accused of having killed the heroine Eularia, and protests frantically, 'It wasn't me! Go and ask her!', while believing that Eularia is in fact dead. In *Il baron todesco/ Le Baron allemand* [The German Baron] he drinks medicine thinking it is soup, and eats a bar of soap mistaking it for cheese.[35] But in later Biancolelli scenarios Arlequin embarks on impersonations of high-status figures: judges, princes, especially medical doctors. The title of one scenario is *Arlequin as Thief, Policeman and Judge*, showing impressive upward mobility during the course of a single story.[36] Here he tends increasingly to mock and undermine such wielders of power, and so to exercise a subversive 'fool's wisdom'. Rather than, or in addition to, simply showing the incomprehensions and inadequacies of a bumpkin from Bergamo, his masquerades satirize the incompetence or corruption of alleged experts and authorities: in particular there are frequent one-line gags about doctors tending to kill more people than they cure. In some plots Arlequin twists the law or falsifies a judgement in order to procure a happy ending for the play's Lovers. Aristotle had not noted the fact that an audience (especially, but not only, an audience of social underdogs) can eagerly turn a stage fool into a stage hero, cheering on his subversions rather than simply deriding them. It is unlikely that early modern clowns were mounting a conscious campaign to refute Aristotle's description of laughter; but the fact that Arlequin could appear perplexingly as both stupid and clever was being recognized. It began to be stated explicitly in comic texts. In Chapter 10 we noted a comedy attributed to Jean Palaprat (1650–1721), performed in 1692 by the Théâtre-Italian and entitled *La Fille de bon sens* [The Sensible Girl]: it was included in Gherardi's collection of 1701.[37] In 1.5 we read the following exchange between Arlequin and Colombine:

> COLOMBINE Haven't you become clever, since I last saw you!
> ARLEQUIN   *(laughs)*
> COLOMBINE And yet you're still pretty stupid sometimes; God forgive me, I
>   think you've got two souls in your body.[38]

Colombine's 'since I last saw you' is metatheatrical: it does not refer to this particular play, but to Arlequin's accumulated appearances in dozens of similar staged fictions. Both the 'souls in his body' were familiar to the Théâtre-Italien's regular audience: one belonged to the mask and the other to the actor (Evaristo Gherardi, in 1692). In *La Fille de bon sens*, Arlequin has moments of complete confusion and stupidity, but in the end he combines victoriously with Colombine to get rid of all her

---

35 The French translation of these notes (by Thomas-Simon Guellette, *c.* 1750) is edited in Gambelli 1993–97: II, 109, 178.
36 *Arlechino ladro, sbiro et giudice*: no. 30 in Gambelli 1993–97: II, 363–75.
37 The play is reprinted in Gherardi 1994–96; and is discussed in Mazouer 2002a: 196–98.
38 'COLOMBINE: Que tu es devenu habile depuis que je ne t'ai vu! ARLEQUIN: Ah! ah! COLOMBINE: Tu es pourtant bien sot quelquefois; et je crois, Dieu me le pardonne, que tu as deux âmes dans le corps' (1.5). See also, in Scott 1990: 380–81, part of a similar dialogue from *Arlequin misantrope* (1696) by Louis Biancolelli.

mistress's unwanted suitors. The audience laughs sometimes at him, sometimes at his victims.[39]

In eighteenth-century Venice, Carlo Goldoni was also aware of the duality between character and performer. In his preface to the comedy *La cameriera brillante* [The Smart Serving-Maid] (1753) he comments on the reluctance of some actors, both amateur and professional, to play unsympathetic parts:

> They don't know, or they don't want to know, that the audience judges a comedy by how well it is performed, and gives equal credit to those who play heroic parts and to those who play hateful parts; and the good actor does not lose personal credit because of playing a bad character, nor does a bad person become better by playing a virtuous one.[40]

In spite of this perception, Goldoni was not always more able than other comic dramatists to negotiate a firm distinction between audience derision and collusion in respect of a strong protagonist. In the same year 1753 he wrote one of his most successful plays, one of the few to have been frequently translated: *La locandiera* [The Mistress of the Inn], the translated title often being *Mirandolina*. Mirandolina is a control freak who despises the queue of men, customers at her inn, who tend (or claim) to fall in love with her. When she encounters a misogynist Cavaliere who boasts of being immune to amorous feelings, she takes this as an irresistible challenge: by praising his attitude, and by proclaiming a strategy of false 'sincerity', she eventually gets through his guard and he succumbs. She then has to beat a hasty retreat when the Cavaliere's suddenly awakened passion leads him to potential violence. The words with which she concludes the play state that she has learned her lesson, and that male spectators should take the story as a warning that they should beware of women like her. Goldoni follows the same line in his preface to the reader: this, he says, is 'the most moral, the most useful, the most instructive' of all his comedies. Honest women will be repelled by its protagonist, and approve of its exposure of such 'deceivers who dishonour their sex'.[41] We are back to the formulation of John Vanbrugh: 'show people what they should do by representing them upon the stage doing what they should not do'. However, the role of Mirandolina is one to which many Italian actresses still aspire; and for two and a half of the three acts, the audience is likely to be on her side, in the way that we so often collude with the skilful trickster against the incompetent loser. It is for the Cavaliere, rather than for his female tormentor, that we feel superior scorn.

---

39 For further notions of 'Fascination and Contempt', with regard specifically to *commedia dell'arte*, see Taviani 2018.

40 'Non sanno, o sapere non vogliono, che i spettatori gustano la commedia se è bene rappresentata, e tanto si fa merito chi fa la parte eroica, come quello che fa la parte odiosa; né il buono perde il merito personale per un cattivo carattere, né il cattivo divien migliore per un carattere virtuoso.'

41 'Fra tutte le Commedie da me sinora composte, starei per dire essere questa la piú morale, la piú utile, la piú istruttiva. [...] Le donne che oneste sono, giubileranno anch'esse che si smentiscano codeste simulatrici, che disonorano il loro sesso'. There are critics who think that this preface is a defence thrown up against anticipated moralistic criticism, and that Goldoni did not mean what he said. I would argue that in any case the ambiguities of the play still remain: Mirandolina, however clever and entertaining, is also cruel and dishonest.

This may effectively warn the male spectator against becoming like the Cavaliere, which is how the moral lesson of a comedy was supposed to work, and is also what Goldoni stresses in his preface. Nevertheless, our reaction to Mirandolina herself may be more complex, especially if we are female: an energetic leading actress, supported by a director with an agenda, can make her more the heroine of the play than its villain. Here even Goldoni, with his vast theatrical experience and his fine critical perception, was unable unambiguously to prioritize comic derision over comic collusion.

In classical comedy generally, therefore, we see an undoubted preference for aggressive mockery and a need for comic victims; but playwrights, theoreticians, and actors rarely managed to produce an experience which conformed exclusively to the official moralistic view that laughter works entirely through derision. It was the contribution of the performer in particular which regularly, and happily, muddied the waters. Here, as at other points throughout this study, we can see artisan skill trumping erudite precept.

Before pursuing further how these questions affected specific themes, we need to look at some nuts and bolts of performance itself. My next two chapters explore ways in which acting techniques, combined with inherited dramaturgical habits, helped to form theatrical expectations.

CHAPTER 18

Component Parts, I: Roman Dramaturgy

Imitating Roman Texts

Certain elements of a classical comic play — both its performed content and its presentation as a written text — were inherited directly from Roman comedy, that is from the scripts of Plautus and Terence as they had been transmitted from antiquity to modern times.

A major motivation for the creation and diffusion of early modern drama, in comedy and in other genres, was the perception that plays written for the stage during Greco-Roman antiquity had been seen as artefacts to be taken seriously.[1] They had been copied, preserved, and transmitted to posterity as significant and prestigious items of literary culture, read and discussed on the same level as epic poetry, lyric poetry, philosophy, and history. During the early medieval period, after the rise of Christianity, texts composed for recitation before an audience had been given little value, or indeed negative value: pronouncements of the early Church Fathers (starting in *c.* 198 CE with Tertullian's *De spectaculis*) had brought the whole practice of theatre performance into disrepute. Eventually dramas with religious content became accepted and mounted by some church and civic authorities, but they did not have what we would now recognize as cultural status. Most were composed anonymously, probably also collectively, and preserved in single texts used for revival by single communities on specific ceremonial occasions. Because of this lack of diffusion, most scripts of religious drama are unlikely to have reached us at all: no one imagined that they could be of any interest in a wider literary world. An important but significantly late exception to this would be *sacre rappresentazioni* in fifteenth-century Florence, which were printed after 1485 and attributed to their individual authors. Here we can see a change of climate already influenced by classical models.

Approaches to the new humanist theatre offered a deliberate contrast to the period we call 'medieval'. In Italy, as soon as dramas began to be composed with an eye to ancient examples, playwrights wanted them to have the same cultural importance as the scripts of Plautus and Terence (and as those of Sophocles and

---

[1] For a succinct account of the effects of Humanism on European drama, see Henke 2017, and more specifically Bishop & Henke 2017: 5–8, 31–32.

Seneca in tragedy). They wanted also to take personal credit for them. The new technology of printing was immediately exploited for the diffusion of authored play scripts alongside other literature. In other European countries such attitudes emerged more slowly and with more opposition. In England it is notorious that when Ben Jonson published his collected *Workes* in 1616, he was mocked for giving such self-regarding importance to mere 'plays'. The ambivalence of that word in English probably did not help his humanistic ambitions. The semantic overlap — between 'play' meaning a stage drama and 'play' meaning a trivial game — does not occur in Italian or French vocabulary. By contrast it is clear that Ariosto, from the beginning of his playwriting career in 1508–09, always intended that *La cassaria* and *I suppositi* should be printed in the form which he authorially preferred. He intended to rewrite them in verse, imitating the Latin models: he disliked the pirated prose versions which appeared in 1510.[2] Subsequent Italian dramatists were equally keen to see their work printed and acknowledged. Preserving and publishing play scripts was an integral part of the project whereby Renaissance culture attempted to imitate that of antiquity. In 1554 there appeared an edited collection, intended to be the first volume of many, of what were reckoned to be the best Italian comedies so far composed.[3] The implication was that serious critical judgement could and should be applied to texts written for the stage; and there was even an element of comparative competition, such as was known to have been present in the drama festivals of classical Athens.

Acts and Scenes; Stage Directions; Prologues

With regard to the presentation of play scripts on paper, it is worth recording to start with some facts which are so simple and obvious that historians rarely get around to writing them down.

Because of the atmosphere of innovation which was attached to the new humanist drama, it went without saying that when classical comedies were written or printed — for actors who might revive them, but also for scholarly readers — they had to resemble the inherited scripts of Plautus and Terence.[4] It was not fully realized that those scripts had already undergone some modification at the hands of copyists and editors in later antiquity, so that exactly how the original dramatists had set them down was (and still is) impossible to discover. It is now thought to be unlikely that Roman comedies were formally divided into acts and scenes. The five-act division was imposed on them later, and eventually expressed as a firm rule in Horace's *Ars poetica*.[5] Many of the earliest Renaissance dramatists seem to have regarded drafting comedies in five acts as compulsory, a sign that the playwright was attempting

---

2   All this is made clear in a correspondence between Ariosto and the Marquis of Mantua in 1524. See Andrews 1991a: 87–90.
3   Ruscelli 1554. The chosen plays were Bibbiena's *Calandra*, Machiavelli's *Mandragola*, and three comedies composed collectively by the Sienese Intronati Academy.
4   The conventions for presenting scenarios for improvisation were inevitably different from those which applied to fully scripted plays. See Andrews 2008: xvi–xviii.
5   'Neve minor neu sit quinto productior actu fabula' [A play should not be shorter or longer than a fifth act] (*Ars poetica*, ll. 189–90).

to imitate classical models and to reject medieval ones. When plays were staged together with expensive supporting (or distracting) *intermezzi* of song and dance, this meant that the action of the play was indeed interrupted by four intervals, though it seems that spectators were not always given time to leave the auditorium to relax, or to perform bodily functions.[6] When there were no such interludes, we generally do not know how performing time was managed for *commedia erudita* — that is, whether or not audiences were given any break between acts.

The earliest Italian attempts at creating neo-classical tragedy showed less unanimity about the five-act structure than did the first comedies. Playscripts in ancient Greek suggested different approaches from those which had been inherited in Latin, and as late as 1598 Angelo Ingegneri registered a perception that Sophocles did not divide the acts of his tragedies into scenes.[7] The first vernacular tragedies in Italian were divided between those which followed a self-proclaimed 'Greek' structural pattern involving no act divisions at all, and others which claimed that five acts plus a prologue worked better. The latter were following precedents which were seen as more 'Roman': they followed the Horatian rule, and imitated the tragedies of Seneca as they had been transmitted. It was the 'Roman' model which prevailed: the assumption that tragedies contained five acts soon became established throughout Europe, lasting until the French Revolution and beyond.

In Italo-French classical comedy, practice was soon more flexible. From the late sixteenth century, Italian professional improvising companies divided their comic shows into three acts rather than five, to judge by those scenarios which have survived in print or in manuscript.[8] *Commedia ridicolosa* plays (see Chapter 5) were poised between the two worlds of script and scenario; and some of them appear in alternative five-act and three-act editions. In France there soon emerged a kind of class division whereby 'lower' forms of comedy had three acts, with many farces consisting of just one, and more ambitious pieces (such as all the comedies of Pierre Corneille) had five.[9] This is a distinction which more or less works for the plays of Molière. In Paris generally, as if to reinforce the cultural hierarchy, the Comédie-Française tended towards five acts (though not in every case), and the Théâtre-Italien used three or fewer. By the time of the 'New' Italian company in the early

---

6 The use of *intermezzi* was most common in lavish court productions in Ferrara and Florence. By contrast the Intronati Academy of Siena, in the person of its controlling spokesman Alessandro Piccolomini (for whom see Chapter 22), opposed the use of interludes; and there would be many performance venues which could not afford them.

7 Ingegneri 1989: 12–13.

8 To explain this, we might be tempted to refer back to the three stages of a dramatic plot — *protasis*, *epistasis* and *catastasis* — detected in (or imposed on) plays by critics in late antiquity. This triple analysis is now seen as having been invented by Aelius Donatus, the fourth-century author of the commentaries on Terence which were available from the start to humanist scholars and playwrights. However, although some professional *arte* actors were certainly well enough educated to be aware of the three categories, it seems more likely to me that the three-act structure responded to the practical demands of acting for a paying public. Two intervals were viable and even desirable, while four were too many. Spanish *comedias* of the Golden Age, whose formats were explicitly responsive to audience demands and preferences, settled permanently for a three-act structure.

9 As late as 1877, in his *Essay on Comedy*, George Meredith wrote (perhaps ironically) that 'five is dignity with a trailing robe; whereas one, or two, or three acts would be short skirts, and degrading' (Meredith & Bergson 1956: 7).

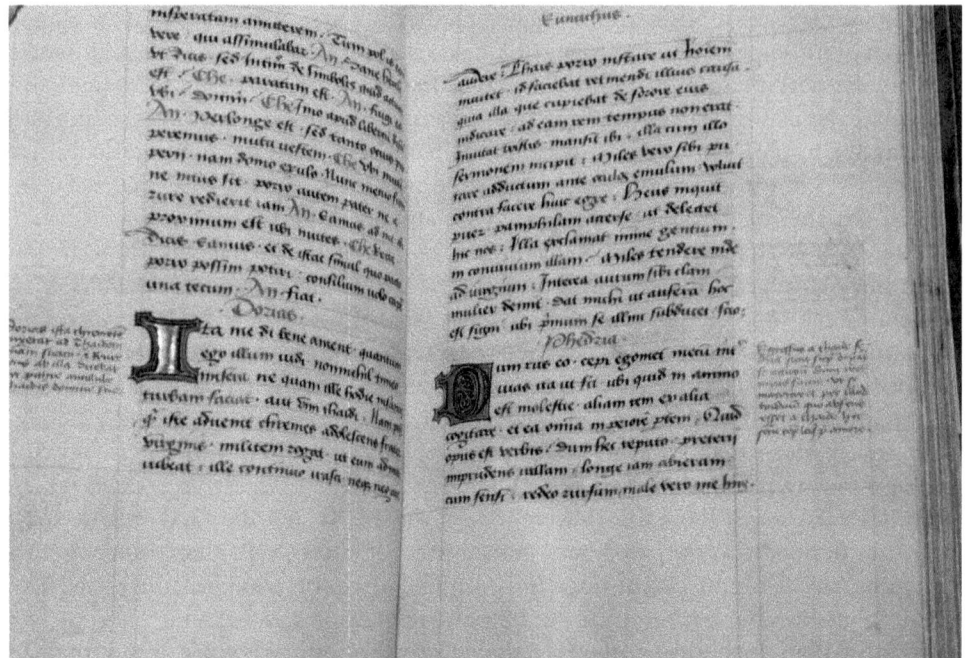

FIG. 18.1. A manuscript of Terence's comedies, dated 1477. The centred headings, each giving the name of the character who will be on stage, mark the beginnings of Act IV, Scenes 1 and 2, of the comedy *Eunuchus*. There are no words for 'Act' or 'Scene', and no numbers.

eighteenth century, Marivaux had almost abandoned writing comedies in five acts, no doubt influenced precisely by writing more often for the Italians.[10]

In Italy itself, we learn from Luigi Riccoboni that audiences around 1700 would have regarded a prose comedy in five acts, as opposed to three, as 'monstrous'.[11] This fact will have influenced Goldoni, who used five acts for his comedies in verse (few of which are revived today), and three for those in prose. Beaumarchais's *Barbier de Séville* achieved its public success when it was reduced from five acts to an unusual four. He reverted to five for *Le Mariage de Figaro*, and for his *drames sérieux* including *La Mère coupable*.

Acts are usually divided into scenes, though the precise meaning of that term differs between modern theatre cultures. In the scripts of Roman comedies, as transmitted in medieval manuscripts, a new 'scene' was marked simply by a revised list of the characters — or at least of those who had lines to speak — who were to be present on stage: there were no explicit stage directions indicating 'Enter Davus' or

---

10   Marivaux wrote two five-act tragedies, but his only comedy in five acts was *Les Serments indiscrets* for the Comédie-Française in 1732. Twenty of his plays, whether or not we can class them as comedies, were in one act.

11   In the 'Proemio' to the scenario *La moglie gelosa*, he says: 'una comedia in cinque atti sarebbe stata creduta un mostro non mai comparso su la Scena Italiana' [a comedy in five acts would have been seen as a monster never presented on the Italian stage] (Riccoboni 1973: 39.)

'Exit Pseudolus' (see Fig. 18.1).[12] This presentation was adopted by Italian *commedia erudita* — though very soon the scenes of printed plays were also given numbers, which had not been the case in texts of Plautus and Terence. The convention remained fairly constant in France as well as Italy throughout the period of classical imitation. 'Scenes' were thus defined by the entrance or exit of one or more characters: performances of Roman comedy had never involved a change of physical scene. (For rehearsals, in fact, it is more convenient to designate a 'scene' by which characters, and therefore which actors, are taking part.) By the eighteenth century, changes of location had become commonplace even in classical comedy: I shall have more to say about this in Chapter 20, when examining how 'unity of place' was observed. In the script on paper, however, scenes were still distinguished and numbered according to entrances and exits rather than by changes of scenography, which occurred less often. When observed punctiliously, the convention could lead to some numbered scenes containing only a single monologue or a couple of short speeches. This practice is different from that adopted by English playscripts, where a change of 'scene' usually implies a change of scene. As is remarked by Suzanne Jones, in England this implies also a break in the action; whereas classical theory was more preoccupied with ensuring continuity (using the French word *liaison*) between successive scenes.[13] It was often maintained that the stage should never be left empty between scenes, as opposed to between acts: this was insisted on by Angelo Ingegneri in 1598.[14] Giovan Battista Andreini, depicting a play mounted within his play *Le due commedie in commedia* (1623), has his on-stage audience whistle in derision in v.10, when a group of professional actors does in fact leave an empty stage because one of their company has gone missing. This implies that at least some theatre spectators were informed at that time about academic rules which claimed to be derived from antiquity.

The omission of entrance and exit instructions was just one aspect of the fact that stage directions were absent from the inherited format of classical scripts. When physical actions needed to be communicated, a way was found of doing so in dialogue, with one character commenting verbally on what another was doing, or on what was happening. As a single typical example we could quote from Plautus's *Menaechmi*. When Menaechmus is taken for a madman, and forcibly restrained by a group of slaves, the dialogue gives us outraged exclamations from the victim himself ('Help! Murder! What's happening? Why am I being set on like this?', etc.), and then from his slave Messenio ('Almighty gods! What do I see? My master man-handled and carried off by a gang of ruffians!').[15] It is almost as if extra lines

12 Because of this convention, non-speaking characters who were certainly present on stage were sometimes not named at the start of a scene. The most obvious example is the unlisted presence of some brothers of Fulvia, in Bibbiena's *La Calandra*, v.7–8.
13 Jones 2020: 19.
14 Ingegneri (1989): 15.
15 'Quid hoc est negoti? Quid illisce homines ad me currunt, opsecro'; and 'pro di immortales! opsecro, quid ego oculis aspicio meis? | erum meum indignissume nescioqui sublimem ferunt' (*Menaechmi*, ll. 997, 1001–02). The translation quoted is that of E. F. Watling (Plautus 1964). My Latin extracts from Plautus and Terence are quoted from the most recent Loeb Classical Library editions (Plautus 2011 and Terence 2001).

were being inserted to make things clear for a reader who is not a spectator: at all events the information is indeed given in such dialogue, rather than via directions in narrative form.

This somewhat inhibiting convention was observed for a long time by play scripts in Italy and France — an early example is III.5 of Ariosto's *La cassaria*.[16] We might speculate that, in the early period of Italian *commedia erudita*, playwrights wanted not only to copy their Roman models but also to distance themselves from the way in which medieval drama was presented. Texts of the new humanist plays had to look clearly different from those of mystery plays or *sacre rappresentazioni*, and the omission of stage directions was one way of ensuring this.[17] By the mid-seventeenth century, Pierre Corneille was already recognizing that the absence of stage directions in published scripts could lead to a lack of clarity both for readers and actors: he suggested adding them in the form of marginal notes.[18] The prejudice against them, if that is what it was, began to disappear in the eighteenth century. It has been observed that, starting with his comedy entitled *L'Envieux* [The Envious Man] (1738), Voltaire began to add directions indicating the tone of voice which a character should use.[19] Meanwhile the Théâtre-Italien in Paris, more dismissive of *classiciste* convention, had been producing scripts which offered detailed descriptions of scenic effects.

Outside potential or nominal acts and scenes, Plautus and Terence usually composed a prologue — an introductory piece of direct address to the audience, containing a comment from the author on the piece about to be performed. In imitation of the ancient sources, prologues were then included in many Italian *commedie erudite*; and there were major theoretical discussions about whether to use them in tragedy (as was done by Seneca, but not by any Greek tragic playwright). The content and purpose of a comic prologue varied considerably. In the earliest years, it might attempt to summarize the plot, or the fictional events and relationships which led up to it — in which case the Italians might call it an *argomento* — but once dramatists had learned to compose efficient scenes of expository dialogue, that function became redundant. Prologues could also contain Roman-style justifications of the playwright's enterprise, which occasionally turned into theoretical dialogues between two people on stage, not dissimilar to some lengthy Inductions which are found in English plays of the Jacobean period. If the prologue was a solo number, the actor who delivered it (and who often also spoke the concluding lines of the play, the '*plaudite*' inviting applause) tended to be playing one of the lower-class, more disreputable characters: the ambiguous derisive-collusive relationship between audience and clown, which I examined in the previous chapter, often resulted in the clown also becoming the master of ceremonies. Prologues are an interesting subject of study in Italian theatre culture in the sixteenth and seventeenth centuries, but

---

16 The relevant sequence is fully translated in Andrews 1993: 43–45.
17 In medieval play scripts, stage directions were often in Latin, rather than in the vernacular used by the play. This may explain the persistence of *exit* and *exeunt* in English theatrical language: English dramatists were less doctrinaire about rejecting input from medieval traditions.
18 In his *Discours des trois unités* of 1660.
19 Peyronnet 1978: 41. See also Goulbourne 2006: 108.

they disappeared from classical comedy once the genre moved to France.[20] There are none in Pierre Corneille or Molière or Marivaux, and they soon vanished from fully scripted Italian comedies too. (There is no surviving textual indication that they were ever used in *commedia dell'arte*: however, the relationship between a scenario text and performance practice is partial and approximate, so we cannot be sure.) French *classiciste* doctrine was uncomfortable with speeches which stepped outside the carefully constructed fiction of the drama: they implied a recognition of the theatricality, and therefore the artificiality, of the enterprise, and so clashed with the drive towards a seamlessly coherent illusion which was seen as making the dramatic experience more 'rational'. (Even the example of Seneca was not enough for them to be retained in neo-classical tragedies by Corneille and Racine.) In hindsight, and in modern revivals, prologues do not appear as a regular constituent part of the Italo-French comedy genre.

Stage Conventions Taken from Roman Comedy

Modern scholars are able to conduct sophisticated analyses of the texts of Plautus and Terence: there is even informed speculation on which passages were and were not performed with a musical accompaniment. The concept of *canticum* in Terence was hinted at in the commentaries of Donatus, but the first humanist readers still took some time to perceive even that Roman comedies were in verse.[21] Early modern comic dramatists paid no attention to notions of *canticum*. Large numbers of comedies were now being composed in prose, and musical settings require metre. The perception of a melodic element in ancient theatre was made by Italian academicians in the late sixteenth century, but in relation to Greek tragedy rather than to Roman comedy: it led to the invention of opera, which as we have seen did not initially relate itself much to the comic genre.

What the new classical comedy did pay attention to, and regularly copy, were some dramaturgical conventions which governed how characters in comedy conveyed information, both to each other and to the audience.[22] In relation to what we would now see as behaviour in normal life, they tend to be implausible; but they wrote themselves firmly for a long time into the compositional and performing practice of modern theatre. They play their part in the 'comic contract' (in the expression of the critic Nicholas Grene), the suspension of disbelief and the acceptance of artificial conventions which make up an unspoken agreement between dramatist, actors, and audience.[23] However, they were not exclusive to comedy, but also used in classical and neo-classical tragedy. I refer here to soliloquies; to asides spoken to the audience; and to scenes involving eavesdropping.

Eavesdropping scenes, where characters listen on stage unobserved to words spoken by others, are the simplest of these devices. In stories which regularly involve

---

20 See Hulfield 2018.
21 See Dane 1999.
22 For accounts of these matters in Roman comedy itself, see the surveys which introduce the latest Loeb editions: Plautus 2011: 1, li–liv; Terence 2001: 1, 6–12.
23 See Grene 1980.

plot and counter-plot, trickery and deceit, they are strategies to be expected. There will be considerable variation as to how convincing they are in realistic terms (especially in an outdoor setting, which was the norm in Roman comedy); but what they depict is not totally impossible, and the audience will be willing to play along. In Plautus the situation can be happily complicated by the fact that those who are being overheard are sometimes aware of the fact, and are therefore saying what they want the eavesdropper to hear, working a counter-deceit on the person who thinks he is outwitting them. A sequence towards the end of *Miles gloriosus* [The Braggart Soldier] (ll. 1216–69) is built around this device: the derided eponymous victim Pyrgopolynices overhears a long charade played out by a courtesan and her maidservant, in which the women pretend to be totally besotted on the soldier who, as they know, is listening to them. In this play the soldier's sexual vanity is targeted even more than his military boasting, and so it is this defining comic fault that makes him believe every word they say.

Italo-French classical comedy also used eavesdropping scenes. An example which goes beyond mere imitation is found in II.6 of *Gl'ingannati* (1532), the pioneering play composed collectively by the Sienese Intronati Academy. On an open front door step, the daughter of the house Isabella is being wooed and eventually kissed by the page boy 'Fabio', who is in fact the play's heroine Lelia in disguise. Two servants observe them with glee, and express reactions which are voyeuristically obscene. In the standard comic setting of a city street, it is assumed that the two sets of characters can be far enough apart but not too far: the lovers are unaware of the watching servants, but the servants can hear them — and both pairs are audible to the audience. More than a century later, Molière wrote IV.5 of *Le Tartuffe*, where the virtuous wife Elmire makes her gullible husband Orgon listen to the attempts at seducing her made by their predatory guest, Tartuffe himself. Up to now, Orgon has been fooled and bewitched by the hypocrite's mask of rigorous piety. In this case Elmire knows that they are being overheard, whereas Tartuffe does not: the pattern of deliberate deception is thus more complicated than in *Miles gloriosus*. The indoor setting also makes the scene more plausible: in life it is easier to hide within earshot under a table, or just behind a door, than round a corner in a street. This scene, together with the story in which it functions, has precedents in a *commedia dell'arte* scenario in Flaminio Scala's collection of 1611: III.11 of Day 31, *Il pedante* [The Pedant].[24] In that version the treacherous (and eponymous) house guest is Cataldo, employed as a family tutor, and the virtuous wife is Isabella, while the person who listens in is not the foolish husband Pantalone but the smart servant Pedrolino. Eavesdropping situations are especially plentiful in Scala's volume, with some scenarios (such as Day 29, *Il fido amico* [The Faithful Friend]) making continuous multiple use of them.[25] It is possible that the relatively mechanical nature of such scenes led them to be used more often in *commedia dell'arte*, where the metatheatrical game of comedy was proclaimed more openly. However, the device appears in a final flourish in both versions of *The Marriage of Figaro*, when Figaro listens in the

---

24   Scala 1976: II, 325; English translation in Andrews 2008: 188.
25   Ibid.: 293–303; 172–81.

dark to the Count apparently seducing Suzanne/Susanna, and does not yet realize that the woman accepting the adulterous advances is the Countess in disguise. As in *Miles gloriosus*, the women concerned in this conspiracy are aware from the start that Figaro is overhearing the action: they want his discomfort to act as a punishment for his unwarranted jealousy.

A more obviously theatrical device, with little correspondence in anyone's reality, is the aside which a character delivers to the audience, revealing what he or she is really thinking or feeling. In comedy, the motivation for hiding the truth might be politeness, or prudence — or simple deceit, when an alternative false story is being circulated. Plautus and Terence provide a surprising number of asides which just aim to keep the audience informed about the speaker's inner reactions or state of mind: comments translated as 'How right you are!' (*Phormio*, l. 718), or 'I'm done for!' (*Phormio*, l. 942), which modern actors might prefer to express with a facial expression or other body language.[26] Their presence in the dialogue might be compared with those spoken words which fulfil the function of stage directions, such as those quoted above from *Menaechmi*. Moreover, the identification of particular words as asides — like the mental insertion of stage directions — was left to the reader or the modern editor. In Italo-French comedy such brief asides were also used. Often the reader, or the actor, is left with the task of spotting them (though in Goldoni's comedies they are printed in parentheses). There is however a wide range of frequency and infrequency of their use among different authors. Italian humanist dramatists sometimes employ them. *Commedia dell'arte* actors, who were their own dramatists, may have used them much more, especially when the more clownish masks were bidding for a confidential relationship with the audience. Improvised verbal texts have not survived, so strictly speaking we cannot tell. Both Molière and Marivaux make some use of 'revelatory' asides, often again in contexts where modern actors and playwrights would have other ways of communicating hidden feelings, or would assume that they could be taken for granted.[27] They are then frequent in Goldoni, who clearly considered them a necessary element of the 'Theatre' through which he expressed his 'World': some of his most sophisticated presentations of social tension, including hilarious scenes in the *Villeggiatura* trilogy of 1761, revolve round fierce frustrated asides from characters whom the pressures of politeness have just forced to say the opposite of what they mean. In those cases the asides themselves convey enjoyable comic tension, and also help with the plays' revelatory satire.

It has to be assumed that words which we now categorize as 'asides' are directed to the audience — they are certainly not addressed to anyone on stage. Does the character (or the performer) who speaks an aside thus recognize that an audience is indeed there to listen? Using more recent terminology, is the use of an aside an open breach of a 'fourth wall' between the auditorium and the fictional events

---

26   'Rem ipsum putasti' and 'nullus sum!'. The translations quoted are by Betty Radice (Terence 1976).
27   See for example Molière's *L'École des femmes*, 1.4, as well as some crucial asides in Marivaux's *Le Jeu de l'amour et du hasard*, in scenes such as II.9.

being enacted? Such a question raises itself even more in the case of a soliloquy, a substantial speech delivered when no other character is present (or known to be present). Do people ever really formulate their thoughts, their feelings, their intentions, aloud and audibly when they are alone? (Does the answer to that question vary, with different habits in different human societies?) Or does a soliloquy — in tragedy as well as in comedy, a speech by Hamlet as well as that of a clown — count as a direct address to the spectators? The issue recurs on a regular basis in Plautus and Terence. We can ignore solo prologues, which can be seen as the playwright or the actors addressing the audience before the dramatized fiction begins. Setting those aside, Roman comedies still remain packed with soliloquies. Slaves tell us what tricks they are planning; lovers express their current agitation; old men generalize about the world and about society — all at considerable length, in carefully composed speeches. Such monologues are then often seen as important passages in the play: those in Roman comedy were extensively mined by critics, from antiquity onwards, for aphorisms worth memorizing, applicable to life in general. To whom are they all talking, if not to the audience?[28]

In Greek and Roman tragedy, it could be claimed that long emotional speeches, and reflections on fate or morality, were addressed to the Chorus, who were always present on stage and who complicated one's perception of how and to whom the action was being delivered. But there is no Chorus in Roman comedy, nor in its Italian or French imitators. When Pseudolus is preparing himself for action with a long military metaphor, or when Euclio is lamenting the theft of his pot of gold, there is no one else on stage to listen. The issue then becomes more complicated when we note that in both Plautus and Terence there are scenes where a character believes he is speaking alone, but where his words are overheard by someone else. In Roman comedy it is possible to eavesdrop on a soliloquy. This gives such speeches a status which arguably has little to do with reflecting real human behaviour. Whether or not we decide to categorize them as being delivered to the audience, they appear as a thoroughly theatrical convention. Soliloquies or monologues did of course become central, almost indispensable, to European dramaturgy in all genres for a long time, and have been seen by actors as vehicles for their most treasured performing skills. They took a long time to disappear: there are soliloquies even in Chekhov.

The range covered by solo speeches in Roman comedy can be conveniently surveyed in a single play, Plautus's *Aulularia* [The Pot of Gold]. The script includes a number of extended passages in which single characters simply tell the audience what is on their mind: for example, Euclio (ll. 178–81, 371–89, 460–74); and a nameless Slave (ll. 587–607). In ll. 475–534 the elderly Megadorus, believing himself to be alone, indulges in a long reflection about getting married and the expense of keeping a wife. His speech is listened to with interest by Euclio, who comments in asides of his own from time to time, and eventually tells Megadorus that he has

---

28   The British actor Timothy West, in workshops, suggests that monologues can be classified as being addressed 'inward, outward, or upward'. The 'upward' address to a deity certainly has to be recognized. I have examined this whole question in relation specifically to the comedies of Pietro Aretino in Andrews 1988.

been 'digesting your very palatable lecture'.²⁹ Later, though, Euclio gets himself into trouble by soliloquizing: he is overheard twice by an unnamed Slave revealing where his precious pot of gold has been stored. The Slave can therefore make two attempts to steal it, and the second is successful.³⁰ Unlike Megadorus, Euclio has not merely been entertaining a passing listener but giving away crucial information — however implausible this is in realistic terms, he has been caught speaking his secrets aloud in the public street. Then once his gold has been stolen, Euclio has a famous despairing soliloquy (ll. 712–30) in which he appeals to the audience for help, and then sees that the spectators are simply laughing at him.³¹

Such unlikely situations are reflected repeatedly in Italo-French classical comedy. Eavesdropping on soliloquies is a theatergram often used in Scala's 1611 scenarios, and we find it as late as 1753 in III.3 of Goldoni's *Servitore di due padroni*. Soliloquies themselves were a device taken for granted (in tragedy, of course, as well as in comedy). In particular, Euclio's monologue of despair is famously imitated by Molière in *L'Avare* (v.7), where the miser Harpagon, having been robbed in a similar way, also appeals to the audience, and also sees that he is being laughed at ('Isn't he [the thief] hidden there among you? They're all looking at me and starting to laugh').³² Italian humanist critics and theorists were divided on the question as to whether characters should be allowed to talk aloud to themselves.³³ When French *classicisme* tried to impose higher standards of rationality, it became conventional in tragedy for leading characters to explain and express themselves to *confidants* and *confidantes*, characters whose sole function in the play was to listen and sympathize. In comedy too, from the very beginning, we see young lovers and old fathers confiding in servants, whose role in the plot might then be more substantial. Nevertheless, in neither genre were soliloquies ever abandoned, even into the rational eighteenth century. Marivaux and Goldoni may have kept them to a minimum, but the popularity of Beaumarchais's Figaro character depended largely on long solo speeches which were undoubtedly addressed to the audience, and which persuaded most spectators that they were listening not very indirectly to the views and personality of the author himself.

The 'fourth wall' issue of whether to include or exclude the audience from the dramatic fiction had none the less been perceived as early as the fourth century. In the 'Donatus' commentaries to the plays of Terence, it is observed that this author 'never makes an actor speak to the public or outside the play, a fault which

29 'Nimium lubenter edi sermonem tuom'; translation by E. F. Watling (Plautus 1965).
30 Euclio's speeches are ll. 608–15 and 667–76, with the Slave reacting immediately afterwards in each case.
31 'opsecro ego vos, mi auxilio | oro, optestor' (ll. 715–16); 'quid est? quid ridetis?' (l. 719).
32 'N'est-il point caché là parmi vous? Ils me regardent tous et se mettent à rire'. Molière's direct knowledge of Plautus can be taken for granted; but some tropes may also have entered the general theatre repertoire from earlier imitations of *Aulularia*, notably *Aridosia* (1536) by Lorenzino de' Medici, which was then copied closely in French by Pierre Larivey in *Les Esprits* (pub. 1579).
33 Ingegneri 1989: 13–14, shows a dislike of soliloquies on grounds of verisimilitude. In a footnote to this edition, Maria Luisa Doglio then points out that Giambattista Giraldi Cinthio had taken exactly the opposite view, in his *Lettera sulla tragedia* of 1583: he saw soliloquies as importing 'gravità reale' ('royal gravity') into a play, and thought that dramatists were wrong to avoid them.

is very common in Plautus'.³⁴ This 'fault' ('vitium') is not in fact avoided by Terence either, if we accept the premise that soliloquies are in a sense addressed 'to the public' ('ad populum'). Terence does write soliloquies, and even has other characters overhearing them. For example, in *Eunuchus* (ll. 549–57) Chaerea's private reflections are overheard and responded to by Antipho. It is probably true, though, that the rascally confidentiality of a Plautine slave was echoed less often by the later dramatist. Humanist commentators and playwrights did not often note, or react to, the rule proposed by Donatus, especially in relation to comedy.³⁵ It may have been instinctively recognized that the comic genre, and particularly this version of it which is ultimately playful and artificial, cannot function according to strict canons of 'fourth wall' realism. A good proportion of the fun offered by stage comedy comes from our confidential colluding relationship with at least some of the characters, and also with their performers (as I have noted in Chapter 17). The comic monologue of a clown is almost always a one-sided conversation with the spectators. In this context it is worth noting that among printed Italian comedies of the sixteenth century, a notably high quota of monologues or soliloquies is to be found in those composed in or around the 1540s for Venetian audiences, by dramatists who were also performers and whose shows and techniques foreshadow *commedia dell'arte*. Ruzante, Andrea Calmo, and Gigio Artemio Giancarli tend more often than other contemporaries to make single characters address spectators directly — explaining themselves, exploring jokes, and chatting in a leisurely fashion. They gave such speeches particularly, but not exclusively, to the star roles which they played themselves. Reading them now, some of these plays can seem to consist of a series of solo numbers linked (more or less) by passages explaining the plot.³⁶

Within our larger history, it then becomes relevant that the expression 'fourth wall' ('quatrième mur') was coined by the French philosopher and dramatist Denis Diderot, who in his *Discours sur la poésie dramatique* of 1758 recommended that actors should observe it. Diderot was a proponent of the new more literary theatre genres — *comédie larmoyante* and *drame sérieux* — which aimed at greater realism, which helped to displace classical comedy, and which certainly stood for erudite values as against those of the *arte*. He may have known that by recommending a fourth wall he was questioning, even trying to forbid, a routine convention of ancient Roman comic dramaturgy.

---

34 'Nihil ad populum facit actorem velut extra comoediam loqui, quod vitium Plauti frequentissimum' (Donatus [& Evanthius] 1902–08: 1, 20). The passage is attributed by Wessner to Evanthius rather than to Donatus.
35 In respect of tragedy, the issue was addressed by Sperone Speroni in 1543 and by Giambattista Giraldi Cinthio in 1544. See Andrews 1988: 156, n. 4.
36 This fact emerges from my own observation of comedies by these authors. I do not know of any published study which addresses the matter.

CHAPTER 19

Component Parts, II: Italian Improvisation

Modular Dramaturgy

After the input from Roman dramaturgy, other typical features then developed in classical European comedy, in terms of how play scripts were constructed. Especially significant were some performance techniques associated with Italian improvisation.

Actors of *commedia dell'arte* were renowned throughout Europe for performing their plays without learning a script. The text of 'Italian comedy' was seen as being improvised by the actors, delivered *a soggetto* in the Italian phrase. *Soggetto* was one of the words used for a summary scenario containing no spoken text, such as Flaminio Scala's fifty printed examples. 'Improvising', however, can be a misleading word: it did not mean inventing a brand-new text every time. *Arte* actors made their careers by assembling in their heads an extended repertoire of speeches and responses which could be recycled in different plays.[1] The story they were enacting was likely also to have been recycled: it was a rearrangement of elements derived from a stock of existing plots, redeploying a limited range of relationships and conflicts between a familiar set of character types. The encounters and emotions depicted in individual scenes were therefore liable to recur from one play to another. Many of the phrases and speeches which performers delivered had been composed in advance, and stored both in the memories and the personal notebooks (*zibaldoni*, or *libri generici*) of individual actors.[2] Performers were identified with single masks, which they played for most of their careers; so familiar forms of words, and frequently expressed emotions, were recast into whatever verbal idiom belonged to the individual role. This method applied equally to actors playing scurrilous clowns and to those playing rhetorically high-flown lovers. *Arte* stage improvisation had little to do with the imaginative exercises which 'improv' designates in twenty-first-century drama schools. It was an artisan skill in which an actor memorized pieces of suitable

---

[1] For more detailed discussions of this performing methodology, see the 'Introduction' in Andrews 2008: xix–xxxii, xxxvii–xlvi.
[2] There are few surviving examples of *zibaldoni*. The notebooks discovered in Spain by Maria del Valle Ojeda Calvo are lists of useful references, rather than composed texts for recitation (see Ojeda Calvo 2007). For items published by Isabella Andreini, see n. 9 below. The notes left by Domenico Biancolelli are described in Chapter 9.

verbal material, and then adapted each item to fit the play or scene being performed. Moreover, although we consider *commedia dell'arte* acting to be based primarily on oral tradition, much of the material in an actor's repertoire was likely to be borrowed from printed sources, either literary or dramatic.

The best *arte* actors read extensively, each of them soaking his or her brain and tongue in the verbal style and concepts which were suitable to the role they played. The following is an excerpt from an all-purpose seventeenth-century prologue which could be attached to any comedy: the serving-maid Ricciolina (hovering between her roles as actress and as on-stage servant) gives the audience an idea of how her company colleagues have prepared themselves behind the scenes:

> In the morning the Leading Lady summons me: 'Hey, Ricciolina, bring me *Fiammetta the Lover*, because I want to study'. Pantalone wants Andrea Calmo's *Letters*. The Captain wants *The Tirades of Capitano Spavento*. Zani wants *Bertoldo's Witty Sayings*, the *Fuggilozio* ['Fleeing Idleness'], and the *Ore di Ricreazione* ['Hours of Recreation']. Doctor Graziano wants the *Sentences* of L'Erborenze, and the *Novissima Poliantea*, Franceschina wants the *Celestina*, to learn how to play the bawd. The Lover wants the works of Plato.[3]

In a culture where learning words by rote played a large part in education, and also in social ritual, much of what these actors delivered on stage was formulaic and memorized. Rather than inventing their lines on the spot, they supplied text which already existed, whether they had composed it for themselves or filched it from elsewhere. They adapted and organized it to deliver the events required by the scenario, to express the required emotions, to realize the required comic effects. In his treatise of 1634, the actor Nicolò Barbieri also underplays spontaneous invention, and highlights second-hand recycling:

> Actors study and fill their memories with a whole load of things — mottoes, conceits, speeches of love, reproaches, despairings and delirium, so as to have them ready for the occasion. [...] There isn't a single good book that they haven't read, no fine conceit that they haven't taken, no formal description of anything that they haven't imitated, no fine epigram that they haven't gathered, because they're constantly reading and leafing through books. Many of them translate speeches from foreign languages and make them their own, many others invent, imitate, and amplify.[4]

---

3   'La matina la Signora mi chiama: "Olà Ricciolina, portami la innamorata Fiammetta, che voglio studiare". Pantalone mi domanda le *Lettere* del Calmo. Il Capitano le *Bravure* del Capitano Spavento. Il Zanni le *Astuzie* di Bertoldo, il *Fugilozio* e l'*Ore di ricreazione*. Graziano le *Sentenze* dell'Erborenze e la *Novissima Poliantea*, Franceschina vuole la *Celestina* per imparare di far la ruffiana. Lo Innamorato vuol l'opere di Platone' (Domenico Bruni, 'Prologhi, parte seconda', undated seventeenth-century manuscript in the Brera Library, Milan). Not all the works alluded to are easily traceable, but one was first printed in 1611.

4   'I comici studiano e si muniscono la memoria di gran farragine di cose, come sentenze, concetti, discorsi d'amore, rimproveri, disperazioni e delirii, per averli pronti all'occasioni. [...] Non vi è buon libro che da loro non sia letto, né bel concetto che non sia da essi tolto, né descrizzione di cosa che non sia imitata, né bella sentenza che non sia colta, perché molto leggono e sfiorano i libri. Molti di loro traducono i discorsi delle lingue straniere e se ne adornano, molti inventano, imitano, amplificano' (Barbieri 1971: 23, 34).

The Italian scholar Siro Ferrone, quoting Ricciolina's prologue, emphasizes in particular the complete absence, from this approach to acting and to dramaturgy, of even the most minimal concept of intellectual property.[5]

The fact that 'Italian comedy' plays were constructed out of such pre-prepared fragments gave their dramaturgy a character which we could describe as 'modular'. Putting together a drama was like choosing beads and threading them on a string, in an order which might be arbitrary and subject to alteration. Or, in another analogy, like dismantling a building and re-arranging the bricks to create a new one.

There were formats and structures which made it easier for improvisers to build scenes in a modular fashion. Some of them left detectable traces in written playscripts. The extent and persistence of their use, and so of their survival in writing, varied from author to author and from place to place. In comedies which had literary or erudite ambitions, traces of modularity tend to decline after the year 1700. When they persisted, they retained an association with Italy rather than France.

Repertoire Items: Set Speeches

Each actor possessed a stock of personal 'numbers' — extended speeches or tirades, to be delivered either to the audience as soliloquies or to other characters on stage. Those others might break in with reactions from time to time, thus providing more variety and more drama; but from the point of view of the person delivering the material, the piece was a single item of repertoire, to be memorized as a unit. It had to attract interest and attention, to thrill or to amuse, and to act as a trademark for the individual performer. Such set speeches, once composed and learned, could be imported into different plots with only minor adaptations.

The collaborative culture of a professional theatre troupe meant that each actor or actress was allowed some space in any given show for his or her own piece of virtuosity, though there was a company pecking order, in which performers recognized as stars by the public had priority. Some shows were devised, and no doubt advertised, to feature an individual's best-known displays. A well-known early example of this is recorded from when the Gelosi company was recruited by the Florentine court in 1589 to contribute to the wedding celebrations of Ferdinando I de' Medici, Grand Duke of Tuscany, to Princess Christine of Lorraine. As we hear from the contemporary chronicler Giuseppe Pavoni, the Gelosi at the time had two leading ladies, Vittoria Piissimi and Isabella Andreini; and each of them naturally wanted to be able to show off in front of the glittering audience:

> This meant that the two said ladies very nearly started a quarrel; because Vittoria wanted them to perform *The Gypsy*, and the other lady wanted them to put on her *Madness*, since Vittoria's favourite role is the *Gypsy*, and the mad role is the favourite of Isabella. However, they eventually agreed that the first play to be performed would be *The Gypsy*, and that the *Madness* would be done on a second occasion.[6]

---

5   Ferrone 1993: 197.
6   Pavoni 1589.

Performance as the 'gypsy woman' would involve a display of sultry emotions expressed in an exotic dialect: the role may have been inspired by Gigio Artemio Giancarli's eponymous comedy *La zingana* (pub. 1545). We hear that the Grand Duke took 'such delight in the novel material performed by Vittoria [...] that he thought of it as a miracle, rather than the invention of a woman'. Pavoni then goes on to give a full account of the plot of *La pazzia di Isabella*, and of Andreini's performance in it, making it clear that the 'mad scene' was this actress's speciality. The story of the play was constructed in order to provoke the scenes in which Isabella ran riot (with her clothes in disarray) and filled the stage with verbal nonsense in a multitude of dialects. Her already existing material was modified for the occasion: Pavoni tells us that there were special insertions in French 'which gave inexpressible pleasure to the Most Serene bride'. Isabella's raving heroines were already famous: she played these same scenes as often as possible, before and after the Florentine wedding, with different dramatic plots being assembled to provide reasons for her character to go mad. In Flaminio Scala's scenario collection of 1611, Day 38 is also a *Madness of Isabella*: a play which tells an entirely different story from what the Gelosi offered in 1589.[7] Its mad scenes for the heroine are summarized, even quoted verbatim (which is unusual in a scenario); but the events which drive her insane are not the ones dramatized in Florence, though in both plays she is betrayed or mistreated by a lover.[8] The two plots have the same title, and offer similar opportunities for Isabella Andreini's entertaining rants, but have little else in common. Isabella herself composed a series of prefabricated scenes for lovers (including one with a mad speech for a male character), which were published after her death by her widower Francesco, her partner on stage in the Gelosi troupe as well as her partner in life. Francesco may have contributed to that volume, and it illustrates the tendency for *arte* actors in general to compose chunks of material in advance, aiming to import them into different scenarios.[9]

Actors and actresses who played Lovers in Italian comedy had a stock of such speeches: as well as insanity, they could express despair, exultation, jealousy, reproach, adoration, and abject apology.[10] The repertoires of other masks would fit their respective stock characters, comic or serious as they might be; and they would reflect the situations which they most often faced, or the verbal and physical skills they most often wanted to deploy. Clownish masks like Arlecchino would patent long solo sequences of nonsense — such as the one recorded from a later time where he catches a fly and eats it with salt and pepper; or the one on which Dario Fo played variations in the twentieth century, involving an unmanageably swollen phallus. Pantalone would memorize and store lamentations based on avarice (leading again to Harpagon's soliloquy in *L'Avare*), or extended paternal reprimands to level against his sons and daughters. A braggart Capitano would

---

7   Translated and analysed in Andrews 2008: 225–38, where there is also a full translation of Pavoni's summary of *La pazzia di Isabella* performed in 1589.
8   See Andrews 2016.
9   Andreini 1616. For more on this material, see Andrews 2013.
10 For typical titles, taken from a manuscript anthology of such speeches, see Andrews 1993: 190–91.

develop overblown narratives of impossible military achievements, expecting them to be undermined in subversive asides by the actor playing the part of his servant. He would also have a stock of predictable excuses for his regular refusals to fight anyone. An actor playing the Dottore composed long speeches of verbally distorted nonsense, mocking academic jargon by twisting it phonetically into scatological or sexual innuendo. All three of these male masks who were not Lovers or Servants had commonplace speeches about the fact that they were in love with unattainable young women: they often excused their weakness by alluding mythologically to the overwhelming power of Cupid, and to the indignities and transformations adopted by the supreme god Jupiter in his serial seductions. (And although English drama is not discussed in this book, it is hard here not to draw analogies with virtuoso solo speeches given to Falstaff: his disquisition on honour and cowardice in *Henry IV Part 1*, v.1; and his appeal to a horn-bedecked Jupiter in *Merry Wives*, v.5.)

The performances in which this material was mostly deployed were for one night only, ephemeral, and not transcribed; but enough evidence has survived for us to be sure that this was how the system worked. I have mentioned in the previous chapter how frequently monologues occur in comedies by Venetian authors of the 1540s who were already foreshadowing *commedia dell'arte* techniques. A little later, material created for the stage by famous clowns (Pantaloni, Dottori, and Capitani, as well as variants on the Zani servant mask) was reissued in pamphlets to be sold to the public, underlining for us the fact that speeches and formulations used in drama could be redeveloped as separate marketable compositions.[11] Soliloquies which appear in scripted *commedia erudita* sometimes express generic opinions and emotions which could easily be recycled, and which sometimes do indeed reappear in different plays. Scenarios for improvisation, paradoxically, are less informative and less explicit: their task was to organize their plot outlines to leave implicit 'insertion points' (in the apt expression coined by Robert Henke) where actors could place their repertoire numbers. They then did not explain exactly what those numbers contained.[12] By contrast, the seventeenth-century texts of what is now called *commedia ridicolosa* (see Chapter 5) are particularly informative about the existence and content of repertoire set speeches: they contain what amount to repertoire numbers transcribed on the page.

Molière's apprenticeship as a dramatist owed considerable debts to the content and methodology of Italian improvisation. In his early farce *La Jalousie du Barbouillé*, he includes the mask of Le Docteur, and in Scene 2 gives him two long tirades which demonstrate both the foolishness of the character and the skill required to portray him. They are virtuoso speeches of self-obsession, tricky to memorize: they have no relevance to the plot, and so could be used in any play whatsoever. They infuriate the other characters on stage, who keep trying to interrupt and curtail them, and

---

11 An evocative English-language account of these compositions can be found in Henke 2002: Chapters 7–10.
12 Some set-piece routines might be alluded to by labels, using the word *lazzo*, plural *lazzi*. The word was then adopted ungrammatically into French, where *lazzi* has become a singular noun. *Lazzi*, or *azzi*, are named in some Italian scenario collections, but the term was never used by Flaminio Scala. For a traditional scholarly approach to this subject, see Gordon 1983.

such explosive frustration is of course part of the fun for the audience. From the same dramatist later on, we have the despairing miser's soliloquy of Harpagon already alluded to. Of all Molière's comedies, *L'Avare* is the one which makes most use of borrowed scenes and gags that have an Italianate background, some of them traceable back to *commedia ridicolosa* plays.[13] Then in texts of the Parisian Théâtre-Italien we can observe a number of transferable set speeches, and intuit the presence of others. From Marivaux on, however, such items become rare in scripts which are authored and have literary pretensions: the eighteenth-century process by which dramatists took back control from actors discouraged the use of material which was transferable. If playwrights knew that some scenes were likely to be expanded with riffs inserted by inventive actors, they did not acknowledge that possibility in the final printed text. In Goldoni's full script of *Il servitore di due padroni*, it is possible to guess where the Dottore could have held up the action with his repertoire verbosity (particularly in II.2); but Goldoni has cut the relevant speeches from his printed version. Beaumarchais's two Figaro plays give great importance to the eponymous character's lengthy monologues, but not a single sentence in them can be traced to an actor's stock material. The voice of Beaumarchais himself was so strong as to persuade the first audiences that they were listening to versions of the playwright's own life and preoccupations: the actor's role was just to learn them and deliver them.

Nevertheless, although movable set speeches disappeared (along with the overall modular approach to dramaturgy) from the scripts of erudite comic dramatists in the eighteenth century, they were still a central feature of the artisan theatre which continued to flourish, on a different cultural level, in Italy and France. Carlo Gozzi, Goldoni's insistently conservative rival, tells us in his *Memorie inutili* that he himself was recruited to write speeches for *commedia dell'arte* actors to memorize:

> I can't give a number to the 'prologues', I've written, or the 'farewells' in verse [...] nor say how many thousands of pages I've filled with soliloquies, despairs, threats, reproaches, prayers, fatherly corrections, and other speeches which come in useful in scenes of improvised comedy, and which the actors call *generici*, necessary for inexperienced actors and actresses to provoke applause.[14]

The theatre public must have been aware that such precomposed material was still being used and transferred from play to play, whether or not they were getting tired of the practice, as Goldoni claimed they were in *Il teatro comico*. There was thus still a recognition, even in the sophisticated eighteenth century, that the culture of commercial theatre still relied considerably on the redeployment of standard verbal formulations of predictable emotions.

The phenomenon was even more firmly entrenched in opera. Over a long

---

13 See Andrews 2006. Many of the individual derivations in *L'Avare* have also been noted by Bourqui 1999.
14 'Non so dire qual numero di 'prologhi', qual numero di 'addio' in versi [...] né quante migliaia di fogli abbia empiuti di soliloqui, di disperazioni, di minacce, di rimproveri, di preghiere, di correzioni paterne e d'altri discorsi ch'entrano a proposito nelle scene delle commedie improvvisate e che i comici chiamano "generici", necessari agli attori e alle attrici non pratici di quell'arte per riscuotere degli applausi' (*Memorie inutil*, composed in 1777 and published in 1797; Gozzi 1984: 32–33).

period, famous singers took possession of successful arias, and forced composers (if indeed force was necessary) to move them from one opera to another, so that the singers themselves could display their best skills. They knew they would reap the rapturous applause of devotees who wanted to hear the same number again. When Handel and Rossini allowed their *prime donne* to do this, or did it for them, they were operating their own version of modular dramaturgy. Eventually composers were writing 'concert arias', separate numbers which expressed familiar emotions and situations likely to arise in a range of different stories: the examples which are now best known are mostly by Mozart. Many of the texts were lifted from existing operas, with libretti by known authors such as Metastasio or Goldoni; in other cases the authorship of the text is now lost. Sometimes the intention was to insert a new aria in a revival of an old opera; in other cases, a dramatic or emotional moment which was recognizable, and perhaps already well-known, was reset separately for the concert hall or salon.[15] Such a habit reflected a process originally established in non-musical drama by sixteenth-century *commedia dell'arte* stars such as Isabella Andreini. Some repertoire speeches in comedy can be seen as independently constructed arias — in many cases effectively 'concert arias' — but without the music.

Repertoire Items: Elastic Dialogues

The principle of modular construction went beyond the redeployment of single speeches. The repertoire of improvising performers also contained memorized sequences involving two-way dialogues and even sometimes larger ensembles. Classical comic plots regularly produced confrontations which — since they involved stereotyped characters expressing standard attitudes — could be transferred between different plots as easily as soliloquies and set tirades. Quarrels and disagreements between Elders and Servants were a sure source of entertainment, and could depend mostly on the fixed personalities of the masks, with little reference to the story being dramatized. Fathers (Pantalone or the Dottore) regularly confronted their sons or daughters about whom those Lovers were going to marry; in some cases it would then turn out that father and son were pursuing the same woman (see Chapter 23). Pairs of Lovers would fall into stereotyped exchanges involving misunderstanding, jealousy, or a heroine's prudent reluctance to be too easily seduced. (They might also vie with each other in rhetorical or learned expressions of devotion, like Lorenzo and Jessica, in *The Merchant of Venice*, v.1.) When such scenes were moved into a new play or scenario, they might never involve repeating exactly the same words every time; but they would still revolve round stock emotions or confrontations expressed in language and imagery which was well-drilled and recognizable. The accumulated repertoire of one actor would dovetail comfortably with that of his or her colleague, so that for many scenes the repertoire was shared or collective. A Lover had rehearsed many times what he or she had to

---

15   With regard to one of Mozart's concert arias, taken from a Metastasio opera, Einstein 1969: 383, suggests that 'everyone knew the text, since it had been composed a hundred times'. Chapter 19 of Einstein's study contains a thorough account of Mozart's concert arias.

say in order to resist a father, and the Elder mask in turn had his ready-made ways of expressing authoritarian outrage. The servant of a braggart Capitano had a stock of undermining asides to the audience, in response to his master's ludicrous fantasies which had been prepared equally carefully in advance. Experience, together with a limited range of stage relationships, made collaboration easy.

If the words were at least partly predictable, so in some cases was the way in which the scene was structured. There is evidence that, as an aid both to memory and to smooth collaboration, a format was often used which was both repetitive and 'elastic'.[16] One simple dramatic cliché offers useful examples of this — showing also in passing how a completely banal event can be made to raise laughs by sheer reiteration, and by injecting an element of suspense. It concerns the apparently uninteresting question of whether a servant character is going to appear, or to open a door, when asked to do so by his or her employer. In an early dialogue, printed in the sixteenth century as a free-standing pamphlet, a Venetian Magnifico (not in this case named Pantalone, though that is the mask we are dealing with) calls repeatedly for Zani from Bergamo to come out and talk to him; and Zani delays his entrance with a series of pointless misunderstandings, heard from off stage:

> MAGNIFICO   [...] Zani!
> ZANI   Yes sir?
> MAGNIFICO   Come out a moment.
> ZANI   What can I do for you, boss?
> MAGNIFICO   Come out here a moment, my dear chap.
> ZANI   Me?
> MAGNIFICO   Thee.
> ZANI   You want *me* to come to *thee*?
> MAGNIFICO   Aye, *thee*, you donkey, get a move on.
> ZANI   At your service, as you *see*. Shall I wear my hat?
> MAGNIFICO   To hell with your hat, put your cap on.
> ZANI   Yes sir*ee*. Er... pardon *me*....
> MAGNIFICO   Now what?
> ZANI   You want *me* to come out?
> MAGNIFICO   Yes, you yourself.
> ZANI   Me myself in person?
> MAGNIFICO   *Yes*, for God's sake, come out!
> ZANI   I'm coming, I've arrived, I'm here, what can I do for Your Honour?[17]

---

16   The material which now follows has been explored in a succession of my previous writings. The notion of 'elastic' dialogue sequences in Italian comedy was proposed in Andrews 1991b: 21–54; and recast more briefly in Chapter 5 of Andrews 1993: 175–85. Both these publications contain longer textual examples than have been included here. For a treatment in French of the phenomenon in a wider context, see Andrews 1998.

17   'MAGNIFICO: [...] Giani! GIANI: Plasí. M: Viene un poco fora. G: Che plasi a Vossignoria? M: Vien un poco fora, caro Giani.. G: Mi? M: Ti. G: Che venga fora mi? M: Ti, sí, cavallo, spàzate! G: Volontiera, messer sí. A patron, volí che porta il capello? M: Che voi fare del capell? Porta la berretta. G: Messer sí. E' vegní a mi. M: Che vustu? G: Volí che vegni mi proprio? M: Sí, ti proprio. G: Mi proprio in persona? M: Sí, in nome di Dio! Vien fora! G: E' vengo, e' son chiluoga: che plasi a la Signoria Vostra?' (text transcribed, with modernized spelling and punctuation, from the diplomatic transcription in Pandolfi 1957–61: I, 174–77.

The basic structure here is one of delay, and the delay is caused by the prolonged reluctance of the lazy servant Zani to do anything at all. The dialogue contains persistent playful rhymes ('Mi... ti... sí...') which my translation attempts to reflect. We all know that eventually Zani is going to come onto the stage. Meanwhile, the actors can make the scene as long or as short as they choose — and it is thus 'elastic'. The technique for prolonging it is repetition, going over the same ground again and again until either actors or audience have had enough. This is a format which improvising actors can pursue without memorizing any verbal text: each of them just has to remember what his/her own character wants to say or do, what game they are playing, and what the conclusion or punchline will be. The conclusion is usually an obvious one — in this case, Zani deciding to enter — and it can function as a safety net if one of them runs out of material.

This is a structure which is easy to perceive when it is transferred from improvisation to a written text. It is enough to identify a repetitive sequence, a notional A-B, A-B, A-B etc., in which the effective content of each A and each B is always the same, although the wording may change every time. The sequence may or may not be concluded by an identifiable punch line, or by an intrusive event such as the entry of a new character which forces the actors to move on. The number of recurrences of A-B is inevitably fixed in a written text; but actors in performance could easily prolong or curtail the exchange, going round the sequence more times or fewer, before the cue or action which concludes it. We could say that the technique of 'modularity', which improvising companies applied to their larger-scale dramaturgy, is used here too on a smaller scale in single scenes or exchanges. In surviving scripted comedy, one of the earliest sets of such elastic sequences occurs in a scene between the braggart Capitan Tinca and his mocking servant Branca, in III.2 of Pietro Aretino's *Talanta* (1542).[18] This play was mounted in Venice, in a context where it is likely that lower-class actors were recruited to fill the more clownish roles, alongside gentlemen amateurs playing parts which involved less undignified buffoonery. Aretino observed the working patterns of the professionals, and reflected them in his script.[19]

Returning to the Magnifico-Zani dialogue, the same routine about summoning a servant, with prolonged delays, recurs in a *commedia ridicolosa* play published in 1617, Giovanni Briccio's *Pantalone imbertonao* [Pantalone Besotted].[20] In 1.4, the young master Tiburzio wants Zanni to come down and let him into the house. But Zanni is having a meal, and puts off moving for 'just one more mouthful... just one more glass of wine...', in a sequence which is potentially elastic. Tiburzio gets furious, and picks up a stick. But then Zanni does not want to open the door because he is afraid of being beaten, and there is a new delaying sequence with Zanni saying 'Promise you won't hit me...?' and Tiburzio trying to convince him that indeed he will not. When Zanni finally opens the door, he does of course get

---

18   See Andrews 1991b: 49–51, where substantial parts of the scene are translated.
19   For the social context of plays mounted in Venice by Compagnie della Calza ('Companies of the Hose'), see Jordan 2014.
20   Briccio 1617. For more details of this play, see Chapter 23, n. 4.

beaten, as the audience has anticipated all along. All of this is fully scripted, but the repetitive elastic structure shows how *commedia ridicolosa* authors were mimicking practices used in improvisation, as Aretino had done in 1542. There are in fact a large number of such examples in the plays of Briccio and Verucci. We then find the same format in Molière's *L'École des femmes* (1662) where, in 1.2, the servants Alain and Georgette are asked to open the door to their master Arnolphe. To start with neither of them can be bothered, and their elastic exchanges are of the 'You go — No, *you* go' variety, with fatuous excuses. Then Arnolphe threatens to starve them as a punishment, so they start falling over each other to open the door, and their contest to get there first causes more delays.

Molière makes quite frequent use of the elastic structure: it is one of the most concrete proofs of how well he knew, and how much he borrowed from, the content and methods of Italian improvised theatre.[21] I have noted that there are sequences in *L'Avare* in particular which use such improvisation structures. Some of the individual instances closely reflect identifiable scenes in Italian *commedia ridicolosa* scripts — most of all in Verucci's *I diversi linguaggi* (1609). (This play also uses the plot device of a Lover taking a job as a servant in the house of his beloved's father — Valère in *L'Avare*, Silvio in *I diversi linguaggi*). However, Molière eventually learned that the format of elastic repetition might be a vehicle for something more than farcical entertainment: on at least two occasions he deployed it to support sophisticated comic perceptions. In 1.4 of *Le Tartuffe*, the master of the house Orgon is returning from a journey. Dorine, the maidservant, tries four times to interest him in the fact that his wife has not been very well. Four times Orgon interrupts with the question 'And Tartuffe?', showing that he is more concerned about his prestigious guest than about his wife. Four times he hears that, by contrast, Tartuffe has been offensively healthy; four times Orgon fails to pick up the sarcasm, and responds with the famous exclamation 'Poor fellow!' ('Le pauvre homme!'). This is one of Molière's most renowned passages of comically revealing psychology, but its dramaturgical structure is in no way realistic — we are unlikely in life to hear people repeating themselves so precisely and so often. The dialogue is a *commedia dell'arte* structure, 'elastic' in that the exchange could just as easily be used three times, or five, rather than four. Then in *Le Misanthrope*, 1.2, we see Alceste trying hard not to give his real unfavourable opinion of a new sonnet penned by his acquaintance Oronte. Three times (but it could be four or five times, or only twice) Oronte asks him 'Do you mean to say…?', attributing to him increasingly brutal points of view, and three times Alceste tries to fend the situation off with 'I'm not saying that' ('Je ne dis pas cela'). Having insisted earlier that social pretence is to be condemned, and that one should always express oneself with absolute frankness, Alceste finds that in practice he is as inhibited as everyone else about being confrontational. Both here and in the scene from *Tartuffe*, a playwright of genius has taken over an artisan device from professional actors, seen its potential, and put it to penetrating use: the

---

21   I have explored this fact in Andrews 1989, where there is a sample list of Molière scenes which contain further examples; and in Andrews 2005, which includes a demonstration of the frequency of the 'elastic' technique in *Le Médecin malgré lui*, 1.

theatrical game of repetition has been used to express a plausible obsession, and plausible evasiveness, in a carefully delineated character.

When we move to Marivaux, we find that the dramatist's attachment to the Théâtre-Italien company did not involve any use of modular dramaturgy, and this particular kind of game-playing is not to be found in his plays. Goldoni does use it, however, in his earlier comedies, most of all in the ones which still make use of *commedia dell'arte* masks. For example, in 1.2 of *La bancarotta* [Bankruptcy'] (1741), the two servants Arlecchino and Brighella have an extended discussion about which different jobs Arlecchino might choose to do if he were not a servant.[22] In *commedia ridicolosa* plays of the previous century, it had been equally clear how working through a list, of any kind, was a frequent excuse for an elastic sequence. Goldoni also wrote passages in *I due gemelli veneziani* [The Two Venetian Twins] (1747–48) which bear signs of such formats. In II.2 there is a prolonged scene in which Arlecchino recognizes Tonino as his master, but Tonino refuses to acknowledge him: the dialogue swings back and forth over the same ground in an elastic fashion, until a temporary conclusion seems — but in the end actually fails — to resolve the dilemma. (Arlecchino's real master is the other twin in the play, Zanetto, and his confusions are similar to those experienced by the two Dromios in *The Comedy of Errors*.) Such scenes disappeared from Goldoni's comedies, along with single repertoire speeches, as his use of the old professional material gave way to comedy of character.

Beaumarchais, following Marivaux, did not use modularity or repetition in his Figaro comedies. However, the chronicle tells us that the actor Dugazon, who created the minor role of the constantly sneezing servant La Jeunesse in *Le Barbier de Séville*, had a tendency to overplay by sneezing more often than the script demanded, and had to be called to order by his dramatist.[23] Inserting sneezes *ad libitum*, to get more laughs, was a procedure which we could still call elastic and modular. Once again we can intuit the persistence, in the eighteenth-century comic theatre profession, of techniques which more culturally ambitious playwrights wished to jettison in their pursuit of new standards of stage realism. I shall be returning to these issues in my final chapter.

Echoing and Mirroring

In the analysis which follows, the word 'echoing' does not refer to the separate phenomenon of 'Echo scenes', in which an off-stage Echo — or sometimes a mocking character from the play — repeats the closing syllables of words delivered on stage in soliloquy, and gives them another meaning. This device (traceable back at least to the 1580s) was used for a while in Italian comedy, in pastoral, and eventually in opera: it could provide either a sentimental gloss on the original statement, or a mocking distortion. Here, on the other hand, we are using the terms 'echoing' and 'mirroring' to describe moments when there is a straight repetition

---

22   *La bancarotta*, Goldoni's third comedy, was mounted in a partly scripted version in 1741 as *Il mercante fallito*, then printed with its revised title in 1757.
23   Descotes 1974: 39–40.

of spoken lines or actions between characters on stage; or when an identical or very similar series of events recurs in more than one scene. The examples now explored should make this clear.

In Goldoni's *Servitore di due padroni* (the surviving full script published in 1753) the heroine Beatrice has been presenting herself to most of the characters on stage as a man named Federigo Rasponi. Only the inkeeper Brighella, and the audience, know her real identity. She has been travelling in disguise to search for her fugitive lover Florindo, thus pursuing a narrative trope launched in 1532 by the anonymous Sienese *Gl'ingannati*. The two masters whom the comic mask Truffaldino is trying to serve at once are the disguised Beatrice and Florindo himself: unaware of each other's presence, they are staying in the same inn. In III.3, Beatrice is persuaded that Florindo is dead, and she breaks into an impassioned lament which makes it clear to any listener who she really is. She does in fact have two listeners on stage: Pantalone and Truffaldino, who are performing the well-established trope of eavesdropping on a soliloquy. They look at each other open-mouthed, and deliver the following piece of dialogue:

> PANTALONE   Truffaldino!
> TRUFFALDINO   Mister Pantalone!
> PANTALONE   A woman!
> TRUFFALDINO   A female!
> PANTALONE   What a turn-up!
> TRUFFALDINO   What a surprise!
> PANTALONE   I'm confused.
> TRUFFALDINO   I'm gobsmacked.[24]

Like the elastic dialogue sequences examined above, this exchange could go on forever; but it has the extra characteristic that each character is saying the same thing. Truffaldino simply has to echo in his Bergamo dialect what Pantalone has just said in Venetian, with the different vernaculars helping to ensure that they do not use the same words. For the actors, and particularly for Truffaldino, this is an even easier routine to sustain than one where they are opposing or contrasting one another. Repeating what you have just heard is not a demanding exercise for an improviser.

As it happens, a structure of mirroring or echoing is operating also on a larger scale in this scene of Goldoni's comedy. Beatrice's outburst of grief in Scene 3 has been caused by Truffaldino telling a pack of lies. He has confused the two sets of luggage for which he is responsible, and a locket emerges containing a picture of Florindo which Beatrice naturally recognizes. The only story Truffaldino can fabricate is that this portrait represents a former master of his who is now dead. In the immediately preceding scene, he was forced into an identical routine with Florindo himself. That same portrait, which Florindo gave some time ago to Beatrice, surfaced in Scene 2 also from a wrong set of luggage. Truffaldino's panicky explanation was that he inherited this piece of property from his previous

---

24 'PANTALONE: Truffaldino! TRUFFALDINO: Sior Pantalon! P: Donna! T: Femmena! P: Oh che caso! T: Oh che meraveia! P: Mi resto confuso. T: Mi son incantà'.

master, who died just a week ago. Florindo had heard that Beatrice had run away in male disguise, so he concluded (correctly) that the 'man' in possession of his portrait must in fact be her.

We thus have two successive scenes with identical structures, as follows:

A. Truffaldino, in the presence of one of his two masters, unpacks a set of luggage belonging to the other employer.
B. Truffaldino reveals the portrait of Florindo, which the employer present on stage recognizes.
C. Truffaldino tries to explain the presence of the portrait, in both cases inventing a story in which his previous master, the owner of the picture, has died.
D. The employer on stage believes that his (or her) lover is dead, and despairs.

Because this is a full printed script, and because Goldoni's whole dramaturgical trend was to move away from stylized improvisation structures, the playwright has made the scenes slightly different: he has not published despairing tirades for each Lover in succession. In Scene 2 Florindo's grief is expressed in a brief aside, as he runs from the room, whereas in Scene 3 Beatrice is given a full virtuoso repertoire speech (an 'aria without music', as I suggested above). However, these scenes which have come down to us in printed form bear unmistakable traces of an improvised scenario in which the verbal echoes would have been more insistent: probably Florindo, as well as Beatrice, would have filled phase D with a lament.

Repetition, echoing, mirroring: these were regular techniques in earlier Italian improvised theatre. As narrative and dramatic devices, they were perhaps culturally fashionable for a certain period of time (modern critics often categorize the trend as 'baroque'), but in any case they can be entertainingly comic.[25] They are also easy to mount in unscripted theatre, where what has just happened once on stage is already there to be imitated for a second time, perhaps with ad hoc variations, by improvising actors. The frequent use of such repetitions, large-scale and small, could be catalogued at some length from Flaminio Scala's published scenarios of 1611, as some examples now show.

Sometimes we find the simple comic trope of one set of characters imitating exactly the behaviour of another, as in this example from II.5 of Scala's Day 37, *La caccia* [The Hunt]: '[Orazio] turns round, sees [Isabella], and runs to kiss her hands. Isabella *gives him a slap, and goes indoors*. Flavio sees Flaminia, and does the same as Orazio did. Flaminia *gives him a slap, and goes indoors*'.[26] The fact that the scenario uses exactly the same words (which I have italicized) to describe each action reinforces the repetition on stage. There are some other scenes where Servant masks

---

25 Such patterns have however been judged *un*fashionable by those performing to twentieth-century audiences. In the classic production of *Il servitore* by Giorgio Strehler for the Piccolo Teatro di Milano (broadcast and recorded by RAI2 television in 1993), the repetitions in III.2 and 3, were toned down, and the two scenes were made to end with firmly different physical gags.
26 Andrews 2008: 218; Scala 1976: II, 379: 'Egli si volge e, vedendola, corre per baciarle le mani. Isabella *li dà uno schiaffo et entra*. Flavio vede Flaminia, fa l'istesso che ha fatto Orazio. Flaminia *li dà uno schiaffo et entra*' (my emphasis). The Marotti edition, like Scala's original printing, does not give numbers to the scenes.

mimic the behaviour of the Lovers, either because they feel the same emotions or because they want to mock their employers. A more elaborate example comes from the Day 16 scenario entitled *Lo specchio* [The Mirror]. A woman named Laura claims to be able to endow a mirror with magical powers: it will present images of things which have happened in the past, and so help to discover who has stolen some missing valuables. The 'magic' is pure deception: what everyone sees 'in the mirror' is really two servants playing games. Act III.14–15 have identical sequences, once again summarized in identical words: III.14, 'Pedrolino, in hiding, looks in the mirror. Flaminia says: "See, there he is!". Everyone looks in the mirror. Pedrolino goes off, laughing'; III.15, 'Arlecchino, in hiding, looks in the mirror. Fabrizio says: "See, there he is!". Everyone looks in the mirror. Arlecchino exits, laughing'.[27] The fact that a mirror is used here in scenes which 'mirror' each other can give rise to heavily complex interpretations from modern critics. Moreover, in 1622 Flaminio Scala's friend and collaborator Giovan Battista Andreini actually wrote a tortuous comedy called *Amor nello specchio* [Love in the Mirror], which uses mirrors as part of a story involving narcissism and shifting identities — a structure on whose complexity modern editors of the play have theorized at length with some justification.[28] That play also contains significant examples of scenes mirroring or echoing each other, both verbally and in terms of repeated patterns of action. In the Scala scenario quoted above, however, there are no identity crises, just a simple, deliberate repetition of the same deceitful trick played by two characters in succession, provoking the same reaction each time from those who are watching.

The most comically creative example of echoing in Scala's scenarios comes in the very competent farce *Il cavadente* [The Tooth-puller] in Day 12. In order to take revenge on Pantalone for an act of violence, Pedrolino organizes other characters in the play to persuade the old man that his breath smells and that he needs to have a tooth extracted. In I.13–18, the message is conveyed by Pedrolino himself, Francheschina, Flavio, the Dottore, Flaminia, and Orazio; and then Arlecchino turns up on cue in Scene 19, disguised as a tooth-puller. The scenario gives no detailed suggestions about how each of the characters in turn should express the bad news. But each actor will have heard the words and tone of voice of his and her predecessors; and each will have the choice of echoing what someone else has done, of playing variations on the way the lie was delivered, or of supplying a deliberate contrast. There is space for genuine improvisation here, in the modern sense of ad hoc invention as well as the *commedia dell'arte* sense of recycling existing material; but the echoing (or blatantly non-echoing) relationship between each encounter is an intrinsic part of the entertaining spectacle.[29]

---

27   Andrews 2008: 94; Scala 1976: I, 175: 'Pedrolino di nascoso guarda nello specchio. Flaminia dice: "Vedetelo, vedetelo!". Tutti guardano nello specchio. Pedrolino, ridendo, si parte. [...] Arlecchino di nascoso guarda nello specchio. Fabrizio dice: "Vedetelo, vedetelo!". Tutti guardano nello specchio. Arlecchino, ridendo, via.'
28   Andreini 1997.
29   Andrews 2008: 64–65; Scala 1976: I, 132–33. My reflections on how this succession of scenes can be played are inspired by what was done by Bristol University students in a videotaped performance of the whole scenario (using the title *The Dentist*) which was available for hire to teachers during the 1980s.

In full classical comedy scripts composed and published by Italian and French dramatists, the devices of echoing and repetition are rare; but if we do encounter an example — as we did in Goldoni's *Servitore di due padroni* — it will have its origin, like other phenomena described in this chapter, in the techniques and disciplines of Italian improvisation.

CHAPTER 20

Observance of *classiciste* Rules

Classicisme avant la lettre

Chapter 7 narrates how rules for imitating the drama of classical Greece and Rome were formally articulated by the French in the seventeenth century, though much of what the French pundits proposed had been first suggested by Italian commentators on Aristotle and Horace. Full-scale treatises and debates about literary and dramatic theory do not appear in Italy until after 1536, when the Greek text of Aristotle's *Poetics* was printed with a translation into Latin, making it accessible to a larger number of humanists. As the decades of the sixteenth century wore on, it became increasingly possible to judge dramatists for their adherence or non-adherence to supposed rules of dramaturgy, including what became codified as the 'three unities'. Later, in France, those guidelines became associated with an institutional authority which had royal backing, the Académie Française — a fact which made them more unitary, more coherent, and more widely obeyed.

The context in which the authors of the earliest *commedie erudite* wrote their plays is less clear to us now, because no formulations of theory had yet been published. There are a few glimpses, however, of discussions which must have been taking place informally, in conversation and in correspondence, between the small number of humanist-educated writers involved. Many of them were probably based on the 'Donatus' commentaries attached to the collected comedies of Terence, but there would have been other sources too.[1]

The earliest and most obvious feature which was adopted from the Renaissance understanding of classical drama was the five-act structure, which I have addressed in Chapter 18. Other precepts which were being considered show through in some early *commedia erudita* texts. In Machiavelli's *Mandragola* (IV.10), Fra Timoteo remarks that the characters are going to stay awake all night: 'And you spectators, don't take us to task, because no one is going to sleep tonight, so there's no break in time between the Acts'. He implies that the spectators might dislike a breach in continuity, or in what was later called the unity of time.[2] Pietro Aretino, often now described as being 'anti-classical' in his approach to drama, nevertheless knew

---

[1] See also 'Introduction' in Beecher 2008–09: 7. Hilger 2007 explores the 'theory' extractable from Donatus.
[2] 'E voi, spettatori, non ci appuntate, perché in questa notte non ci dormirà persona, sí che gli Atti non sono interrotti dal tempo.'

the rules which were being suggested by his colleagues, and sometimes treated them with irony. In the Prologue to *La cortigiana* [The Courtiers' Play] (the printed version of 1534), he waves aside a prohibition against characters appearing on stage more than five times during the play. We can also deduce Aretino's awareness that direct address to the audience was disapproved of (by 'Donatus', see Chapter 18). On this point he became more willing to conform: in the 1534 printing of *La cortigiana* he systematically corrected the tendency of his earlier manuscript version to allow characters to break the 'fourth wall'.[3] (Machiavelli's Fra Timoteo had of course violated it in the lines just quoted above.) It was in the prologue to *La cortigiana* that Aretino was perhaps the first practitioner to query whether rules formulated for the theatres and the societies of ancient Greece and Rome were entirely suited, word for word, to sixteenth-century Europe: 'Apart from that, don't be surprised if the comic style is not followed according to the required rules, because in Rome we live in a different way from how they lived in Athens'.[4] In fact throughout the three centuries covered in this study, there were sceptics who argued for a more flexible response to the ancient treatises, pointing out that practices which Aristotle and Horace had condemned were nevertheless enjoyed by contemporary audiences. Such dissenting views were expressed from time to time in all the theatrically active countries of Europe; and in Spain Lope de Vega distanced himself explicitly from the alleged 'rules'.

A significant feature of early Italian comedies is the tendency for prologues to justify, defensively or not, the principle of imitating, and borrowing from, the works of Plautus and Terence.[5] The most cogent justification was that Plautus and Terence themselves, in a process which was called *contaminatio* in Latin, had been imitating and adapting Greek plays by Menander and others, the genre known as Athenian New Comedy. A second phase of *contaminatio* was now proclaimed in Renaissance Italy as creating yet another 'new comedy'. The very first two words of Ariosto's verse prologue to the very first printed *commedia erudita*, the 1508 prose version of *La cassaria*, are in fact 'Nova comedia'. In a prologue to Bibbiena's *Calandra*, first staged for the court of Urbino in 1513, the question of plagiarism is turned into a joke. In paraphrase: 'People accuse our author of stealing from Plautus, but he says that if you go and look at Plautus's stuff, you'll find it's all still there, so nothing has been stolen'.[6]

As the rules ascribed to classical comedy became better known, playwrights had to make more conscious decisions about how seriously to take them, and about how to interpret them in detail. When the arguments became serious and polemical in seventeenth-century France, more attention was paid to tragedy and to epic poetry.

3   See Andrews 1988.
4   'Oltra di questo non vi maravigliate se lo stil comico non s'osserva con l'ordine che si richiede, perché si vive d'un'altra maniera a Roma che non si vivea in Atene.' *La cortigiana* is set in Rome in the 1520s, so it is the contemporary city, rather than ancient Rome, which is being referred to.
5   As well as *La cassaria*, treated here, see for instance the prologues to Bibbiena's *Calandra* (1513), Machiavelli's *Clizia* (1525), Ruzante's *La vaccaria* (1533), and Lorenzino de' Medici's *Aridosia* (1536). Many more could be cited.
6   'E che ciò sia vero, dice che si cerchi quanto ha Plauto e troverassi che niente gli manca di quello che aver suole. E, se cosí è, a Plauto non è suto rubbato nulla del suo.'

Comedy was the poor relation in terms of moral and artistic prestige: it escaped some of the more wearisome attempts to legislate in detail, but was not entirely exempt. The first comic dramatist to express a coherent train of thought, in relation to the *règles*, was Pierre Corneille (who also wrote tragedies): in 1660 he published a series of retrospective assessments of his own reprinted comedies, and expanded more generally on the subject in a set of treatises, including a *Discours des trois unités*. Overall in these works he talks much more about tragedy, but does occasionally refer to his own comedies. His original preface to *La Veuve, ou le Traitre trahi* [The Widow, or the Betrayer Betrayed], published in 1634, had already hinted at slightly maverick interpretations of the unities in particular.

We can review here, one by one, how each of the three unities was observed during the history of classical comedy. Codified exhaustively by French *classicistes*, these principles had been largely invented by Lodovico Castelvetro, in his commentary to Aristotle's *Poetics* published in 1570.

Unity of Time

According to Chapter 5 of Aristotle's *Poetics*, the action of a tragedy attempts as far as possible to confine its action to 'a single revolution of the sun'. This statement is offered as a contrast to the unlimited amount of time which can be covered in an epic poem. Renaissance readers of the treatise took it as a prescriptive rule, rather than a simple observation of what was generally being done in tragedies of Aristotle's time. They assumed also that a rule which applied to tragedy should also apply to comedy, knowing that any writings which Aristotle might have dedicated to that genre are now lost.

No unity of time had been observed by medieval plays, especially those presenting extended accounts of the lives of saints or heroes: their action could sometimes amount to a complete dramatized biography. The humanists wanted to end all that, and follow the Greco-Roman models. Notoriously, Shakespeare took no notice: his first history plays (a genre which had few parallels in Italy and France) can cover events lasting for decades, and the denouements of the romances *The Winter's Tale* and *Pericles* resolve tensions which have built up over many years.

Whatever problems were sometimes experienced by tragic dramatists, those composing classical comedies did not find the unity of time difficult to observe. The stories put on the comic stage tended not to involve long-term development either in characters or in situations; and it was entertaining to compress multiple conflicts and deceptions into what was presented as a short period of time. The tension was ratcheted up, the characters were made more amusingly desperate, and the quality of comic energy (*vis comica*) which had been sought also by the dramatists of antiquity was made more forceful and hilarious by a sense of urgency. This is one of the ways in which comedy relies on a level of implausibility, even of fantasy.

There were theoretical disagreements about how literally to take Aristotle's 'single revolution of the sun', in particular as to whether the action should last for twenty-four hours or twelve. Pierre Corneille referred to this argument as 'cette dispute fameuse' ('this well-known dispute'), and tended to take a relatively relaxed

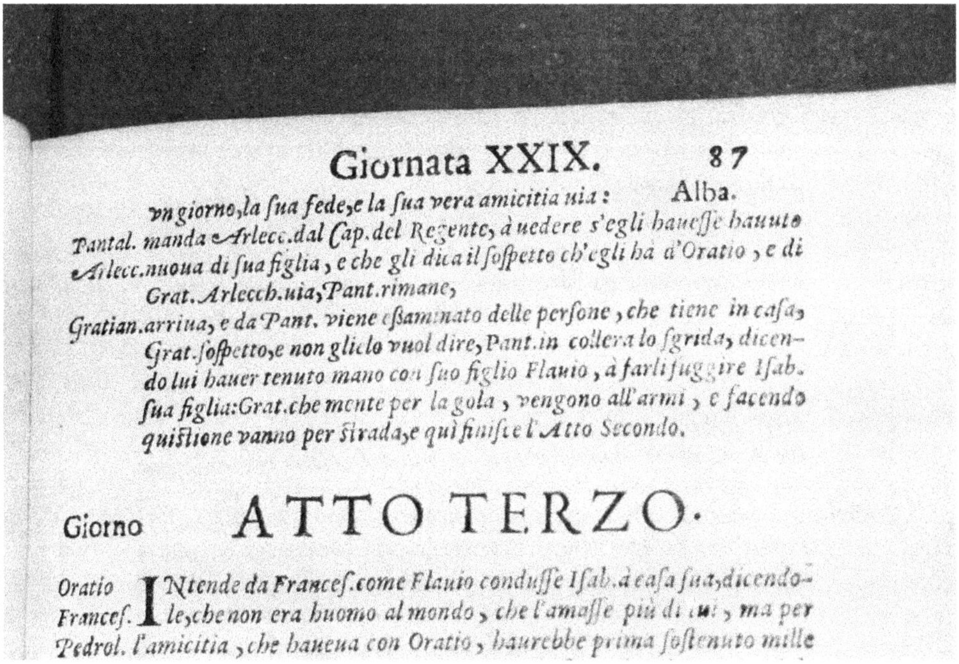

FIG. 20.1. A page from the 1611 printing of Flaminio Scala's scenarios. The words 'Alba' (dawn) and 'Giorno' (day) show the passing of time: like other similar indications in the volume, they appear to be last-minute insertions by the printer.

view of the matter. In fact he was prepared to state of his comedy *La Galerie du Palais* (1631–32) that the five acts should take place on five consecutive days. This was a piece of explicit resistance which was not followed by many others.

In the earliest Italian comedies, the story often ran from sunrise to sunset; and in court performances this might be signalled visually by having a painted sun move, act by act, across the top of the stage or proscenium arch. Alternatively, as in Machiavelli's *Mandragola*, the twenty-four hours could include things which happened during the night, with implications which had to be sorted out in the morning. This was an especially useful structure for the more scurrilous adultery tales, of which *La mandragola* is one: illicit nocturnal couplings, or failed couplings, would be the climactic moments of the story from which everyone then had to recover. Night sequences are central to some *commedie erudite*, from *La mandragola* (c. 1518), via Ruzante's *La moscheta* [Posh Talk] (c. 1529), to Gian Maria Cecchi's *L'assiuolo* [The Horned Owl] (1549). They also occur in Flaminio Scala's scenarios, signalled by his 1611 printer with a firm *Notte* in the margin, sometimes followed later by *Alba* for sunrise or *Giorno* for daytime (see Fig. 20.1). The fact that characters cannot see each other properly can help to produce farcical confrontations, including mistaken identities, leading people to end up in beds where they did not intend to be. Later on, however, Molière, Marivaux, and Goldoni tended not to feature such scenes in their plays: as I noted in Chapter 17, the scurrility quotient of comedy was tending to decline. A relatively decorous example of night-time intrigues is offered none the less in the final act of our last great classical comedy, *The Marriage of Figaro*, in both its spoken and operatic versions: the concluding sequence involves confused and confusing encounters in the dark in the grounds of the Almaviva palace. Throughout our period it was of course difficult or impossible to vary the illumination, either in candle-lit theatres or for open-air stages, so part of the fun was actors' ability to mime the fact that they could not see.

The main risk involved in observing the unity of time was that in some cases it might seem unconvincing to fit quite so many events into an alleged twelve or twenty-four hours. This may have been why Corneille was prepared to extend his own time-scale to a radical degree. He was amusingly scathing in his *Discours* about tragedies by Aeschylus and Euripides which pack too much action into their dramatized day, including transfers of armies over long distances — observing thus that the rule allegedly derived from ancient examples had been spectacularly broken by the ancients themselves. In comedy, however, such implausible concentrations provided entertainment value and did not provoke controversy. *The Marriage of Figaro* itself, a play where the frantic succession of plots and counter-plots might certainly invite such objections, was originally titled by Beaumarchais *La Folle Journée*, or 'The Day of Madness'. That label could be attached to most of the comedies composed in classical style over nearly three centuries.

Unity of Place

'As for the unity of place,' said Corneille in his *Discours*, 'I can find no such precept in Aristotle nor in Horace'.[7] Modern scholars such as René Bray agree with him.[8] It was in fact the influential Italian commentator Julius Caesar Scaliger (Giulio Cesare della Scala, 1484–1558), in the sixth book of his Latin *Poetices* published posthumously in 1561, who said, 'It is not the sign of a prudent poet to arrange things so that one travels from Delphi to Athens or from Athens to Thebes in a moment of time ... so fast that an actor scarcely has time to breathe'.[9] He may have been expressing a personal opinion, rather than quoting an imagined authority.

Nevertheless, the unity of place came to be taken as seriously as the other two unities. There are at least two possible reasons for this. Firstly, the unity of time insisted on a short fictional duration for the action of a play, based ultimately on what audiences were told they could accept as reasonable and plausible. A concentration in the time-span could seem automatically to imply concentrating also on a single space. This indeed was how Corneille chose to explain it. Secondly, simple observation showed that in ancient dramatic texts the scene was not signalled as changing. Comedies were set in a single urban street or square, often showing the front doors of houses where some of the characters lived. Tragic actions took

---

7   'Quant à l'unité de lieu je n'en trouve aucun précepte ni dans Aristote ni dans Horace.'
8   Bray 1931: 257.
9   'Nec prudentis est poetae efficere ut Delphis Athenas, aut Athenas Thebis momento temporis proficiscator [...] adeo cito vix ut actor respirandi tempus habeat' (quoted in Lawton 1949: 133).

place in named cities or princely dwellings, or other places equally precise — as for example in *Oedipus at Colonus* by Sophocles, which is set in an identifiable rural location outside Athens. In some plays there may have been more vagueness or fluidity in these settings than Renaissance readers were able to perceive. But it was clear that ancient stages did not offer physical changes of scenery, so — as in the case of Aristotle's 'single revolution of the sun' — what in antiquity had been a habitual practice was reinterpreted as a rule. When the rule became codified, there were (as for the unity of time) disagreements about how strict it should be. Some authorities argued that a slight shift in location — from indoors to outdoors, from one room to another — was acceptable provided everything took place in the same town. Corneille's view was that you could include places within any distance which could be physically travelled within twenty-four hours. Others insisted that once a single space had been identified, it should not alter.

There were however significant changes from 1500 to 1800 in how the unity of place was observed in Italian and French comic drama. They depended as much on the history of scenography as on theoretical proposals.

In the first decades, there was no alternative to sticking to a fixed scene, because early Italian Renaissance stages (like ancient ones) were unable to alter their scenery during the course of a performance. Moreover, the launch of *commedia erudita*, in Ferrara at the start of the sixteenth century, had coincided with the launch of a genuinely new and much appreciated approach to scenography. The techniques of linear perspective, discovered and developed by Renaissance painters during the previous century, had made it possible to mount an entrancing visual illusion: a painted stage backcloth supported by wings could persuade the audience that the action was taking place in a single location, plausibly represented. The scenery might even portray a particular recognizable city. By doing things this way, Renaissance designers were distancing themselves from previous practice, from what modern historians refer to as 'mansion' scenography. In much medieval drama, a set of successive locations, relating to different episodes of the story, had been alluded to simultaneously in a fixed scene which contained a range of different images or structures. Both actors and audience were prepared to relate imaginatively just to one place at a time, and mentally discard or postpone the other 'houses' or 'mansions'. The most obvious example of this method is the placing of Heaven at one end of the stage and Hell at the other in large-scale religious drama.

In this respect, as in many others, the humanists wanted to challenge their immediate predecessors, and to create a visual context which the French would come to call more 'rational'. Ariosto's *La cassaria* was mounted in 1508 in front of scenery depicting 'a part of a town in perspective, with houses, churches, belfries and gardens', in the words of a spectator of the time.[10] The set was the work of a well-known painter, Pellegrino da Udine; it had the appeal of being up-to-date in terms of its style and techniques; and it created a model which was immediately

---

10 'Una contracta et prospectiva de una terra cum case, chiesie, torre, campanili e zardini' (letter from Bernardino Prosperi to Isabella d'Este, 8 March 1508). The document is quoted in many Italian histories of theatre; in particular Davico Bonino 1977–78: I, 413–14.

LIBRO SECONDO.
Della Scena Comica.

Quanto alla dispositione de i Theatri, & delle Scene circa alla pianta io ne ho trattato qui a dietro, hora delle Scene in perspettiua ne trattarò particolarmente, & perche(com'io dissi)le Scene si fanno di tre sorte cioè la Comica per rappresentar comedie: la Tragica per le tragedie, e la Satirica per le Satire, questa prima sarà la comica, i casaméti della qua le uogliono essere di personaggi priuati, come saria di cittadini auocati, mercanti parasiti, & altre simili persone. Ma sopra il tutto che non ui manchi la casa della Rufiana ne sia senza hostaria, & uno tempio ui é molto necessario. per dispor re li casamenti sopra il piano, detto suolo: io ne ho dato il modo piu a dietro, si nel leuare i casaméti sopra li piani, come nella pianta delle scene massime, come & doue si dee porre l'Orizonte. Nientedimeno acciò che l'huomo sia meglio instrutto circa alle forme de i casamenti: io ne dimostro qui a lato una figura laquale potrà essere un poco di luce a chi di tal cosa uorrà dilettarsi. Pur in questa essendo cosi piccola non ho potuto osseruare tutte le misure. Ma solamente ho accennato alla inuentione per auuertir l'huomo a saper fare elettione di quei casamenti che posti in opera habbino a riuscir bene come saria un portico traforato: dietro delquale si uegga un'altro casamento come questo primo, li archi del quale son di opera moderna. Li poggiuoli, altri li dicono pergoli: altri Renghiere: hanno gran forza nelle faccie che scuriano, & cosi qualche cornice che li suoi finimenti uengono fuori del suo cantonale tagliati intorno & accompagnati cò l'altre cornice dipinte: fanno grande effetto, cosi le case che han gran sporto in fuori riusciscono bene: come l'hostaria dalla luna qui presente, & sopra tutte le altre cose si dee fare elettione delle case piu piccole, & metterle dauanti: acciò che sopra esse si scuoprano altri edificii, come si uede sopra la casa della Rufiana, l'insegna della quale sono li rampini, o uogliam dire hami, onde per tal superiorità della casa piu a dietro, uiene a rappresentar grandezza, & riempisse meglio la parte della scena, che non farebbe diminuendo se le summità delle case diminuissero l'una dopo l'altra, & benche le cose qui disegnate habbino un lume solo, da un lato nondimeno tornano meglio a dargli il lume nel mezo: percioche la forza dei lumi si mette nel mezzo, pendenti sopra la scena, & tutti quei tondi, o quadri che si ueggono per gli edificii sono tutti i lumi artificiati di uarij colori transparenti: de iquali darò il modo da fargli ne l'estremo di questo libro, le finestre che sono in faccia sarà bene a mettergli de lumi di dietro, ma che siano di uetro, & anco di carta: ouero di tela dipinta torneran bene. Ma s'io uolessi scriuere di tutti gli auuertimenti che mi abbondano circa a tal cose, io sarei forsi tenuto prolisso, però io le lassarò nell'intelletto di coloro che in tal cose, si uorranno essercitare.

FIG. 20.2. 'The comic stage' (*La Scena Comica*), from Sebastiano Serlio's *Secondo libro d'architettura*, proposing an all-purpose stage set to be used for any classical comedy. This 1560 printing of the book was dedicated to the King of France (either François II or Charles IX).

seized on by the theatre designers of sixteenth-century Italy. In 1545, Sebastiano Serlio's *Secondo libro di perspettiva*, part of a multi-volume treatise on architecture, printed illustrations of what the author proposed as three sets of fixed stage scenery, respectively for comedy (see Fig. 20.2), tragedy, and 'satyric' or pastoral drama. Some editions of this treatise were published with facing-page translations into French. Serlio's proposals were regarded for a while as definitive — even though, in 1545, there had been as yet few performances of tragedy, and none at all of 'regular' pastoral plays in five acts.[11] So, after the use of fixed perspective sets had been acclaimed in practice, the notion of an unchanging set for a classical drama was accepted also as a theoretical premise: it did after all harmonize entirely with developing ideas about unity of place. Serlio's illustrations appeared in a work whose theory was based on that of the ancient Roman architect Vitruvius: this gave them an authority which was in fact spurious, since there was no evidence that Greek or Roman theatres had used painted perspective scenery.[12]

In sixteenth-century Italy, therefore, both scripted and improvised comedies set all their action in a public street or square surrounded by houses. This in spite of the fact that their action was often filled with encounters which were desperately private, and which would have been better staged indoors. Plausibility was further strained by the fact that in real Italian society women above a certain class could not leave their houses without a chaperone, and would certainly not be seen wandering about alone in a public place or conversing outdoors with the young men who pursued them. Balcony scenes were slightly more convincing, with the man in the street and the woman up on a practicable piece of scenery depicting the front of her house. The social and moral risk implied by a heroine stepping into the street could increase the comic subversion and suspense; but the tensions within a family so often implied by a comic plot, especially those between fathers and their offspring, remained under-explored. A modern reader is left feeling that Italian comedy was left seriously hampered, almost waiting to be given permission to set at least some of its scenes indoors. This impression is reinforced, in the hindsight of a historian, by the fact that the technical limitations which had originally imposed a fixed set were quickly disappearing.

During the middle and late sixteenth century, in subsidized Italian court theatres, designers and technicians developed the ability to mount rapid changes of scenery, along with exciting effects such as ships moving across the stage on waves, and characters (especially pagan deities) being flown in on chariots or clouds. All these facilities were fully available, and eagerly used, for the interludes mounted at the famous Florentine wedding celebrations of 1589 (when Isabella Andreini performed her mad scenes with the improvising Gelosi company, as narrated in Chapter 19). The *intermezzi*, full of music and dance and moving scenery, were offered between the acts of a standard five-act scripted comedy, *La pellegrina* [The Pilgrim Woman],

---

11 Giraldi Cinthio's tragedy *Orbecche* was mounted in Ferrara in 1541; Agostino Beccari's five-act pastoral *Il sacrificio* in 1554, also in Ferrara.

12 There were references in the classical authorities Vitruvius and Pollux to changes of scene, achieved by revolving *periaktoi*. However, these were mentioned in a context of spectacular effects which did not on the face of it apply to comedy. See Hoxby 2017: esp. 170–71.

attributed posthumously to Girolamo Bargagli but in fact the collective work of the Sienese Accademia degli Intronati. After each interlude, the unmoving set of *La pellegrina* (a townscape depicting the city of Pisa) was restored to the stage for the next act; and the same routine may have been applied to the improvised comedies (*La zingana*, and *La pazzia di Isabella*) offered by the Gelosi. So an unchanging scene was still obligatory for classical comedy; but that genre was now being interleaved with other kinds of theatrical entertainment which took no notice of Aristotelian criteria.

In his treatise of 1598, Angelo Ingegneri was still assuming that a fixed set was expected in the mounting of all three classical genres: tragedy, comedy, and pastoral. Nevertheless from the 1580s on, in Italy and then later in France, the sober classical notion of unity of place, so easy to achieve scenographically, was competing with the availability of flexible visual effects in what were sometimes categorized as 'machine plays'. These, by definition, involved regular and spectacular changes in a story's location. Audiences enjoyed the new technology, whenever it came at affordable prices or was paid for by courts and rulers. One can detect a long-lasting tension, in what theatres offered during the seventeenth and eighteenth centuries, between classical theory and commercial practice: 'regular' plays in classical genres demanded one visual approach, but there were other stage spectacles which worked quite differently. Opera in particular was characterized from its very beginnings not only by its setting of words to music but also by a high level of spectacle and scenic invention: a fact recognized by Giovan Battista Andreini in his 1622 preface to *La Ferinda*, his failed comic libretto. Comedy was insulated from the issue by the fact that its plots were determinedly domestic and urban, and did not invite splendid settings or supernatural interventions.

In this field, as in many others, it was Pierre Corneille who was a major innovator. The action of his comedies never strays beyond the city walls of Paris; but it shifts, scene by scene (either implicitly or explicitly), to wherever it makes most sense for the relevant encounters to occur. Some scenes still take place in the public street, but others are set indoors. This is already clear in his second comedy, *La Veuve*; and in *La Suivante* [The Lady's Attendant] (1634) a new indoor unity of place is established, with the whole play being set inside the house of the character Géraste.[13] Corneille thus accepts the logic of verisimilitude, in a dramatic genre where so many of the verbal exchanges are private rather than public.

Scholars have shown how some comedies of Molière also began to move the action indoors, challenging the hegemony of the fixed outdoor setting.[14] Their evidence is based on frontispiece illustrations to published editions of the time. In plays such as *Le Misanthrope*, *Le Tartuffe*, and *Les Femmes savantes*, Molière had the action take place inside a family home (see Fig. 20.2). On other occasions he hinted, by one visual means or another, at shifts between outdoor and indoor spaces in what

---

13 The settings of all Corneille's comedies can be conveniently surveyed via the pages devoted to them in the compendium edited by Vuillermoz 1998.
14 The story is followed in hard physical detail in Herzel 1978. For a briefer account, see Clarke 2006: 15–36.

Fig. 20.3. Frontispiece for Molière's *Le Malade imaginaire*, showing scenery for an indoor setting.

Fig. 20.4. Frontispiece for Molière's *L'Avare*: behind the indoor space on stage there is an opening towards Harpagon's garden, to which characters are stated to have access.

was effectively the same locality: different parts of the same house and garden (as in *L'Avare*, see Fig 20.3), places inside a house and then out in the street. Modern critics have made the point that in some of Molière's masterpieces a struggle to own a domestic space — to occupy it, or to control it — is a way of characterizing the comic contest. Certainly a full dramatization of domestic conflict, together with a more plausible presentation of the feelings of female characters who could not step out into the street, was made much easier by an indoor setting.

From then onwards, it became an unquestioned habit to locate each scene in a comedy wherever it logically belonged, and in particular to shift from outdoors to indoors when necessary. Corneille's approach became standard. Characters might appear inside one or more houses, and then outside in the street. They still never moved beyond the limits of a single town. Texts which provide examples of this practice include those produced by Regnard and Dufresny for both the Comédie-Française and the Théâtre-Italien, and scenarios for improvisation by Luigi Riccoboni, drafted both before and after he moved from Italy to Paris in 1716. Riccoboni acknowledged that audiences preferred a degree of variety, as well as plausibility: his criterion for accepting scene changes was that movement between the fictional locations could be comfortably achieved within the twelve hours he thought were prescribed by the unity of time.[15] Marivaux, on the whole, observed unity of place more strictly and tended to choose a single location — indoors, as often as not — where all his encounters could take place. Goldoni was happy to move between the open street and a succession of different indoor settings, all within the same locality: *Il servitore di due padroni* is a good early example, and the *Villeggiatura* trilogy an equally good late one. Beaumarchais's *Barbier de Séville* starts in the street outside Dr Bartholo's house, and then moves indoors for the subsequent three acts; while *Le Mariage de Figaro* is set in a series of different spaces in the Almaviva palace, concluding (as noted above) outside in the garden, in the dark.

Normal practice in the eighteenth century was thus not to reject the unity of place, but to treat it with flexibility. Meanwhile, outside the genre of traditional comedy, the new French genres which we can broadly call 'sentimental comedy' were increasingly concentrating on stories which were firmly domestic, and reinforcing the preference for indoor stage settings. It can be remarked that Voltaire was interested in the possibility of simultaneous settings in different places, an effect which scenographic techniques had long made achievable if it was wanted. It was partly due to his influence that, from April 1759, spectators were finally banned from sitting on the stage at the Comédie-Française.[16] This practice, which clearly interfered with any serious *classiciste* preservation of a full dramatic illusion, is one which readers now tend to forget when assessing dramatic texts composed during this period.

---

15 See the Proemio to the scenario *Il filosofo deluso* [The Disillusioned Philosopher], in Riccoboni 1973: 105–06.
16 For both these points regarding Voltaire, see Goulbourne 2006: 207–08.

Unity of Action

The unities of time and place were constraints applied to dramatic compositions, and not to literature presented on the page. The prestigious genre of epic poetry was expected to narrate events which were more wide-ranging than those found in a play, while the other genres of imaginative literature which claimed classical antecedents — principally lyric poetry — did not involve narrative at all. (The novel in prose had hardly developed, and was not recognized as a separate or even respectable form of literature, during the period when *classicisme* was being articulated in France.) Unity of action, however, was a quality which might be demanded of any kind of literary composition. It was a broader, and also vaguer, principle; and in René Bray's account it has some precedence, having been considered as a theoretical concept earlier than the other two unities.[17] A demand for a 'unified' story, or for what we might just call 'coherence', appears in Chapter 8 of Aristotle's *Poetics*: he applies it in the first instance to epic poetry rather than to drama. His concentration on tragedy rather than comedy leaves some questions open: to what extent does the appeal of a comic play depend on individual episodes or moments, rather than on a single overarching narrative? I shall address that issue in my final chapter.

A determination to make dramatic structures coherent and focused, rather than fragmentary, was an important part of the *classiciste* campaign. The need for unity of action was firmly supported by Pierre Corneille. In the *Discours des trois unités*, he suggested an interesting criterion by which one could judge whether the action of a drama possessed unity or not: 'unity of action in comedy consists of the unity in the intrigue or in the obstacle to the main characters' intentions, and in the unity of peril in tragedy, whether the hero succumbs to it or escapes it'.[18] At the risk of a certain clumsiness, my translation sticks as close to Corneille's words as possible, because those words are important. He proposes that the circumstances against which protagonists of plays have to struggle, to which their actions in the story are opposed, have to be sufficiently focused for us to feel that the play is telling a single story, rather than several stories. This implies a recognition that both comedy and tragedy involve a contest or combat. In tragedy the protagonist is faced with 'peril', and usually loses the fight; in comedy the main characters confront an 'obstacle' or an 'intrigue', and they win. In Chapter 8 of the *Poetics*, Aristotle had expressed things differently: 'if the presence or absence of something makes no apparent difference, it is no real part of the whole'. That is not a difficult principle to understand or to observe, but in comedy it can inhibit free-wheeling entertainment. As I shall argue also at the end of this book, incoherence and digressions in the plot can be a part of the fun. It takes a particularly skilful dramatist to dispense with such variety while still keeping the audience amused.

In Italian *commedia erudita* there are many examples of scripts which involve separate 'perils' or 'intrigues' for different sets of characters, and where the dramatic

---

17 Bray 1931: 240.
18 'L'unité d'action consiste, dans la comédie, en l'unité d'intrigue ou d'obstacle aux desseins des principaux acteurs et en l'unité de péril dans la tragédie, soit que son héros y succombe, soit qu'il en sorte.' This comes in the first paragraph of the *Discours des trois unités*, and is quoted in Bray 1931: 247.

action is therefore short of strict unity. In the influential *Gl'ingannati*, the amorous tribulations of the heroine Lelia are accompanied by some irrelevant farcical encounters between lower-class characters, particularly those between the serving-maid Pasquella and the ludicrous Spanish soldier Giglio. Aristotle would quickly perceive that the absence of those scenes would 'make no apparent difference'; and indeed the Spaniard was cut completely from Charles Estienne's French translation of the play.[19] Later Italian 'serious comedies' preferred a structure whereby the misfortunes of a range of contemptible comic characters ran in parallel alongside those of the Lovers, with links between the two stories which could sometimes be superficial. The heroes and heroines faced dilemmas which were treated in moralistic or sentimental vein; the more clownish characters (especially lustful old men and braggart Capitani) were tempted into exposing themselves to merciless ridicule. Influential examples of scripts which worked in this way started with *Erofilomachia* [The Battle of Love and Friendship] (1572) by Sforza Oddi, and continued with the comedies of Giovan Battista della Porta.

There is a second feature of *Gl'ingannati* which might be seen as violating unity of action. The play concludes with two marriages rather than just one, though, since identical twins are involved, they resolve a single set of confusions. Here too the play set a pattern for subsequent scripts in which there were two pairs of lovers whose happiness needed to be achieved.[20]

Both these trends were particularly appropriate for Italian artisan professionals. *Arte* troupes employed two male Lovers and two leading ladies, and wanted parts for all four of them in their plays. (In the shows mounted later in Paris by the Théâtre-Italien, casting was more flexible and two pairs of Lovers were not always used.) There was also a growing distinction in those same professional companies between 'serious' and 'funny' roles — *parti serie* and *parti ridicole*. To begin with, that hierarchy was less formally recognized than it became in eighteenth-century *opera buffa*; but a variety of tones had audience appeal. There were thus practical and commercial reasons for later Italian comedies to combine moments of high-flown sentimental or moralistic rhetoric with scenes of clowning and slapstick humiliation, and the unifying links between the two strands were not always tight. The range of plots offered in Flaminio Scala's scenarios, as well as those which appear in scripted *commedie gravi* of the later sixteenth century, make all these tendencies clear.

When the precept of unity of action became recommended by French theorists, it had a substantial effect on the plots of comedies which aspired to observe the *classiciste* rules. Pierre Corneille's denouements usually still involve marriage between two couples rather than one; but the intrigues, misunderstandings, and deceptions are tightly constructed so as to make all the main characters intermesh, and the story always appears as indivisible. Corneille never then added any separate farcical sub-plots: he himself recognized that his comedies lacked 'personnages ridicules'.

---

19   Estienne 1540. Rayfield 2021b argues that the cut was motivated by a diplomatic wish not to appear anti-Spanish.
20   None the less, this practice is condemned as a breach of the Unity of Action by Girolamo Bartolommei Smeducci in his *Didascalia* (Bartolommei Smeducci 1658).

In Molière we usually have only one pair of Lovers, not two. However, Molière was ready to use a denouement where the union of a young master and a young mistress was accompanied by a marriage between their two servants. Such plebeian couplings had been relatively frequent in later Italian printed comedies, and they are common in Flaminio Scala's scenarios. It soon became a recognized trope, even an expected one, in comedies written for the Comédie-Française; and it was adopted also by Marivaux.

Many of Goldoni's comedies conclude with a wedding between two servants whose employers are also getting married: it is perhaps less common, though not exceptional, to find a Goldoni comedy containing two pairs of middle-class Lovers. Beaumarchais's Figaro comedies are sharply contrasted in this respect. *Le Barbier de Séville* concentrates firmly on the problems of Comte Almaviva and Rosina, in Aristotelian fashion and with no distractions. *Le Mariage de Figaro* makes the union of the servants Figaro and Suzanne the focus of the plot, with the reconciliation of the Comte and Comtesse almost a by-product: true to its perceived revolutionary tone, the play reverses the importance of the servant and the master. But *Le Mariage de Figaro* also contains a range of plot digressions (Basilio pursuing Marceline, Chérubin pursuing both the Comtesse and Fanchette, the relationship between Marceline and Bartolo), which Da Ponte and Mozart decided either to reduce or to cut altogether. Because a sung episode takes up more time on stage than an equivalent spoken one, comic operas required simpler plots. Thus they observed unity of action more closely than did some non-musical comedies.

CHAPTER 21

Comedies and their Societies: Satire?

> Plays of Menander survive today precisely because his style of comedy could be lifted from its original time and place and remain meaningful in worlds far removed from fourth-century Athens. — SANDER M. GOLDBERG[1]

The term 'satire', with its Italian and French equivalents, is traced back to Latin words (*satira*, *satura*) meaning 'medley' or even a kind of 'salad': the term was first applied to compositions which were not theatrical, such as the poems of Juvenal.[2] The existence of the mythological figure of the satyr (*satyrus*), and of 'satyr plays' which were mocking parodies of tragedy in ancient Greek drama, led in the early modern period to some confusion: it is via this route that the word has acquired its usual modern meaning. Rather than attempt a meticulous theoretical definition (which would involve distracting attempts to distinguish 'satire' from other terms such as 'parody' or 'lampoon'), I shall use the word as it is employed now in common parlance. So here it denotes any artistic representation which, in its intention or in its perceived effect, presents a recognizable aspect of human behaviour in an unfavourable light. In comic drama this is usually done by exposing people or institutions to ridicule. The implied tone of voice can vary from moral outrage to mere amusement. Audiences can be entertained by their own feelings of superior derision, whether or not they take the matter seriously. Moreover, satire does not always contain a revolutionary or reformist message. It is possible to satirize ideas or behaviour that are innovative, in order to defend traditional values or the status quo.

I noted in Chapter 17 that the function of comedy formally approved in early modern Europe was the 'castigation of vice through laughter'. I quoted John Vanbrugh: comic plays showed people 'what they should do', by dramatizing 'what they should not do', presenting undesirable actions and attitudes in a humiliating light. All this presupposes that characters and behaviour ridiculed in a comedy reflected something which the audience would recognize. Somebody, somewhere, was being taught a lesson; and that somebody should not be too far away. This is how classical theory related comedy to what I am now broadly calling satire. Very frequently we speak in particular of *social* satire. Where that expression is appropriate, it implies that stage mockery is directed at things which an audience

---

[1] Goldberg 2007: 130.
[2] For a quick summary of this, see the 'Introduction' in Quintero 2007: esp. 6–10.

saw as happening, or at types of people they saw as existing, in their own contemporary society. Classical comedies were mounted in a succession of times and places, and they therefore related to many different contemporary societies. Between 1500 and 1800, we would expect substantial changes in what comedies chose to mock or expose — when, that is, there was a social target at all. Many comic playwrights did aim to portray an identifiable society, to operate on a level of immediate topicality to which their audiences could respond. Others, however, might not do this, or might claim that they did not. Any desire to portray the 'here and now' was balanced against another assumption: namely, that certain traits of human behaviour were universal and recurrent, and could be caricatured outside the context of a particular time and place. Many targets of human ridicule were seen as perpetually inherent in human nature. Lust, greed, self-deception, stupidity, and ignorance are always with us and always laughable, irrespective of any passing social structures or patterns. Molière's *Tartuffe* contains the line: 'Envious people will die, but envy never will'.[3] Not all comic dramatists felt moved — and some did not feel permitted — to switch their attention from the universal to the particular.

Such hesitations were supported by another prejudice transmitted from the Greco-Roman world. We have seen that a historical distinction was made between Greek Old Comedy, represented by the plays of Aristophanes, and the New Comedy of Menander and others on which Terence and Plautus had based their Latin plays. The transition from Old to New was seen as a desirable reform — partly because Aristophanes was too scurrilous and obscene in general, but also because his comedies often openly targeted living people. The example which we now know best is the caricature of Socrates in *The Clouds*; but there were other Athenian public figures whom Aristophanes directly attacked by name. When Italian Renaissance dramatists undertook to revive Roman-style comedy, with the 'Donatus' commentaries as their guide, they began with an assumption that it was unacceptable to attack or caricature identifiable people. Unsurprisingly, rulers and people of influence, some of whom would be in their audience, agreed with them. Throughout the history of classical comedy in Italy and France, the relationship between comedies and their societies was conducted with some delicacy.

A starting-point for surveying that relationship, and how it changed or developed, is to note where comic dramatists chose to locate their fictional stories, or indeed to note whether there was a named location at all. The comedies of Plautus and Terence, though composed for a Roman audience, were always set in a notional Athens. On the face of it this was because everyone knew that they were adaptations (*contaminationes*) of Athenian originals. In addition, though, it is easy to guess that such satirical references as they made to Roman habits and behaviour were prudently softened by the pretence that they were not portraying Rome.[4] Leaping forward nearly two millennia to the plays which chronologically conclude

---

3   'MME PERNELLE: Les envieux mourront, mais non jamais l'envie' (*Le Tartuffe*, v.3).
4   In fact it is now thought that the presentation of ridiculous Greeks, tricked and manipulated by their own slaves, pandered to a specifically anti-Greek prejudice in the Roman audience. Whether this perception was shared by humanist scholars, in their own readings of Plautus and Terence, is not clear.

this present study, we see Beaumarchais using the same approach. In *Le Barbier de Séville* and *Le Mariage de Figaro* the dramatist cushioned his criticism of hierarchical French society by setting his action in Spain.

Between Terence and Beaumarchais, or at least between Ariosto and Beaumarchais, we can catalogue a considerable amount of diversity in the setting of a comic drama, in terms of its distance from, or proximity to, the place where its audience lived. This points to an equal diversity in the extent to which comedies indulged in topical satire.

Italian *commedia erudita*

Ariosto's original *La cassaria* in prose was composed in 1508 with a close, even pedantic eye on Roman models; and this included setting it in the eastern Mediterranean rather than at home in Ferrara.[5] The location is given as 'Metellino', that is Mytilene on the island of Lesbos. This could be seen as placing the action in the ancient Greek past, distancing it in time as well as in space; but detailed textual references make it more probable that Ariosto was thinking of contemporary Mytilene, ruled by the Ottoman Empire since 1462.[6] This level of exoticism makes it easier for the audience to swallow the rather un-contemporary Plautine plot, in which the two young rakes want to purchase from a pimp the two slave girls after whom they are lusting. The play still contains a small number of satirical jabs at purely Italian targets, in imitation of Plautus's occasional references to Rome.[7] A year later, in 1509, Ariosto had acquired the confidence to set his next comedy, *I suppositi*, in his and his court audience's home town of Ferrara. Here we have a single young male protagonist pursuing a girl whom he wants to marry, and whom he has made pregnant. Thus, in only the second example of *commedia erudita*, the main intrigue has been brought to revolve around marriage rather than an anachronistic form of concubinage. Compared with *La cassaria*, the play has a more contemporary feel. It also satisfies a public taste for something approaching romance, as established by well-known patterns from medieval literature which had not been there to influence Plautus. In a sixteenth-century Italian urban space, the characters behave in ways which the audience can recognise, and they even discuss problems which relate to living in Ferrara. Of Ariosto's subsequent comedies, two were again set in Ferrara and one, *Il negromante* [The Magician] (1520, revised 1528), in Cremona, 130 kilometres away as the crow flies. In particular *La Lena* (1529) is a hard-hitting comedy which depicts types of social and sexual exploitation which some of its audience might have found uncomfortably close to home. It also alludes, in farcical detail, to the corruption of low-grade law-enforcers in Ferrara.[8] It is striking that

---

5   Angela Casella's presentation of the play in Ariosto 1974: xiii–xix, makes this clear. As well as large-scale borrowings in terms of plot, Casella cites seventy-nine specific textual derivations from Plautus and thirty-one from Terence.
6   When Ariosto rewrote the comedy in verse, for performance in 1531, he moved the setting to 'Sibari', the ancient Greek city of Sybaris in southern Italy which in his time no longer existed. His motivation for this is hard to guess.
7   Casella lists these satirical jabs in Ariosto 1974: xvii–xviii.
8   For a more detailed account of *La Lena*, see Andrews 1993: 83–87.

Ariosto felt able to compose this for the court of the Este duke, who commanded such officers. This may have been partly because he was a very trusted courtier, with a kind of gentlemanly jester's licence; but also because satirical jibes delivered to a coterie audience have a different resonance from those offered to the general citizenship. The episode acts as a reminder, relevant to all discussions about satire and its reception, that such material can be seen as more or less tolerable, more or less subversive, according to who is speaking and who is listening. What might rank as sedition in public can be taken as loyal criticism in private.

Subsequent erudite comedies, performed in Italian courts and academies during the sixteenth century, do not often follow Ariosto's lead in this respect. Stage depictions of, and even verbal references to, social or political characteristics of an identifiable community are relatively rare. Allusions to real rulers, or to real people of any sort, are rarer still; and when they occur, they are always carefully complimentary.[9] Some comedies did set their action in the audience's own home city: Florentine comedies were quite often set in Florence. In Venice there were playwrights who created a unique fashion for local linguistic parody: they paraded on stage the diverse ethnicities which were to be found in this most multi-national of Italian sea-ports. The accents of merchants and sailors from Dalmatia, Greece, and Germany were meticulously and derisively copied, alongside the speech of Venetians themselves and the dialect of peasants from the Paduan mainland close by.[10] There was no corresponding attempt, however, to make any comment on state institutions in Venice, or on its characteristic social structures — apart from sometimes depicting typical street thugs (*bravi*, or *bulli*), whom everyone was happy to see denigrated. These multi-lingual Venetian comedies played a part in the debates which created, and then disputed, the existence of an Italian literary language; and they also contributed to the linguistic diversity of *commedia dell'arte*. Such issues could not then overflow into classical comedy performed outside Italy. In so far as the stage presentation of accents and dialects contained a satirical element, this too was untranslatable and could not acquire a larger European dimension.

There was an alternative tendency in Italian comedies of this time to set themselves in a different city from where they were performed — a place which the audience might know by reputation, but where the misbehaving protagonists could not be seen as alluding slanderously to individuals or families in the audience. The Sienese Accademia degli Intronati, whose comedies were highly praised and much imitated, usually adopted this policy. Their most influential play of all, *Gl'ingannati*, was set in the northern Italian city of Modena, ruled by the Este dukes who also controlled Ferrara. The reasons for this specific choice have been debated and are still not clear. After that, in the equally successful *Amor costante* [Constant Love] (1536), *Alessandro* (1544–45), and *La pellegrina* (eventually staged in Florence in 1589), the Academy preferred to use the Tuscan city of Pisa, not too

---

9   A strong maverick exception to all these generalizations is Pietro Aretino (1492–1556). His early comedy *La cortigiana* contains scathing mockery of papal Rome as he knew it in 1525; and the next one, *Il marescalco* (1533) narrates a version of a practical joke played (perhaps in reality) by a Duke of Mantua. See the accounts of his comedies in Andrews 1993: 66–77, 154–60.

10 The two principal authors of Venetian multilingual comedy, Andrea Calmo and Gigio Artemio Giancarli, are surveyed in Andrews 1993: 144–54.

distant but possessing the advantage of being a sea-port like Venice, and so open to the arrival and departure of wanderers or fugitives in the fictional story. Much scripted *commedia erudita* thus shared the reluctance of the Latin dramatists to place their action too close to home, and so risk their characters being confused with real people. The comic flaws of the characters could indeed be seen as universal rather than particular, and details of their behaviour could simply reflect the habits and attitudes shared by residents of most urban communities in the peninsula.

Those communities differed from each other politically, belonging to the separate states which constituted 'Italy' at that time. Local features of society and government were not often referred to in the plays: as well as being potentially subversive, such references would have limited the number of venues in which a comedy could be revived (as the epigraph chosen to introduce this present chapter reminds us). The larger events of Italian politics did, however, sometimes provide a narrative background or pretext for the stories. Dramatists used real political and military upheavals — which in sixteenth-century Italy were frequent and sometimes disastrous — to explain the disruptions inflicted on families. Long-lost relatives were then discovered in 'agnitions' revealing their true identities (see also Chapter 26). Events such as the Sack of Rome in 1527, or civil conflicts in cities such as Genoa or Palermo which might force families into exile, gave a background to such much-repeated narrative tropes. No opinion is ever expressed in the plays about the rights or wrongs of wars or of family feuds, when they are historically true: they just provide a patina of plausibility. In other stories, family separation is blamed on the perils of long sea voyages, undertaken by members of the urban merchant class to which the protagonists of comedy usually belonged. Italian cities had long participated in, and indeed to some extent had created, a commercial network in which families had branches and contacts throughout Europe and the Mediterranean. In addition, Italian comic plots might acknowledge the looming presence of the Ottoman Empire, just across the sea. In Turkey, in Egypt, and closer to home in north Africa, the community of Islam faced Christian Europe in a cold war which could easily break into hotter conflict. Captives were often taken, and subsequently ransomed. Episodes like this were exploited in dramatic plots. Audiences in different cities had no difficulty in recognizing facts which might apply to their own lives, irrespective of the varying political structures of their home towns.

These Italian communities also had many social habits and attitudes in common. In directing how their characters behaved, comic playwrights portrayed the preoccupations which governed how members of real families treated each other. The insistent anxiety about family reputation, which included most of all the preservation of a daughter's virginity before marriage, motivates many of the fathers in these plays, and their actions and choices would be seen as normal by all Italian audiences. Like Leonato in Shakespeare's *Much Ado About Nothing*, patriarchs can be seen switching from almost homicidal rage to relieved affability, as their understanding of their daughters' situation alters (see also Chapter 23). Such changes of heart are recognized as having their ridiculous side, but there is no suggestion that they, or society in general, could or should find another way of reacting. The same applies to plots where Lovers manage to get into bed with each other, forcing their Elders to accept a fait accompli and allow them to marry (see also Chapter 24). The situation can be dramatized amusingly, and the young people have defeated their elders as in comedy they are expected to do; but in real society, as well as on stage, the parents would have to make the same decisions, and the plays never suggest that another approach would be possible.[11] In that sense, they reflected social reality, but cannot be said to satirize it.

Comedies also accepted without question, and exploited for purposes of entertainment, that the lower classes in early modern societies had less honour to lose than their masters did. Not only do servants have a comic licence to play aggressive and deceitful tricks on their employers, but female servants (*fantesche*) have lower thresholds of sexual propriety than most female Lovers. When Juliet's Nurse, in Shakespeare, advises her to accept what is imposed on her and marry the County Paris, she is deploying a level of pragmatism which is shown by Italian stage nurses and servants in *commedia erudita* and later also in early opera. Juliet's obstinate fidelity to Romeo reflects what an Italian stage heroine would also insist on, especially in the more thoughtful and moralistic *commedie gravi* of the later sixteenth century. Plays were reinforcing the values which society claimed to be operating, rather than trying to cast doubt on them; and this was also true regarding the different standards expected from different social classes. Comic derision can both entertain the audience and keep its victims in their place. Again, this process cannot be called satire.

The single area where *commedia erudita* did loose off some critical salvoes, at least in its earlier decades, was against mercenary or misbehaving clerics. One of the first and most influential comedies, Machiavelli's *Mandragola*, features the corrupt Friar Timoteo. In III.11 he preaches a famously tendentious sermon to the virtuous wife Lucrezia, persuading her that to commit adultery will not be a sin if she aims to produce an heir for her husband. In other plays, such as *Gl'ingannati* (1.5), the alleged louche habits of monks and nuns are explored with some relish, in long speeches or conversations involving servant characters. There are in fact some historical examples, in sixteenth-century Italy, of scandals which led to the dissolution of individual monasteries and convents, so such attacks were not completely without basis. At the same time, satire of the clergy had also become a literary trope dating back at least to Boccaccio's *Decameron* of the fourteenth century. We may wonder whether cliché depictions of sexually rampant priests, monks, or nuns had a bawdily relished but partly fictional status — like images of equally randy milkmen, scoutmasters, and vicars, in schoolboy jokes told in twentieth-century England. Are we really condemning such miscreants, or vicariously enjoying what they do? There could be a delicate balance between derision and collusion, in the terms I pursued in Chapter 17. However, religious authorities soon came to take these attacks at their face value, as slanderous subversions which threatened clerical authority and

---

11   This is made clear, with chronicled examples, in Ruggiero 1985. There will have been minor differences in law between the various Italian states and communities, but they all shared general principles.

needed to be slapped down. It is notable — and relevant to the subsequent history of classical comedy — that new rules of censorship, launched in the atmosphere of the Catholic Counter-Reformation, actually banned from the theatre all depictions of, and references to, members of the clergy. The Sienese comedy *La pellegrina*, much referenced in this present chapter, was originally composed in the 1560s, and contained some scathing comments about licentious monks which (to a modern reader, at least) carry more resentful weight than the earlier equivalent passages from *Gl'ingannati*. *La pellegrina* was offered to the Medici Grand Duke of Tuscany, and initially put away in a drawer. When a later Grand Duke got married in 1589, it was chosen to be the showpiece of the massive wedding celebration (along with the improvised plays of the Gelosi company, discussed in Chapter 19). At that point the manuscript text was carefully purged of all its anticlerical diatribes.[12]

For the most part, then, *commedia erudita* was making use of a familiar social framework rather than satirizing it. Dramatists set their stories in a contemporary world — in 'an Italian city' whose name was not always very important — in order to connect with their audience. They needed to make palatable and comprehensible a genre which had first been conceived in a substantially different culture. The events portrayed were mostly playful fantasies, heavily circumscribed by the limitations of genre; and in practice their entertainment value was more important than any real plausibility, although theorists of this period did not say so. A modern setting could bestow on the plots, and on the behaviour of the characters, a kind of surface verisimilitude. On the other hand, with very limited exceptions, Italian comedies were disinclined to ask awkward questions about their societies. They preferred to deploy their derision against perennial human foibles.

Italian Scenarios

In terms of satire, as in most other respects, the plots used in their scenarios by professional Italian companies differ very little from those of *commedia erudita*. The generalizations just offered above are all applicable also to early *commedia dell'arte*. The forty comic scenarios published by Flaminio Scala in 1611 dramatize the same kinds of story as do the printed comedies on which they are heavily based. They too are set in 'an Italian city', whose name often seems chosen at random but with Rome used more often than anywhere else. The other towns referenced are mostly in the northern half of the peninsula, reflecting what we know about the touring routes of the troupes in which Scala operated. However, three of the scenarios are set in Spanish-ruled Naples — this reflects either the political and economic importance of that city, or (in addition) the influence of comedies by the Neapolitan Giovan Battista Della Porta.[13]

Any single choice of setting which Scala came to record in print for a given

---

12   The history of this text, now a well-known case study, appears in Borsellino 1974: 107–19; the relevant essay is entitled 'Il manoscritto della *Pellegrina*'. See also Chapter 25 below.
13   The full list of Scala's settings for comedy reads as follows: Bologna, three scenarios; Florence, five; Genoa, two; Mantua, one; Milan, one; Naples, three; Parma, one; Perugia, three; Pesaro, two; Rome, sixteen; Venice, two; and one in a villa in the Paduan countryside.

scenario might reflect the fact that it was once staged in the town concerned; but it is equally likely to be irrelevant. The manager of an *arte* company — the *capocomico*, who devised scenarios by assembling and copying plot theatergrams filched from existing plays — wanted to be able to mount the successful ones in a series of different places, and so there was no point in homing in satirically on one society in particular. In individual performances, we can easily assume that local references, local jokes, even small pieces of local satire would have been imported ad hoc by Zani, Pedrolino, and Arlecchino. We cannot expect to find traces of such insertions in the surviving scenario texts. Moreover, granted that a company's activities, and even the tolerance of its presence in the town, depended entirely on approval by civic, princely, or ecclesiastical authorities, we can also assume that seriously critical comments about the host community would be carefully avoided. Insertions in which the local audience were flattered are much more likely.

The more we read Italian *arte* scenarios, and the more we look at visual depictions of the improvising masks in action, the more we can be struck by their element of self-referential repetition.[14] Pantalone and Zani, even Isabella and Orazio, operate in a world of theatre which is constantly recycled: on the large scale in its choice of plots and relationships, and on the small scale in its use of actors' existing repertoire. Much later in 1750, as I have previously observed (see Chapter 13), Goldoni made a character remark: 'the audience knows what Arlecchino is going to say before he opens his mouth'. The audience probably started knowing this, or at least anticipating some of it, quite early in the history of *commedia dell'arte*. They knew it because Arlecchino's world was familiar and self-contained. The predictability of the genre (as I argue also in Chapter 22) came to be something which the public wanted and enjoyed, just as music-hall audiences in Edwardian Britain wanted to hear the star performer sing yet again the song which was her trademark. In Italian comedy the repetition seems indeed self-referential. Arlecchino does what he does on stage, firstly because he *is* on stage and not in the real world, and secondly because he is Arlecchino. His back story is not what his character is said to have experienced earlier in this particular fiction, it is what the mask has done in other shows for other audiences. The bumpkin from Bergamo adrift in an urban environment, who may once have been portrayed by the mask, has become an increasingly distant point of reference.[15] To be satirical, a drama has to be 'theatre about society'; Italian *commedia dell'arte* was most often 'theatre about theatre'.

---

14   The illustrations themselves came very quickly to be self-referential in their turn: images and postures were recycled across a number of visual genres. All this has been made clear by the researches of M. A. Katritzky, especially in her monograph Katritzky 2006.
15   Arlecchino was not originally from Bergamo, but in this respect his mask became assimilated to other Zani servant figures. This was true both for Italian and French audiences.

Seventeenth-Century Paris: French Comedies

Touring companies had to relate to all audiences, or to none in particular. In the seventeenth century, most of the French theatre scripts which survive were created for Paris. Suddenly comedies were being aimed a regular returning audience, and both dramatists and performers knew in advance whom they were addressing. This awareness had a radical effect both on the actor-dramatists of the Théâtre-Italien and on major French playwrights.

I have suggested in Chapter 6 that the quiet revolution which Pierre Corneille brought to comic drama, effectively recreating it in a new French manner, included establishing a relationship between his characters and an identifiable social and physical environment. Corneille's first two comedies, *Mélite* and *La Veuve*, do not identify their setting, but a Parisian location seems implicit. His next two are entitled *La Galerie du Palais* and *La Place Royale*, places in the city where much of the action takes place, and which were entirely familiar to his audiences. Then *La Suivante* and *Le Menteur* [The Liar] are also explicitly set in Paris.[16] The young protagonists of Corneille's comedies reflected social and moral questions being faced precisely at that time by the upper bourgeoisie of the city. In a society attempting to reconstitute itself after decades of upheaval, and where Cardinal Richelieu in particular was seeking to create a new behavioural image for France as a whole, the emotional confusions of these characters may have been capable of provoking indulgent laughter, but they also provoked thought. Whether we want to call this sort of social commentary 'satire' is open to question — it involves at least as much encouragement towards virtue as discouragement of vice. We can however claim to see Corneille's comedies as mirroring attitudes and responses which his spectators were either experiencing for themselves or observing in those around them. The plays contained a fresh topicality, in a limited and delicate area of behaviour, which few if any Italian comedies had attempted.

The controversies which Molière faced during his career sprang from the fact that the public — both his supporters and his enemies — assumed that his plays were inextricably connected to trends, and even to people, in the Parisian life of their day. Some critics have since argued that those assumptions were exaggerated, that the essence and force of Molière's comedies do not lie in programmed satire, but in pure comic structures which work independently of a particular time and place.[17] The fact that they do contain such qualities is indeed an important reason why they still work for audiences whose times and places are different. Nevertheless, when Molière's comedies were first produced they were often a talking point, and much of the talk they provoked was about just whom they were satirically portraying.

---

16   *La Suite du Menteur* (1644–45) is set in contemporary Lyon. It depicts the protagonist Dorante as having fled from the Parisian marriage with which *Le Menteur* apparently concluded.
17   In homage to a personal academic debt, I refer here particularly to the study by W. G. Moore entitled *Molière, A New Criticism* (Moore 1964). Moore accepts that Molière's comedies do contain satire; but he argues that their guiding principle is aesthetic rather than moral, and that Molière's personal opinions are both indecipherable and irrelevant. See also the brief concentrated account of Molière in Moore 1969: 17–21.

This is clear from the two one-act plays which he mounted in 1663, *La Critique de l'École des femmes*, and *L'Impromptu de Versailles*, plays which respond head-on to current attacks. (*L'Impromptu de Versailles* contains a use of the verb *satiriser* which corresponds more or less to its modern meaning.) *La Critique de l'École des femmes* depicts the arguments which the comedy *L'École des femmes* had been provoking since its premiere the previous December: portraying a *salon* debate, Molière creates characters who represent or caricature the contrasting points of view. In *L'Impromptu de Versailles*, he actually puts himself and his troupe colleagues on stage, using their real names, and shows them attempting to rehearse a sketch which Louis XIV has commissioned from them at very short notice — hence the 'impromptu' of the title. Both plays deal directly with public assumptions that *L'École des femmes*, and Molière's comedies in general, contain comments on contemporary social behaviour and literary opinions. In both of them Molière insists that there is indeed satire in his plays, but that it is general and not particular. Those who feel targeted by his caricatures, and who take offence, are admitting that they do possess the faults being depicted; but so do many others, and no identifiable person was being referred to. This accepts as an opening premise that the comedies are indeed about contemporary society, and that types and classes of people — but not individuals — in seventeenth-century Paris are being made to look ridiculous.

In 1664 and 1665, in *Le Tartuffe* and *Dom Juan*, Molière took explicit aim at what he called 'hypocrisy', suggesting that as well as true religious faith there existed a false devotion, exploited for self-seeking purposes. This could in theory have referred to a generalized undesirable human tendency, on a par with avarice or arrogance, which might affect anyone anywhere. But the attack was immediately taken to be more topical and specific: some powerful groups of religious people, referred to broadly as the *dévots*, decided that he was aiming at them. (In the context of the Counter-Reformation censorship referred to above, we should note that the character Tartuffe is not actually a cleric: he is a layman who professes intimidating levels of piety.) *Le Tartuffe* was banned for five years, until Louis XIV overrode the objections and explicitly permitted a revised version to be mounted in 1669. *Dom Juan*, however, was taken off the stage and not seen again in Molière's lifetime. This is not the place to unpick the issues concerned, or to propose modern standards of judgement; but these events can leave us in no doubt that Molière's comedy was seen by his own audiences and critics as relating firmly to contemporary France, or contemporary Paris. Molière's defence was that he was observing well-established classical parameters: he was following (we could now say, though he did not) the same rules as his Italian humanist predecessors. Comedy was supposed to ridicule vice in general, and this was acceptable provided that it did not name particular victims. Such claims may sometimes have been disingenuous. Regarding *Les Femmes savantes* (1672), historians suggest that the two ludicrous poets Trissotin and Vadius are depictions of real people. In *L'Impromptu de Versailles*, Molière mischievously took the opportunity — granted that he was casting himself as himself — of showing that he could imitate and make fun of the recitation styles of some leading actors in rival companies, individuals who are openly named in the surviving stage directions.

Seventeenth-Century Paris: The Italians

The Italian comic actors in Paris began by trading on their exotic appeal. This might have meant that they offered comedies which referred to a foreign reality; but if that was ever the case, it did not last for long. Audiences prefer to know what their actors are talking about, or narrating about, and especially to know what they are joking about.

We have two main sources for the content of shows mounted by the Théâtre-Italien, before they were run out of town in 1697. We have, in a later French translation, eighty-one partial scenarios assembled by Domenico Biancolelli for his role as Arlequin between 1667 and 1680. Then there are extracts from fifty-six plays in the *Théâtre italien* collection started by the next Arlequin, Evaristo Gherardi: it was expanded into six volumes in the 1701 printing.

Biancolelli's notes were probably memory aides written just for himself. He was noting for future reference, in case he had to do it again, which of his routines and speeches he had used in which play. It is thus hard to see which, if any, of the stories in which he performed had an overall satirical content. Sometimes, indeed, it is hard to decipher what the story was at all. What we can observe, however, is an increasing tendency for the fictional Arlequin to disguise himself as figures of power and social status — judges, doctors, gentlemen, even princes — and subject them to ridicule (see also Chapter 17.) His judges deliver verdicts which are nonsensical, both in their substance and in the parodic language they use. His doctors, anticipating or following Molière's *Malade imaginaire* [The Imaginary Invalid], speak gibberish and do more harm than good to their patients. He impersonates gentlemen in ways which are so un-gentle that they belong to a world of fantasy. There may be some swipes at the excesses of aristocratic pretension (especially with regard to duelling, which royal authority was attempting to ban); but the message is equally that if you are a pleb then you remain plebeian, and can never manage convincingly to sound or look like one of your betters.[18] There is more clowning here than coherent social criticism. Even clowning, though, has to relate to the perceptions and prejudices of an audience. In that Parisian society (as in many other societies), resentments felt against the legal system in particular were easy to turn into caricatures which, deep down, sound more angry than indulgent.

This becomes immediately apparent when we open Gherardi's *Théâtre italien*. The items assembled in its first volume are scenes in French possibly composed by the dramatist Fatouville for Italian shows mounted between 1682 and 1692.[19] The plays' titles imply worlds of fantasy, sometimes from classical mythology: Arlequin as Mercury; The Matron of Ephesus; Arlequin as Jason searching for the

---

18   There are signs, though, that Biancolelli himself knew what he was doing, and was not operating from a position of surly ignorance. He knows when his Latin is incorrect, and when his mythology is garbled.
19   The birth date of the Norman writer Anne Mauduit de Fatouville (who was male, despite his baptismal name) is not known: he died in 1715. As the first composer of 'Scènes françaises' for the Italian actors, he is seen as having helped to create the troupe's subsequent house style: cf. Mazouer 2002a: 165–85.

Golden Fleece. I have noted in Chapter 10 that much of this involved theatrical parody, mockeries of plays and operas recently mounted in more serious theatres. But the various dream worlds also contain sarcastic attacks on Parisian habits and institutions; and in the first volume the dramatist is especially keen to take aim at the legal profession. He had been famously preceded, no doubt among many others, by Molière, who in II.5 of *Les Fourberies de Scapin* had given to the play's eponymous rogue character a succinct aggressive tirade about how anyone involved in a lawsuit faced corruption and exploitation at every level.

We can briefly survey one of Fatouville's examples. The story of the Matron of Ephesus, taken from the *Satyricon* of Petronius, would mean nothing at all to an audience of the twenty-first century; but the Théâtre-Italien was ready to use it as a starting reference for its paying public of 1682, parodying its presentation in another theatre. Arlequin is initially given the role of the rough soldier who persuades the widowed Matron that she should stop grieving suicidally over her husband, and return to the delights of life and of love. 'However,' he says in French, 'I haven't always been of such low social rank: I was once assistant clerk to a *procureur*' (a class of advocate in the French legal system). The Matron immediately tells him — in Italian, because she is really 'Eularia', Orsola Cortesi, who plays Innamorata roles in the Théâtre-Italien — that by sheer coincidence she has an uncle who is a *procureur* about to retire. Because she likes Arlequin so much, she is willing to buy him the practice which her uncle is giving up. This arbitrary and incoherent device leads to a series of sketch scenes in which Arlequin takes the name Grapignan, and practises the trade of *procureur* with blatant ruthless corruption. He complains at his clerk for putting more than two words on each line while copying documents, because the copying fee was calculated per line of text. He offers (for a stiff payment) to get a street thief out of trouble by bribing two false witnesses. When a Hatter and a Pastrycook quarrel violently in the street, they visit Grapignan for legal advice and he takes payments in kind from both sides. How far such a picture was seen as literally true, rather than comically exaggerated, we cannot now tell. Whatever the case, there is a level of clownish stylization which places these scenes in a frame of unreality. Grapignan is being impersonated by Arlequin, and the spectator knows who Arlequin is — a comic actor who plays entertaining games.[20]

The plays of the Théâtre-Italien tended to operate on this level. They were full of digs at the corruptions and idiocies of Parisian society, but their depictions were absurd and over the top. A systematic dismissal of classical *vraisemblance* made it possible to claim that none of the attacks were really serious. There is a paradox in the fact that, compared with the Comédie-Française, the Italians could sometimes offer harsher (though more fragmentary) criticism of French society, precisely because they ignored the rules of composition which aimed to bring drama close to perceived reality. In Fatouville's *Arlequin Jason* (1684), the classical witch Medea rantingly lists 'Sergeants, Scribes, Advocates, Commissioners, Clerks of the Court' among the hellish demons whom she can conjure up for her black magic.[21]

---

20 This view of the overall effect is supported by Mazouer 2002a: 180.
21 'Sergens, Clercs, Procureurs, Commissaires, Greffiers'.

Medea is a playful fiction from an unreal literary world, and so she was immune to the outraged counter-attacks provoked by more realistic portraits of gruesome characters, like Molière's Tartuffe and (as we shall see immediately below) Lesage's Turcaret.

Fatouville was not the only contributor of texts to the Italians; and the legal profession was not their only target. Theatre historian Virginia Scott observed the following when characterizing *Arlequin misantrope* (1696), one of the last titles in the sixth volume of Gherardi 1701: 'The satire marshals most of the targets commonly struck by the Comédie-Italienne: frivolous aristocrats, ambitious bourgeois, bumptious peasants, magistrates, petits marquis, braggart soldiers, coquettes and abbés, and singing and dancing masters are, in turn, held up to ridicule'.[22] It is partly because of this detailed topicality, which today's audiences cannot follow, that the plays of the Italians in Paris have not survived as part of a modern legacy. In 1697, the authorities were at last persuaded that the company had gone too far; but the Regent brought the Italians back to Paris in 1716 after the death of Louis XIV, satisfying what must have been popular demand.

Eighteenth-Century France

After Molière's death, comedies written for the Comédie-Française had to cope with his continuing reputation: many sources show how a dramatist could either be criticized for imitating him too closely, or condemned for not writing as well as he did.[23] Plays varied considerably in terms of how specific their satirical references were; but most of them assumed, without necessarily pressing the point, that their spectators would recognize representations on stage of the French world which they too inhabited. The eighteenth century would then add variety and detail to the types of satire which were attempted. With an increase in variations on, or departures from, the classical comedy format, there was more willingness to include direct and legible lampoons of living people. However, such targets tended to be writers and thinkers, participants in cultural controversies, rather than figures of political authority. A playwright did not attempt to portray or criticize the king, or his ministers, or indeed his mistresses; and the clergy as a class remained untouchable.

Topical satire in French drama after 1700 was in fact frequent and often intense; and it was not restricted to plays which labelled themselves as comedies. The range of experimental non-tragic plays composed by Voltaire is especially interesting here, even though they have now rarely been seen as meriting revival. Voltaire set plays in ancient biblical Israel (*Saül*, pub. 1759), in classical Athens (*Socrate*, pub. 1762), and in sixteenth-century Picardy (*Le Droit du Seigneur*, pub. 1760); but such semi-fictional settings were always a veil for satire on eighteenth-century France. Each of these plays launches unmistakable (but usually non-personalized)

---

22 Scott 1990: 380. *Arlequin misantrope* is tentatively ascribed to Louis Biancolelli, son of Domenico and brother of Pierre-François.
23 This point is well summarized in Goulbourne 2006: 19–20.

attacks against the French 'Establishment' — whether legal, social, or cultural.[24] Other dramatists took a similarly varied approach. A play offered to the Comédie-Française might be turned down by the company, but end up being performed privately in an aristocratic house. In the Paris Fairs, subversive shows with overtones of Carnival were flourishing; and after 1716 Parisians could once more enjoy Italian productions at the Hôtel de Bourgogne. In all these venues there were continued doses of detailed, often ephemeral, satire.

One comedy which is less ephemeral is *Turcaret* (subtitled *Le Financier*) by Alain-René Lesage (1668–1747). The eponymous protagonist, mocked by the script, exposed and defeated by the events on stage, is a remorselessly greedy man who exploits and ruins everyone with whom he comes into contact, mostly by acting as a loan shark. He is also obsessed with concealing his low social rank. His selfish traits are sufficiently human, in the worst sense, to be detachable from a particular historical moment; and a modern revival can make fun of him, and convey the story, without significant problems.[25] Nevertheless, the play works on the surface through references to its original audience's contemporary life. It includes caricatures of lower-class Parisian tradespeople (the Comédie-Française was becoming fond of such cameo roles), and some of the funnier scenes exploit the clash of attitudes and behaviour between the capital city and the provinces. In an echo of Molière's confrontation with the *dévots*, real *financiers* took objection to *Turcaret*, perceiving that they and their normal practices were being systematically attacked. They tried unsuccessfully to bribe Lesage into withdrawing the play; and they had enough influence to make the Comédie-Française uneasy about staging it. In the end the Dauphin, son of Louis XIV, echoed the earlier attitude of his father towards *Le Tartuffe* by issuing in 1709 an express command that the French actors should perform *Turcaret* immediately.[26]

Marivaux and Beaumarchais, the major French comic dramatists of the eighteenth century, had strong opinions to pursue about the society in which they lived, but in theatrical terms they presented them in very different ways.

In essays and novels, Marivaux was a keen publicist for his views about social justice. He was concerned about how masters treated servants, in what was of course a firmly hierarchical society; and he was capable of pursuing hesitantly feminist ideas about how men treated women. These subjects are inherently dramatizable, and lie at the heart of the comedy plots which Marivaux inherited from the Italo-French tradition: they could have been explored by a critical look at comedy Lovers, at the fathers or guardians of young stage heroines, and at encounters between Pantalone and Arlecchino. In fact Marivaux's attempts to broadcast his opinions on stage did not come in classical comedy form. He composed three experimental prose dramas which have attracted some understandable interest from modern directors,

---

24 See the relevant chapters of Goulbourne 2006.
25 An English-language version with a Yorkshire slant, *For Love or Money*, was composed by Blake Morrison in 2017 for the Northern Broadsides company: it was intelligible and successful.
26 This 'Grand Dauphin' never succeeded to the throne: both he and his son, 'le Petit Dauphin', failed to outlive Louis XIV, who died in 1715. Louis XV was therefore the great-grandson of his predecessor the Sun King.

but which in the 1720s were too removed from audience expectations to succeed as stage spectacles. All three involve characters being uprooted from their normal communities to a remote island, where they have to confront their attitudes and prejudices — sometimes compelled to do this by fictional societies whose practices are proposed as utopian. In *L'Île des esclaves* [Slave Island] (1725), the exiles are not even from contemporary times but from ancient Athens: the aristocrats are indeed the owners of slaves, not the employers of servants. In *La Colonie* [The Colony] (1750), the shipwrecked protagonists flee from an unnamed 'conquered land': in their exile they are made to examine the exploitation of women by men. In these plays normal behaviour and expectations are questioned by reversing roles between classes, or between genders; but in both cases the status quo is restored at the end, with a hope that exploiters and oppressors will have learned a lesson.

Before *La Colonie* had come an even more surprising fantasy, *L'Île de la raison* [The Isle of Reason] (1727). Here a group of marooned Europeans from a range of social classes are obliged to examine the 'rationality' or otherwise of their normal behaviour. The play demands some impossible stage effects, in which characters become taller or shorter as they become more or less rational: when the text was finally published, Marivaux acknowledged that it should be read rather than staged.

When remaining within the performable comic genre Marivaux generally refrained from preaching, or from formulating explicit criticisms against the real structures of his own society. He showed sympathy with female characters, and even with masked servants like Arlequin, simply by giving them lines which examined their inner feelings and took them seriously, a dramatic strategy which in its time was devastating enough (see also Chapter 25), but which avoided topical references to Paris or France. An early example is *La Double Inconstance* [The Double Infidelity] (1723). A Prince is courting the peasant girl Silvie, to whom Arlequin is betrothed: a lady courtier, Flaminia, is recruited to redirect Arlequin's affections towards herself, while the Prince works to persuade Silvie (rather than tyrannically force her) to love him. The project is successful on both sides, and I shall show in Chapter 22 that Marivaux explores the shifting emotions involved with some care. This play, composed for the Italians, has a setting which is unnamed: we do not know what imaginary country this Prince rules. Issues about how rulers are entitled to rule thus remain generalized and abstract, kept at arm's length from the real kingdom of France and its absolutist constitution. In fact not many of Marivaux's comedies actually state that they are set in eighteenth-century France, even though most of them portray habits and assumptions familiar to their audience. They can be set in 'a country house', 'in front of the Countess's château', and around similar unspecified aristocratic residences, and once in a 'Barcelona' which is as short of recognizable local colour as is the Athens of Plautus.[27] The first Marivaux comedy which admits that it is set in Paris is *Le Jeu de l'amour et du hasard* of 1730 (see also Chapter 11). In so far as Marivaux was asking awkward questions about eighteenth-century society, he was raising issues which applied to behaviour anywhere in

---

27 The comedies referred to here are *La Surprise de l'amour* (1722); *La Fausse Suivante* (1724); and, for 'Barcelona', *Le Prince travesti* (1724).

Europe, and concentrating carefully (like Italian *commedia erudita*) on the general rather than the specific. This would not have stopped his audiences seeing that his comedies contained social criticism and satire; but they would have found it harder than did Molière's audiences to gossip about possible targeting of individuals. As well as being implicit rather than explicit, the satire was general, theoretical, even 'philosophical', as befitted an Enlightenment *philosophe*.

Then Beaumarchais incorporated in his first two Figaro plays many coruscating comments about social classes and their underlying structures, but he chose, or pretended, to set his action in Spain rather than France. The pretence fooled nobody. When Figaro queried whether noblemen were competent enough to be valets (*Le Barbier de Séville*, 1.2), it was never assumed that he was referring exclusively to Spanish hidalgos. It was French theatregoers' enduring distrust of their own legal system which was addressed by the farcical court case in *Le Mariage de Figaro* (III.12–20). The Count, pursuing his own vendetta, presides over a fatuous judge passing a sentence against Figaro. With overtones of farce or *opera buffa*, the dramatist then twists the story so that Figaro risks having to marry his own mother. The state censors, along with Louis XVI himself, knew exactly what was being implied. It is not clear whether the play's setting in an obviously fictional Spain eventually enabled it to be passed for performance, but Beaumarchais may have hoped that it might help. For *La Mère coupable*, the conclusion of the Figaro trilogy which is a *drame* rather than a *comédie*, he moved his Almaviva family to post-Revolutionary Paris, with the Count having renounced his title and adopted the rank of citizen. This back story had become politically correct in the 1790s. It allowed the play to concentrate on a plot with few satirical implications: it explores personal guilt and redemption, and portrays the machinations of an adversary who is more of a villanous individual than a comment on a social class.

In spite of their formulated unease and resentments about *ancien régime* society, neither Marivaux nor Beaumarchais offered workable visions of a political system which might replace it. In contrast to the views expressed by Danton and Napoleon about *Le Mariage de Figaro* — 'killing the nobility', and 'The Revolution in action' (see Chapter 14) — we might note a remark by Russell Goulbourne: 'Marivaux and Beaumarchais are not revolutionaries; their plays are not political manifestos. Like Molière, they knew that it is comedy's job to be against things, not for them'.[28] Ridicule can be cleansing, refreshing, certainly entertaining; but it rarely manages to replace its derided target with something more palatable. Some eighteenth-century dramatists created denouements in which immoral characters swore to reform themselves in the future: in such cases they were stepping outside the comic genre and being influenced by the new sentimental modes.

---

28 Goulbourne 2007: 152.

Goldoni and Venice

With Carlo Goldoni, the relationship between his comedies and the society which their dramatist inhabited is often close and deliberate. That society was mainly, but not exclusively, Venetian (we have seen in Chapter 13 how he set some plays in other Italian cities in order to broaden the perspective). There have been many studies of Goldoni which explore his views on the merits and failings of key social classes in Venice, ideas which developed and altered as Venice itself changed. All in all, researchers into social history and behaviour will find more hard information embedded in his comedies than in any of the other plays examined in this volume.[29]

In his earliest comedies Goldoni showed a tendency to make his characters preach on stage about moral behaviour. In *I due gemelli veneziani* [The Two Venetian Twins] (1747–48), the clever virtuous twin Tonino delivers a tirade about the desirability of marriage (II.12), and another (III.6) about how male friendship is more important than a man's love for a woman (see Chapter 24).[30] Tonino presents himself in this play as a *cortesan*. This was a Venetian word which Goldoni adapted to a concept of his own. In his first two plays he used it to promote a recommended pattern of social and moral behaviour: the *cortesan* imitates the best aspects of an aristocratic code of conduct without the arrogance of the nobility. This image was not pursued much in subsequent plays; but we have noted (see Chapter 13) how the playwright recreated the Pantalone mask for a while as a relatively sober figure — less farcically derided than it had formerly been, and linked via a new element of realism to attitudes which might be adopted by the Venetian merchant class.[31] (For a different aspect of this presentation of the mask, see Chapter 22). A major contribution to Carlo Gozzi's dislike of Goldoni's comedies was a perception that they recommended a relaxation or revision of the hierarchical boundaries between ranks in society. Gozzi's reaction may have been dictated partly by his own paranoia; but he cannot have been alone in feeling that Goldoni had a message to convey about how Venetians and other Italians should treat each other. We can relate such ideas to the French Enlightenment, having seen them approached also by Marivaux and Beaumarchais.

Nevertheless it is possible to see a strongly conservative streak in Goldoni's plays, especially as regards the marital and sexual relationships which are a central issue in standard comic plots. I shall treat this more fully in Chapter 24. For the moment we can note the late comedy entitled *Gli innamorati* [The Lovers] (1759), written in Italian and set in Milan. This depicts a rocky relationship between the engaged couple Fulgenzio and Eugenia, each of whom is determined to read into small details of the other's behaviour signs of coolness and potential infidelity. The plot works us ingeniously through a series of misunderstandings and cross purposes, which the couple's friends and family either provoke unintentionally or attempt to block. The extent to which these episodes will be amusing to a modern audience,

---

29 This is abundantly clear from the extensive study Günsberg 2001.
30 See also Andrews 1997b.
31 This subject is pursued by Guido Davico Bonino in his introduction to Goldoni 1976. The perceptions have been shared and developed by a number of other scholars.

rather than tedious and exasperating, will depend very much on how the play is directed and performed; but in his preface Goldoni assumes that we will both laugh at them and derive a salutary lesson. He hopes that young people with similar jealous tendencies will learn from this comedy how stupid it is to seek or create such suffering for themselves:

> Poor misguided youth! Wanting to torment yourselves for love! Wanting the balm to turn into poison! Utter madness. Young people, see yourselves mirrored by these Lovers I am showing you. Laugh at them, and don't make other people laugh at you.[32]

Goldoni thus takes for granted Hamlet's metaphor of a mirror, to describe the relationship between drama and the real world. He also accepts the classical definition of comedy and its social function: we laugh at the people portrayed on stage and learn not to be like them, not to be laughed at in our turn. We have observed in relation to his earlier *La locandiera* (Chapter 17) that the real dynamics of comic theatre — poised between derision and collusion, between disapproval and admiration — can in fact be more complicated; but in 1759 Goldoni claims still to be signing up to a simple definition of what his plays are doing. In *Gli innamorati* his target is a feature of human behaviour which, also in canonical fashion, can be seen as perennial rather than linked to a particular society or historical moment. In other comedies, however, he prompted Venetian and Italian audiences to pay more attention to what was happening around them in their own contemporary time and place.

---

32 'Povera gioventú sconsigliata! Volersi tormentar per amore! Voler che il balsamo si converta in veleno! Pazzie, pazzie. Specchiatevi, o giovani, in questi Innamorati ch'io vi presento; ridete di loro, e non fate che si abbia a rider di voi.'

CHAPTER 22

Characters and Masks

A 'mask' is a fixed stereotype which recurs from one play to another, largely unchanged and with the same name. Its identity is based on exterior features: visible, audible, and behavioural. In western theatre history, masks belong to the artisan theatre genre now called *commedia dell'arte*. By contrast, we may expect the more erudite or literary types of comedy to offer 'characters', who possess more individuality and more inner psychological coherence. However, in the real practice of early modern stage comedy, the difference can be blurred. The classical comic genre was launched by humanists who sought to generalize about human behaviour, and to divide people into categories or types. Looking back at this period of theatre, terms such as 'mask', 'stereotype', and 'role category' are difficult to separate clearly. This is an issue which needs examining in detail.

Facial Masks

Some ground can be cleared by summarizing what is known about the use and non-use of facial masks in performances of early modern comedy.

In ancient Greece and Rome, masks were worn by all actors in all genres of theatre. The evidence for this comes from written references, from painted vases, and from carved reliefs which decorate ancient theatre buildings (see Fig. 22.1). Early modern scholars did not have as much evidence as we do, but they had enough for the broad facts to be understood. Because Renaissance performing spaces were so different from ancient ones, humanist scholars reacted with some hesitation to the idea of masks (and also of special stage footwear — buskins for tragedy and socks for comedy). Writing in the 1590s, Angelo Ingegneri discouraged the use of masks. He thought they made actors into 'talking statues', blocked facial expression, generally looked unnatural, and interfered with clear verbal delivery.[1] It was not recognized that Greek and Roman masks were designed partly as megaphones, to help project voices in large open-air theatres.

Such opinions from the late sixteenth century may not reflect what was thought at the time of the first experiments in neo-classical comedy mounted by Ariosto,

---

[1] 'Perché elle, rendendo gl'istrioni nella ciera quasi statue parlanti, non lasciano ch'altri scorga le mutazioni dei volti, cagionate dalle variazioni degli affetti; oltra che le medesime impediscono bene spesso la pronunzia' (Ingegneri 1989: 28).

FIG. 22.1. Ancient theatrical masks: carvings on the Roman theatre in Myra, Turkey. The open mouths were designed to help the projection of the actor's voice.

Bibbiena, Machiavelli, and others. Frustratingly, we have no visual depictions of *commedia erudita* performances, only pictures of stage sets without any actors. Strictly speaking, we do not know whether the first comedies were played in masks or not, or indeed anything else about how early actors in courts and academies were dressed. In Nicola Grasso's *Eutychia* (1513), the actor delivering the prologue pretends to be embarrassed by something he has just said. 'Look,' he says, 'my face has gone all red. I'll go and fetch a different one, so you can say it wasn't me'.[2] Two of Ariosto's prologues use the word *maschera* in ways which are not so concrete, but which could raise similar questions.[3] Surviving depictions of humanist theatre productions are rare, and the first ones are surprisingly late. They are friezes on the Teatro Olimpico of 1585 in Vicenza; and they claim to show recent performances of tragedies both ancient (Sophocles's *Oedipus Tyrannus*) and modern (Giangiorgio Trissino's *Sofonisba*). The actors in these monochrome paintings (some from as late as 1596) are shown with their faces bare.

On the artisan side, Italian improvised theatre is well known to have involved masks: it was sometimes designated at the time as *commedia delle maschere*. Facial

---

2 'Vedeti com'io mi son in viso arrossito. Vado adunque a farmi un'altro, acciò diciate che non sia stato io.' (Grasso 1978). These concluding words of the 'Prologue' appear on fol. III verso of the original printing.

3 The plays in question are the first version of *La Lena*, and the second version of *Il negromante*, both performed in 1528.

FIG. 22.2. A modern copy of a *commedia dell'arte* mask: it covers only the upper part of the actor's face, leaving the mouth free for normal speaking.

masks were not worn by every stereotyped figure on the *arte* stage. The Lovers were never masked; the Elders and the male Servants always were. For the most part, female servants — *fantesche* in Italy, *soubrettes* in France — were not masked. Boastful Capitani, to judge from surviving illustrations, might or might not wear masks. Altogether, from the very beginning of the *arte*, we see a foreshadowing of the eighteenth-century distinction between 'funny roles' (*parti ridicole*, masked), and 'serious roles' (*parti serie*, unmasked). The Capitano stood on the borderline between the two categories: some denouements allowed him to marry one of the female Lovers.

Stage masks are generally felt to diminish, or limit, the vulnerable humanity of stage figures who are set up to be derided by the audience. The equivalent French tradition had been for such characters to disguise the face with flour, a practice which continued in the white-faced Pierrot and the circus clown. The name of the eponymous Barbouillé in Molière's early farce can translate as 'Doughface'. When the Italians arrived in France, there were thus two versions of a comic facial screen. Molière was lampooned for allegedly slavish imitation of Tiberio Fiorilli's

Scaramouche; but the much-reproduced picture which supports this accusation (see Fig. 8.1) shows both actors bare-faced, so Fiorilli may have stopped wearing his Italian mask. Molière is in fact documented as possessing a mastery of comic facial expression, which gave him a recognized advantage over actors whose faces were covered in flour or leather. By the late seventeenth century, in Paris, it would seem that masks on stage were Italian and bare faces were French. Perhaps, also, bare faces and more realistic costumes belonged to 'high comedy' obeying erudite *classiciste* rules, while grimaces fixed in leather, accompanied by equally fixed uniform costumes, belonged to artisan farce.

Italian *arte* troupes stuck to their masks for *parti ridicole* throughout the eighteenth century. In France they remained a badge of Italian identity. Marivaux included Arlequin and others, wearing what they usually wore, in the comedies which he wrote for the Théâtre-Italien. The Comédie-Française did not use masks, and nor did Beaumarchais. Within Italy, touring companies using the masks still proclaimed the identity of 'Italian comedy'. Goldoni wrote scenarios for the genre at the start of his career, and then included Pantalone, Arlecchino (or Truffaldino), and Brighella in many of his early scripted comedies. Under his influence, and that of other dramatists such as Pietro Chiari, types of comedy which did not involve masks were at the same time being introduced to Italy. Meanwhile companies like that of Antonio Sacchi continued to exist, in Venice and elsewhere, with actors still trained to play the old stereotypes. We have seen (in Chapter 15) that Carlo Gozzi was able to write for Sacchi's troupe in the 1760s, mixing the masked figures with bare-faced characters from fantasy and fairy-tale.

The leather masks of Italian comedy bore little relationship in their physical structure to those of Greek and Roman theatre. They did not represent full faces with open mouths, but only covered the top half of the face (see Fig. 22.2). The mouth and the lower jaw were free to deliver speech in a normal fashion, so Angelo Ingegneri's objections about poor audibility were misplaced. He made no other detailed judgements about the style and practices of *commedia dell'arte*, though he expresses a predictable lofty contempt for the theatre of the artisans to whom he referred as 'istrioni mercenari'.

Scientific Study of 'Characters'

In classical Athens, the successor to Aristotle as head of the Peripatetic school of philosophy was Theophrastus (*c.* 371–287 BCE), later called the 'father of botany' and a pioneer in the study of the natural world. Predictably, his scientific method involved taxonomy, dividing phenomena into categories and organisms into species. Correctly or not, Theophrastus was credited after his lifetime with a book which categorizes human beings according to their traits of personality and behaviour: we know it under the title of *The (Ethical) Characters* ('Ηθικοὶ χαρακτῆρες). The work contains thirty brief outlines of moral and social types, sometimes suggesting what they might typically say, and so inventing dialogue for them. It can be seen as the first surviving attempt at systematic writing on behavioural psychology. Examples of his specimens are a 'Flatterer', a 'Boastful Man', and two different versions of what we would now call a 'Miser'. None of the thirty essays depicts a woman.

Theophrastus was a contemporary, perhaps even a friend and mentor, of the Athenian playwright Menander (see the Frontispiece), whose name is associated with the rise of New Comedy. It is debatable how much connection there was between the descriptive taxonomy of the philosopher and the stereotyped creations of the dramatist; and on that subject scholars in the sixteenth century would be short of evidence. No complete play by Menander was yet available for study, though it was known in general that Plautus and Terence were transmitting New Comedy material by the process called *contaminatio* (see Chapter 21). What seems undeniable is that the existence of *The Characters* as a surviving Greek text will have supported the humanist inclination to create and collect descriptive generalizations about types of human being. This aspiration is consciously present also in neo-classical drama, comedy included.

In the early modern period, *The Characters* attracted both translators and imitators in English and in French.[4] By far the most influential work of this kind was *Les Caractères, ou les Mœurs de ce siècle* by Jean de La Bruyère (1645–1696). From a first edition of 1688, which contained 420 character-sketches or *remarques*, this compilation proceeded to an eighth edition of 1694 which raised the total to 1,120. Initially inspired by the Theophrastus original, *Les Caractères* left its model far behind. It grew into an encyclopaedic survey of contemporary society and behaviour (*Les Mœurs du siècle*), which now has a place in the canon of French literature of the classical period. Comédie-Française dramatists, and others such as Marivaux, would know La Bruyère's portraits and his accompanying moral reflections; though both Corneille and Molière died too soon to see them.

There is no room in this volume for a detailed study of how playwrights might have been influenced by, or might have borrowed from, compendia of 'Characters' by Theophrastus, La Bruyère, or others. It must simply be acknowledged that the existence of such writings helped to create an intellectual climate which favoured the registration and classification, in scientific style, of different human temperaments. People could be grouped into 'types', and they could be identified by speech and behaviour which were also 'typical'. The work of both dramatists and actors could be influenced — or, as they would have seen it, aided — by this approach to psychology.

Stock Characters and Stock Material

In sixteenth-century Italy, a disproportionate influence on the development of comic drama was provided by the small city republic of Siena. The comedies created and published by its Accademia degli Intronati, starting with *Gl'ingannati*, created a stock of theatergrams which then recurred in Italian plays and scenarios for decades afterwards: the play was also influential abroad. The Academy was

---

[4] English imitations include Joseph Hall's *Characters of Vertues and Vices* (1608), Sir Thomas Overbury's *Characters* (1614–16), and Bishop Earle's *Essayes and Characters* (1628).

especially innovative in the sympathetic attention which its plots paid to the predicaments and emotions of female characters (see Chapter 24).[5]

It has been established by the researches of Daniele Seragnoli that the Intronati composed their scripts collectively, with different members responsible for successive stages of drafting.[6] However, a presiding figure, whom we could call the Academy's guru, was the humanist polymath bishop Alessandro Piccolomini (1508–1579). Two Intronati plays — *Amor costante* [Constant Love] (1540) and *Alessandro* (1545) — were attributed to him as author when they were printed. Piccolomini's wide-ranging interests predictably included dramaturgy and the practicalities of mounting stage performances: he translated Aristotle's *Poetics*, with a commentary. He has a lunar crater named after him, because he was also an astronomer, one of his major works being entitled *La sfera del mondo* [The Sphere of the World] (1561). With a level of irrelevance which is hard to explain, it was in the dedication to later editions of this volume that he told a friend about a project he was pursuing, of which no other details or documents have survived. In modern terms, Piccolomini was compiling a database of speeches and scenes which could be used in comic drama. Its essence is explained in the following extract:

> First of all I had listed and described most of the types of person who can be, or normally are, represented in comedies, according to those distinctions which are usually found for various reasons in the ordinary life of men: that is to say, according to blood relationships, like fathers, sons, brothers, nephews and such like; according to diversity of fortune, such as rich and poor, servants and masters; of age, such as old, young and children; of profession, such as lawyers, doctors, soldiers, pedants, parasites, whores, bawds, merchants, and so on; of emotional state, such as angry, amorous, fearful, bold, confident, desperate, and so on; of habit of mind, such as miserly, prodigal, just, prudent, foolish, jealous, fickle, boastful, arrogant, cowardly, and other such; and in this way I was making a survey of all those types of character and background which can represent in comedies the ordinary life of men. Now, to each one of these characters I had planned to attach first of all sets of monologue scenes, which although all different from one another would all be adjusted to the decorum and quality of the people represented. And then, linking and coupling these characters in various ways, as it were father with son, master with servant, servant with servant, lover with beloved, procurer with procured [...]. I had planned to create various scenes for each of these couples, having an eye always to decorum, with verisimilitude in relation to the persons represented; and to adapt the scenes to various concepts and different inventions, so that they could be applied to many different stories, with just small additions and omissions which would be relevant to whatever story was being handled.[7]

Piccolomini's erudite approach to dramatic composition strikingly resembles the artisan methods of the professional actors who, around the year 1561, were becoming established on the Italian scene. We know that individual *arte* actors accumulated

---

5   See also Andrews 2010; and for *Gl'ingannati* in particular, Andrews 2008: xxxv.
6   Seragnoli 1980: passim.
7   Alessandro Piccolomini, dedicatory letter to *La sfera del mondo* (Venice: Varisco, 1561). The whole Italian text of the letter is reproduced in Seragnoli 1980: 98–100.

in their personal repertoire precisely the kind of material suggested in the above extract. The difference is that Piccolomini proposed to do it for every type of role which he could imagine being useful, rather than compose a *libro generico* for just one performer. In both cases the underlying assumption is that speeches and dialogues were recyclable — that the same situations would recur in different comedies, and so the same verbal text could be used repeatedly with 'small additions and omissions which would be relevant to whatever story was being handled' ('con levar solo o aggiungere qualche cosetta, che potesse fare a proposito di quella favola che si avesse per le mani'). Was this aristocratic playwright imitating the professionals? It is hard to believe that he would admit such a thing, given the huge social prejudices which separated him from 'mercenary' actors. Alternatively, were Pantalone, Zani, and Isabella learning from Piccolomini, or from the teamwork methods of his Intronati Academy? That is less inherently implausible, granted the strong desire of the best professional troupes to attain upward cultural and social mobility; but there is no evidence for it. The date of 1561 leaves the question wide open: we have no way of determining just how soon the creation of actors' personal repertoires became established in the craft of *commedia dell'arte*. But Piccolomini's account suggests that the compositional practices which I call 'modular dramaturgy' (see Chapter 19) were beginning also to underpin playwriting in academies and courts. Indeed, a survey of the plots of comedies printed in the second half of the sixteenth century makes it abundantly clear how often particular stories and situations were liable to recur.[8] Professor Louise George Clubb had every reason to coin the now indispensable term 'theatergram', to draw attention to such reusable units of character, relationship, and storyline.[9]

It is in fact hard to determine whether Piccolomini's project was intended to be useful for actors, or for dramatists, or to be an academic exercise. What is relevant here is that his assembly of material was based on the 'types of person who can be, or normally are, represented in comedies'. We can note in passing that the only female categories listed are whores and bawds. His material was to be categorized, in his order of presentation, by family status, social status, age, profession, 'emotional state' ('qualità di affetti'), and 'habit of mind' ('abito d'animo') — this last expression relating to what we would call 'temperament' or indeed 'character'. His use of the concept of *decoro*, and the adjective *verisimile*, reflects how those terms were applied in literary theory based on Aristotle and Horace. The Latin word *decorum* designated what was 'proper' or 'suitable', in several senses. It came to define what was decent and respectable, and so permitted on stage; but its primary meaning was a demand that a fictional character should speak and behave in a manner which conformed with, and expressed, the sort of person he or she was supposed to be. 'Decorum' overlapped with 'verisimilitude', with French *vraisemblance*; and in the extract above we see both words used in the same sentence.

---

8   Such a survey can be conducted by reading through the summaries in Mango 1966. Plot recyclings are particularly evident in plays by Florentine dramatists. Mango's 181 listed comedies represent about two-thirds of those which are now known to have been printed.
9   Clubb 1989: passim.

Already in 1561 Piccolomini was signalling a tendency for stage comedies to deploy what we now call 'stock characters', and a desire to accumulate for them equally 'stock' material in terms of speeches and dialogues. His project shows a desire to classify human beings into groups or types, as Theophrastus had done in antiquity.

I suggest that there may be some parallels with Italian improvised masks; but in addition, Piccolomini's approach presages some later professional practice with regard to scripted theatre, especially that of the Comédie-Française. For centuries after its foundation in 1680, the contracts of employment favoured by that company involved broad classifications of roles, assigned to its performers according to talent and personality but also according to age. Each actor worked under a named role category or *emploi*, designated by terms such as *jeune premier/ première, père noble, duègne, soubrette* etc. Such divisions have existed informally in many theatre cultures in many countries; but in the Comédie-Française they were bureaucratized and written into the employment system. They lasted well into the twentieth century. In a lecture given by a French academic in 1962, I heard a vivid description of how an ageing actor might be distressed and traumatized by the company's collective decision that he should be moved from *jeune premier* roles to the category of *pères nobles*.[10]

How far did such stereotypes, created by and for actors, influence the approach of comic dramatists who flourished after Alessandro Piccolomini? The answer no doubt varied widely among individuals; but any playwright who was composing for professional companies would have been aware of how roles were distributed. Those who wrote for the Comédie-Française are unlikely to have used, or confessed to using, a data-bank of stock material such as Piccolomini was proposing. They were seeking a level of originality; and they would have been motivated partly by the desire to differentiate themselves from the rival Italian practice which involved fixed masks. Nevertheless, in most cultures, including our own, commercially marketed drama thrives on clichés. When composing speeches and dialogues, even Molière, Marivaux, Goldoni, and Beaumarchais will have been making some use of words which everyone expected to hear spoken — by lovers male and female, by servants, by housewives, by fathers of families, by lawyers (honest or corrupt), and by a range of other human types regularly involved in comic plots.

Italian Masked Stereotypes

The characteristic of a 'mask', in Italian improvised theatre, is that its stage personality already exists, and is already familiar, before a play is devised or performed. The mask often dictates, or overrides, the details of the story being dramatized. Pantalone, Zani, Isabella, and the rest had back stories already constructed in the minds of their public. In any given performance, the things which they had done and said before, on 'this' stage and other stages, dictated what audiences expected of them, and took precedence over any antefact to the plot currently being narrated. This was just as true of the unmasked Lovers as it was of the more clownish

---

10 In 2019, the French Wikipedia entry <https://fr.wikipedia.org/wiki/Emploi(théâtre)> listed twenty-eight different role categories.

parti ridicole. The roles played by stars such as Isabella Andreini, and by her male counterparts taking names like Flavio and Orazio, have left less of an impression on subsequent theatre history than Pantalone and Arlecchino. This is because their names were not so often transferred from one generation to another, and because they impress themselves less on posterity through grotesque visual inventions. Evidence suggests, however, that actors of both sexes in Lovers' roles had followings of adoring fans, just as has been the case in the twentieth and twenty-first centuries for film stars who take similar romantic parts. Fans have pre-conceived images of their idols, and have expectations of how they should look, speak, and behave (on stage or on screen) to maintain the personality which makes them so popular. Isabella and Orazio were 'unmasked masks', recognizable to the theatregoers of their day: they inhabited the same stage world as Arlecchino, the Dottore, and the Capitano. Each of them possessed an identifiable personal style and virtuoso skills which distinguished them from their competitors, just as Greta Garbo was firmly different from Barbara Stanwyck or Katharine Hepburn.

The inner psychology of Italian stage masks was fluid, or in a sense non-existent. As has been said of figures in myth and religion, they possess attributes rather than psychology.[11] They were defined as much by their outside appearance, costume, and behavioural style as by a coherent set of attitudes and emotions. Pantalone was expected to be both miserly and lustful; but the relative importance of those two traits varied according to the story being performed. Equally variable was the nature of his attachment to his children, which the plot might oblige to be more or less possessive and autocratic, more or less genuinely affectionate. In Flaminio Scala's scenarios, the servant Pedrolino appears in forty-nine out of the fifty scenarios, including all but one of those which are not comedies. He is sometimes loyal to his employer, sometimes extremely treacherous; sometimes sentimental, sometimes brutally mocking; he can also swing in a single play from being courageous to being cowardly. It was simply required that he should do and say everything in a recognizably 'Pedrolino' manner: more important than psychological consistency were his voice, his characteristic dialect, and his physical style. This approach was shared later by the protagonists of early film comedy, both human and animated. Charlie Chaplin's 'tramp', who is not always a tramp, also alternates rapidly between bravery and cowardice, but is held together by his costume, appearance, and mannerisms. Donald Duck is always irascible, because that is one of his attributes; but he fluctuates wildly in respect of his desires, attachments, and emotions.

Analogies between Italian masks and cartoon cinema can be extended further. The more clownish roles of *commedia dell'arte* took on a life of their own in the popular imagination, to the extent that images of them could be used in contexts outside the theatre and outside individual stories. Pictures of Arlecchino, Pantalone, and the rest were used in commercial products such as gaming boards and almanacs: the assumption was that purchasers knew who these characters were, and enjoyed being reminded of them. There are even some sequences of drawings which do

---

11 An observation borrowed from A. S. Byatt, writing about mythology in a *Guardian* review, 6 August 2011.

seem to recount theatrical plots, almost analogous to modern cartoon strips. The most famous example, the *Recueil Fossard*, much reproduced and discussed by modern scholars, is dated as early as 1577.[12] This set of woodcuts was not designed for reproduction and sale; but elsewhere the Italian masks were depicted and exploited commercially in much the same way in which figures from cartoon film (created by Disney and by other firms) have been marketed since the mid-twentieth century. The technologies of mass production were less potent in the 1600s; but allowing for that difference of scale we could say that the figure of Arlecchino/ Harlequin was being reproduced in diverse contexts, across national boundaries, just as Mickey Mouse, or Tom and Jerry, have been more recently. An impresssion of Harlequin's character might be known even to people who could never visit a theatre. The extent to which existing folk traditions influenced the creation of these figures is less clear than some scholars claim; but it is certain that, once they had taken shape, the theatrical masks made their own entry into popular culture and perhaps even into folklore.

When the Italian comedy took root in France, the masks became as familiar there as they were back home, and developed independent versions of themselves. Flaminio Scala's Pedrolino, 'little Peter', was a tricky energetic Zani-type mask developed by the Modenese actor Giovanni Pellesini (1526-c. 1615). The French for 'little Peter' would be 'Pierrot'; but we associate that name with a white (flour-covered) round face and a costume with a white ruff, a mask popularized by the actor Giuseppe Geratoni. In the scripts of the Ancien Théâtre-Italien his main characteristic is comic stupidity. The romantic childlike pathos of the 'Pierrot Lunaire' image is a nineteenth-century creation: images of this Pierrot, also called Gilles, had been inherited from the early eighteenth century via Watteau and other illustrators. It is hard to trace him back to Italy — either in his physical appearance and costume, or in the sentimental character which later became attached to him — but Pierrot was a French mask created by Italian performance methodology. There is an unbroken line of descent to English 'Pierrot shows' of the early twentieth century, but that history lies outside our present scope.

Character Names

Names such as Zani, Pantalone, Dottor Graziano, Franceschina, Arlecchino, and Pierrot were thus attached to stage figures who existed independently of single plays, because they were constantly redeployed in new ones. To begin with, the name of each mask may have been associated with a single actor. Even early names for Lovers, such as Isabella, Flavio, and Lelio, tended for a while to evoke a particular performer — in those three cases, Isabella Andreini, Flaminio Scala, and Giovan Battista Andreini. Later, some French actors created individual masks of their own, the most notable being Jodelet (Julien Bedeau, see Chapter 6), and

---

12   See the numerous illustrations in Katritzky 2006. A gaming board appears as her plate 38, and illustrations from monthly almanacs as plates 64–67. The *Recueil Fossard* is reproduced in, among other places, including studies of the *commedia dell'arte*: Duchartre 1929 and Molinari 1985. See also Katritzky 1989.

Sganarelle who was entirely invented and performed by Molière. The Italian *parti ridicole*, however, were robust and popular enough to survive the disappearance of their original performers: in Italy and in France, over more than two centuries, actors without number incarnated the roles of Pantalone, Arlecchino/ Arlequin and Dottor Graziano, for audiences in equally innumerable places. On the French side, we have noted (see Chapter 10) the long survival of the servant role Crispin, performed by the Poisson father and son. For the stage profession, and for the theatregoing public, a mask was identified quite sufficiently by its name. That name carried with it a series of automatic expectations regarding exterior personality, behaviour, and costume; and within Italy, always very importantly, also regarding dialect or linguistic register.

Even outside the Italian masked tradition, certain names for characters in comedy had a tendency to recur, though this is less true of *commedia erudita* scripts of the sixteenth century. In French comedies, starting particularly with Pierre Corneille, there was a vogue for invented names based loosely on the Greek language, a clearly 'classical' choice which had a generalizing feel, and put the characters at a distance from contingent social reality. Molière and others offer many elderly fathers named Géronte (from the Greek γέρον, 'old'), and many young lovers called Dorante, Éraste, Cléante/ Cléonte, Léandre, beside the more French-sounding Valère. This 'Hellenic' fashion appears in scripts for the Comédie-Française both before and after 1700. Female names might sometimes follow the same trend, but were more often recognizably French — Élise, Julie, Lisette — though the names Angélique and Isabelle suggest influence from, or overlap with, an Italian tradition. In the eighteenth century, Marivaux made some use of the Greek-style names, though he was often writing for Italian performers who already possessed stage names and personalities. He called some of his aristocratic characters simply 'La Comtesse', 'Le Prince', or 'Le Chevalier', with no personal names at all. In Italy, Goldoni's early comedies offer a confusing number of heroines named Rosaura — for example *La donna di garbo* [The Well-behaved Lady] (1743), *I due gemelli veneziani* (1747), *La vedova scaltra* [The Crafty Widow] (1748). All these roles were written for the same actress, Teodora Medebach, who used Rosaura as her stage name. Later, as he moved away from stock repertory and from the influence of masks, he sought more variety in his nomenclature. Beaumarchais's Figaro plays cannot enter this survey, because all three of them deal explicitly with the same central characters at successive stages of their lives.

In general, the recurrence of names may sometimes have been associated with the recurrence of identifiable performers; but it also suggests a continued humanist search for the 'typical', for repeated characteristics in more or less repeated roles. Even outside *commedia dell'arte*, it implies a level of stereotyping which was associated with the division of parts into *emplois*, and may sometimes not have been far from the rigidity associated with masks.

Care was generally taken to avoid giving offence to real people or families. Characters with plausible surnames are relatively rare in comic scripts. In plays which aim at any level of realism, surnames are avoided altogether. Implausible surnames, bearing a satiric edge, were more common, especially in more farcical

French compositions, and most of all in the Théâtre-Italien. An easy laugh could always be raised by a name beginning with *Sot-*, meaning 'fool' or 'idiot': Monsieur and Madame De Sotenville [Foolintown] are the snooty parents-in-law in Molière's *George Dandin* (1668). (This was of course also a regular practice in English Restoration comedy: we can remember Pinchwife, Horner, Mrs Loveit, and Sir Fopling Flutter.) The lower classes had been given comically allusive names from early *commedia erudita* onwards: *Gl'ingannati* has servants called Spela [Pluck], Scatizza [Stoke], Crivello [Sieve], and Stragualcia [Squint].

Masks and Characters

The masks of *commedia dell'arte* have exercised a fascination over some theatregoers and practitioners ever since they were presented and discussed by nineteenth-century French scholars such as Maurice Sand. They have been adapted in different artistic media — visual arts, opera and ballet, as well as spoken drama — to create mysterious worlds of grotesque fantasy. Sometimes they have been depicted sentimentally or to express cheerful subversion; but at other times in less comforting vein, particularly when they are presented as puppet-like figures manipulated from outside, or condemned without any choice to predictable emotions and actions.[13] More recently, the theory and practice of 'improvisation' in theatre training has used modern visions of *arte* masks as a starting-point for acting techniques which remain influential, the best-known practitioner being Jacques Lecoq (1921–1999) in Paris. Both audiences and drama students can find this approach to theatre joyous and liberating, in ways which may recall the function I attributed in Chapter 10 to the Théâtre-Italien: a therapeutic form of game-playing which turns its back on adult social behaviour and produces insights of its own.[14] These performance methods all began essentially in the twentieth century, and they have their own rationale and their own virtues. In relation to the early modern theatre discussed in this book, the extent to which they are or were 'authentic' (or 'historically informed', to use the less pretentious term now preferred by musicians) is a complex issue which cannot be pursued here. It must be pointed out, though, that *commedia dell'arte* improvisation, as I have described it particularly in Chapter 19, was a disciplined craft skill, based on preparation and careful memorization of repertoire material. It was very different from the imaginative challenges posed by 'improv' in modern drama schools — and even more different from recent theories and techniques of 'Applied Improvisation'.[15]

---

13 The example which springs to mind is the Stravinsky ballet *Petrushka* of 1910–11. A group of twentieth-century Italian dramatists, now known as the *grotteschi*, explored the notion that human beings are constrained by socially-imposed masks. They foreshadowed the drama of Luigi Pirandello.
14 From direct experience, I can refer to enjoyable performances in the 1980s by Carlo Boso's TAG Teatro company; and more recently to workshop sessions conducted in England by Ludovico Nolfi. Ferruccio Soleri (b. 1929) has made a prestigious career as Arlecchino, with the Piccolo Teatro di Milano. A typical discussion in English of relevant methodology is Grantham 2000. For more theoretical approaches, see Robbins Dudeck and McClure 2018.
15 A similar opinion to mine is offered in more detail by Schmitt 2020: 91–94. The essays in Balme, Vescovo & Vianello 2018 emphasize the differences between the myths and imitations of

We cannot be fully sure, then, how far modern reconstructions of *arte* masked figures are accurate in detail. Some of the details to be imitated will in any case have changed many times over the period 1540–1760 and in venues as different as Munich, Venice, Naples, and Paris. At all events, the essential features of a mask in any given time and place included fixity and predictability — even though performers were constantly seeking for novelty and comic surprise in their detailed material. In fact predictablility constituted part of their appeal: spectators went to see Pedrolino, Isabella, and Arlecchino (or Arlequin) because they knew what to expect and knew that they liked it. The same could be said of Charlie Chaplin and Buster Keaton.

The stories which were dramatized by *commedia dell'arte* companies were adapted to accommodate the fixed characteristics and popular routines of members of the troupe. In some cases, indeed, the insertion of familiar masks would dictate the tone of the story. Day 18 of Flaminio Scala's scenarios published in 1611 is entitled *Li tragici successi* [The Tragic Events]: it presents a story of lovers from feuding families, which has similarities to the story of Romeo and Giulietta as narrated by Matteo Bandello and dramatized by William Shakespeare. As the title suggests, and despite being labelled as a comedy, this drama contains episodes of tension and menace: two sets of lovers, rather than just one couple, are threatened with death or disaster before they are rescued and a happy ending is engineered. In fully scripted form, the show would have been classed as a *commedia grave*. The heads of the feuding families, however, are not called Montague and Capulet (or Montecchi and Capuleti), but Pantalone and Dottor Graziano. There is just one street confrontation between them, described in 1.6: 'Pantalone with lanterns lit, sees Graziano armed; they parade in front of each other in tough-guy style and then insult each other; and all exit'.[16] The fact that we are dealing with those two familiar masks would force this scene to be comic, despite the loftier tones sought by other parts of the play. Pantalone and the Dottore were not associated with noble dignity. Their costumes and postures, and their caricature Venetian and Bolognese dialects, would convey their quarrel in a manner impossible to take seriously.

In *commedia erudita*, character depended on plot. If the story was one in which a servant outwitted a master, then the servant was shrewd and the master was stupid; if on the other hand the attempted trick was going to fail, then the audience would laugh at the servant's incompetence. If an old father was lusting after someone unsuitable, then his attitude to his wife was irritated and dismissive; but if at the same time his wife was being pursued by younger men, his possessive patriarchal jealousy was unlimited and his rage hilarious. At other times (as will be seen in my next chapter) the father would simply be stereotypically obsessed with his family honour, which depended on the behaviour of his womenfolk, and so his actions and emotions would be dictated by what the dramatist had decided those women would

---

commedia dell'arte and its historical reality: see in particular the contribution of Piermario Vescovo (Vescovo 2018).

16 Andrews 2008: 108; Scala 1976: I, 189: 'Pantalone con lanterne accese, vede Graziano armato; fanno spasseggiate da bravo poi si dicono villanie; e tutti via'.

do. A young lover would express passionate sentiments towards his chosen partner, using rhetoric which proclaimed that if he could not win her, he would rather die. The story might reward him with success; but if it turned out that the girl was after all his long-lost sister, then his attitude changed in an instant. A serving maid might be affectionately loyal to her mistress... or not, depending on whether she was being bribed, or whether the heroine's desires and interests clashed with her own. The theatergrams of plot which *commedia erudita* adopted became increasingly repetitive and predictable, and the limited range of situations curtailed the available range of responses, emotions, and temperaments. By the end of the sixteenth century, as far as we can judge, scripted comedies were losing their edge and their interest precisely for this reason. The masks of improvised plays were equally predictable, but they maintained their appeal for longer — perhaps because of a performance style which was more anarchic, energetic and scurrilous; perhaps because their audiences accepted the game and demanded less novelty.

The classical comic genre's move from Italy to France may therefore have rescued it from terminal decline. From Pierre Corneille onwards (as I argued in Chapter 21), stage comedy became more penetrating and more reflective of recognizable contemporary society. It was the French, moreover, who developed both the practice and the theoretical label of 'comedy of character', an early obvious example being Corneille's *Le Menteur* [The Liar] (1643). French playwrights increasingly sought to make character dictate plot rather than vice versa. Close analysis of individual plays may now suggest that this attempted reversal was often cosmetic: in the end the entertainment still depended on the creation and release of comic tension, on dramatic personae who first faced apparently insoluble problems and then, under the author's control, found relief from them in the denouement. If a plot structure does not hold the public and keep it guessing, then a comedy is likely to fail. There was nevertheless an increasing tendency for French comedy titles to be psychological or behavioural definitions of their protagonists. We see this from Corneille's Liar and Molière's Imaginary Invalid, via Gamblers of both sexes (*Joueurs* and *Joueuses*) treated by Dufresny and Regnard, to the Babbler and the Prude investigated by Voltaire (*L'Indiscret*, 1725; *La Prude*, 1739). In Italy, Goldoni explicitly proclaimed the virtues of 'commedie di carattere'. His numerous defining titles range from a Prudent Man and a Crafty Widow (*L'uomo prudente* and *La vedova scaltra*, both 1748), via a Gambler and a True Friend (*Il giuocatore* and *Il vero amico*, both 1751), through to a display team of four Yokels (*I rusteghi*, 1760) and the incurably bad-tempered *Sior Todero brontolon* (1762). It is then not surprising that in Paris, writing in French, he came up with a Gruff Do-Gooder (*Le Bourru bienfaisant*, 1771) and an Ostentatious Miser (*L'Avare fastueux*, 1776). It made sense for dramatic investigations of character, which often claimed the status of philosophical inquiry, eventually to pursue theses about contradictory impulses in a single person.

Many historians of European literature and drama have perceived a steady increase in writers' ability to endow participants in fictional stories with levels of 'inner life', and for readers or spectators to relate to them with 'empathy'. Depending on the interests and knowledge of the relevant scholar, different moments and causes have been identified for the launch of this tendency; and it has been traced and described in different ways in respect of literary fiction and of drama.[17] Debates may continue over details, precedence, and chronology; but it is difficult not to recognize the existence of such a long-term trend, starting somewhere in the early modern period and developing through Romanticism into modernity. In fact classical stage comedy was resistant to such developments: it was not naturally driven towards intimate revelations from characters who seek audience sympathy. Laughter was (and is) more easily provoked by depicting human beings from the outside, by an approach which is mocking, judgemental, and behaviouristic. Molière's Miser, Harpagon, may have been presented in modern times (by critics and by stage directors) as a tortured soul who might attract human sympathy, but I would argue that this approach is anachronistic, that it deploys a type of sensibility which would never have occurred to Molière or to his audience, and that the soliloquy in IV.7 of *L'Avare* aimed to provoke nothing but derisive laughter.[18] Nevertheless, after the turn of the eighteenth century, the most innovative and influential French and Italian comic dramatists did begin to analyse the private feelings of their characters, and did invite from the spectator a new balance between mockery and sympathy. They were inevitably affected by cultural trends around them: the cult of *sensibilité*; the rise of *comédie larmoyante* and *drame sérieux*; and (as I shall argue in my final chapter) the rise of the prose novel. We can demonstrate the point here by offering two examples from after 1700, in each of which a playwright pushed a mask in the direction of becoming a character.

I have suggested in Chapter 10 that in the Parisian Théâtre-Italien the Arlequin mask was slowly stripped of its specifically Italian characteristics, and laid open to whatever personality traits, and whatever passing impersonations, his actor and his dramatist chose to deploy. When a new Arlequin, 'Thomassin' Visentini, was recruited to the revived company in 1716, he was faced with some complex fresh dimensions offered by the equally new playwright Marivaux. The fixed exterior mask was made to acquire and explore some fine-tuned inner emotions. This started in 1720 with *Arlequin poli par l'amour* (summarized in Chapter 11); but an even better sign of the development came in 1723 with *La Double inconstance* (see Chapter 21). In a plot framework which contains elements of fairy-tale, Arlequin and his fiancée Sylvia are abducted by the Prince of their unnamed land, and removed from their rustic village to a luxurious palace. The Prince has fallen in love with Sylvia, but is prevented by his own laws from taking her by force. He mounts a campaign to inveigle both the young lovers into changing their affections, thus producing the 'double infidelity' of the play's title. Sylvia is slowly persuaded to accept him, as he woos her using an incognito recalling Dandini in the Cinderella story. In parallel, Arlequin falls for the court lady Flaminia, who starts by working as her Prince's

---

17 Drawing on preceding scholarship, Chapter 14 of Shapiro 2005 suggests that the 'inward' characteristics of Hamlet's soliloquies are partly inspired by the *Essais* of Montaigne. A similar seminal influence is attributed to Cervantes's *Don Quixote* by Egginton 2016. Egginton refers to a body of critical writing which (in n. 15 on p. 189) he calls 'empathy theory'.
18 This is what the speech actually says it has done: 'Ils me regardent tous et se mettent à rire'. I refer again to Andrews 2006: esp. 129–31.

FIG. 22.3. In Goldoni's *L'amor paterno*, characters in fashionable contemporary clothes are accompanied by Pantalone, in his traditional costume dating back to the sixteenth century. The play was written for the Italian company in Paris, after Goldoni left Venice in 1762.

agent, but decides anyway that she is genuinely attracted to the masked country bumpkin.

Marivaux allows Arlequin to retain some of his traditional stereotyped behaviour. He has moments of noisily childish weeping (one of Visentini's specialist *lazzi*); he uses his slapstick to beat Trivelin, who has been assigned to him as an unwanted valet; and he shows his usual weakness for good food and wine, though stopping short of the animal-like gluttony which characterized earlier Arlecchini. However in other crucial scenes — the ones which develop his side of the plot — he becomes more intelligent and more emotionally articulate than had been normal for the mask. On the one hand (as noted in Chapter 21), it is he who expresses the vein of social satire which Marivaux injects into the comedy: he asks innocent questions, which logically undermine the values of eighteenth-century aristocracy.[19] More personally, Arlequin is guided by his dramatist through a succession of ambivalent feelings regarding his first love Silvia and her replacement by Flaminia. He conveys those feelings in the precise revelatory language of which Marivaux was a master. Most of all, he moves through stages of self-deception in which he fails to recognize what his sentiments really are, mistaking the beginnings of his attachment to Flaminia for mere comradeship. This lack of self-awareness is plausible, and transcends the puppet-like characteristics of a figure constrained by a leather mask. Nevertheless, Visentini was still wearing the mask, in this as in all his other appearances for Marivaux. The exact tone and effect of his performance in 1723 can now only be dimly guessed at. It is clear, though, that some degree of movement from 'mask' to 'character' was involved in this comedy, and it continued in others by the same author.

I have also mentioned (in Chapters 13 and 21) how in eighteenth-century Venice Goldoni decided to humanize, or to make more complex, the mask of Pantalone which was one of the bedrock components of 'Italian comedy'. A striking sign of this transformation comes early in his career, in the short comedy which is being rehearsed by a troupe of semi-fictitious actors in the manifesto play *Il teatro comico* of 1750. It is entitled *Il padre rivale del figlio* [The Father as Rival to his Son], and because it is a play within a play, its content has rarely been analysed separately. As the title indicates, Pantalone and his son Florindo are in love with the same young woman: Rosaura (yet another use of this name by Goldoni), daughter of Dottor Graziano. As we would expect in classical comedy, it is Florindo who marries her; and this predictable outcome is supported by the heroine's father, who is less grotesque and more rational here than we expect the Dottore mask to be. The Dottore in fact urges Pantalone to accept the outcome with dignity, and to behave as 'an honest, wise and prudent man' ('da uomo onesto, da uomo savio e prudente'). Pantalone's response to this is worth quoting in full:

---

19   Social criticisms of this sort, based on a false naïvety, were fashionable at the time, as is shown by other plays included in Briasson's multi-volume *Nouveau Théâtre italien* (1718–25). One can cite two plays by Louis François Delisle de la Drevetière, both performed in the 1720s: *Arlequin sauvage* (*Nouveau Théâtre italien* 1733: II) and *Timon le misanthrope* (III). *La Double inconstance* itself was printed in volume III.

PANTALONE Yes, all right, I'm a gentleman, I'm a man of honour, I am fond of this girl, and I want to make an effort to demonstrate the love I feel for her. Florindo will marry your daughter; but because I've looked at her with desire, and can't forget her, I don't want to put myself at risk by having her in my house and living in a permanent hell. Florindo, my son, may Heaven bless you. Marry Miss Rosaura, because that's what she deserves, and make your home with her and with her father for as long as I live; and I shall make over to you an honest and sufficient allowance. Daughter-in-law, since you couldn't love me, then love my son. Treat him with love and kindness, and forgive the weakness of an old man who was dazzled by your good character even more than by your beauty. [...] Ah, my heart is choked, I can't manage any more! (*He exits.*)[20]

Rosaura reacts with compassion: 'Poor father, I'm sorry for him' ('Povero padre, mi fa pietà').

There is a massive distance between the pathos with which Pantalone is presented here and the derisive mockery which would have been directed at the mask during a similar denouement in a seventeenth-century *arte* scenario. Pantalone is trying to learn the lessons of his own unsuitable behaviour, to express those lessons to himself and to interiorize them. He is articulating the need first to recognize his own feelings, and then to repress and reject them. He is going to do things which he does not want to do, because he recognizes that they are correct. The rhetoric of his speech belongs more to a French *drame sérieux* than to a *commedia dell'arte* performance. Goldoni will have known that he was operating a quiet revolution, turning a masked figure of fun into a character with whom an audience might seek some empathy.

In plays by Marivaux and Goldoni, there is what we now see as a strange mixture of attempts at social realism and the continued use of masked stage figures, comfortably familiar to the audience but with roots in the past and in theatrical fantasy (see Fig. 22.3). The resulting visual, tonal, and linguistic incongruities seem to have been comfortably accepted by audiences.

---

20 'PANTALONE 'Sí ben, son un galantomo, son un omo d'onor, voggio ben a sta putta, e voggio far un sforzo per demostrarghe l'amor che ghe porto. Florindo sposerà vostra fia, ma perché vostra fia l'ho vardada con qualche passion, e no me la posso desmenteghar, no voggio metterme a rischio, avendola in casa, de viver continuamente all'inferno. Florindo, fio mio, el cielo te benediga. Sposa siora Rosaura, che la lo merita, e resta in casa con ela e co so sior pare, fina che vivo mi; e te passerò un onesto e comodo trattamento. Niora, za che no m'avé volesto ben a mi, voggié ben a mio fio. Trattélo con amor e con carità, e compatí le debolezze de un povero vecchio, orbà piú dal vostro merito, che dalle vostre bellezze. Dottor caro, vegní da mi, che metteremo in carta ogni cossa. Se ve bisogna roba, bezzi, son qua. Spenderò, farò tutto, ma in sta casa no ghe vegno mai piú. Oimè! gh'ho el cuor ingroppà, me sento che no posso piú. (*Parte.*)' (Goldoni, *Il teatro comico*, III.7).

CHAPTER 23

Children and Parents

> Bad relations between fathers and sons were, alas, not uncommon. Comedy took them for granted. — A. R. Burn[1]

This statement was made with regard to the period in ancient Athens which is most often described as 'classical': the age of Pericles, and then of Aristophanes, leading up to the Peloponnesian War. It applies equally well to early modern Europe.

We can start with an exemplary scene of family confrontation. It exposes a father-son rivalry like the one Goldoni used in 1750, but it was composed more than a century before. In an early scene of a comedy, Pantalone consults his son Tiburzio on questions of marriage. First the two of them agree comfortably (in a scene of elastic repetition, going through a list) about the qualities which a woman should possess if she is to be mistress of a household. Then Pantalone speaks of the good character of Olimpia, daughter of their neighbour Coviello. Tiburzio, who is in love with Olimpia, cannot believe his luck; and he enthusiastically endorses that lady's suitability to become, in his father's words, 'wife of one of us, and authority over both of us'.[2] Dottor Graziano, present at this conversation, is entrusted by Pantalone to approach Coviello as a go-between. Again, Tiburzio is in full agreement, until the following speech from Pantalone:

> PANTALONE And if Coviello raises any difficulty, because I'm old, just advise him that it is only right for the man to be a bit older than his wife. Because where there are years, there is wisdom; and where there is wisdom there is true authority.[3]

We in the audience have been expecting this all along. Pantalone has made his desires clear in a previous scene, and we have been anticipating the moment when his son will discover the truth. Tiburzio is of course shocked and outraged. A quarrel immediately follows. (This is also structured in repetitive elastic units: Graziano agrees alternately with both sides.) Tiburzio is banished from his father's house; and the basis is set up for a predictable story-line, in which we know who will win the contest but look forward to seeing how it will happen.

---

1   Burn 1966: 256.
2   In Venetian: 'moier de un, e governatrice de do'.
3   'PANTALONE: E se Coviello facesse quanche difficultae per esser mi vecchio, conseiello, che xe dover che l'huomo tenga qualche anno d'avanzo, perche dove xe i anni, ghe xe anca el senno, e dove xe el senno, xe el vero governo' (Giovanni Briccio, *Il Pantalone imbertonao*).

This scene is taken from a *commedia ridicolosa* play (see Chapter 5) by Giovanni Briccio: *Il Pantalone imbertonao*. Its first edition is dated 1620; it was then reprinted in a series of different versions down to 1673.[4] The text could thus have been read by Molière, who used the structure of the above scene in 1.4 of *L'Avare*: young Lover Cléante has his hopes raised and then dashed by his father Harpagon in relation to young Mariane, with their conversation going through the same elastically structured stages. It is a type of encounter which was liable to be repeated throughout the history of classical comedy. The clash between generations was a central element in the genre; and ever since Plautus's *Mercator* and *Casina*, rivalry between father and son for the favours of the same young woman had been one of the familiar plot-lines which expressed that clash. We find it in Machiavelli's *Clizia* of 1525, in several other Florentine comedies, and then particularly often in *arte* scenarios. So far, so unsurprising; but Briccio's scene is a useful example for two reasons. It shows the figure of Pantalone, a mask associated with *arte* improvisation, appearing in a fully scripted play; and it also offers a dialogue in a multi-lingual Italian script whose outline then recurs in a French comedy.

What should be surprising, on the face of things, is that ridiculous old Pantalone is stating opinions which in his time were unexceptional, and even encapsulated in the prevailing social order. Older men married to younger women were a norm in ancient and then early modern Europe (and continue to be so today in some cultures). Rather than being matters of romantic youthful choice, marriages were patriarchally arranged for the social and financial benefit of families, and for the sexual benefit of patriarchs. Many mature men in Briccio's audience would have agreed with this speech, and would have acted on the principles it expresses. A seventeenth-century Pantalone, however, is not a theatrical figure who attracts approval — he is a mask (or a stock character) set up to be derided. We know he will not marry Olimpia, and that Tiburzio will obtain her instead, because that is how comedy works. His opinions are normal for the time, but they have been put in the mouth of a stage figure defined in advance as a loser.

In a classical comedy it is unthinkable that the Elders should win and the young Lovers should lose. Often the Elders will end up soundly humiliated, though this is not always the case. Pantalone may be persuaded more gently (as in my Goldoni example in the previous chapter) that his desires were unacceptable; or indeed he may discover that he was amorously pursuing his long-lost daughter. Equally often there is no sexual rivalry between father and son: Pantalone's resistance to his child's marriage can be based on motives other than his own lust. But in all cases we are presented with the younger more vigorous characters winning the contest, and so with a symbolic transfer of power to the next generation. This is so even if (as was often the case in Plautus) the lovers themselves are weak or incompetent. They may gain their victory through the deceits and machinations of servants, or through sheer circumstantial luck — including, again, the revelation of lost family relationships — but some kind of victory is guaranteed.

4 The play appears in two versions, either in three acts or in five; and sometimes with the alternative title of *Pantalone innamorato*. In the five-act version, the scene quoted is II.1; in the three-act version it is 1.15.

The sheer predictability of this pattern, its contribution to the expectations shared by everyone when the curtain went up on a comedy, underlines the element of fantasy which the genre always contained (and still contains). Comedy provided (and provides) an alternative world, partly insulated from reality. In its carefully selective way, it overrode, subverted, or disregarded some of the practices and attitudes which operated in its audience's society, even if, as has been seen in Chapter 21, its story might claim to be set in that society. The area of social and emotional behaviour in which it did this most often was the battle between generations. In this chapter I shall unpick some of the relationships depicted under this heading, and note some changes, over three centuries, in how the issues were portrayed. Always underlying such stories is a conscious inheritance from Roman comedies, in which elderly Simo or Demipho were outwitted and deprived by young Calidorus or Antipho.[5] (I shall treat in Chapter 25 the contribution made to the contest by the slaves Pseudolus or Phormio — the class conflict involved invites separate examination.)

Generational Politics

In dramatizing a story which culminates in the younger generation defeating or even overthrowing the old, it is possible for a playwright to be pursuing an agenda which is larger and more immediately topical. Comedies play with generational 'politics', in the sense of strategies and skirmishings between older and younger characters; but some of them could be alluding to politics in another sense. There might be an old generation in charge of a state or a community, and a young generation which would like to replace it. In that case, a comic drama which portrays private family matters might stand for something of more public significance.

Some critics and historians have argued that this happens in a few Italian *commedie erudite* of the sixteenth century. They have seen Machiavelli's *Mandragola*, and then some Florentine comedies of the 1530s, as containing veiled allusions to a series of revolutions and confrontations in the city state of Florence. A republic was replaced in 1513 by the imposed governance of the Medici family. A shorter-lived republic threw the Medici out again in 1530; but it was quickly crushed by an alliance of local and imperial troops. The new Medici ruler Alessandro, given the new title of Duke of Florence, was then murdered by a younger member of his own family, but he was replaced by another relative, Cosimo, who became Grand Duke of Tuscany and sired a long-standing dynasty. During these upheavals, documents show that the contending factions could be distinguished at least partly by age or generation. For example, it was claimed that those who had the courage to fight for the republic of 1530–33 were the younger men, while their fathers preferred not to risk their wealth and status. One of those who argued this, from exile, was Donato Giannotti (1492–1573), author of the comedy *Il vecchio amoroso* [The Old Man in Love] (composed *c.* 1533). The young man who assassinated his ducal cousin in 1537 was Lorenzino de' Medici (1514–1548), whose comedy *Aridosia* (named after

---

5   Plautus's *Pseudolus*, and Terence's *Phormio*.

its miserly old father Aridosio) had been performed before Duke Alessandro just the year before. In these cases it is tempting to see an overlap between dramatists' political opinions or actions and the content of their comedies.[6]

More diffuse interpretations, but of a similar kind, have been proposed in relation to comic drama composed in sixteenth-century Venice. The Venetian governmental and social hierarchy was not beset by upheavals, but it involved a very clear-cut, efficient system of gerontocracy, whereby members of the ruling families proceeded smoothly up a career ladder of successive public offices which was regulated on grounds of age. It has been suggested by Anthony Ellis and others that comedies such as those of Andrea Calmo (1510–1571), which feature extended mockery of old men in love, acted as a kind of safety-valve for young patrons and spectators. Ellis suggests that 'comedy reconfigures conflict as play', and that here a specific social conflict can be identified.[7] From another angle, it has been noted by Peter Jordan how young aristocratic Venetians were prevented by their elders from marrying, so that the family wealth would not be split between lines of descendants. The *commedia dell'arte* figure of Pantalone, distinguished from the start by his Venetian dialect, can be seen as a kind of revenge caricature by the young against the old. The old man's sexual pretensions (and the prominent codpiece which formed part of his costume) were a more central characteristic of the mask than was his mercantile avarice.[8]

In close studies of comic drama in particular times and places, these critical approaches undoubtedly have a part to play. When dealing with the whole comic genre, however, I am more concerned with the sheer persistence of inter-generational conflict in plays written in many different places between 1500 and 1800. Resentment against parental control, especially in wealthy families, is indeed probable in sixteenth-century Venice, but it was equally likely in all the other Italian states of that time. It would continue to be provoked by the patriarchal systems of Italy and France until the French Revolution and beyond. In stage performances, the fictional victory of the young over the old had (and perhaps still has) a permanent ahistorical attraction.

In the overall history of classical comedy, therefore, the depiction of father-son discord may sometimes have a political or socio-political dimension, but very often it does not. When reading French comedies of the seventeenth century, it is hard to associate this plot theatergram with any wider public confrontation involving opposed generations. Certainly the Théâtre-Italien in Paris would never risk becoming involved in major political debates, under this or any other heading. In eighteenth-century France, when plays tended to offer more satirical content, the situation perhaps becomes a little more complex. Likewise Goldoni, in eighteenth-century Venice, was certainly pursuing in his plays a series of social and political agendas in which comparisons between past and present habits, between older and

---

6   Cf. Ellis 2009: esp. Chapter 3. Ellis makes use of earlier critical bibliography in Italian. Political interpretations of Machiavelli's *Mandragola* have a long history.
7   Ellis 2009: Chapter 4. The quotation is from p. 100 and it draws on ideas propounded by the anthropologist Turner 1982.
8   For these observations see Jordan 2014: esp. Chapters 7 and 8.

younger ideologies, played a part. In the end, with regard to such questions, each individual play has to be treated on its own merits. As a rule, though, comic plots appeal to audiences by observing the principle inherited from Aristotle, Horace, and Donatus: that comedy should concern itself with private relationships rather than with public affairs. Machiavelli's *Mandragola* remained popular, and was often revived, in a series of different Italian locations and states during the sixteenth century.

Nevertheless, in dramatizations of the face-off between parents and offspring, the choices and preferences of comic playwrights did pass through phases which need to be registered. These include some important distinctions relating to gender.

Sons and Fathers

All Terence's comedies involve dealings between a father and a son. In Plautus the quotient is rather lower: only around half of his surviving plays include any active parental relationship (excluding the discovery in a denouement of lost children who had not previously been recognized). Nevertheless, we today, along with humanist scholars earlier, are likely to conceive an overall picture of Roman comedy as a genre which tells stories about families, with more concentration on fathers and sons than on spouses or siblings.

In ancient Roman law, heads of households had an absolute power, which we would now see as brutal, over their families and dependents. In early modern Europe, much law was still based on Roman precedent, and the same powers were retained in theory and often in practice. However, the precise details of laws and customs, in single nations or city states, are not often relevant to what happens in comedies. In many cases, fathers are shown as persistently overbearing and authoritative simply because — in so many human societies, across the world and across history — there has been a general presumption that this is what tends to happen. Patriarchy, as we now label it, is found almost everywhere. (In England, where the legal system was not so obviously of Roman derivation, Plautine and Terentian family intrigues made just as much sense as they did in Italy and France.) Since comedies are about desired marriages, or couplings, this is the subject on which fathers and sons usually disagree. In Plautus the son is often chasing an enslaved concubine; in Terence, and in most early modern comedy, the young man wants to marry a young woman of his choice. We have seen that the father's opposition is sometimes due to the fact that he fancies the same woman; but just as often his motivation is based on money, or simply on a desire for control. In Italian plots, both scripted and improvised, there are many cases of the parental blocking character having his own idea about which daughter-in-law would bring his family the best dowry. Equally often (as in Ariosto's *Lena* of 1529), there is no obvious reason at all why the Lover's preference should be opposed: the father just has the knee-jerk attitude that he, rather than his son, should make such decisions. In *commedia erudita* the young man's chosen bride often turns out to be perfectly suitable. Meanwhile his clandestine relationship with her may have made her pregnant, a situation which we see as early as 1509 in Ariosto's *Suppositi*, and which is then frequent in *arte* scenarios.

The task of comedy was to laugh at family tyrants, and to deprive them on stage of the power they held in real life. The easiest way to do this was to concentrate on those characteristics associated with old age which could easily be made laughable: bad temper, avarice, and inappropriate lust. Historians can now quote early modern theories of physiology and medicine, which said that as we get older our organic balance changes in the direction of 'cold' and 'dry' humours.[9] Some members of theatre audiences would have known about these; but even if they did not, there were standard assumptions about how old men behaved which did not need learned theories to explain them, and which were based on observation as well as social prejudices. The stereotypes were constantly repeated, and were fixed most of all in the more mechanical figures of masked improvised theatre. Pantalone was lustful, greedy, and cunning, but was always defeated nevertheless. Dottor Graziano was bumbling, self-centredly arrogant, and able to turn sheer repetitive tedium into a quality to be laughed at. Even the braggart Capitano, less firmly associated with a particular age bracket, carried into early modern comedy the Greco-Roman characteristics of the *alazōn*, the character who is blindly convinced of his own superior qualities, and doomed on stage to show that he does not possess them. The characteristic most firmly associated with the old man on stage was in fact self-delusion, and it was this which assigned both Elders (*Vecchi*) and Soldiers (*Capitani*) to the category of *parti ridicole*.

Among patriarchal readers and spectators there were always people, and institutions, who objected to authority figures being made ridiculous. In sixteenth-century Italy, one theorist and critic who was explicit about this was Bernardino Pino da Cagli, whose views on subversive comedy I have quoted in Chapter 17, and who sought laboriously to establish an inoffensive form of comic drama. There were in addition moralists, writing on both sides of the Alps (and of the English Channel), who thought that 'inoffensive theatre' was a contradiction in terms: their objections to comedy certainly included the fact that heads of families in this genre had their status constantly undermined. Their arguments did not carry the day, and comedy continued to be supported and mounted by patriarchal monarchs and aristocrats, even by controlling senior clerics such as Cardinal Richelieu, during the seventeenth and eighteenth centuries. Slowly, though, during the latter half of our history, it became less common to ridicule old fathers simply because they were old. We have already noted that in the comedies of Pierre Corneille the older generation plays little part, and the Lovers have to negotiate with each other and with their own emotions more than with their parents. In the eighteenth century, Marivaux continued the same tendency. Between those two playwrights, however, came the influential comedies of Molière, where Elders were defeated as soundly as they had been in Italian plays and scenarios.

What Molière did was to shift attention away from a purely generational conflict to a chosen satirical issue: he put his stage Elders in the wrong for reasons other than their age. He created fathers whose resistance to their son's (or, as we shall see, their daughter's) choice of partner arises from foolish personal obsessions of their own.

9   I refer once again, among other sources, to Ellis 2009.

Monsieur Jourdain wants to marry his child into the nobility; Harpagon is concerned only with the amount of dowry he can rake in; the hypochondriac Argan wants to get a medical man into his family; Orgon is hypnotized by the apparent sanctity of his manipulating guest Tartuffe. In many cases the play's title makes clear where the principal comic attack is being directed: *Le Bourgeois gentilhomme*; *L'Avare*; *Le Malade imaginaire*; *Le Tartuffe, ou l'Imposteur*. A patriarchal family head in Molière's audience could accept the humiliation on stage of a character with whom he might otherwise identify: 'Of course, ordinary sensible fathers should be obeyed — but not that one, because he's an idiot'. In Venice in the following century, many Goldoni comedies sought similar reactions: after a succession of Pantaloni he presented the deeply unpleasant Sior Todero (who is a grandfather rather than a father), and the ineptly resistant old-fashioned yokels of *I rusteghi*. It is noteworthy, though, that Goldoni is careful to ensure that his patriarchs are defeated gently, using forms of words which allow them to retain some level of dignity. In Molière's denouements, by contrast, there is rarely any sign that the errant father acknowledges his fault, or seeks to reform himself.

In any given time and place, the triumph of sons and the defeat of fathers on stage could be a covert expression of resentments and jealousies — sexual as well as financial and social — felt by a particular generation of young men towards their elders. Comedies offered a pre-existing template, a fantasy bubble world already created by the genre. By determinedly seeking to provoke laughter, they enabled such conflicts to be 'reconfigured as play', however destructive they might sometimes be in reality. The scenarios of *commedia dell'arte* in particular were deliberately unspecific about the societies which they might reflect, and so could be manipulated on each occasion to suit a chosen context or mood. Individual audiences, even individual performers, could use the format to vent frustrations more derisively and subversively than later dramatists like Goldoni would recommend. As time went on, though, the purely farcical tone of improvised artisan shows became almost a separate genre from the more reflective approach offered to polite society by erudite playwrights. In the latter plays the tendency over the decades was for father-son relationships to become portrayed with more even-handedness, and via less wildly stereotypical caricature. Some dramatists remembered and imitated Terence's *Adelphoe* [The Brothers], in which two mature men disagree about whether sons should be raised with harsh discipline or with a light rein, thus contrasting an irritable and obstructive father with a more benign one. Of the Italian and French plays which develop this theme, we could single out Lorenzino de' Medici's *Aridosia* (1536), already mentioned in this chapter, and both *L'École des maris* (1661) and *L'École des femmes* (1662) by Molière. However, the Molière examples relate to the education of women rather than men. The change of gender demands a shift in the terms of discussion.

Daughters and Fathers (and Guardians)

Fathers and sons were seen as being in simple competition with each other. In comedies sons fought their fathers for autonomy, for control, for money, or for the possession of a woman. The relationship between daughters and their parents was affected by the extra constraints placed on female sexual behaviour. In early modern European society (as still in some other societies), if an unmarried daughter was labelled in public as unchaste she destroyed the honour of her whole family. The responsibility for maintaining that honour rested with her father, and it logically followed that a father who failed to control his daughter was treated by society with the same derision as was directed at a cuckold who could not control his wife. In real life he had the right and even the duty to take punitive measures; and if those measures were violent, even lethal, then he was treated by the law with a degree of leniency.

These attitudes regularly underlie the behaviour of fathers in comedy. English-speaking theatregoers are exposed to the same ethic in Shakespeare's *Much Ado About Nothing*, a play set in Italy and based on an Italian short story which had wide diffusion. In IV.1, young Hero is accused of entertaining an illicit lover on her balcony. Her fiancé Claudio brutally rejects her: he throws her back in the face of her father Leonato, who himself is reduced to despairing, incoherent anger. When she faints and may be dying, Leonato says that if she were to recover he would 'strike at [her] life'. When he is persuaded to investigate whether the accusation is true or false, he still says 'If they speak but truth of her, | these hands shall tear her'. There are Italian *commedie erudite* in which outraged patriarchs approach similar extremes, including two influential ones from Siena. In *Amor costante* (1536) attributed in print to Alessandro Piccolomini, Guglielmo plans to poison Lucrezia whom he has taken paternally under his wing, along with the lover (in reality her husband) with whom she has been found in bed: he knows that this act of 'vengeance' must be kept secret from the authorities, but he is still determined to perform it. In *La pellegrina* (1589) attributed to Girolamo Bargagli, Casandro finds his daughter Lepida in bed with her brother's tutor, and is urged by Lepida's furious suitor to kill them outright: milder counsel prevails, but the lover is still likely to end up condemned to the galleys. In these three examples — Shakespeare as well as the Sienese plays — misunderstandings are cleared up in time about what really happened, or about people's true identities, and a happy ending ensues. In *La pellegrina* (as also in the earlier *Gl'ingannati*) the father's outraged description of what he has just seen in the bedroom is scripted so as to provoke prurient laughter. Nevertheless, stories of this sort were 'reconfiguring as play' emotions and reactions which were plausible and not inherently amusing.

Old fathers who are frantically angry about what their daughters have done, or may have done, are common in Italian play scripts and scenarios of the sixteenth and early seventeenth centuries. An exaggerated performance style would present them entirely as figures of fun, especially since the audience knew they were watching a comedy and that all would eventually be resolved. As the genre moved to France, and then into the eighteenth century, we can see a tendency for mechanical caricatures of extreme emotion to give way to more nuanced portrayals. Molière's obsessive tyrannical fathers are trying to rule daughters as well as sons, though the threatened sanction is permanent removal to a convent rather than violence. Harpagon in *L'Avare* is as much at odds with Élise as he is with Cléante. In *Le Tartuffe*, Orgon is determined that Mariane should marry the villainous Tartuffe himself. In IV.3, Mariane pleads eloquently against this match, saying she would actually prefer to become a nun. In an aside famously full of comic irony, Orgon struggles against any impulse to pity her: 'Come now, be strong, my heart, no human weakness!' ('Allons, ferme, mon cœur, point de faiblesse humaine'). Molière often shows more clearly than his Italian predecessors how closely comedy can play with situations which could be tragic: the pain and cruelty with which his fathers threaten their children has sometimes been hard to digest, in judgements offered by post-Romantic critics.[10] In presenting *L'Avare*, *Le Tartuffe*, and other such plays, modern directors can choose, and have chosen, to move their productions away from a purely comic tone. That is their choice and their privilege, and it can work for a modern audience. In a purely historical assessment, however, it should be recognized that on stage almost anything can be made funny, or be made serious, according to the style in which it is performed; and in the seventeenth century if a play was a comedy, then the actors delivered it in a comic manner. In surviving scripts, complete or partial, from the Paris Théâtre-Italien, there are passing caricatures of both fathers and daughters who maintain a kind of guerilla war against each other, with regard to marriage and other matters. The tone in which this material was treated made it difficult to take either side of the contest very seriously; but the comic convention tended to push the audience towards deriding the Pantaloni and the Docteurs, and colluding cheerfully with the Colombines and Isabelles. The rebellious daughters manipulated events, often using implausible fantasy disguises, in order to get their own way. The young women, but not the old men, were given the chance to take the spectators into their confidence in witty scenes of conspiratorial chat.

In any case, as the decades passed daughters in high comedy tended to become less brusquely treated by their fathers. As also in relation to fathers and sons, Pierre Corneille and Marivaux dealt seldom, if at all, with such clashes. By around 1700, Luigi Riccoboni was struggling between conservative values which insisted on daughterly obedience, and a more liberal view whereby fathers should note 'to what risks they expose their children when they want to marry them off purely according to their own interests'.[11] He must have been influenced by the long-

---

10 Introducing an edition of *L'Avare* for English students, Ronald A. Wilson can find nothing funny at all in 'a father who suspects his own children of being capable of stealing his money', and says 'there can be nothing either more distasteful or tragic than the dispute between Harpagon and Cléante over the hand of Mariane' (Molière 1949: xlvi–xlvii). This is an extreme (and very un-Gallic) example, but it stands at one end of a polarity of critical and directorial reactions. By contrast, in the Paris production by Jean Vilar which I saw in 1962, the family quarrels were made vigorously grotesque and hilarious.
11 'A quali rischi espongono i figli quando vogliono maritarli solo con le mire del proprio interesse' (Riccoboni 1973: 82; in his remarks on the scenario *Il muto per spavento*).

standing comic tradition in favour of young lovers, to which he knew his audiences would respond. In his plots, however, he explicitly refrained from offering stories involving elopements, let alone pre-marital fornications (for which see Chapter 24). In Venice, Goldoni's treatment of parental relations was probing and even moralistic, sometimes showing that there might be faults on both sides. Youthful passions and attachments in Goldoni are treated critically, and may give way to matches which are socially and financially appropriate. Giacinta in the *Villeggiatura* trilogy is eventually persuaded that her irrational attraction to Guglielmo makes no sense either for her or for her family. Giacinta's father Filippo is presented as comically weak and indecisive: in this area as in many others Goldoni was able to leave stereotypes behind.

Comedy could also treat another type of opposition between a young female and an older male. A legally appointed guardian could have just as much power over his ward as a father had over a daughter; and in addition he might have sexual designs on her which were not prohibited because they were not incestuous. The Wicked Guardian, like the Wicked Stepmother, is a stereotype existing both in fairy tales and popular culture generally, as well as in the theatre. His motivation is usually a combination of greed for the girl's dowry and simple lust; so his destiny is to be defeated like a tyrannical father. I know of no sixteenth-century Italian play or scenario which develops this relationship (though in those texts it is not uncommon for a lecherous old man to discover just in time that the maiden he has been pursuing is his long-lost daughter). In the legacy passed on to us by the classical comic genre, the first memorable predatory guardian is Arnolphe in Molière's *L'École des femmes*: the preceding *École des maris* ranks as a more cautious experiment with the format. Arnolphe tries to groom Agnès into his idea of a perfect wife. He starts by being calculating but ends by falling genuinely in love, which makes him more ridiculous, rather than less. His educational blueprint fails, of course, and Agnès meanwhile has been secretly courted by Horace. The same situation was then famously developed by Beaumarchais in *Le Barbier de Séville*, where Bartholo tries unsuccessfully both to woo and to control his ward Rosine. Between those two well-known comedies there may be an unexplored iceberg of more neglected plays; but one of its observable tips is certainly Jean-François Regnard's *Les Folies amoureuses* (1704), whose status as a likely source for *Le Barbier de Séville* is noted in Chapter 14.

In earlier Italian comedies, the situation of an old man in unwelcome pursuit of a young woman had been treated regularly in a different theatergram: the one where a father offers his daughter in marriage to a conveniently rich elderly friend. The opening scene of *Gl'ingannati* is a dialogue between Virginio and Gherardo in which the former's daughter Lelia is betrothed in her absence to the latter. Such a conversation subsequently became a common formula for a scripted opening scene. It included some unconvincing boasts by the proposed elderly bridegroom about his continuing sexual prowess, with some quiet scepticism expressed by the bride's father. When *commedia erudita* became *commedia dell'arte*, the play might open with Pantalone and the Dottore each promising his daughter to the other, thus leading to a double level of contest and intrigue after which the daughters, the *Innamorate* of the company, succeed in marrying the *Innamorati* of their choice. This trope leads us back again to Molière and to the very Italianate plot of *L'Avare*. Harpagon wants Élise to marry old Anselme, who will take her without a dowry. Anselme turns out to be the long-lost father of Élise's suitor Valère, as well as of Mariane who is being courted by both Harpagon and Cléante. By favouring the obvious happy ending, and bestowing his new-found children on their chosen partners, Anselme enters the category of 'benign father', contrasting with Harpagon in another echo of Terence's *Adelphoe*.

Mothers

Fathers who are not benign, or who at least start their play in the role of a blocking character, are at first sight the norm in classical comedy. Are they then counterbalanced or opposed by sympathetic or supporting mothers? This can sometimes be the case, but the benign mother is not a standard figure in the genre.

It is easy to form the impression that while fathers are almost omnipresent in comedy, mothers are largely absent. In fact neither of those statements is quite true, even in the Roman sources. Six Plautus comedies contain mothers in their cast, but there is no clear tendency as to the part they play in the story, or as to how they treat their sons or daughters. The same can be said of Terence, whose three roles for mothers have less dramatic profile than those of Plautus. A mother in Roman comedy can be an outraged campaigner against a philandering husband, and can sometimes take her son's part against his father; but she can equally be resigned or stoical, or take little initiative.

In Italian *commedia erudita*, there are again more mothers in the casts than we hear about in many standard critical surveys, and their contribution to the plot is just as varied as in the Roman comedies which they are often copying. Equally, there are many such comedies which have no mother roles.[12] It is interesting that the comedies of the Sienese Accademia degli Intronati, influential and admired in their day, do not bring any mothers on to the stage, despite a certain proto-feminist bias (which I shall address in the next chapter) in their treatment of young heroines. By contrast in one Florentine comedy — *La sporta* [The Basket] (1543) by Giovan Battista Gelli — the single matronly character of Eunomia in Plautus's *Aulularia*, on which the play is closely based, is expanded into three separate widows, each intervening in the plot in different ways. Altogether, Italian humanist playwrights had not inherited any uniform picture of how to present mothers on stage, nor of the kind of contribution they might make to the story. *Commedia dell'arte* troupes never formulated a masked or stereotyped version either of a matriarch or of a grotesque crone, and there was no old woman's repertoire of speeches or dialogues for an actor's commonplace book. Pantalone and the Dottore rarely have wives; Orazio and Lelio, Isabella and Flaminia, rarely have mothers. Since the *arte* repertoire, and the *arte* cast of characters, became a default version of resources for a standard comic

---

12 Manes 2011 is based on a thorough statistical survey of mother roles in *commedia erudita*. In her main critical analysis, she devotes her attention to just five plays.

plot, Italian and French comedies of the seventeenth and eighteenth centuries show a tendency either to omit mothers altogether or to treat them with more freedom and variety than is conceded to the other family roles. In Pierre Corneille and in Marivaux there is in any case little focus on parental relationships generally.

We have surveyed the typical Molière comedies where a foolish father is the target of the comic attack. The mothers of these families, when they exist, do not observe any single pattern. Some wives have sense enough to see through their husbands, and so to favour the marriages which their sons or daughters desperately desire. Madame Jourdain is derisive of her *bourgois gentilhomme*; Elmire proves to the besotted Orgon that Tartuffe is a villain rather than a saint. Harpagon the miser, however, is a widower (a loss which some modern directors have used as his psychological back story). Argan the *Malade imaginaire* has a young second wife, Béline, who almost qualifies as a Wicked Stepmother — a role which classical comedy could easily have picked up and made into another stereotype, but which in fact appears very rarely.[13] In *Les Femmes savantes*, as a satisfying variation on Molière's usual formula, it is the mother Philaminte who is blindly devoted to her self-image as a woman of culture, and who tries to bully both her husband Chrysale and her daughter Henriette into accepting a match with the ridiculous poet Trissotin.

Of Goldoni's comedies, around a quarter contain characters who are mothers or stepmothers. (A patriarch with a second wife was not uncommon in real society: the first wife could plausibly have died in childbirth.) The extent to which maternal feelings or actions are important to those plays varies, though Maggie Günsberg sees a tendency for maternal love to be represented as excessive, and to subvert the 'proper' claims of paternal authority.[14] By contrast, two other Goldoni titles — *La madre amorosa* (1754), and *La buona madre* (1761) — allude to portrayals of mothers who are 'loving' and 'good'. Significantly, both these female protagonists are widows, operating with no masculine support; and both have to conduct struggles and sacrifice themselves, so as to provide their children with acceptable marriages. As I have noted more generally, Goldoni presents the matches as being successful in terms of social propriety and financial viability, rather than of romantic love.

In the two versions of *The Marriage of Figaro*, which I see as concluding my narrative, the victory of offspring over parents is replaced entirely by the triumph of lower classes over their employers. Count Almaviva is an exploitative aristocrat, not a tyrannical father. This alternative form of subversion was equally inherent from the start in the fantasy world of classical comedy: I shall treat it at more length in Chapter 25.

---

13   She is, however, a central figure in three of Goldoni's lesser-known comedies. See Günsberg 2001: 114–17.
14   Ibid.: 113–24.

CHAPTER 24

Women and Men

The treatment of women and of gender relationships on stage is a subject self-evidently central to the material studied in this book. The denouement of a classical comedy usually involved either a marriage or an illicit coupling between a woman and a man, and the dramatic action skirmished around both parties' efforts to achieve such a goal. Moreover, the long-standing presence of actresses in European or 'western' theatre has its historical roots in the Italian professional companies who helped to create the comic genre.[1]

Female Performers

Until the final decades of the last century, studies of *commedia dell'arte* often underplayed the fact that the Italian troupes introduced women performers to the European stage, and that in doing so they fought against and defeated enormous social prejudice. We would not be taking for granted the existence, and arguing about the significance, of Sarah Bernhard, Greta Garbo, Maria Callas, Marilyn Monroe, and Vanessa Redgrave, had it not been for the laborious achievements of sixteenth-century pioneers such as Isabella Andreini (and the early singers Vittoria Archilei and Francesca Caccini). In the Greek and Roman theatre on which classical plays modelled themselves, all actors were male. In the civilizations of China and Japan — which, like Europe and the West, have considered theatre to be a form of high culture — the use of actresses was controversial and mostly forbidden, at least until the twentieth century. That last fact has no direct bearing on what happened in sixteenth-century Europe; but it acts as a reminder that most human societies around the world have asserted patriarchal control over women's bodies and personalities, and have restricted their public display. This was as true in Italy and France in the 1540s as it was in other times and places. Nevertheless, in those countries, actresses did begin to appear on stage.

In September 1548, the city of Lyon welcomed its new King Henri II, and his Queen Caterina de' Medici, with a lavish series of events and displays which were then recorded in a number of documents and reports.[2] The contribution of the

---

[1] I stick to the word 'actress', despite the recent English fashion for making 'actor' gender-neutral. Italian and French, being grammatically gendered languages, still unavoidably use *attrice* and *actrice*.
[2] This whole *Entrée*, which lasted many days, is thoroughly researched in Scève 1997, and also treated in Rayfield 2021b.

city's large Italian expatriate community was a performance of Bibbiena's *Calandra*, a comedy which dated from 1513 and had already been printed a dozen times. The players were invited in specially from Florence, Queen Caterina's home city. The diarist Pierre Bourdeille, seigneur de Brantôme (c. 1540–1614) states unequivocally that the performers included women as well as men — 'comédiens et comédientes'. He was only about eight years old in 1548, and was reporting (as he says) from people who were present; but he is very definite about the presence of the actresses, acknowledged to be 'rare in France'. His informants particularly commended the women's verbal delivery: they were 'very pretty, spoke very well and in a graceful manner'.[3] We are left uncertain about whether women performed the somewhat scurrilous female roles in the comedy itself, or whether they just recited some of the allegorical and encomiastic verses which were composed separately for the show's lengthy *intermezzi*. Either way they must have been well prepared, and have performed before: it is unlikely that women who so impressed French noblemen were displaying their skills in public for the first time. This first staging in France of an Italian *commedia erudita* ranks also as the first documented appearance, in either Italy or France, of female performers in a public spectacle which claimed high cultural status.

There is then no doubt that actresses became a normal component of Italian troupes during the middle part of the century. A document registering 'Lucrezia of Siena' as a formal member of a theatre company dates from 1564.[4] In the winter of 1566–67, two well-established *arte* companies were visiting Mantua, each of them relying on an established female star and one of them actually being directed by the *prima donna* Barbara Flaminia.[5] The first famous Italian actress, Vincenza Armani, lived from 1530 to 1569 and was celebrated after her death in a special compendium of tributes and poems.

In France, a notarial document survives from 1545 (earlier than the *Calandra* performance in Lyon) confirming that Marie Ferré (or Fairet), 'wife of a *bateleur*', was legally enrolled as a performer in a company run by one Antoine de l'Esperonnière.[6] The word *bateleur* suggests a street entertainer or even street vendor, so we are not dealing here with high-status material like *Calandra*, or like the plays produced during the 1567 Mantua season which were based on prestigious literary sources. Marie Ferré may have displayed her talents and her body in very unrespectable ways. We also know that early visits to France by Italian touring troupes often blatantly exploited the sexual attractions of their women performers.

Objections to actresses were based on the notion that exposure of a woman's body, and even of her voice, was a surrendering of that body and that voice to public possession, therefore undermining their patriarchal ownership by a husband

---

3   'J'ay ouy dire à plusieurs seigneurs et dames, que si la tragi-comédie de ce grand cardinal fut belle, elle fut aussi très-bien représentée par les comédiens et comédientes, qui estoient très-belles, parloient très-bien et de fort bonne grâce' (Brantôme 1867: 256–58).
4   The full text is in Taviani & Schino 1982: 183–84.
5   Private correspondence about this eventful theatre season is reprinted in D'Ancona 1891: II, 449–54. It is also discussed in Nicholson 1999.
6   Lacour 1921: 6–7, with reference to two archival studies printed in the nineteenth century.

or father. Respectability, both cultural and social, was associated with female 'modesty'; and so (at least in an initial conservative view) it was safer for women not to be involved at all — though there were exceptions for all-female contexts such as nunneries, or for shows given to closet audiences which kept the event within the family. Any woman displaying herself more widely was automatically associated with prostitution: it demeaned the woman, and tempted the male spectator into unseemly thoughts of lust. Somehow, in European culture, this assumption became softened or modified, though for a long time it did not entirely disappear. The exclusion of actresses from truly respectable status ended only with the acceptance of wider sexual freedom for all women. The fact that such changes began and were tentatively accepted in sixteenth-century Italy is still something of a mystery; but those changes did occur, and they permanently altered the nature of western theatre.[7]

According to recent speculations, the earliest Italian actresses (certainly including Vincenza Armani) are in fact likely to have been prostitutes: they were probably recruited from the ranks of so-called 'honest courtesans', women trained in the art of entertaining cultured upper-class clients not only with sexual services but with recitations and songs. They learned courtly skills of improvisation, both in music and in verse, which were easily transferable to *commedia dell'arte*. It is even possible that the celebrated Isabella Andreini (1562–1604) may have started from this background, and that her successful campaign to redeem the image of herself and her profession was a massive achievement of rebranding. By the time she died in 1604 Isabella was a figure of high culture, a published lyricist and dramatist, mentored by poets, an elected member of a (usually all-male) Academy, and protégée of princes and cardinals. She was as famous in France as she was in Italy. Her Italian publications were reprinted in French translations, and she accumulated a clique of adoring fans who hailed her talent as more divine than human.[8] When she died in Lyon in 1604, the city gave her a civic funeral, and a medal was struck in her honour by a French sculptor (see Fig. 24.1). As well as achieving a high cultural profile, she showed that actresses could be mothers of stable families, and that their children (in her case, actor and dramatist Giovan Battista) could go on to work in the same profession, following a model which applied to normal artisan trades, or *arti*.

Professional actresses (and also female singers in opera) thus became accepted in Italy, and were then exported to Spain and to France. We know that in England they were banned until after the 1660 Restoration. (It is now strongly argued by Pamela Allen Brown, however, that the existence across the Channel of the star actress, or *diva*, radically altered the approaches of Elizabethan and Jacobean playwrights to female characterization.)[9] They never ceased to provoke controversy, in countries both Catholic and Protestant.[10] In the mid-seventeenth century, the diatribes of the

---

7   For a view on this by an Italian scholar, see Ferrone 2014.
8   The poet Isaac du Ryer wrote in 1604: 'Je ne crois point qu'Isabelle | soit une femme mortelle, | c'est plutôt quelqu'un des dieux | qui s'est déguisé en femme' [I do not believe that Isabella is a mortal woman, rather she is one of the gods disguised as a woman] (Du Ryer 1610: 15).
9   Brown 2021: passim.
10 Church opposition to professional theatre in Italy is the subject of the second part of Taviani 1970. See also Laiena 2021.

FIG. 24.1. Medallion by Guillaume Dupré commemorating Isabella Andreini, issued after her death in 1604. The reverse side shows an allegorical figure of Fame, with two trumpets.

Jesuit writer Gian Domenico Ottonelli exemplify clerical suspicion of any theatre which did not have a religious content: he was especially ferocious about women performers.[11] On the one hand, a professional actress was arousing lascivious desires in all male spectators (including Ottonelli himself, to judge by his tone), offering attractions presented as utterly irresistible. On the other hand, given especially that she was being paid for her self-display, she was branding herself irredeemably as a potential or actual whore. In France, the same opinion was expressed by the priest Francesco Maria del Monaco, personal confessor of the king's first minister Cardinal Mazarin.[12] The cardinal took no notice, but instead supported the re-admittance of Italian companies to Paris in the 1640s. On the other side of the controversy, Italian actors such as Giovan Battista Andreini and his wife Virginia Ramponi mounted calculated campaigns proclaiming the virtue of actresses.[13] In addition, in a treatise of 1614, the actor-manager Pier Maria Cecchini used arguments relating to family and sexual morality to support the use of female performers. He said that it was less scandalous to employ a woman rather than a boy to play female roles, provided she was then properly chaperoned offstage by her family; because a young boy who had displayed himself as a female was more likely to wander out on his own and be enticed 'by virtuous words [...] into places where immoral acts took place'. This is an interesting acknowledgement of the sexual ambivalence of cross-dressing (see Chapter 26), and of the possibility that boy actors too might arouse lascivious desires.[14] Whether Cecchini persuaded any fire-breathing misogynistic clergyman to change his mind is perhaps unlikely.

Before the rise of professional actresses, Italian *commedia erudita* in courts and academies took it for granted that female roles would be played by boys. It is not in fact clear when, if ever, these gentlemanly productions accepted female performers. For example, at the famous Florentine wedding celebrations of 1589, the artisan Gelosi troupe advertised the virtuosity of Isabella Andreini and Vittoria Piissimi (see Chapter 19); but there is no record of who mounted the centrally featured production of *La pellegrina*. That Sienese *commedia grave* includes important female roles, but we do not know who performed them. In the early seventeenth century, *commedie ridicolose* (see Chapter 6) were composed in a style which deliberately imitated the content and methods of professional shows; but they were composed for amateur academies, and it is unclear how they were staged and whether women were allowed to participate. In seventeenth-century Paris, however, women were regular members of the licensed professional companies who performed Corneille, Molière, and Racine.[15] Molière in fact married a member of his own troupe, in

---

11 Ottonelli 1655. The first editions of the various volumes appeared between 1646 and 1652.
12 Del Monaco's views are quoted (in Latin) in Taviani 1970: 189.
13 On the joint strategy of this couple, see Laiena 2021.
14 'Tuttavia fu concluso esser assai meglio, & di manco scandalo la donna; poiché ben guardata, e dalla propria honestà e dall'interesse dell'honor del marito, si sarebbero fuggiti quei scandali che possono esser partoriti dalla libertà di quel garzone, che fuori di casa può incontrarsi in persona, che con parole virtuose lo conducesse in luoco dove si consumassero fatti vitiosi' (Cecchini 1614; quoted by Pandolfi 1957–61: III, 358).
15 A useful study, containing an extensive bibliography, is Scott 2010.

circumstances which attracted some misleading scandalous accusations. Thereafter, there were admired female stars in both the Comédie-Française and the Théâtre-Italien; and by 1700 the presence of actresses was taken for granted in European theatres and opera houses, excluding the States of the Church, where women were banned from public performances until 1798. Their acceptance did not make them entirely respectable: their private lives were regularly the object of salacious gossip. For many generations, even into the twentieth century, highly cultured actresses, as well as lower-class showgirls, often relied on the protection of leading male members of society to whom they were sexually attached. In England such men included the future King Edward VII.

Constantly under pressure from the male gaze and from male requirements, female stage performers were thrust into an insecurity which produced a need for self-justification. It could also lead to undignified bouts of competitive jealousy. The first production of Goldoni's *La madre amorosa* was postponed from 1754 by a quarrel between two actresses about their respective ages — which of them should play the mother, and which the daughter? ('Worthy of a comedy in itself,' recalled Goldoni in his preface.) Such sensitivities in the acting profession were not (and are not) limited to the female sex; but the patronizing scrutiny of a society controlled by men had an infantilizing effect on at least some of the women who were subject to it. Such scrutiny, and such prejudices, would also regularly impinge on the portrayal of women in scripts written by male dramatists.[16]

The participation of women in European theatre cannot have failed to affect, and broaden, the development of female roles, in classical comedy as well as in other genres. At the same time, early modern society was pervaded at all levels by the attitude which modern feminists call 'essentialism', the conviction that there are permanent fundamental differences in nature, psychology, and behaviour between male and female human beings. This view was so ingrained as to be shared by women as well as by men. In theatre, essentialism was inherent in the public's attitudes towards actresses; and it constantly informed the process by which female roles were conceived and created by male dramatists.

Female Characters

Machiavelli's *Clizia* was first staged in a private house outside Florence in 1525. Its prologue includes the following warning to male spectators:

> This play is called *Clizia*, because that's the name of the girl who is being fought over. Don't expect to see her, because Sofronia, who has brought her up decently, doesn't want her to come outside. So if there's anyone here who fancies her, he'll have to do without.[17]

Machiavelli is true to his word: Clizia is pursued sexually by both Sofronia's

---

16 For a parallel account of all these matters in the English theatre, where professional actresses were only accepted after 1660, see Howe 1992: esp. 32–36 and 56–62.

17 'Questa favola si chiama *Clizia*, perché cosí ha nome la fanciulla, che si combatte. Non aspettate di vederla, perché Sofronia, che l'ha allevata, non vuole per onestà che la venga fuora. Pertanto se ci fussi alcuno che la vagheggiassi, arà pazienza.'

husband and her son, the discovery of her true identity provides a happy ending, but she never appears on stage. The same is true of the eponymous 'heroine' of Plautus's *Casina*, on which the plot of *Clizia* is openly based. Similarly in Terence's *Andria*, the mistreated young woman from Andros named Glycerium who gives the play its title is never seen by the audience; though she is heard crying from indoors as she gives birth to a child whose status the denouement will happily determine.

We have seen in the previous chapter that Roman comedy sometimes chose to develop the characters of older women, especially mothers of families. When it came to the young women whose marriage or concubinage was the issue around which the intrigue revolved, Plautus and Terence were more cautious. Experienced courtesan characters could be given plenty to do on stage, as in the case of *Miles gloriosus* (particularly the eavesdropping scene described in Chapter 18); but younger girls, respectable or not, tended either to be kept off stage or depicted as silly, giggly, and without any initiative. Their presentation was no doubt influenced by the fact that they were being caricatured by male actors wearing masks.

Many Italian humanist comedies are similarly inhibited with regard to female roles — they are sometimes also mocking and misogynistic.[18] Machiavelli's decision to keep Clizia off stage was followed by a number of other playwrights, especially in Florence where overt imitation of the ancient models was a notably important feature of comic dramaturgy. In Ferrara Ariosto too, despite his pioneering approach to other matters, was conservative about depicting women. His only strong female role is an unsympathetic one: the strident, promiscuous, and unscrupulous Lena, in the eponymous play first drafted in 1529 — her name suggests that she was a female distortion of the grotesque pimp figure (*leno*) in Plautus, played almost as a pantomime villain. Outside Ferrara and Florence, however, from early in the history of *commedia erudita*, female roles were given more stage time and more sympathy. A leading role in Bibbiena's *Calandra* is the girl Santilla, disguised as a boy. She appears alongside the unsatisfied wife Fulvia who is energetically pursuing an adulterous affair with Santilla's twin brother. At one point Fulvia also dresses as a man, and in III.7 she glories openly in the extra freedom which that gives her. This brash farce, which was much revived (as in Lyon in 1548), is based more on Boccaccio than on Plautus, and its characters are by modern standards cartoon-like. Also significant in the long term were the plays of the Intronati Academy in Siena, which introduced romantic (or romanesque) elements into classical comedy and decisively raised the profile of female characters both heroic and subversive.[19] Lelia, the heroine of the influential *Gl'ingannati* is in male disguise like Santilla, and serving the man with whom she is in love (like Shakespeare's Viola, for whom she is a recognized source). Her part is written so as to hold a balance between mischievous trickery and appealing emotion. The cast of *Gl'ingannati* includes other strong women — the nurse Clemenzia and the serving maid Pasquella — who play active parts in the plot. Subsequent comedies by the Intronati gave increasingly more controlling initiative to central female characters, a tendency typified by

18   For a more detailed (though selective) account, see Andrews 1997a.
19   For analyses of Sienese comedies, see Andrews 2010; also Andrews 1993: 89–108, 227–33.

the sentimental comedy *La pellegrina*, composed in the 1560s but not staged until 1589. The eponymous heroine, Drusilla, holds the stage disguised beneath a veil, in anguished conversations with an apparently unfaithful husband, who believes her to be dead and does not recognize her. In a complex cast of characters, Drusilla is the one who retains moral consistency and authority. In any case, during the middle decades of the century the Sienese trend had been followed more widely in Italy by the genre sometimes known as *commedia grave*, which often portrayed young women who were determinedly and even heroically faithful to partners to whom they were betrothed or secretly married. The amount of stage time granted to them still varied, however; and as late as 1598 Angelo Ingegneri was prepared to state in a treatise on play-writing that it was not proper to admit 'virgins and honest women' on to the stage of a comedy: he thought that such characters were more suited to the fantasy world of pastoral drama, which occupied a middle way between comedy and tragedy.[20] It was in pastorals and tragedies, Ingegneri thought, that women could acceptably be shown giving theatrical expression to high-flown emotion ('nobili affetti').

Ingegneri's views may or may not have been typical for 1598, but his expressed dislike of 'mercenary' actors shows that a distinction was still perceived between the professional companies which used actresses and respectable academic theatre. In the longer term it was the *arte* troupes, including their female stars, that were creating the enduring default formats for future comedy. As well as regularly expressing 'nobili affetti' in the two more serious genres, the skills of the great divas were being deployed in comedies which offered a wide variety of tone. The scenarios of Flaminio Scala, printed in 1611, show us among many other things the remarkable range of stylistic tones which featured in the career of Isabella Andreini: there is little doubt that in his collection Scala wanted to pay retrospective tribute to his much-appreciated colleague who had died in 1604, and to memorialize her repertoire. I have already treated her famous 'mad scenes' (in Chapter 19), but they were just one glittering fragment in her kaleidoscope.[21] As well as moving the audience to tears with her plight and her madness, we can find her commanding the stage with intellectual wisdom (like Drusilla the *pellegrina*); storming the stage as a vengeful lover; as a daughter pregnant out of wedlock, intriguing in pure comedy style to capture her man; and as a tricky adulterous wife deploying sexual double-entendres.[22] Moreover, in thirteen scenarios out of Scala's fifty, Isabella appears in male disguise, sometimes with very little narrative pretext, as though this was something which her public appreciated and expected to see.

For an audience, women dressed as men on stage offered possible sexual overtones, or undertones, which I shall discuss in Chapter 26. A more fundamental point is the extra freedom which cross-dressing provided to female characters, in the context of plots which were fancifully romanesque or farcical but which tried to

---

20 Ingegneri 1989: 7; where pastorals are described as 'mezzane fra l'una e l'altra sorte di poema'.
21 Scala's *La pazzia di Isabella* is Day 38 in his collection; he then allows her to repeat the same skills in the only scenario which is classified as a tragedy: Day 41, *La forsennata principessa*.
22 These stories occur, in the order listed here, in Scala's Day 36, Day 25, Day 21, and Day 6. For Isabella's repertoire generally, see also Andrews 2013.

FIG. 24.2. Frontispiece to Goldoni's *Il ritorno dalla villeggiatura*, from an anthology published in 1761. Depicting Act III Scene 9, it shows a social gathering in which women make up the majority.

maintain a patina of social realism. In real Italian society, young unmarried women from affluent families never went out of their houses unchaperoned. Streets and squares were the preserve of men, and of lower-class women providing services for their social superiors: house servants on errands, vendors peddling their wares, and others (including prostitutes) who had no choice but to be out there. Different urban spaces were thus differently gendered, at least for the upper ranks of society; and for as long as convention placed the action of comedies out of doors, that fact was a constraint on the actions and conversations which playwrights could depict. Even in the world of comedy, where the means by which lovers achieved their goals involved severe stretches of narrative imagination, it could be hard to develop female roles convincingly if they could only appear on balconies or front doorsteps. A young woman disguised as a page boy, or as a male traveller from another city, might not be something which theatre audiences had seen in their own lives; but it became accepted as a fictional device to allow a heroine to take initiatives, to pursue her chosen young man, even to take revenge against an unfaithful lover, without provoking the automatic question 'Where are her family, then?' In sixteenth-century Italy, scripted *commedia erudita* and improvised scenarios such as those of Scala had to manage what in those days seemed to be an inflexible rule: that action took place in public spaces (because that was always the case in Roman comedy), and that the scene on stage did not change (because of the unity of place).

I have described in Chapter 20 how the strict unity of place eventually crumbled, first in France and then in Italy, and how in particular the audience's gaze was redirected from the street or square to the domestic interior. Once action could take place indoors, the regular participation of women, of any age or social class, ceased to raise questions of verisimilitude. Plots involving cross-dressed heroines became less frequent, though they did not disappear altogether. Marivaux's *La Fausse Suivante* has the heroine Silvia disguised as 'Le Chevalier' in order to test her lover's sincerity — she exposes him as mercenary and unfaithful. The fact that Silvia acts without any kind of family constraint on her liberty is given little explanation. Even Riccoboni, in his unpublished scenario *Il filosofo deluso*, has a heroine going out in male disguise in search of her lover. Riccoboni's own inhibitions about such immoral behaviour led him to argue at length, and somewhat incoherently, that he had kept the episode within acceptable bounds.[23] In Goldoni's *Il servitore di due padroni*, Beatrice travels disguised as her brother, who she knows is dead, in order to track down her fugitive but faithful lover Florindo; there are similar situations in *La donna di garbo* (1743) and *Il frappatore* [The Con Man] (1745). It may be significant that these are early plays composed by Goldoni for masked acting troupes. They show only a selective attention to realism and to social morality, and accept greater levels of stylized game-playing, redolent of the comic opera libretti with which the playwright had begun his career. As that career moved forward, his plays increasingly showed fathers and mothers insisting that their daughters should behave properly and accept family control.[24] Such concerns are rarely expressed

---

23 Riccoboni 1973: 104.
24 The first three chapters of Günsberg 2001 give overwhelming evidence of how often such concerns are voiced on stage in Goldoni's comedies.

in French comedies, and one can gain the (perhaps incorrect) impression that women were less strictly monitored in France than in Italy. In Pierre Corneille and in Marivaux (but not so much in Molière) we do see women circulating socially without guardianship, in contexts which we would not find in Goldoni. It may also be the case that French dramatists were less inclined to show patriarchal anxieties and values being articulated on stage in open dialogue.[25]

At the same time, during the seventeenth and eighteenth centuries, social gatherings organized by women, or giving them a high profile, were increasingly a feature of polite society: the implications of the French word *salon* are now well known. Because such events were becoming normalized, they were depicted in comic plays, with a range of attitudes and tones. In Molière's *Les Femmes savantes*, women's attempts to impose artistic judgements are treated with aggressive satire. By the time of Goldoni, groups of women on stage featured regularly in comedies (see Fig. 24.2), with the tone of their presentation varying according to the theme of the play.

In terms of plum roles for actresses, the legacy of classical comedies to the modern stage is less rich than we might hope. Nevertheless, the *canovacci* of Flaminio Scala give an impression of how strongly Italian professional *prime donne* were capable of taking over a stage and dominating a plot. Since they are scenarios and not scripts, this can remain only an impression: we have few examples of the words which they delivered, which would better explain how they achieved what they did. In France, the comedies of Corneille and Molière give scope for female characters to take the initiative and express their feelings. In many of Molière's plays the liveliest female roles are those of serving maids: he contributed greatly to the establishment of the *soubrette* category in the *emplois* of French comedy (see Chapter 22). In addition, though, he left to posterity the challenging role of Célimène in *Le Misanthrope*, the virtuous but tricky Elmire in *Le Tartuffe*, and the determinedly verbose 'learned ladies' of *Les Femmes savantes*. Marivaux's writing makes demands on actresses, because the purpose of so much of his drama is to investigate, analyse, and sometimes to undermine the detailed feelings of lovers both male and female. Goldoni has bequeathed to the modern repertoire the strong but ambivalent figure of Mirandolina in *La locandiera* (see Chapter 17). Beaumarchais's Rosina, in *Le Barbier de Séville*, is spirited but also frustrated; then in *Le Mariage de Figaro* he created supreme roles for women in the Comtesse and Suzanne.

Since I am presenting the classical comedy format as being subversive, with younger characters defeating their elders and servants tricking their masters, it can be asked to what extent the genre shows women winning a contest against men. In a study of Goldoni, a simple but relevant scheme of analysis was constructed in Italian by Mirella Saulini. She identified, in each play analysed, the 'project' set up by the intrigue, the 'subject' character who drives it and the 'object' character against whom the plot is directed. It is then easily perceivable whether the plotter comes out as a 'winning subject' or a 'losing subject'.[26] In the plays she selected,

---

25 In a play mounted by the Italians in 1693 (*Les Originaux, ou l'Italien*, by Houdar de la Motte), Arlequin is given satirical comments (in French) on a stereotypical view that Italians control and seclude their women much more than do the French. See Mazouer 2002a: 211.
26 Saulini 1995. The terms used by Saulini are *progetto*, *soggetto*, and *oggetto*; and the *soggetto* can end

the female 'winning subjects' are more numerous than the male ones. The validity of such large-scale conclusions depends on the range and relevance of the plays used as samples; but it is clear that Saulini's survey could be carried out (time and determination permitting) on all the comedies composed in Italy and France between Ariosto and Beaumarchais. The number of female winning subjects registered over three centuries of drama would be high, granted what I have noted in the previous chapter: the strong tendency of marriages desired by young women in these plays to be successful in the face of parental opposition. Those marriages involve sons as well as daughters, however, so they represent victories for a generation rather than for a gender. What I see as increasing, during those three centuries, is a tendency for female characters to be sympathetic, to be emotionally clever, to be morally perceptive, to get the audience on their side — often in comparison with male counterparts who are weaker, more confused, or less trustworthy. Many women in classical comedy, especially in the eighteenth century, command the stage even if they cannot rule the society to which they belong. Beaumarchais's Comtesse and Suzanne are the climax of a development which began with Lelia and Drusilla in the Sienese plays mentioned above. It is a trend familiar also to English theatregoers who know Shakespeare's Portia, Rosalind, and Viola, various triumphant heroines of Restoration comedy, and Oliver Goldsmith's Kate in *She Stoops to Conquer*.

The creation of attractive young heroines has to be set alongside an alternative tendency for older women in comedy to be grotesque caricatures, especially if they have any ambition to attract or impress men. The ridiculous figure of Bélise, in Molière's *Les Femmes savantes*, is an example still well known in modern revivals. The text of the aria given to the housekeeper Berta in II.6 of Rossini's version of *Il barbiere di Siviglia* (the character has no equivalent in the Beaumarchais original) can sound to modern ears as a harsh piece of mockery based on ageism and sexism. In English comedy, Molière's Bélise is paralleled by Goldsmith's Mrs Hardcastle and Sheridan's Mrs Malaprop. It is in the nature of humour, and of humanity, that fictional creations which are potentially cruel can also be funny.

In relation to more positive depictions of women, the difference between ruling the stage and commanding in real society still has to be recognized. Saulini, surveying female winning subjects in Goldoni, admits that their victories are limited to domestic, and particularly marital, affairs: '[woman] is not a loser in the face of man [i.e. of individual men in the plays], but she still is in the face of society'.[27] We cannot expect, and we do not find, comedies between the sixteenth and eighteenth centuries which recognize the huge weight of impotence which patriarchal society lays on women. The nearest we get to it is in the last play included in this study. In *Le Mariage de Figaro*, the mature woman Marceline is initially treated as a figure of fun: she quarrels with Suzanne and shows sensitivity about her age, like Goldoni's actresses in 1754. Then she discovers that Figaro is her long-lost son: she had been seduced, but never married, by her employer Dr Bartholo. (She does not appear

---

up as *vincente* or *perdente*.

27 '[La donna] non è perdente nei confronti dell'uomo, ma lo è ancora in quelli della società' (Saulini 1995: 31).

with Bartholo in *Le Barbier de Séville*.) Unexpectedly, in III.16, the farcical revelation having first been hilariously exploited, Marceline breaks into a tirade about the oppression of women, and the condemnation of their sexual errors on the basis of a double standard: 'Unfeeling men, who brand the playthings of your lust with the stigma of your contempt: we are your victims. It's you who should be punished for the mistakes in our youth — you and your magistrates'.[28] Marceline's speeches were cut from the 1784 premiere at the Comédie-Française; but Beaumarchais included them all in his printing of the play, marking them as unperformed. Two years later in *Le nozze di Figaro*, Da Ponte and Mozart reduced the scene to a less aggressive Act IV aria by Marcellina, 'Il capro e la capretta', which recommends loving and harmonious behaviour between the sexes. This in its turn is often now omitted in performance, probably to avoid holding up the action.

Love in Classical Comedy

The vast majority of classical comedies involve plots which intrigue for, and achieve, a male-female coupling which was wished for by the pair concerned. Feelings of love, or at least of desire, are thus the driving force of the story. We might expect those feelings to be expressed at some length on stage in the plays covered in this narrative, and their nature or essence explored in the dramatic writing. This is not often the case. Stage plots which are driven by love do not necessarily result in plays dealing with the subject of love. Nevertheless, between the sixteenth and the eighteenth centuries there were changes in the presentation of erotic emotion, developments which are predictable granted the altered approaches to character and psychology which I traced in Chapter 22. There are also arguably some longer-term differences in this respect between Italy and France. There exists a detailed monograph entitled *Love in the Theatre of Marivaux*.[29] Its existence is not surprising, and other scholars have analysed Marivaux from similar angles; but it is hard to imagine a whole volume on the same theme being devoted to any of the other playwrights treated in this book, apart perhaps from Pierre Corneille whose comedies are generally less studied.

For English-speaking audiences, expectations about the treatment of love in early modern drama are unavoidably presided over by the precedent of *Romeo and Juliet*. In Shakespeare we see the couple meet for the first time and fall in love; exchange immortally passionate speeches in the balcony scene and after their wedding night; and then express desire, hope, and finally desperation, in successive stages of their long-drawn-out tragic denouement. A simple twist in the plot (or the removal of a twist) could easily have led them to a happy ending involving reconciliation between their families, in which case their story would resemble an Italian *commedia grave*. If Shakespeare had written that play instead, the earlier scenes could remain

---

28 'Hommes plus qu'ingrats, qui flétrissez par le mépris les jouets de vos passions, vos victimes! c'est vous qu'il faut punir des erreurs de notre jeunesse; vous et vos magistrats'. The English translation quoted is by David Coward (Beaumarchais 2003: 165).
29 Papadopoulou Brady 1970.

unchanged, and extended emotional speeches could still be included, but with rapture replacing despair at the end. Such an alternative *Romeo and Juliet* would still be exceptional for its era, however, not only in the poetic skill and intensity of its love scenes, but in the fact that it includes them at all.[30] It is a play conceived and composed by a writer some of whose reputation was already invested in his privately circulated love sonnets. Such mergers between dramatic and lyric poetry are not a characteristic of classical comedy.

In fact hardly any Italian or French comedies depict a first meeting between the lovers whose marriage will provide the denouement. In a majority of cases, interaction between them during the play is likely to involve arguments and misunderstandings, scenes which make fun of the over-sensitivity of people in love. Such amused detachment is more typical of the genre than is any deep emotional empathy: in one of the earliest examples, Machiavelli's *Mandragola*, the lover Callimaco is given overblown soliloquies which encourage laughter in the audience rather than sentimentality. Scenes of misunderstanding, of resentment, or of despair followed by reconciliation, contained more dramatic mileage for a comedy than did amorous harmony. There is a baseless quarrel between lovers Cléonte and Lucile in Molière's *Le Bourgeois gentilhomme* (III.8–11). This is typical of Molière; and indeed one of his early comedies, less revived today, is entitled *Le Dépit amoureux* [Lovers' Pique] (1656), and revolves entirely round such confrontations. I have mentioned (see Chapter 21) the Goldoni comedy entitled *Gli innamorati*, and its mockery of pointless jealousies.

The absence of first encounters actually occurring on stage can be partly explained by the unity of time: if an action is to be contained within twenty-four hours, it is simpler to assume that a passion already exists and to concentrate on its outcome. In the first scene of *La mandragola*, Callimaco narrates to his servant Siro how he fell in love some time ago while in Paris with the virtuous Florentine wife Lucrezia, just on the strength of hearsay reports about her. This is a strange but not unfamiliar trope, inherited by Renaissance drama from the medieval novella. A few Italian comedies and scenarios dramatize the start of a love affair in rather un-Shakespearean balcony scenes, where a lover pleads his cause from the street, and is treated by his beloved at her window with cautious resistance even if she is attracted to him. Such dialogues reflect stereotypes of the male predator and the female prey, and also the gendering of urban social space referred to above. They are rhetorical exercises for both the hero and the heroine: they exploit standard patterns of speech or thought which entered the memorized and recycled repertoire of the acting profession (see Chapter 19). Nevertheless, most erudite comedies and artisan scenarios prefer to start with relationships already established. Balcony scenes, especially in improvised *canovacci*, are likely to involve tensions or quarrels between lovers. Alternatively they may be used for farcical deceptions. In one of Flaminio Scala's scenarios, the *innamorata* Flaminia delivers from her window a speech of love addressed apparently to Orazio, but in fact to Flavio whom she prefers and

---

30 The single important theatrical model which preceded, and probably influenced, Shakespeare's various wooing scenes is found in the staged fantasies of John Lyly, which do not belong to the comic genre.

who is standing further back in the street.³¹ This is a cross-purpose gag frequently exploited in Italian comedy, not always in scenes for lovers, and not always with the use of a balcony.

A central perception about different phases in the history of classical comedy is the extent to which love is, or is not, acknowledged to involve bodily desire. In Plautus and Terence there are no inhibitions about alluding to sexual couplings or even rapes. Some of the female characters are prostitutes; and I have mentioned scenes such as that in Terence's *Andria*, where Glycerium is heard giving birth off stage. That situation was imitated or echoed by some Italian humanist comedies, such as Lorenzino de' Medici's *Aridosia*, where the girl concerned gives birth in a nunnery. The fact that a love relationship has become physical, with the heroine sometimes already pregnant, is an element in many plots of *commedia erudita* plays and *arte* scenarios, beginning with Ariosto's *I suppositi*. When this is not the starting-point, the machinations of the lovers and their conniving servants may still be aimed at getting the couple into bed with each other and presenting their families with a fait accompli. Both in theatre and in real life, such a situation would force parents into agreeing to a rapid marriage in order to maintain respectability. In v.5 of *Gl'ingannati*, this strategy culminates in a gratuitously bawdy climax, where a young girl listens through a house wall to Flaminio and Lelia making love, and reacts with some comments which entertain by being innocently perplexed ('Oh! One's saying "Wait for me". They must be going somewhere. And there's the other saying "Be quick then!"').³² Another explicit plot device is the 'bed trick', whereby characters are deceived in the dark into ending up in bed with a person they have not chosen: this can be done to consolidate a marriage, to procure an unwanted adultery, or to steer an intended adulterer back to coupling unwillingly with his wife.³³ Italian commentators expressed regular disapproval of 'rapes and adulteries' ('stupri e adulterii') on stage, and attributed them to the vulgarity of lower-class professional actors; but in fact such elements were not absent from literary scripted comedies.

Things changed noticeably in France, after the principle of *bienséance* became part of the formalized classical rules. Under the supervision of the Académie Française, overt sexual references disappear from approved classical comedies, starting with those of Corneille. This was the case despite the absence of prudery from the native French tradition of farce. Here we must stress the words 'approved classical comedies': the more anarchic Théâtre-Italien had fewer inhibitions about using double entendres, though their language — at least as recorded in print — was wittily allusive rather than vulgarly explicit. I have already recalled (in Chapter 17) how few smutty allusions occur in Molière. Marivaux does not refer

---

31   *La fortunata Isabella*, I.11–13, Day 3 in the Scala collection. The scenario is not included in Andrews 2008.
32   'Oh! Dice uno: "Aspettami". Si debbono voler partire. Odi l'altro che dice: "Fa' presto tu ancora"' (*Gl'ingannati*, v.5).
33   The plots of twelve of Flaminio Scala's forty comic scenarios are resolved by pre-marital couplings. Ten out of the forty involve some kind of 'bed trick', not always used to consolidate a marriage.

even distantly to physical sexuality: the desires and hesitations which he and his characters explore are expressed as being felt by the adoring and perceiving eyes, or by the metaphorical flaming heart, rather than by the rest of the body. The most extreme level of intimacy ever referred to is a man kissing a woman's hand. As this level of refinement took hold on polite eighteenth-century culture, pre-marital sex disappeared from comic plots. Goldoni's reforms were based on moral principles and on a knowledge of French theatre, and he observes the same *bienséances* as does Marivaux. In eighteenth-century comedy it was Beaumarchais who came closest to the physical realities of desire and seduction. In the last act of *Le Mariage de Figaro*, the purpose of the Comte's rendezvous with Suzanne under the chestnut trees is unambiguous, even if the words used are not physically explicit. When the Comte proposes hiding in a pavilion, the Comtesse (who is not, as he thinks, Suzanne) objects that it will be dark in there: his answer (both in Beaumarchais and in Da Ponte) is 'So what? We're not going to read anything'.[34]

Love and Friendship

One theme which was treated quite often in the plots of sixteenth-century Italian comedies, both scripted and improvised, was a clash between the claims of love (heterosexual) and friendship (homosocial). A familiar narrative trope from medieval romance and novella was that of a young man who surrenders the woman he loves to a close brotherly friend, who loves her too. There is a well-known example in Boccaccio's *Decameron*, the story of Tito and Gisippo in x.8. This story-line is not usually associated with those classical comedies which survive in the modern repertoire; but it did in fact linger and recur in the genre, more in Italy than in France.

The theme was launched most effectively in 1572, in a play by the lawyer-dramatist Sforza Oddi entitled *Erofilomachia*, a title which claimed to be Greek for 'The Battle of Love and Friendship'. In so far as we can designate *commedia grave*, 'serious comedy', as a separate Italian sub-genre, Oddi might almost be credited with inventing it, though its roots stretch back earlier than 1572. He was followed most particularly by the Neapolitan dramatist Giambattista Della Porta, in plays composed between 1550 and 1614.[35] The struggle in a character's mind between the claims of love and of duty was a popular subject for early modern drama, for tragedy even more than for comedy: it was still going strong in nineteenth-century Italian opera, for example in Verdi's *Aïda* (1871). In tragedies the contrast was most often between love and political loyalty, or patriotism; in comedies the political dimension was rare, and the tension was between love for a woman and fidelity to a male friend. (A contrast between amorous desire and duty to a parent tended of course to be treated with less solemnity.)

---

34 'LA COMTESSE: Sans lumière? LE COMTE: A quoi bon? nous n'avons rien à lire' (*Le Mariage de Figaro*, v.7). Da Ponte's libretto for Mozart follows the French closely: 'CONTESSA: Al buio, signor mio? CONTE: È quello che vogl'io; | tu sai che là per leggere | io non desio d'entrar!' (*Le nozze di Figaro*, IV.11).

35 The principal study of Della Porta's plays is that of Clubb 1965.

After Italian *commedia erudita*, the artisan professionals followed suit as they usually did: nine of Flaminio Scala's scenarios involve a conflict between love and friendship.[36] A closing sequence of Scala's Day 34, *Il finto cieco* [The Man Pretending Blindness] is an example of how often amorous dilemmas in this period were resolved not by close attention to characters' inner feelings, but by a rigorous exterior code in which people were seen to have almost legal rights over each other. In III.12, the heroine Isabella instructs all the other lovers how they are going to untangle their particular knot of cross-purposed passions and obligations:

> Isabella, after remaining in thought for a long time, turns to Flavio and says to him that since he has shown the greatness of his soul by giving what he most loved in the world to another man, then she will let him see that she is in no way inferior to him, by also giving away what she loved most. She lays formal claim to Flavio, then bestows him on Flaminia. She adds that she gives herself, as Flavio's property, to Orazio; telling Orazio that he should give his sister Flaminia to his greatest friend Flavio. Orazio and Flavio agree to what Isabella has proposed, give each other their promises and embrace each other, saying that they will persuade their fathers to agree.[37]

The improbable plot convolutions which lie behind this proposed 'happy ending' need not be explained here: what stands out is how it is dictated by perceived social and moral rules, rather than by what we would now recognize as love. We can also note the authority given to the female protagonist Isabella, and the fact that she implacably imposes on herself and on others a set of standards which, among other things, appears anti-feminist to a modern reader. The whole scene stands in massive contrast to how a plot might be resolved if it were composed by an eighteenth-century dramatist influenced by *sensibilité*.

In France, initially, the morally thoughtful comedies of Pierre Corneille were still ready to address the struggle between love and friendship, alongside the other dilemmas in which their dramatist was interested. The theme is relevant to *La Veuve* (1631–32); *La Galerie du Palais* (1632–33); *La Suite du menteur* (1644–45); and to *La Place Royale* (1633–34), where the protagonist Cléandre has a monologue in 1.3 about the conflict between his love for Angélique and his friendship for Alidor. (This scene is made to stand out by being composed in stanzas (*stances*), a more varied semi-lyrical metre than the standard alexandrine couplets.) After Corneille, neither Molière nor Marivaux highlight the same theme; nor does it appear in the Figaro plays of Beaumarchais.

The subject continued to interest Italian dramatists. Riccoboni addressed it in three of his six unpublished scenarios, one of which is entitled *La vera amicizia* [True

---

36 Days 2, 5, 9, 19, 22, 27, 29, 30, and 34.
37 Andrews 2008: 200; Scala 1976: II, 353–54: 'Isabella, dopo l'esser stata sopra pensiero, rivolta a Flavio, li dice, poich'egli ha voluto mostrar la grandezza dell'animo suo con dare ad altrui quello che piú egli amava al mondo, ch'ella li vuol far conoscere non esserle punto inferiore, col donar anch'ella quella cosa che tanto amava, togliendosi Flavio e donandolo a Flaminia soggiungendo che come cosa di Flavio, si dona ad Orazio, dicendo a Orazio che doni Flaminia sua sorella a Flavio, suo carissimo amico. Oratio, e Flavio si contentano di quanto ha proposto Isabella, si danno la fede, s'abbracciano, dicendo che disporranno i padri a contentarsi'.

Friendship]: the importance of male bonding, and its precedence over heterosexual love, was one of the conservative values which he thought comedies should proclaim.[38] We might not associate the topic with Goldoni in his most successful surviving comedies, but at the very start of his career, when he was more inclined to preach at his audience, he was as emphatic on the subject as was Riccoboni. In *I due gemelli veneziani*, the hero Tonino, the 'clever' twin of the two, perceives that he is being deceived by his friend Florindo, who is his rival over a woman. He reacts in III.6 with a long moralistic soliloquy. It includes the following statements, in Venetian dialect:

> TONINO [...] The law of friendship is the most sacred thing on earth. [...] Love of women is based on a passion of the lower senses. Love of wealth is based on a corruption of nature. The love in friendship is based on real virtue — and yet the world gives it so little value. Pylades and Orestes don't serve as examples any more, to friends in modern times. Faithful Achates is just a subject for jokes.[39]

There is an element of misogyny here (supported with classical references) which characterizes our retrospective view of eighteenth-century Illuminism. It was equally detectable in the sixteenth-century humanist ideas which preceded the Enlightenment. Over three centuries, each of these thought systems in turn affected classical comedy — they acted as a resistant counterbalance to the genre's more subversive aspects, those which might liberate women on stage and give them some respect and some initiative.

Marriage

It can be a rueful observation (in relation to life, as well as to theatre) that the urgent desire of a couple to come together and get married then leads to marriage itself; and that in the long term marriage may or may not be a happy ending. With regard to classical comic theatre, it is hard not to note that there are just two stories which are most often told: the tale of the couple who triumph over the odds to become husband and wife, and the tale of the wife who is determined to cuckold her husband. The latter version was pushed out of respectable comedies relatively soon in the genre's history, but it lingered for longer in popular farces involving *commedia dell'arte* masks. The troupe in the well-known opera *I pagliacci* (1892) is shown touring with a standard story of Colombina cheating her husband Pagliaccio with her lover Arlecchino. (Ruggiero Leoncavallo, who wrote his own libretto, specified that the action takes place in southern Italy between 1865 and 1870.)

Wives who seek lovers, in stereotypical versions of the story, are most often dissatisfied with their husbands through being faced either with tyrannical jealousy

---

38 Riccoboni 1973: 155–82.
39 'L'amicizia xe la piú sagra leze del mondo. [...] L'amor delle donne el xe fondà sulla passion del senso inferior. L'amor della roba el xe fondà sul vizio della natura corrotta. L'amor dell'amicizia xe fondà sulla vera virtú; e pur el mondo ghe ne fa cussí poco conto. Pilade e Oreste non serve piú d'esempio ai amici moderni. El fido Acate xe un nome ridicolo al dí d'ancuo.' For more on this speech, see Andrews 1997b.

or with sexual impotence. Such situations arose from the frequent pairing in real society of old men and young women (see Chapter 23). This is not a trope derived from Roman comedy: it came into early modern literature and drama from various forms of medieval narrative. The most obvious source was again Boccaccio's *Decameron*: stories such as II.10, where an abducted wife refuses to be ransomed by her decrepit husband, and prefers to stay with her sexually active kidnapper. Literary laments by unsatisfied or ill-treated wives had become a separate identifiable genre of lyric poetry or song, ascribed to a *mal-mariée* in French or a *malmaritata* in Italian. They also appeared as long speeches in prose narratives, and were easily transferred to those erudite comedies which chose to dramatize entertaining adulteries. Bibbiena's Boccaccesque *Calandra* (1513) contains the furiously frustrated wife Fulvia. Bibbiena was from Florence, and *malmaritata* speeches recur in Florentine comedies such as Giannotti's *Il vecchio amoroso* (1533), in III.6, and Cecchi's *L'assiuolo* (1549), in IV.3.[40] In *La Calandra*, Fulvia's virtuoso speeches include a general complaint about her situation in III.7, but also a witheringly aggressive tirade in III.12 when she finds her husband Calandro attempting an adultery of his own. This too was a direct borrowing from Boccaccio (III.6), and became a useful repertoire contribution to knockabout comedy.

I noted in the previous chapter that roles for mothers were thin on the ground, and that an older woman was not a fixed role in a *commedia dell'arte* troupe. This contributes to the fact that classical comedies offer relatively few studies of marital relations as such, particularly in plays written by Italian dramatists. The French farce tradition had been keen to dramatize vigorous hostile bickerings between husband and wife, but the legacy of Roman comedy did not push plots in that direction. Some of Molière's wives may be fed up with the stupidity of the husbands who are the comic targets of their plays; but of these long-suffering women it is only Orgon's wife Elmire who takes any initiative, in order to expose the hypocrisy of Tartuffe. An interesting exception to these patterns is *Les Femmes savantes*. Here the comic target is the wife Philaminte rather than the husband Chrysale; and the scenes which show Chrysale's evasive tactics, when faced with the wife whom he is afraid to resist openly, are among Molière's funniest. The play in fact opens with a discussion about marriage between the two sisters Armande and Henriette. Armande claims to be rejecting the body, and vulgar human frailties ('bassesses humaines'), in favour of purely Platonic attachments; Henriette comes as close as *bienséance* permitted to expressing desire for a sexual union: 'a husband, children, a household' ('un mari, des enfants, un ménage'). The undermining irony here, as Henriette well knows, is that Armande has been in love with the man who is now courting Henriette.

In less refined comic writing, it was assumed as a matter of course that all young virgins, of all classes, were obsessed with the desire to get a husband. The plays which were unequivocal about this were those of the Parisian Théâtre-Italien, less constrained by *bienséance* than their erudite rivals. In addition, the Italian actors

---

40 It should be noted, however, that in the best-known Florentine adultery comedy of all, Machiavelli's *La mandragola*, Lucrezia is bullied against her will into her liaison with Callimaco.

and their French dramatists were happily subversive on the subject of marriage as such. There are countless comments and gags, delivered in a knowing tone across the footlights, which assume that marriage is a kind of confinement from which both husbands and wives are constantly trying to escape. A picture is painted of a society which functions on the basis of institutionalized adultery. Parisian spectators seem to have been happy to enjoy this as an escapist carnival version of their own lives. Given that Italian dramatists, earlier and later, were not inclined to create the same atmosphere for their own native public, it is striking how subversive and sarcastic Italian actors were prepared to be in their presentation of French marital behaviour. I have suggested in Chapter 10 that, being by definition outsiders and almost outlaws, they had an unwritten licence to play games with their audience's self-image.

Neither Marivaux in France nor Goldoni in Italy was prepared to conduct close analyses, entertaining or not, of relations between husband and wife. In Beaumarchais's *Mariage de Figaro*, however, there emerge questions which had been repressed during the previous two and a half centuries of the comic genre. In *Le Barbier de Séville*, the dramatist had presented a standard tale of Comte Almaviva and Rosine triumphing over Dr Bartholo to achieve their desired marriage. *Le Mariage de Figaro* shows that same relationship turning sour: the Comte has become a predatory philanderer, and the Comtesse Rosine is deeply unhappy. She is tempted in her turn by the charms of the young aristocratic page-boy Chérubin. These disharmonies are triumphantly and wittily resolved, through a series of deceits and disguises which belong firmly to the comic tradition (see also Chapter 26). Before his denouement, however, Beaumarchais delivered a subtle debate about how marital partners should behave to each other, including the implication (which is perhaps very eighteenth-century, even very French) that women have a duty to retain men's affection by adding 'variety' to their bedroom behaviour.[41] No other comedy in the classical mode attempts anything remotely similar in the way of comments on the married state, let alone in the way of sexual advice. *Le Mariage de Figaro* is both a supreme achievement of the genre and its final point of arrival.

The celebration named in the titles of Beaumarchais's *Mariage* and Da Ponte's *Nozze* is the wedding of two servants, even though the existing marriage of their noble employers is also closely examined. All through the history of classical comedy and of *commedia dell'arte*, there was the possibility of unions between lower-class characters, to complement those of their superiors. Pedrolino or Arlequin pursued, and sometimes married, Franceschina or Colombine. Such events were treated in a variety of tones, from the derisive to the sentimental. Relationships between social classes are as central to the comic genre as those between genders; and they form the subject of my next chapter.

---

41 For a full discussion of this, I refer again to Andrews 2001.

CHAPTER 25

Servants and Masters

In early modern Europe, as in most of history, work could only be performed by the human hand, by manipulated tools, or by trained and guided animals. All civilizations therefore functioned on divisions of labour which produced a hierarchy. There were those who did the work, wielded the tools, or guided the animals; and there were those for whom that work was done, who were kept alive by muscle power which was not their own, so they could concentrate on other contributions to society — typically commanding, fighting, buying and selling, thinking, or creating. Some of those who were being served managed to get a free ride, and were not contributing anything at all. (It is doubtful whether any of those statements can be consigned exclusively to the past tense.)

This archetypal situation, inevitable as it may be, produces tensions, differences, and conflicts between those who work and those who benefit from their labour. In narrative or dramatic art, such confrontations can be presented on a sliding scale of tones, from intensely serious to utterly farcical. In stage comedy it is obvious which end of the tonal scale is likely to predominate. In the classical genre, in this thematic area as in others, dramatic practice and emphasis showed some changes from the sixteenth to the eighteenth centuries.

Dramatizing Hierarchy

In both Roman and early modern times, the vast majority of subordinate oppressed workers in society were those who produced food from the fields. Classical stage comedy, however, dealt almost exclusively with urban families in city streets and houses: plays dealing with rural societies were rare, and those which do occur have an air of deliberate novelty. Slaves in Plautus and Terence, and paid servants in comedies from Ariosto to Beaumarchais, are mostly providers of domestic service. The work which they routinely do is almost never mentioned in detail, not even cooking, which in Roman comedy involved calling in specialist caterers for wedding banquets and similar functions. Hired comedy cooks in Plautus are dramatic stereotypes, cameo roles providing their own rough entertainment. They were occasionally imitated by erudite Italian playwrights, but did not become regular comic characters or masks. In the comedies studied here, servants of both sexes — *servi* and *fantesche*, *valets* and *suivantes* — wait on their employers personally, run errands and carry messages for them, take initiatives to support them (or sometimes to hinder them) in their love affairs, and offer advice which may or may not be confidential. Servants also keep watch on doors, and so can admit or repel visitors.

There is rarely any allusion to the cleaning, laundering, bed-making, horse-tending, table-waiting, and similar duties which would occupy the time of their real equivalents. Dealing with chamber pots may be mentioned in less inhibited comedies, if they are emptied out of the window on to someone's head.[1] We can find just two notable exceptions to this kind of omission. Both of them occur in plays still frequently revived, but none the less both stand out as rarities. In III.1 of Molière's *L'Avare*, Harpagon lines up the servants of his household and makes it clear what they should not spend his money on, effectively providing a set of one-line 'miser jokes' against himself. The audience thus hears details of domestic arrangements which are being ludicrously curtailed: inadequate food and drink, servants' liveries with embarrassing holes in them, underfed horses, insufficient candles. Then Goldoni's *La locandiera* contains a justly famous sequence in III.1–6. As she irons sheets for her inn, Mirandolina conducts a complex game, holding at arm's length both the Cavaliere whom she has tricked into falling in love with her, and her employee Fabrizio who considers himself promised to her in marriage. As irons are fetched back and forth from being heated on the hob in the next room, her domestic task becomes both a displacement activity and a psychological weapon, in a masterly exercise of dramatic choreography which probably has no equivalent in any other work of theatre. In the comic genre overall, this exceptional scene underlines how rarely the ordinary work of a household is depicted or even mentioned on stage.

In terms of how subordinates are treated by their masters, there is a detectable difference between the status and predicament of slaves in ancient Rome and of paid servants in later times. Roman slaves are threatened with dire punishments — severe flogging, the treadmill, being sent to the quarries — which did not usually apply between 1500 and 1800 CE. However, in early modern times employers were still perfectly entitled to beat or whip their servants. Slapstick violence was expected to be part of comedy, including *commedia erudita*: the first example of a master beating a servant on stage is in Bibbiena's *Calandra* when Calandro beats Fessenio in III.3; and although the spectators are on Fessenio's side against his idiot master, they are still expected to enjoy the knockabout spectacle. Two centuries later, such amusements still appear in early plays by Goldoni: Florindo beats Truffaldino in *Il servitore di due padroni*, I.13.

Those scenes are based on social reality: when servants manage to subject their masters to physical harm, we enter a world of licensed comic fantasy. We can expect subversion and reversal to be a key component of comedy; but as our history progresses, we find it expressed less often in outright violence. As part of his reforms of comedy, Goldoni rejected such scenes as both implausible and socially unacceptable — they breached 'decorum' in all senses of that word. The fact that he expressed himself so firmly shows that there were still practices to disapprove

[1] This happens in *Gl'ingannati*, IV.6, an erudite academic comedy.

of: such theatergrams were still common in improvised Italian comedy. It is easy to trace them back to the scenarios of Flaminio Scala. In *Il cavadente* (see also Chapter 19), Pedrolino's dental revenge on Pantalone is triggered by an unrealistic scuffle between them, in which Pedrolino gets bitten on the ear. There are similarly clownish encounters in those scripted *commedie gravi* which combined a farcical sub-plot with more serious romantic issues faced by the Lovers. In France, there was considerably less violence between employers and employees in approved classical comedy. Neither Corneille nor Marivaux used it very much, though Marivaux makes the occasional exception for his Italian Arlequin character, who beats Trivelin with his slapstick in *La Double Inconstance*, III.2. The slapstick was part of a Harlequin's uniform, both in France and in Italy, so he was almost obliged to use it on somebody. For Molière, we have seen (in Chapter 17) how Boileau referred to the scene where Géronte is beaten in a sack in *Les Fourberies de Scapin* (see also Chapter 27), so as to distinguish the master playwright's low farce from his high comedy.

The subordination of female slaves or servants to their male masters could be sexual as well as economic. In ancient Rome female slavery was simply assumed to involve sexual slavery. In Plautus and Terence, the young giggling girls pursued by inadequate young lovers (as in Plautus's *Pseudolus*) are the legal property of a pimp, whose stage role was the that of a stock villain. Within a real domestic household all sorts of exploitations could occur legally, but the Roman dramatists show little interest in them. Italian *commedie erudite*, by contrast, sometimes assumed openly that a female servant would end up in bed with her male employer. In fact, early modern social history is full of real cases of this relationship, with illegitimate children produced as a result. An early relevant example is Ludovico Ariosto himself, who acknowledged the son he had fathered by a servant and helped to find him a respectable career. Then Ariosto's *La Lena* is centred around an exploitative liaison between the bourgeois Fazio and the lower-class Lena, which has not produced any offspring but is presented as unsavoury on both sides. In some other Italian comedies, female employees take it for granted that they will have spent time in bed with their patriarch employers, not always showing much resentment at the fact. The resulting banter between the relevant characters is written as mildly derisory but ultimately quite comfortable; and in relation to the plot it is incidentally entertaining rather than having a high profile. The earliest and most influential example (once again) is *Gl'ingannati*, in scenes where the nurse Clemenzia gently derides old Virginio for his declining sexual prowess. The message in this brand of comedy was that such relationships were to be expected, and that lower-class women — unlike the heroines whom they might be looking after — had no honour to lose and had to put up with it. Such situations disappeared from classical comedy, both in Italy and in France, from the seventeenth century on.

Underlying the dramatic portrayal of employers and their employees was an ingrained prejudice about differences between them. Along with the 'essentialism' about gender mentioned in the previous chapter, there were similar assumptions about social status.[2] Just as men were seen as essentially different from women, there was believed (at least for the purposes of fiction) to be an inherent, detectable difference between people born into upper and lower classes. Gentlefolk had inherited qualities of courage, courtesy, and generosity; if they failed to display those qualities, they might be blamed and punished on stage. The lower orders could be forgiven for being cowardly and self-seeking: there was something almost wrong if they were not. Noble or bourgeois heroines were obstinately faithful to their sworn love of one man, and clung to those obligations in the face of threats and difficulties; their plebeian nurses (like Juliet's nurse in Shakespeare) advised them to take the easy way out, and marry the person whom their family had chosen.[3] In fairy tales as well as in drama, long-lost children of noble or royal families stood out from their fostering environment because of a naturally inherited grace and refinement which overrode the deficiencies of their upbringing. (In Shakespeare's *The Winter's Tale* (IV.4), Perdita behaves in a way which 'smacks of something greater than herself' as compared with the shepherds who have reared her.) The English word 'clown', etymologically, meant 'countryman' or 'peasant'. To an upper-class audience, the lower classes were inferior by nature as well as by nurture, and potentially funny by definition. The main defects which were manipulated to provoke laughter were ignorance, incompetence with words, unbridled sexuality, and most of all gluttony. Food was a real and constant problem for the poor: the lower-class preoccupation with it was transformed into a cartoon-like comic obsession. All these traits were inseparable from the routines of a *commedia dell'arte* 'Second Zani' such as the various incarnations of Harlequin.

This was a predictable mockery of the subordinate classes, which catered for the prejudices of a relatively affluent audience. I have shown in Chapter 23 that there were also some derisive stereotypes for the employers of such servants, the elderly fathers who were going to be defeated in the standard comic contest. In Italian improvised theatre the two most durable masks were Pantalone, with his merchant's avarice and his inappropriate lust, and the Dottore, with his unshakable fantasies of intellectual superiority. These fixed caricatures lay behind many of the more thoughtful and probing attacks mounted against bourgeois fathers by Molière, by subsequent Comédie-Française playwrights, by Goldoni, and by Beaumarchais in *Le Barbier de Séville*. The idea of identifying and mocking behaviour identified as aristocratic took longer to be accepted, and for some time it was more common in French than Italian comedy. Italian satirical targets did not include comic noblemen, at least not before French dramatists such as Molière began to show the way. After 1700, Riccoboni thought that such a character had to be treated with some care, producing 'a mixture of the noble and the comic', whereas servants on stage were automatically funny.[4] Goldoni learned from his French models that such satire was possible; and he incorporated it into those of his comedies which proclaimed

---

2   Class essentialism in Goldoni is addressed by Günsberg 2001: 184–85.
3   This contrast is explored in Clubb 1989: Chapter 3, as the theatergram which she labels 'Women as Wonder'. We can add that the trope also became a cliché in seventeenth-century Venetian opera.
4   In his 'Proemio' to the scenario *Il giocatore*; see Riccoboni 1973: 129.

or assumed the virtues of the industrious Venetian merchant class, in contrast to a rather sour portrayal of that city's effete and ineffective nobility.[5]

In the light of all this, when a lower-class figure posed as one of his superiors (it was usually a male character who did this), the laughter provoked always cut both ways, in terms of who was being cheered on and who was being derided. To be sure, there was a subversive glee, for proletarian spectators and perhaps for others, in seeing a servant take command and give orders to masters; and it was also enjoyable to see the pretensions of masters undermined and rendered ridiculous by the servant's caricatures of high-class language and manners. In most cases, however, the impostor failed to keep up the pretence for very long: his 'essential' vulgarity made it easy to see through him, so that in the end the audience could laugh at his failures and put him back in his place. Plots and tricks like these are found most often in material from the Paris Italians, including the summarized scenes in the notebooks of Biancolelli (see Chapter 21). In Gherardi's *Théâtre italien* compilation, there is a play entitled *Arlequin empereur dans la lune*, in which the star clown does indeed present himself in one scene as an emperor from the moon. However, he eventually confesses that he is illiterate: 'We Emperors don't spend time reading, that's too middle-class for us'.[6]

A more nuanced approach was taken when employer and employee temporarily changed places, each one pretending to be the other. The origin of this dramatic idea is found in Plautus's *Captivi*, where the prisoner of war Philocrates and his slave Tyndarus exchange identities in order to negotiate a complicated ransom. The play is acknowledged by critics, and by Plautus himself in his prologue, to pursue themes of trust and honesty which are unusually serious for comedy. Because of this Latin model, early modern comedies which use the device tend not to question either the loyalty of the disguised servant or his ability to keep up the pretence.[7] The earliest example of the trope is the second comedy in our history, Ariosto's *I suppositi*, in which young Erostrato swaps identities with his servant Dulippo, is employed in the house of his beloved Polinesta, gets access to her, and seduces her. The device was then applied by Shakespeare (but without the sexual consummation) to the characters Lucentio, Tranio, and Bianca in the sub-plot of *The Taming of the Shrew* (c. 1593). The Ariosto play had previously been translated by George Gascoigne as *Supposes* (1573). In this theatergram generally, both impostors may risk serious penalties if they are discovered, as they are in *I suppositi* and also in the influential *La pellegrina* (performed 1589) by the Intronati Academy. Later in Marivaux's *Le Jeu de l'amour et du hasard* (see Chapter 11), the identity switch is performed by both the male and the female lovers and their servants. Here, typically for Marivaux, the emphasis moves away from the mechanics and perils of trickery to analyses of true emotions and true identity. The fathers of the two young lovers are colluding

---

5   See Günsberg 2001: Chapter 4.
6   'Nous Empereurs, nous ne nous amusons point à lire, cela est trop Bourgeois pour nous'. The play appears in Gherardi 1701: 1.
7   Scarron's *Jodelet, ou Le Maître valet* (1643, see Chapter 6) is something of an exception: like various Harlequins in disguise, Jodelet shows limited competence in his attempts at aping the nobility.

with the deception from the start, and so there is no risk of their imposing brutal punishments.

There is of course an underlying implausibility in this whole device of identity exchange, as in all stories of disguise, a fact which I shall explore further in my final two chapters.

Servants Defeating Masters

Just as sons and daughters tend to triumph over fathers in the classical comic contest (see Chapter 23), so servants are expected to outwit their masters and achieve a temporary subversion of power. That at least is the pattern which the average reader may absorb from Roman comedies. The slave Pseudolus who gives his name to Plautus's comedy tricks his master Simo out of large sums of money, so that the young master Calidorus can gain possession of the girl with whom he is besotted. Calidorus is wimpish and useless, and has to rely entirely on the slave's greater intelligence.[8] In monologues addressed to the audience, the slave presents his schemes as a kind of military campaign in which he is going to be the victor. It is often now stated that these relationships were simply transferred to early modern Italian comedy, and then especially to *commedia dell'arte*: Arlecchino (or Pedrolino, or Scapino) tricks and defeats Pantalone (or the Dottore), so that young Isabella and Orazio can get married in the face of their parents' opposition. Such plots are indeed very frequent, and they were a significant part of an audience's expectations in an early modern theatre auditorium. They are not found, however, in every play or in every scenario. To start with, the apparent requirement of comedy — that the social hierarchy, as well as the generational one, should be undermined on stage — clashed with the alleged moralistic purpose of classical comedy (see Chapters 17 and 21), and with the 'essentialist' assumption that the lower classes should entertain by being incompetent. Then later, in the eighteenth century, comic dramatists were facing, accommodating, and even proposing some serious new questions about what should be the proper relationship between masters and servants.

The very first Italian *commedie erudite* do indeed present lower-class characters who drive the plot and defeat the aims of their employers or patrons.[9] Ariosto's *La cassaria* features tricks played by the servant Vulpino and the con man Trappola in a plot quite reminiscent of *Pseudolus*. In *I suppositi* we have described above the exchange of identities between Erostrato and Dulippo. Bibbiena's *Calandra* revolves entirely around deceptions mounted by Fessenio, who is pretending to serve one master while working for another. The essential trick in Machiavelli's *Mandragola* is devised by the parasite Ligurio, and its main victim is the foolish lawyer Nicia. However, such patterns were not uniformly repeated for long. Already in Ariosto's later comedies of the 1520s the outcome of the class struggle is more complex:

---

8   An ageing generation of British television viewers may remember these stereotypes being faithfully reproduced in the farcical series *Up Pompeii!* (1969–70), starring Frankie Howerd as the slave Lurcio.
9   See Schironi 2013.

schemes mounted by servants do play a part in those stories, but the solution is reached just as much by luck and confusion as by intrigue. Modern Italian critics have seen the Machiavellian contrast between arbitrary Fortune and human initiative (*Virtù*) as a subject addressed by sixteenth-century comedies, and they have noted that Fortune is likely to control the final outcome as often as not.[10] When more romanesque elements were introduced into comic plots — wandering heroes and heroines, uncertain identities, moral dilemmas involving fidelity — the extent to which servants procured happy endings varied even more greatly. This wider range of narrative tropes was then transferred to *commedia dell'arte* scenarios. Without having attempted a statistical analysis, one can come away from reading Italian comedies, scripted and improvised, with the impression that stories in which servants defeat masters constitute around half the total number. In the other half, servants either attempt intrigues which fail, or else are present in the play purely to provide entertainment. As later in the Parisian Théâtre-Italien, the 'triumph' of Arlecchino/ Arlequin and his servile colleagues was not so much that they always won the comic contest mounted by the story, but rather that they always won the attention and the hearts of spectators.

If a servant is to mount tricks and control the plot, then he (or sometimes she) needs to be clearly more capable than at least some of his or her employers. Sometimes this extends to a more general show of perception or intelligence, for example when servants can see through the deceptions of blocking characters who are deceiving their masters, or when they help to channel the audience's mockery of a master who is a comic target. In Ariosto's *Il negromante* (1520 and 1528), the magic powers claimed by the eponymous charlatan are taken seriously by young Cinzio and doubted by his servant Temolo; but this balance of opposing perceptions was not then taken up very often by other Italian dramatists. It was developed later by Molière, especially through his emerging brand of *soubrette* role for a female servant. Dorine makes a substantial and entertaining contribution to *Le Tartuffe*: she sees through Tartuffe's hypocrisy from the start, and does her best to persuade her young mistress Mariane to stand up for herself and to stop quarrelling with her lover. The idiocies of Monsieur Jourdain in *Le Bourgeois gentilhomme* are mercilessly mocked, with helpless laughter, by his serving maid Nicole; and many of the 'miser gags' levelled against Harpagon in *L'Avare* originate from servants. In *Le Malade imaginaire* (1.6), Toinette is explicit about her right to contradict her hypochondriac master Argan: 'When a master has no idea what he's doing, then a sensible maidservant is right to correct him'.[11] Earlier Italian comedy had been more reluctant to attribute perceptive intelligence to the working classes. Things changed later: Günsberg shows how Goldoni was willing to give to the 'first Zani' mask of Brighella the role of a sober advisor to his social superiors.[12]

---

10   The opposition between *Fortuna* and *Virtù* is a central thesis of Machiavelli's renowned political treatise *Il principe* (composed 1513, published 1532). The meaning given to *Virtù* — masculine skill or initiative — makes it inappropriate to translate the word as 'Virtue' in English.
11   'Quand un maître ne songe pas à ce qu'il fait, une servante bien sensée est en droit de le redresser.'
12   Günsberg 2001: 186–87.

In terms of agency within the plot, Pierre Corneille drastically reduced the importance of servant roles, as he concentrated on the moral and emotional dilemmas of their masters and mistresses. Other French playwrights were more willing to borrow and adapt a more traditional Italianate approach. Molière invented his own unmasked mask, Sganarelle, to whom he gave a series of very different narrative functions in plays which range in length and substance from five acts to one. In his more truly classical comedies, there are some servants who participate in tricking their masters and bringing them to heel, but (like Dorine in *Le Tartuffe*) they are often working or arguing in conjunction with the wives or offspring of their victims. For example, in *Le Bourgeois gentilhomme*, the scheme to deceive Monsieur Jourdain is orchestrated by the valet Covielle (a name derived from the Italian mask Coviello), but it is the young lover Cléonte who actually disguises himself as a Turkish prince. Other French comedies, before and after Molière, offer a mixture of servant roles and personalities who can be sometimes more and sometimes less Plautine or Italianate, more involved or less involved in deceptive schemes. I have noted (in Chapter 14) Regnard's *Les Folies amoureuses*, in which the determined schemer Crispin works hard against the equally obstinate lustful guardian Albert, and in the process introduces himself in a manner which foreshadows Figaro. Marivaux, as has also been seen, made deliberate use of Italian comedy performers, and especially of Arlequin (Tommaso Visentini) and Trivelin (Pierre-François Biancolelli). However, the use he made of these masks did not usually revolve around trickery directed against employers (or princes), and certainly not around a victory of the servant over the master. I have remarked earlier that Marivaux was more interested in portraying the human emotions of servants alongside those of their superiors; and his experimental philosophical sketches expressed a serious reforming interest in class relationships, attacking the mistreatment and contempt which subordinates often suffered. Meanwhile Riccoboni, first in Italy and then in France, tried to adapt his comic plots to what he saw as appropriate for polite society. His surviving scenarios contain servants (Arlecchino and Trivelino) who entertain by being confused and incompetent, but whose actions have little impact on the intrigue.

In Venice, Goldoni moved in a similar direction to Riccoboni. In order to win the confidence and support of audiences and actors, his earliest plays had to acknowledge the extent to which masked insubordination was rooted in the tradition of Italian comedy. He then moved steadily away from depicting tricky insolent servants who take the initiative. He may have started in 1745 with Truffaldino in *Il servitore di due padroni*; but in later years his attention was directed elsewhere, though he was prepared to offer quick cameo portrayals of grotesquely comic street hawkers and domestic retainers. Even Truffaldino, the desperately mendacious servant of two masters, does not achieve any victory: from his point of view, the play is just a suspenseful postponement of the moment when his lies and inventions all collapse.

Nevertheless, and despite these eighteenth-century tendencies to realism, to reform, and to *sensibilité*, it was still expected that in a more robust traditional farce an astute servant should defeat an elderly affluent victim on behalf of a pair of struggling lovers. The format returns with a vengeance in Beaumarchais's *Barbier de Séville*. Then in *Le Mariage de Figaro*, it is the servant's own marriage which is at stake, at least as much as that of his employers, the Count and Countess of Almaviva. In those two comedies, Beaumarchais took the truly revolutionary step of convincing the public that the personality and opinions of the servant Figaro could reflect those of his creator. Looking back over a 280-year tradition of classical comedy, one can ask how often in previous plays servants had been given any opinions at all.

Servants with a Point of View: Derision and Collusion

At the start of Lorenzo Da Ponte's *Don Giovanni* libretto for Mozart, the servant Leporello is grumbling to the audience about his subordinate status. He works in all weathers, he tells us, for a master 'who is never satisfied', and who is currently dallying upstairs with yet another woman, while he himself has to stand outside on guard. He thinks it's time that their roles were reversed: 'I want to play the gentleman, | I don't want to serve any longer!'.[13] In launching his Don Juan story with this now familiar number, Da Ponte was not the first dramatist to push that tale in the direction of the classical comic genre — almost contaminating the fiercely satirical tone of the Spanish morality fable. A grumbling speech from a servant, of either sex, had been a standard item in comedy from the very beginning: improvising actors playing Zani, Arlecchino, or Franceschina would possess multiple versions in their personal repertoire. Often they would complain about the especially hard time that servants had to undergo if their master or mistress was in love: the audience would be entertained by examples of wildly passionate and inconsistent behaviour, and the problems it caused. The trope can be traced, like so many others, back to *Gl'ingannati*. In I.5, the servant Spela describes the attempts of his old master Gherardo, who sees himself as a potential bridegroom, to make himself look young and attractive; and in II.2, Pasquella recounts how young Isabella has been expressing her frustrated physical desires with actions which border on the obscene (quoted in Chapter 17).

Every time a servant was given a speech or a reaction which mocked his or her employers, or which expressed resentment or contempt, the response of an audience was likely in the past to have hovered between the attitudes of derision and collusion which I discussed in Chapter 17. Such potential ambivalence may now be less clear to modern spectators of these plays. We no longer belong to the society that the play depicts, we do not have to respect its hierarchies, and our own world (we think) is more egalitarian. We have subscribed to the theatrical 'comic contract' implicitly proposed by such comedies, which in addition to a suspension of disbelief invites a suspension of social rules in favour of more subversive modes of enjoyment.[14] In most cases, the employers who are being targeted are characters at whom we are supposed to laugh anyway. For early modern audiences, however, the same questions applied as I raised in Chapter 23, about parents being opposed

---

13   'Notte e giorno faticar | per chi nulla sa gradir; [...] Voglio fare il gentiluomo, | e non voglio piú servir!' (Da Ponte 1956: 195).
14   I refer again here to Grene 1980.

and defeated by their offspring. A majority of parents in the audience might also constitute a majority of employers, who would not tolerate insubordinate servants in their normal lives. This is especially true with regard to fully scripted Italian comedies in the sixteenth century, most of which were performed in courts, academies, and other social groups where the spectators represented an affluent ruling class. They may have participated in the 'comic contract' in relation to stage events and denouements; but any expression by a servant character of large-scale class hostility would be more problematic. Mockery of a fictional employer, whom the comedy was portraying as ridiculous to start with, was acceptable. Resentment about the very fact of occupying a servile role would be another matter. In fact statements equivalent to Leporello's 'voglio fare il gentiluomo' are rare in *commedia erudita*. The examples which I shall now briefly introduce stand out as atypical: the fact that they exist at all is of great interest, but they did not then contribute to a standard comic repertoire.

The Paduan dramatist Angelo Beolco (*c.* 1502–1542), better known as 'Ruzante', has featured in my pages less than he deserves. Many of his comedies do not adhere closely to classical patterns: he often ignores family-based plots, and he is most famous for his hard-hitting portraits (or caricatures) of rustic peasants, rather than of city-based characters from the Roman comedy mould. He is nevertheless (for those readers and performers who can deal with his archaic rural dialect) the supreme maverick genius of sixteenth-century Italian comedy.[15] Ruzante's peasant characters, especially in confidential monologues to the audience, are known for supporting a set of values proclaimed as 'natural', in opposition to the assumptions and practices of sophisticated urban society. The audience reaction which they invite holds a shifting position between derision of, and collusion with, their verbal and ideological simplicity. Ruzante's peasants are sometimes refreshing, sometimes just entertainingly silly. Not many of them appear in a simple master-servant relationship with an employer; but in II.1 of *La vaccaria* [The Cowherd's Play] (performed 1533, published 1551) the characters Truffo and Vezzo muse briefly on the short straw which they have arbitrarily drawn in life, compared with more fortunate classes:

> TRUFFO   A bit of 'natural' is worth a whole bag of logicals and philosorificals. [...] That lot think that no one can do anything without running off to look at a book first.
> VEZZO   If only the wheel turned, and the cards were reshuffled, and we had all the loot and they were where we are now! We'd be the Harry Stottles then; and when we said something, everyone would shut up and listen like crazy. [...]
> TRUFFO   They can say what they like, these rich bosses, but they can't do without us, 'cos if we weren't there to be the servants, they couldn't be the masters.[16]

---

15   The definitive English-language study of Ruzante is Ferguson 2000. I have attempted to depict him more briefly in Andrews 1993: 125–41.
16   'TRUFFO: Un buon snaturale è miegio assé che tante luòriche e filuòriche. [...] El ghe par mo che co' i no la tuole zò de qui so libri a perlo, i no sapi far gnente. VEZZO: Oh, se la rua o le carte

This last observation, which one might call 'proto-Marxist', is an insight rarely expressed at that time. It is however reflected at greater length in one play to which I have often referred: the Intronati comedy *La pellegrina*, attributed to Girolamo Bargagli and performed at the Florentine wedding celebrations of 1589. In III.4, for no reason really demanded by the plot, there is a long debate between two male servants about what they owe, or do not owe, to their employers. Carletto upholds a textbook set of values, in which he should be totally loyal to his master: 'What should be closer to me than my master's interests? [...] true service, Targhetta, comes more from the soul than from the body'.[17] Targhetta has no patience with this feudal attitude, proposing instead what in modern terms sounds like a trade union doctrine:

> TARGHETTA   Loyalty? That's a word that the bosses are always coming up with, so as to get themselves served better. Why should you give loyalty to someone who treats you badly, orders you about with no consideration, gets mad at you for no reason, holds back your wages, and then would sacrifice you a hundred times over for a hunting dog or a falcon? [...] If all the servants organized themselves together, they'd have to treat us properly. How else would they manage?
>
> CARLETTO   And if the masters all organized themselves and agreed not to take on any servants, how would *we* manage? How would anyone manage without anything to eat?
>
> TARGHETTA   And if they didn't have anyone to serve them, how would *they* manage?[18]

In 1589, for its performance and its publication, the text of *La pellegrina* had undergone some major changes, compared with the original manuscript which survives from the 1560s. Some scenes satirizing corrupt clergy were censored, but II.4 was left unaltered.[19] Whether that scene was then actually performed before the Grand Duke and his guests we cannot know: evidence of that sort about productions never survives from the sixteenth century. It has simply to be observed that socio-political (or socio-economic) debates like that between Carletto and Targhetta are not found (to my knowledge) in other published Italian comedies of the period. It seems

---

desse volta, e che nu aessàm la roba e igi fosse co' a' seón nu! A' paressàm Stuòtene nu tuti, e co' a' faelessàm, tuti ne scolterae per una smaravegia. TRUFFO: Faze pur, sti richi, co'i vuole, ch'i no pò fare senza nu; perché se nu a' no foessàm famigi, igi no serae paruni' (Ruzante 1967: 1071). The dialect used is a version of Paduan peasant speech which is no longer extant.

17   'CARLETTO: Che cosa è piú mia propia, che l'interesse del mio signore? [...] Il vero servire, Targhetta, è piú con l'animo che col corpo' (Girolamo Bargagli, *La pellegrina*; Borsellino 1962–67: I, 494).

18   'TARGHETTA: Che fedeltà? Cotesta è una parola che hanno sempre in bocca i padroni per farsi servir bene. E che fedeltà si dee servare a chi ti tratta male, ti comanda senza discrezione, s'adira con teco senza proposito, ti fa stentare il tuo salario e talora per un bracco o per un falcone darebbe cento delle tue vite? [...] Se i servitori s'accordassero tutti insieme, bisognerebbe pure che ci trattasser bene. Come farebbono? CARLETTO: E se i padroni s'accordassero tutti a non pigliar servidori, come la faremmo noi? E chi non ha del pane, come la farebbe egli? TARGHETTA: E se non avessero chi gli servisse, come la farebbon essi?' (Bargagli, *La pellegrina*; Borsellino 1962–67: I, 495–96). There is a translation (not used here) of the whole scene by Bruno Ferraro in Bargagli 1988: 95–98.

19   See also Chapter 21, and the crucial essay on this play in Borsellino 1974.

unlikely that they would be mounted often in improvised masked theatre either, granted that the professional companies were always looking over their shoulders to fend off disapproval from those authorities who might pay them, or at least permit them, to perform. The grumblings and resentments of Zani, Arlecchino, and Franceschina, along with their temporary triumphs over masters, did invite a form of collusion. But it was a collusion which belonged firmly on the stage and not to reality. Those masks inhabited a dream world, in which comedy supplied — at most, for some spectators — a few moments of wishful thinking.

Servants in Molière are closer to reality: as observed above, their understanding of the world can be better than that of their employers. Unlike Carletto and Targhetta, though, they are never made to interrogate the social system which makes them servants in the first place. Other playwrights composing for the Comédie-Française followed the same pattern. In the Parisian Théâtre-Italien, the world dominated by Arlequin and Colombine was still essentially a theatrical bubble, like that of their predecessors in Italy: when the masked characters expressed wild radical opinions about how society should be run (some of them perhaps distantly reminiscent of passages in Ruzante), they were playing fantasy games. Satirical presentations of Parisian life, like the depictions of the legal system described in Chapter 21, never tried to formulate alternatives, or to suggest how the injustices and the corruptions might be overturned.

I have noted, also in Chapter 21, that the emergence of Enlightenment ideas in the eighteenth century began to make some dramatists more thoughtful about the behaviour of masters towards servants, and about the claim of the latter to be treated as human beings with equal, or comparable, rights. Most of Marivaux's opinions on this subject were expressed in his journalism, and in less generically comic plays such as *L'Île des esclaves* (see Chapter 21). I have remarked in addition how comedies such as *La Double Inconstance* and *Le Jeu de l'amour et du hasard* explore the feelings and attitudes of Arlequin with more respect than was normal in *commedia dell'arte*, perhaps promoting him from a 'mask' to a 'character'. Marivaux participated in a more general tendency to allow lower-class figures to ask awkward questions, from a position of ignorance and naïvety, about power relationships in civilized society.[20]

It was the Figaro plays of Beaumarchais which broke a major mould, by shifting the point of view in the direction of Figaro himself, the protagonist who is a member of the servant class. To conclude this chapter I shall consider an even more extreme case of a stage servant expressing a point of view: one which challenges and even perplexes a reader (or a spectator, or a listener) as to the reaction it might provoke in audiences in its own time. This dramatic moment was not conceived by Beaumarchais, but grafted on to his original story by Da Ponte and Mozart.

In both versions of *The Marriage of Figaro*, play and opera, the character Don Basilio is a dependent, probably salaried, of Count Almaviva. His ostensible function is as a music teacher, but this fact remains mostly in the background; more obviously, he intrigues and pimps on behalf of his master, and spies hopefully on other people's relationships. In Beaumarchais he has his own sub-plot, being interested

---

20 See Chapter 22, n. 19.

in marrying Marceline: Da Ponte's libretto wisely cuts out this distraction. In the opera he remains a blocking character, in that the Count uses him to pressurize Susanna with messages of sexual invitation accompanied by bribery or blackmail. His limited role in the plot of Da Ponte's *Le nozze di Figaro* puts him in the category of 'comically unpleasant'. We can find some of his reactions entertaining, especially in the sequence of Cherubino and the armchair in Act I, but we are not invited to be on his side.

For a moment, in the final act of the opera (IV.7), Basilio unexpectedly takes centre stage. He suggests that Figaro must tolerate the Count's designs on Susanna. The world is full of husbands who have to put up with cuckoldry, especially when the adulterer is a person of greater power:

> BASILIO In this world, my friend,
>   attacking great men head on
>   has always been dangerous.
>   They give you ninety percent, and still they've won.[21]

Basilio then delivers a solo aria ('In quegli anni') which lays out his philosophy: the only way to survive in a threatening world is to adopt the role of a harmless despicable fool. Allegorically he recounts how Milady Patience ('Donna Flemma') bestowed on him the precious gift of an ass's skin. It sheltered him from a raging tempest, and when he was faced by a beast threatening to devour him, the vile smell ('il fiuto ignobile') of the donkey hide was so repellent that the predator lost its appetite and went away. Humiliations, dangers, shame, and death ('onte, pericoli, vergogna e morte') can all be fended off by presenting oneself as an ass. The first performance of *Le nozze di Figaro* was given before Emperor Joseph II and his whole glittering court: not an auditorium which would readily identify itself with the shady Don Basilio, and certainly not a collection of people who would let themselves play the fool in order to avoid danger. Basilio's 'philosophy', in the eyes of aristocratic spectators, is one of cowardice: it seems calculated to reinforce their superior contempt. Nevertheless, it is not enunciated merely in a passing recitative: Da Ponte and Mozart obliged their noble patrons to hear it expressed in a lively full-length musical number. Those patrons may have rejected Basilio's sentiments out of hand, but they had to listen to him first. They were made to hear how a lower-class dependent saw the cards stacked against him in the poker game of life, by the 'ninety percent' which they, the noble spectators, owned and manipulated. More than three centuries later, in a society which sees itself as less oppressive, we may sometimes still recognize (aided or not by the approach of a given performer) how ideologically complex Basilio's aria is: a survival strategy which is unattractive, but which may perhaps work, proclaimed by a character who has made us laugh but who himself is unsympathetic.[22]

---

21 'BASILIO: Nel mondo, amico, | l'accozzarla co' grandi | fu pericolo ognora. | Dàn novanta per cento, e han vinto ancora'. Full text of the aria in Da Ponte 1956: 171–72.
22 In a response which may be more personal, we may also experience the orchestral flourish, with which Mozart concludes the aria, as a derisive gesture to the rest of the world, or to the audience.

In modern performances, Basilio's defiantly 'ignoble' aria is often omitted, along with the less aggressive feminist number which Mozart gave to Marcellina (see Chapter 24). *Le nozze di Figaro* is a long opera by modern standards, and directors often assume that their audience will not want to wait much longer for the central characters to attain their final reconciliation. Marcellina and Basilio are judged to provide awkward digressions. Da Ponte and Mozart nevertheless chose to create both items, and to challenge (in ways which may or may not have seemed jocular) contemporary hierarchies regarding gender roles and social class. There were limits of tolerance here which the classical comedy format had long been challenging. The two dramatizations of 'Figaro's Wedding', with music and without, move away from a comic game which is comfortable fantasy towards discomforting facts about real society. The arias of Marcellina and Basilio could not have been written before the eighteenth century, when comedy was becoming more reflective and more analytical.[23]

In other respects Beamarchais's story, which provides a climax to my history of the genre, remains firmly anchored in a central narrative tradition. The intrigues pursued by Figaro and Suzanne and the Countess are the devices which had always been at the heart of the comic genre: deceits, lies, and disguises. Disguise in particular will be the focus of my next chapter.

---

23   For different reactions to these two arias, see Allanbrook 1982.

CHAPTER 26

Disguise and Mistaken Identity

Comedy thrives on misapprehension. Almost all classical comedy plots contain at least one moment when a character is in error. Someone on stage believes something to be true which is false, or believes something to be false which is true. Such errors could be central to classical tragedies too: Aristotle in his *Poetics* gives great importance to an act of recognition (anagnorisis, ἀναγνώρισις), which alters the previous assumptions made by protagonists such as Oedipus in Sophocles. These disruptive errors, and their correction in key theatrical moments, were passed on to early modern tragedy, tragicomedy, and *opera seria*.

In comedy, confusions may be due to an accidental combination of circumstances — as I remarked in the previous chapter, some comic plots are driven more by the caprices of Fortune than by intrigue. Very frequently, though, a mistaken belief is created by another character, in a deliberate act of deceit: comedy also thrives on trickery. When this is so, spectators always know what the trickster is doing, and can see the situation from his or her point of view: comedy does not involve confusing the audience. Part of the essential experience is that we know more, or better, than the characters whom we are watching. Our superior derisive enjoyment can override, perhaps temporarily, any general sympathy which we may be invited to feel for one character as against another: if an endearing romantic heroine gets things wrong, and therefore says or does something silly, then we still laugh at her.

Tricks, lies, and misunderstandings thus prevail in most of the plays included in this history: they come close to defining the classical comic genre. In Ariosto's *Cassaria* and *Suppositi*, servants spread false stories in order to bring lovers together, and the audience has to remember who is deceiving whom, and how. The experience has not seriously changed 270 years later in Beaumarchais's *Barbier de Séville*, where the lies told by Figaro and Rosine about clandestine letters become frantically complicated and contradictory, and again the audience is challenged to keep up. Throughout three centuries the ingenuity of playwrights, and then of improvising actors, was devoted to inventing more and more surprising fabrications. The chief focus of my present chapter is to observe that, in comedy between 1500 and 1800, one particular type of trick or error is especially characteristic: that is, intrigues and misunderstandings regarding a person's identity. By contrast, in the huge amount of comic drama which has been created and enjoyed in the twentieth and twenty-first centuries for theatre, cinema, and television, tricks and lies continue to be a staple component of what is enacted, but disguise and mistaken identity are rare.

The number of examples which could be discussed places a strain on attempts to cover this subject in a single chapter.[1] The following pages can only hint briefly at the typologies which might be explored. In all cases it has to be recognized that there is a metatheatrical element alongside all the other effects and functions which can be explored. All actors take delight in impersonating characters; the audience has come in order to watch them doing so; and virtuosity is proclaimed on one side and appreciated on the other. If there is impersonation within the fictional plot, as well as within the performance space, then that can increase the fun. On both levels, we can note the remark of Suzanne Jones, that 'the pleasure of a disguise sometimes derives from the awareness of the true identity of whatever lies beneath it'.[2] Audiences enjoy *not* being deceived.

Comedy is more open about all this than other genres. I have already examined in Chapter 17 the double relationship constructed in comic theatre, not only between spectator and fictional character but also between spectator and performer. This was much exploited in the Parisian Théâtre-Italien: Charles Mazouer describes a 'paroxysm' of multi-levelled role-playing in 1683, when Italian actors on stage played the part of other actors who were performing a parody version of Racine's *Bérénice*, and in the process giving mocking imitations of a third group of actors.[3]

Long-lost Relatives

In classical comic plots, the only type of information which was sometimes concealed from the audience until the end was the existence of lost or unknown family relationships. In *commedia erudita*, these were such a regular feature of the story that dramatists sometimes commented sarcastically on the convention in metatheatrical prologues. The audience might well guess them in advance, if they were signalled early on by a father remembering the disappearance of a child, though not every relevant play offers such a clue. If an old man in the cast list had an adopted daughter or ward, she would almost certainly turn out to be the long-lost daughter of his elderly neighbour. When this was discovered in an anagnorisis, the consequent realignment of characters would unravel an otherwise insoluble tangle of contrasting desires. This was especially the case when an old man discovered that he was sexually pursuing his daughter, or a young man found that the object of his lust was his sister. Sometimes a comic heroine could also fall in love with her brother: young women were of course never shown as attracted to older men. There was an emotional myth attached to those situations, whereby the instinctive call of a blood relationship had been mistaken for romantic attraction: this idea always induced the characters to accept the situation immediately, once it had been explained to them.

---

[1] Forestier 1988 devotes more than 650 pages to 'disguise and its avatars' in French theatre — of all genres, not only comedy — just between 1550 and 1680. His categories and analyses are pertinent, but far more meticulous than can be accommodated here.
[2] Jones 2020: 178.
[3] Mazouer 2002a: 260–61; the play, by Fatouville, was appropriately entitled *Arlequin Protée* (1683).

In Roman comedy long-lost daughters are a recurrent feature. In Terence, there are the characters of Glycerium in *Andria*, Philumena in *Hecyra*, and Pamphila in *Eunuchus*. In Plautus, I have noted (in Chapter 24) the case of the eponymous Casina, imitated in Machiavelli's *Clizia*. The young women in question tend to be kept off stage: they are the object, and even the prize, of contests between relatives and suitors, but do not participate themselves. In Plautus's *Epidicus* there is a complex deceit whereby lies are told about the young women Telestis and Acropolistis: it is claimed that Acropolistis is the long-lost daughter of a man who is not in fact her father. Early modern comedies then reprised these situations, often explaining family separations via back stories which had a patina of plausibility: Italian political upheavals, or capture by Turkish pirates (see Chapter 21). Tales involving captivity in Constantinople, Cairo, or Algiers are common in scripted Italian comedies and in scenarios for improvisation. (In the real-life theatrical profession, Francesco Andreini, 'Capitano Spavento' and husband of Isabella, had served some time as a prisoner of the Turks.) Such stories, with their vein of pleasurable exoticism, held their popularity into the eighteenth century and even beyond, giving rise to operas by Mozart (*Die Entführung aus dem Serail*) and Rossini (*L'italiana in Algeri*).

Nevertheless, denouements and solutions involving long-lost relatives eventually became rare in plots set at home in Europe, especially among French dramatists pursuing an erudite agenda. They do not feature in Corneille's comedies; Molière offers just one example in *L'Avare*, where the sudden late appearance of M. Anselme to claim both a son and a daughter, with a long explanatory narrative for which there is no earlier preparation, is a symptom of how that comedy was constructed rather hastily out of much-repeated Italian material.[4] This may be one explanation for *L'Avare*'s mediocre reception in 1668: more sophisticated French audiences might see this last-minute revelation as a worn-out expedient. Marivaux did not use the trope, being perhaps less interested in families as such. The public nevertheless remained familiar with it, and able to be amused by it. When Beaumarchais in 1784, followed by Da Ponte and Mozart in 1786, had Figaro revealed as the unrecognized son of Marceline and Bartolo (stolen by gypsies, another over-convenient explanation which was often used), the tone is satirical: we are invited to enjoy and deride a comic device which has had its day, rather than to take it seriously.

There are two points to be made about this 'unconscious disguise' (as Georges Forestier calls it), which puts a character in a position of not knowing his or her true identity.[5] Firstly, the 'identity' which is hidden is in today's terms social, not psychological. Valère in Molière's *L'Avare* does not become a different person, in our view, when his father appears to claim him; but his economic status is transformed, as is his role in a society where the most important fact about any individual is the family to which he or she belongs. In ancient Rome (or in the Athens which Plautus and Terence pretended to be portraying), and then in early modern Europe, who your father was dictated who you were, and what you were permitted to do,

---

4 See Andrews 2006. Anselme's long-winded narrative recalls the fifth-act speech of Massimo in the first (1520) version of Ariosto's *Il negromante*.
5 'Déguisement inconscient', in Forestier 1988: 44–54, and elsewhere.

including whom you might be permitted to marry. In the real life of those times, if anyone could have been convincingly revealed as a 'long-lost relative', then the implications of the discovery would be far from trivial.

Secondly, and precisely because blood relationships were so important, they were deeply felt. An early modern audience could be emotionally affected by scenes of discovery and reconciliation which healed a previously wounded family. The overall effect would depend on the dramatist's tone and intentions, and on the style adopted by the performance. Revealing Figaro as Marceline's long-lost son comes across as a cheerful absurdity, and most productions have probably presented the episode as such. Nevertheless, earlier comic plays and scenarios have denouements involving family recognition which are treated sentimentally and seriously. We should remember, in the twenty-first century, that if actors and directors choose we can still be moved to tears in Shakespeare's *Twelfth Night*, when Viola and Sebastian rediscover each other.

That example recalls how some classical comedies played with another type of 'unconscious disguise': the phenomenon of identical twins.

Twins on Stage

Before it inspired Shakespeare's *Comedy of Errors*, Plautus's comedy *Menaechmi* had repeatedly fascinated comic dramatists in sixteenth-century Italy. A lost twin arrives for the first time in the town where his brother resides. The confusions caused for the twins themselves and for others, and the accusations which can then be laid against each one of them, are an endless invitation to comic invention, and guaranteed to provoke laughter. Spectators know exactly what is happening, and enjoy their superior amusement at the ridiculous but explicable mistakes made by everyone on stage.

This plot template appeared early in *commedia erudita*, in two of its most influential plays: Bibbiena's *Calandra* and *Gl'ingannati* by the Intronati Academy, both of which were reprinted and restaged for many decades. In these cases an element was introduced which was not Plautine at all, but which was also then much imitated: confusions were caused not by two male brothers, but by a brother and a sister who were still identical twins. (The fact that this is biologically impossible may or may not yet have been known; but the idea was embraced with enthusiasm in the world of Italian comedy.) A sister could only then be mistaken for a brother if one of them, for some of the time, had been cross-dressing. I shall address that device at the end of the present chapter.

Among Italian comedies printed after the 1530s, at least eight were inspired by *Menaechmi*: some of them altered the original plot or 'contaminated' it with elements taken from elsewhere, while others were little more than straight translations of Plautus. Two or three *commedie erudite* imitated Plautus's incomplete *Bacchides*, which presents female twins. In 1622, one of the plays published in Paris by Giovan Battista Andreini was *Li duo Leli simili*, which has identical male twins both called Lelio (as those in Plautus both answer to the name Menaechmus). This composition is described elsewhere by its author as being a scripted version of a scenario originally composed by his father Francesco.⁶ Plots involving twins in fact appear quite often in *canovacci* for improvisation, as a simple survey of their titles makes clear. There are three examples in Flaminio Scala's 1611 collection: Scala's Day 1, *Li duo vecchi gemelli* [The Two Old Twins], which involves twin Pantaloni; Day 17, *Li duo Capitani simili* [The Two Identical Captains]; and Day 25, *La gelosa Isabella*, a variant on *Gl'ingannati*, with twins of opposite sexes. This last example shows on the one hand how memorable that original play was, and on the other hand how few scruples existed about altering such well-known plots and combining them with others. In a separate manuscript collection of scenarios from Venice, there is an item based even more closely on *Gl'ingannati*: it bears the title *Intronati*, showing confusion between the title of the play and the name of the Academy which composed it.⁷

A major distinction regarding such plays and scenarios relates to whether the twins are allowed to meet on stage (as they do in *The Comedy of Errors* and in *Twelfth Night*). Bibbiena's *Calandra* involves two encounters between its identical siblings: one (III.23) where both are in female dress, and another (V.1) when they are dressed as men. In each case, another character hovers confusedly between them. The authors of *Gl'ingannati*, by contrast, keep the male and female twins firmly apart, to the extent of offering an anticlimactic conclusion to the comedy with no proper family reunion on stage.⁸ The only reason for this must be a decision to cast the same actor (a boy in 1532) in both parts. The scenario imitations of the Sienese play, by Flaminio Scala and in the Venetian manuscript, follow the same policy, whereas Scala's other two *canovacci* involving twins have them appearing together, with the twin Capitani even squaring up to fight a duel with each other. In other *arte* scenarios, games are played with three or even four *simili*. The use of identical facial masks would make them easy to present (as would also have been the case for the Roman masked actors in Plautus). However, there needed to be some way for the audience to know which twin was which, even though other characters on stage could not distinguish them: it is rarely apparent from surviving texts how this was done. In the printed script of Andreini's *Li duo Leli simili*, which uses two actors rather than one, the characters are designated as '*Lelio' and 'Lelio', with and without an asterisk, which is of no help to a spectator.

French plays imitating *Menaechmi* were then also composed, some based on Italian scenarios and some more independent. In particular, comedies entitled *Les Ménechmes* were published by Jean de Rotrou (1636) and Jean-François Regnard (1705). Both are in verse, and both end (as in Plautus) with the twins meeting on stage. Rotrou stays close to his Latin source; but Regnard's adaptation makes a typically eighteenth-century effort to insert social and psychological details. One of the twins is called Le Chevalier, his brother Ménechme comes unexpectedly into Paris from the provinces, and the two are given strongly different personalities.

6   The play is named as 'suggetto di Francesco Andreini mio Signor Padre, e dicitura mia', in the introduction to Andreini's play *La centaura*, also printed in Paris in 1622.
7   'Scenari per il teatro di San Cassiano', seventeenth century (Biblioteca Correr, Venice, MS 1040). The collection is now edited by Alberti 1996. There are also scenarios entitled *L'intronati* in the seventeenth-century Corsini and Locatelli collections.
8   This fact was first brought to light in Andrews 1982.

That last strategy was then followed by Goldoni, in his highly virtuosic *I due gemelli veneziani* of 1747/48.[9] His Tonino is witty and morally aware, and his Zanetto stupid and cowardly: he relied on his leading actor Cesare d'Arbes to play both parts convincingly. Goldoni would have been aware that Italian *arte* scenarios often invited such a doubling of roles, though he may not have traced the practice back to *Gl'ingannati*. He also made the decision to have foolish Zanetto poisoned by the villain Pancrazio, and actually to die on stage. He knew that a comic death scene was a risky enterprise, but he assures us in his preface that D'Arbes managed to carry it off.

Whenever twins are played by the same actor, the audience is bound to concentrate most of all on the sheer virtuosity of the game: on how the dramatist solves the practical problems which he has set for himself, and on how well the performer differentiates the two roles. Involvement in the characters' emotions becomes secondary, and it is rare generally in the plays derived directly from *Menaechmi*. By contrast, in 1.2 of *The Comedy of Errors*, Shakespeare's Antipholus of Syracuse sees himself as 'a drop of water | that in the ocean seeks another drop'; and in *Twelfth Night*, Viola more than once conveys her sense of loss at the assumed death of Sebastian. Such confessional insights into feelings of loss or incompleteness are what we expect from Shakespeare: they do not belong to the expected tonal range of comedies from early modern Italy and France.

Deliberate Disguise

Unconscious disguise can produce much fun and laughter: conscious disguise involving deliberate deceit is so endemic to classical comedy that it would need a whole volume to survey its use over three centuries.[10]

Once again, the roots are found in Roman comedy. There are, for example, a series of complex impersonations in *Pseudolus*. Pseudolus pretends to be a slave of the pimp Ballio, attempting unsuccessfully to persuade the messenger Harpax to pay him some money. Simia, a clever slave, is recruited to pretend to be Harpax himself. Then the real Harpax arrives and is accused of being an impersonator in his turn. All these mechanisms were imitated in early modern comedies and scenarios. The phenomenon then spread to a much wider range of disguises, from calculated ones like those in *Pseudolus* to inept attempts at deception which rebound and land the impersonator in trouble. In Scala's scenarios we have characters disguised as messengers, tinkers, chimney sweeps, dentists, lunatics, gypsies, and respectable pilgrims of either sex. In Italian comedy generally there are plots in which older men have simply adopted a new name, in order to avoid pursuit by enemies. A young heroine may conceal her identity (sometimes, but not always, also concealing her gender) in order to pursue or test a lover. This trope appears with cross-dressing

---

9   For a discussion of this comedy, see Andrews 1997b.
10   Peter Brand, who published a series of articles on the subject, wrote: 'in a recent survey of just over eighty of the better-known Italian comedies of the sixteenth century I found conscious disguise in approximately three-quarters of them' (Brand 1993: 191).

in *Gl'ingannati*, and was popular in Italian scenarios; it survived, via Marivaux's *La Fausse Suivante*, through to Goldoni's *La donna di garbo* and *Il servitore di due padroni*.[11] Without cross-dressing, disguised heroines are found in plays such as the Sienese *La pellegrina* and Marivaux's *Le Jeu de l'amour et du hasard*.

Disguise was frequently adopted either to facilitate or to frustrate a sexual encounter. A young man would take the role of a servant in his beloved's household, in order to get near her, as in Ariosto's *Suppositi*, then Shakespeare's *Taming of the Shrew*, then Molière's *L'Avare*, with other examples in between. A jealous husband might test his wife's fidelity by trying to seduce her in disguise: this happens in Ruzante's *La moscheta* (c. 1529). On the other side there was the 'bed-trick', where a hopeful adulterer was foiled by his wife: in a denouement derived originally from Boccaccio, he ended up coupling with her in a darkened room, instead of with the woman he had hoped to seduce. In the *Marriage of Figaro* story, this deception is mounted against the Count Almaviva when his wife presents herself as Suzanne, though their encounter does not quite reach the bed-sheets. In less sexually cautious Italian plays and scenarios, the bed-trick might sometimes have little to do with marital relations: starting with Aretino's *La cortigiana* (first version 1525), it could be a humiliation imposed on a ridiculous character by cheerful conspirators, who would arrange for the victim to find himself in bed with someone less desirable than the person he was hoping for. The mocking enjoyment which such plots provoked has a background in the fantastical disguise trick dramatized by Plautus in *Amphitruo*, where the god Jupiter seduces a virtuous wife using his divine magic, taking on the appearance of her husband. Perhaps surprisingly in a Christian era, some early modern dramatists were attracted by this story: Molière produced a version in his 1668 *Amphitryon*. The fact that Jupiter as Amphitruo is accompanied by Mercury disguised as the servant Sosia, producing confrontations between the real Sosia and the false one, was a tempting format for actors who specialized in comic servant roles: Molière himself played his rewritten French Sosie, probably basing the performance on his trademark role of Sganarelle. (Shakespeare, of course, offered his own dialogue between servants who are physically identical, with the two Dromios facing each other through a closed door in *The Comedy of Errors*.)

A device which was common in Italian comedy, scripted and improvised, was what, for want of an accepted label, we could call the 'Bad Disguise Trick'. In IV.2 of Shakespeare's *Merry Wives of Windsor*, Sir John Falstaff makes his second attempt to seduce Mistress Ford in her home. When Master Ford arrives and he risks discovery, the fat knight is manipulated into disguising himself as a real named person who might plausibly be visiting — the 'old woman of Brainford'. He is made ridiculous enough by having to appear as a woman, and one of low social rank, but his female tormentors have condemned him to further humiliation: Master Ford knows and detests this person, and beats 'her' out of the house. Falstaff has been made to adopt precisely the disguise which will expose him to attack; but he has to endure what happens, because he would be even worse off if he revealed

---

11   For a full survey of disguise, including cross-dressing, in Goldoni's comedies see Günsberg 2001: 134–46.

who he really is. This stratagem has roots in earlier Italian comedies (as indeed do other elements in *The Merry Wives of Windsor*). In the Sienese *Alessandro* (1544), old Costanzo is persuaded to disguise himself as a tinker, and is driven violently from the house of a married woman whom he is pursuing. Some similar Venetian examples may or may not slightly pre-date that play. The Bad Disguise Trick was then used in other *commedie erudite* — including, at that time, 'serious' *commedie gravi*, which were not averse to combining the lowest and most mechanical slapstick with more sentimental and moralistic stories for the heroes and heroines. The trick was often played on Pantalone or the Capitano in *arte* scenarios: it is used in six of Flaminio Scala's *canovacci*. It then faded out of erudite classical comedies in the seventeenth and eighteenth centuries.

In more general terms, impersonations and pretences about identity remained popular with comic dramatists and librettists throughout the eighteenth century: they were never frozen out by new standards of psychological or social plausibility. In 1768, at the age of twelve, Mozart set to music a text entitled *La finta semplice* [The Woman Pretending to be Simple]: the libretto has been attributed to Carlo Goldoni. In a sleeve note to a 1991 recording, the Italian musicologist Franco Piperno comments on the large number of comic opera titles which contain variants on the Italian word *finto*, meaning 'false' or 'pretended' or 'fake'; a list which could be expanded, he notes, by the words *falso*, *supposto*, or *creduto*.[12] He estimates roughly that there could be well over 150 such titles up to 1799, and lists a string of various 'false' attributes flaunted by protagonists, which include geographic or ethnic provenance, occupation and skills (such as fake doctors or fake magicians), and marital status (fake wives or fake widows). There are also many examples of feigned illness or insanity. In particular, as in that first Mozart opera, characters will pretend to be a different sort of person from what they really are; a trope which takes us back to Molière's hypocritical Tartuffe, and to the ancestors of that figure in Italian comedies such as Aretino's *Lo hipocrito* (1542).

Titles including the word *finto* appear in lists of seventeenth-century Italian scenarios. Flaminio Scala has nine of them in his forty comic *canovacci*; the Locatelli manuscript collection has ten, out of one hundred titles in all genres. By contrast, the word appears hardly at all to designate fully scripted *commedie erudite*; and French comedy titles do not often contain variants of the word *faux*. This split, just in respect of titles, between scripted comedies on the one hand and scenarios and comic opera libretti on the other, is both curious and misleading. Pretence and play-acting are regularly used in higher forms of comedy: indeed the moral intention of a more didactic playwright can be to mock and condemn such deceit, as Corneille does in his two comedies about a compulsive liar. The plethora of fakes in eighteenth-century comic opera may signal a tendency in more light-hearted genres of entertainment to celebrate and enjoy disguises rather than to disapprove of them: we return here to the uneasy relationship between derision and collusion which I discussed in Chapter 17.

---

12 Piperno 1991.

It is not hard to find comic sub-genres which prioritized collusion over derision. The Parisian Théâtre-Italien offered a genre of comedy which took particular delight in multiple masking and rapid switches of role for both performers and characters. Just one of their surviving texts can function as an example. In 1696, the year before they were expelled from Paris, the Italians put on a play by a dramatist calling himself Boisfranc: the title was *Les Bains de la Porte Saint-Bernard* (a leisure area on the outskirts of Paris, where there was bathing in the river Seine).[13] The cast list contains many standard roles for a classical plot: the lovers Octave and Angélique, her father the Docteur, and servants Colombine, Arlequin, Pierrot, and Scaramouche. The intense levels of deceit and trickery in the story mean that impersonations come thick and fast. Scaramouche disguises himself as an antiques dealer, and then as a boatman; Arlequin presents himself as a demon, as a medical doctor, as a *procureur* (cf. Chapter 21), and even as a sculpted Triton on a fountain. All these tricks are deliberate attempts by one character to deceive and confuse other characters within the chaotic story. In addition, however, there is the role of Madame de la Fredindaillerie, a predatory middle-aged woman who is trying to get into bed with the Docteur's young son Léandre. It is stated in the cast list that this role is to be played by Arlequin. This is not a disguise motivated by trickery: Madame is a separate character with her own existence and desires. But Arlequin is the actor who must play her, as well as everything else he has to do, retaining his black mask and showing glimpses of his normal patched costume. We have here an Arlequin who is 'Protean' (to use the word often adopted at the time: see Chapter 10) on two different levels at once. On the one hand, the fictional servant Arlequin adopts various disguises in order to trick and bemuse the Docteur, and the audience colludes with that as part of the story. On the other hand, the actor who is usually Arlequin (Évariste Gherardi in 1696) plays a role which is not Arlequin, while remaining blatantly identifiable, and the audience colludes metatheatrically with the game which the company has chosen to play. The very rapid changes of costume imposed on Gherardi would have added to the fun. In other plays for the Italian troupe, Colombine was given equally complex multi-levelled roles.[14] It will not have escaped notice that she and Arlequin, and other members of their troupe, thus furnished extra entertainment by pretending to change their gender.

Cross-dressing (and Cross-casting)

Cross-gender disguise can function on two different levels. As in the play by 'Boisfranc' just examined, a performer can be recruited, for one reason or another, to play a role of the opposite sex. Alternatively, in the story enacted, a character can disguise his or her gender to deceive other characters. Indeed, it is possible for both things to be happening at once. Shakespeare's Rosalind was a boy actor

---

13 Mazouer 2002a: 222–24, cautiously identifies this author as Germain Boffrand (1667–1754), better known as an architect. The play is the subject of a whole chapter by Mazouer (2002a: 220–42), and has a full critical edition in Gherardi 1994–96.
14 For a full survey of Colombine and her role-switching, see Mazouer 2002a: 245–63.

playing a girl who pretends to be a boy; and the same applies to the seminal role of Lelia in *Gl'ingannati*. Female roles were played by boys in Italian court and academy productions for most of the sixteenth century. In fact, a succession of different casting practices in early modern theatre makes the subject of cross-dressing more varied and complex than it might appear, and it would be harder to summarize and to interpret if I were studying anything other than non-musical comedy. In the English Restoration theatre, the newly accepted actresses were often seen playing male 'breeches' roles in tragedy and tragi-comedy: this complicates one's automatic assumption that women were finally introduced on to the English stage just in order to play female characters more realistically.[15] The practice of *travesti* (to use the French term) seems to have been less common in Italian or French spoken drama in the seventeenth and eighteenth centuries. It was not unknown, however: I shall shortly look at the high-profile example of Beaumarchais's Chérubin. Then in *opera seria*, the popularity (outside France) of castrato singers radically altered audience expectations. The cast lists of the Italian operas produced by Handel in London, in the early eighteenth century, show that high-voiced heroic male roles could be given indiscriminately to male or to female stars, depending on their vocal qualities and their personal availability.[16] In modern productions they can still be performed either by mezzo-sopranos or by counter-tenors.

In *commedia erudita*, intriguing and titillating effects could be produced by cross-dressed casting, before the acceptance of female performers. In *Gl'ingannati* (II.6), not only did a boy actor play Lelia disguised as a boy, but Lelia as 'Fabrizio' was wooed and kissed by another boy actor playing Isabella. Like Olivia in *Twelfth Night*, Isabella thinks she is in love with a young man. Unlike Olivia's, her approach is explicitly sexual; and it is watched voyeuristically, with obscene comments, by a pair of scurrilous male servants. Intriguingly, this is the first love scene mounted on stage in any Italian drama. Its multiple levels of gender identity can be seen to appeal to, or to taunt, the homosexual and even paedophile proclivities which comic dramatists claimed were frequent among Italian courtiers, and among private tutors employed in affluent households.[17] A little later, cross-dressing by actresses in improvised scenarios was less multi-layered; but it would still have involved some sexual titillation for the male viewer (or voyeur). The virtuous Isabella Andreini often appeared in male dress, to judge by words she uses in one of her own sonnets, and by the frequency with which her character dresses as a man in Flaminio Scala's scenarios: thirteen out of forty comic *canovacci*.[18] These 'breeches roles',

---

15 See Howe 1992: 56–62.

16 Jane Glover remarks on 'how fluid theatrical stereotypes had become', when narrating last-minute cast changes for Handel's *Radamisto* in 1720 (Glover 2018: 91).

17 Ariosto makes not entirely jocular accusations to his courtly audience in his prologues to the prose *Suppositi* and to *La Lena*. As regards private tutors and their boy pupils, there are some unmistakable allusions in *Gl'ingannati* itself, attached to the Pedant character Messer Piero. At a distance from drama, and from comic writing of any kind, Ariosto sadly commented on paedophilic tendencies among Humanist scholars in his *Satira VI*, ll. 22–33.

18 The relevant scenarios are Days 10, 11, 14, 16, 18, 24, 25, 26, 27, 30, 34, 35, and 40. The sonnet is the introductory one to Isabella's *Rime* (1601), where she confirms that her appearances 'nei Teatri' were 'or donna e ora uom' [now woman, now man].

together with many others over the next two centuries, had the obvious attraction of showing more of a woman's anatomical outline, parts which were normally concealed by full skirts.[19] We have seen (in Chapter 24) that female characters gained greater social freedom, in their fictional plots, by dressing as men: on the other hand the real actresses who performed them were exposing themselves to the exploitative male gaze.

We should note, however, that cross-dressing in Italian comedy was not one-sided. Mango 1966 summarized the plots of 181 Italian scripted comedies of the sixteenth century (which is about two-thirds of the titles which can now be identified). Through his summaries we can trace twenty examples of female characters dressing as men; but also twenty-two cases in which a male character dresses as a woman, usually as a device to get himself accepted in a place, or in company, which would normally exclude him. The Latin source for such gender-based trickery was perhaps Terence's *Eunuchus*, where young Chaerea pretends to be a eunuch in order to be allowed into the house containing Pamphila. Actresses wearing breeches and showing off their legs was a spectacle which certainly had a sexual content. Boys dressing as women might sometimes have had a titillating appeal, but men in drag are often expected to be just grotesquely amusing, and they can be mockingly misogynistic: I have referred (in Chapter 24) to the character of Lena in Ariosto's eponymous comedy. The comedies of Giambattista Della Porta, composed and performed in the late sixteenth century, sometimes revolve around cross-sexual disguise; but the scripts suggest that their emphasis is on deception and intrigue, rather than on sexual ambiguity as such.[20]

Whatever effect was sought, male characters dressed as females are relatively rare in scenarios for Italian *arte* companies, which no longer used boy actors. Later on, though, we have noted how male masks in the Paris Théâtre-Italien could often appear in female dress — as women, but also as goddesses or allegorical figures (see Chapter 10). The reverse was also true: Colombine could appear as the god Apollo alongside Arlequin as the female Muse of Comedy. We might see this as entertaining nonsense, rather than as sexual teasing. In higher comedy, as already remarked, cross-dressing of any kind became increasingly rare. Nevertheless, in Goldoni's late *I rusteghi*, a group of rebellious wives dresses and masks young Felippetto as a girl in order to escort him into the house of his fiancée Lucietta. Her father has insisted that in accordance with traditional practice the couple should never even see each other before their wedding, but the female caucus decides that such rules are out of date. In *commedia erudita* such disguised intrusions would regularly lead to full sexual contact, even pregnancy. In Goldoni, and in eighteenth-century comedy in general, there is no such impropriety. Felippetto looks amusingly gauche in his skirt, but any sexual implications of his cross-dressing are underplayed or non-existent. No compromising pre-marital contact between him and Lucietta will occur in the

---

19   Cf. Howe 1992; and on cross-dressing in general, Günsberg 1997.
20   I refer in particular to Della Porta's *La fantesca* and *Cinzia*, printed respectively in 1592 and 1601. Details of their composition and performance dates are uncertain; and we also know little about how the female roles were cast.

company of the ultimately respectable married women who chaperone him; the engaged couple will simply be reassured about each other. It remains the case that the central plot device of *I rusteghi* is a deceit involving a disguise. This places the play still firmly in the classical comedy tradition: it is a piece of game-playing on stage which, like all such impersonations, remains improbable in realistic terms.

There are also moments in *Le Mariage de Figaro* when attempted trickery involves cross-sexual disguise. The page boy Chérubin is recruited by Figaro in an attempt to entrap his master Comte Almaviva: disguised as a young girl, he is to keep a rendezvous with the Count who will be hoping to meet Suzanne. The device of substituting a page boy for a girl, in or near the bed of a hopeful sexual predator, can be traced back to early Italian comedies such as Machiavelli's *Clizia* and Aretino's *Il marescalco*. In both those plays the substitution is presented in terms which are graphic and even obscene. In Beaumarchais, Chérubin's planned impersonation has to be called off, following the events which occur in Act II in the Countess's bedroom — after that sequence of frantic lies and near disasters involving a half-dressed Chérubin, it becomes too risky to involve him any further. As a separate piece of mischief, Chérubin then does dress up as a visiting shepherd girl in Act IV, managing to receive a kiss on the forehead from the Countess before he is rapidly unmasked. These episodes involve some ambivalent sexually teasing moments, especially in II.4–9 when Suzanne starts giving the page boy a feminine coiffure, and remarks on the girlish delicacy of his skin. But the cross-dressing in the fictional plot of *Le Mariage de Figaro* is less significant than the cross-casting proposed by the dramatist himself.

For his published script of 1785 Beaumarchais composed a very long preface, and added some guiding comments about the characters of the comedy. He prescribed that Chérubin should be played by 'a pretty young woman', commenting that 'we don't have in our theatres any young male actor mature enough to grasp all [the role's] subtleties'.[21] This instruction has mostly been followed in stagings down to the present day; and Da Ponte and Mozart followed it too by giving the role of Cherubino to a female mezzo-soprano (rather than a to counter-tenor or castrato, voices seldom if ever used in comic opera).[22] Beaumarchais's authorial casting decision and his stated reasons for it are unprecedented in the history of stage comedy, or at least no precedents have been documented. Effectively he was saying that a woman would be able to play a male adolescent more expressively, even more realistically, than a man. There is a string of assumptions here about gender characteristics both in life and on stage, which there is no space to analyse here. We can wonder, though, whether Beaumarchais fully understood the effect of his decision, in terms of what Chérubin might then represent to spectators in the theatre. The young page boy is an incarnation of rampant testosterone, restrained only by the post-chivalric verbal style and manners of eighteenth-century polite

---

21 'Ce rôle ne peut être joué, comme il l'a été, que par une jeune et très jolie femme; nous n'avons point à nos théâtres de très jeune homme assez formé pour en bien sentir les finesses.'
22 Howarth remarked that 'occasional departures from tradition, by casting a male Chérubin, have been notably unsuccessful' (1995: 193). Nevertheless, the risk was taken in a Manchester production of 2002 directed by Helena Kaut-Howson, when the actor Samuel Barnett managed remarkably well.

society. In 1.7 he delivers a bewildered speech expressing his indiscriminate reactions to almost any woman he sees; it was then brilliantly transformed by Da Ponte and Mozart into the aria 'Non so piú cosa son, cosa faccio'. Both in the play and the opera, the fact that confused male desire is communicated by a female voice allows the character to speak for both sexes: any member of the audience can respond — with whatever mixture of detached amusement and inner recognition — to the urges which he (or she) is describing.

Disguise as Fantasy

Disguise is a fundamentally implausible stage device which belongs to comic fantasy: in real societies and families, now and in the past, attempts to pass oneself off as someone else are and were unlikely to succeed.

This fact may have been increasingly recognized as the eighteenth century wore on. There arose a detectable divergence between 'higher' and 'lower' comedy, when it came to representing false or mistaken identity. In the plots of *arte* scenarios and comic operas the fantasy was maintained, and entertaining disguises continued to be central. In comic opera they are so frequent as to seem almost obligatory, as the recurrence of Italian titles with *finto* in them makes clear. On the other side, non-operatic comedies with literary ambitions began to treat them with more caution, or in a more reflective manner. The difference appears in the two Figaro plays, as Beaumarchais moved from farcical comedy towards *drame sérieux*. In *Le Barbier de Séville* (which had first been conceived as a comic opera), Comte Almaviva disguises himself twice in order to get into the house of Bartolo and Rosine, first as a drunken soldier with a forged billeting document, then as a teacher of music. These attempts are amusing but basically unconvincing, and neither of them is successful. In *Le Mariage de Figaro*, we have mentioned the equally unsuccessful attempts to disguise Chérubin as a girl. The final intrigue of the play comes when the Comtesse and Suzanne exchange identities, and these impersonations are given a new dimension, inviting a moral judgement from the audience. As I argued in Chapter 14, the fact that they swap clothes but cannot entirely disguise their voices produces significant and revealing reactions from their male partners. The fickle Comte Almaviva fails in the dark to see (or to hear) that he is talking to his wife. Figaro, overhearing them, believes for a while that the Comtesse is indeed Suzanne; but then faced with Suzanne herself he immediately recognizes her voice, despite her wearing the Comtesse's clothes. The opera gives us the same scenes, with the same implications.

As the classical comedy genre struggled to meet new criteria of psychological and social *vraisemblance*, disguises and impersonations on stage became less frequent and less unthinkingly festive. *Le nozze di Figaro* has been described as 'a voyage of self-discovery', in which 'with the help of a liberal dose of disguise people can be themselves'.[23] This kind of inquiry into personal identity is not often what classical comedy is about: the genre has a different set of virtues. Comic impersonations are

---

23   The stage director Nicholas Hytner in a radio interview, quoted in Cairns 2007: 122–23.

charades viewed from outside, rather than inside, the personalities of the characters depicted. They are games which the audience enjoys most of all for the comic release provided by perceiving, but not sharing, other people's errors.

In his Figaro plays Beaumarchais in fact confronted and then crossed a frontier between classical comedy and new emerging forms of drama — between mocking theatrical game-playing based on exterior caricature and more intimate psychological inquiry which claimed greater realism. Frontiers are meeting-places as well as barriers, and in *Le Mariage de Figaro* he managed to exploit the pleasures of both modes. In my final chapter I shall argue that classical comedy had been torn, for much of its history, between coherence and plausibility on the one hand and escapist enjoyment on the other.

CHAPTER 27

Erudite and Artisan Comedy

The story of classical comedy started with Italian *commedia erudita* and was then rapidly invaded by *commedia dell'arte*. These twin roots of the early modern genre gave rise to two intertwining strands of its history.

Starting in 1508, an ancient form of staged entertainment was successfully revived by educated amateur authors for an audience of their peers. They aimed to recreate an ancient Roman theatre experience, and to obey Greek and Roman prescriptions, both of these being reconstructed from texts up to two thousand years old. The comedies they produced were not untheatrical. One of their revered models was Plautus, an actor turned playwright who knew how to write for an audience. His early imitators — Ariosto, Machiavelli, Bibbiena, Aretino, Ruzante, and the Intronati Academy — studied his comic vitality, and matched it in scripts which had a similar stage appeal. Nevertheless, their dependence on written sources meant that they occupied a territory where drama is treated as a branch of literature. In the face of a preceding medieval culture which had given no status to theatre scripts, Humanist authors were insisting that plays should be preserved, studied, and respected like other literary texts, as had been the case in antiquity. Quite soon, however, Italian professional troupes wrested the controlling baton from dramatists and passed it to actors, who needed to satisfy paying spectators whether they were educated or not. What still linked the two theatrical strands was that the same plot formats and character stereotypes were raw material both for erudite dramatists and for artisan actors. Moreover, there was soon a regular interchange between them, each side absorbing influences from the other. The *erudita* and *arte* brands of comedy, parallel and competing, coexisted and overlapped in Italy from as early as the 1540s. Then they both passed recognizably into France.

From those early decades on, Italian and French theatre practitioners might want to identify themselves more with one of the two sides, but they could rarely ignore or dismiss the other. Dramatists with a literary education, aiming to produce comedies which observed classical rules and social inhibitions, learned from the artisan professionals which structures and devices functioned best on stage. Improvising companies, seeking only to entertain, were aware of the pressures exerted by those classical rules and by audiences who knew them; so the Italians in Paris labelled their theatre building with a moralistic Latin motto, *Castigat ridendo mores*.

Many of my previous chapters show how, after around the year 1700, comic playwrights were moving the content of their plays in directions which were more refined, and perhaps more literary. They purged their plays of elements seen as immoral or vulgar; and they introduced more detail and consistency into their attempts to portray society and human psychology. Both these preferences were at the same time characterizing 'sentimental comedy', 'tearful comedy', and *drame sérieux* — the eighteenth-century theatre innovations which helped to bring classical comedy to an end. Nevertheless all dramatists, classically comic or not, were still entrusting their scripts to professional actors who practised an artisan skill.

The reflections offered in this concluding chapter give examples of ways in which the erudite and artisan strains in classical comedy competed, clashed, sometimes gave way one to another, but in the end always coexisted.

Reality and Fantasy

At the end of the last chapter, I observed that one of the most characteristic plot elements in classical comedies, the use of disguise by one person to trick another, is deeply implausible in relation to what we can imagine getting away with in real life. This is a fact which applies to comedy in general: it impinges equally on the erudite and artisan strains.

By 'reconfiguring conflict as play' (see Chapter 23), comedies project a world which is not only theatrical but inescapably fictional and often fantastic. However much they may allude to phenomena which spectators recognize from their own world, they transform those phenomena and then function at arm's length from them. This is because of the need to provoke laughter. When audiences laugh at what they see or hear on a stage, it is because the writers and/or the performers have worked to make them do so. They have taken perceivable reality and distilled it, polished it, exaggerated its ridiculous contrasts, perfected its timing, generally endowed it with an artistic (indeed aesthetic) surface. Reality is mocked but also enhanced, to make it more amusing; and then sometimes it is abandoned altogether. Comedies which aim to be satirical, of individuals or of society, may pretend in Hamlet's words that they are 'holding a mirror up to nature'; but close inspection always confirms that the mirror is distorted or decorated. Successful comedy is better written and better performed than 'nature': it teases out from the natural world what might be intrinsically funny, and leaves the rest behind.[1]

All this applies as much to classical European stage comedy between 1500 and 1800 as to comedy in other times and places. Examples can be selected from an endless list.

In Machiavelli's *Mandragola*, the foolish husband Nicia is told that there is a potion of mandrake root which will instantly enable his wife Lucrezia to become pregnant; but that the first man to sleep with her after she has drunk the potion will die. To protect himself, he is persuaded to commit murder by picking up a casual stranger

---

[1] It is worth noting that although these remarks might contribute to a theory of comedy, they relate only to theatre and do not belong to a wider theory of laughter, or of humour. Humour and jokes function in a more complex set of social interactions than is covered by actors facing an audience (which means that Freudian theories of humour, among others, are rarely relevant). Laughter itself is not always even deliberately provoked by another person. In this larger context, I am inclined to agree with Beard 2014: 39: 'No statement that begins with the words "All laughter is..." is ever likely to be true'.

from the street, and putting that man into bed with Lucrezia; however, he fails to recognize that the man conveniently kidnapped is Callimaco, the youth who is desperate to seduce Lucrezia. Meanwhile, his pious wife is bullied by her confessor, Fra Timoteo, into believing that going to bed with this stranger will not be a sin. However many satirical gibes *La mandragola* may contain against idiotic lawyers and corrupt clergymen in Florence (along with a misogynist caricature of female gullibility), no audience can believe, on sober reflection, that the events which it portrays could really happen.

In Molière's *Le Bourgeois gentilhomme*, Monsieur Jourdain is obsessed with aristocratic status, and determined that his daughter must marry someone who bears a noble title. His daughter's preferred suitor, Cléonte, disguises himself as a dignitary from Turkey (no less), and mounts an elaborate ceremony to invest Jourdain with the invented Ottoman title of *mamamouchi*. How Cléonte and his tricky servant Covielle manage to acquire, at very short notice, the supporting friends (fully rehearsed in their parts), the musicians, the costumes, and the equipment to create this pantomime is something we do not ask: we know perfectly well that they come from the personnel and the property basket of Molière's theatre company. Jourdain's self-absorbed snobbery is a real human trait, worthy of comic inquiry; but the details with which it is first exaggeratedly expressed and then ludicrously defeated are sheer fantasy.

Marivaux's *Le Jeu de l'amour et du hasard* (see Chapter 11) seems to be set in a plausible version of eighteenth-century France; but in that historical context, could its dual exchange of roles between employers and servants have succeeded even for five minutes? Especially with Arlequin's mask and costume clearly visible through his upper-class disguise?

In *The Marriage of Figaro*, the play and then the opera, we may find it easy to believe in the desires and the frustrations of the four central characters; but can we also believe that a real countess could persuade her husband, even in the dark, that she is her maid Suzanne?

Arguably it was only Goldoni, in his later comedies from the mid-1750s onwards, whose insistence on portraying social and psychological 'Truth' reduced the deceptions employed by his characters to a level which is less fantastical and sometimes almost credible. The plot of the *Villeggiatura* trilogy of 1761–63 (cf. Chapter 13) is driven not by deceit but by levels of ineptitude shared by all its main characters. Rather than mounting implausibly ambitious campaigns of trickery, the *villeggianti* are constantly on the defensive against each other and against their own weaknesses: they amuse us by displays of evasiveness, pique, and self-deception. The element of comic enhancement lies in the implausibly tight pattern which Goldoni builds out of his banal mishaps and confrontations. Underneath this combinatory artifice, the central story of the trilogy — the emotional struggles and dilemmas of its protagonist Giacinta — is not often funny. The denouement is not a 'happy ending', and it leaves no characters who are winners.

Consciously or not, Goldoni was expressing the swan-song of a genre. The outcomes of previous classical comedies and scenarios had involved winners as well as losers, and their triumphs were achieved through contrived devices and events, pieces of theatrical magic containing a touch of fairy tale, to which audiences reacted (and still react) with a willing suspension of disbelief. At the same time, over nearly three centuries in Italy and France, dramatists aiming to write 'high' comedy had to balance this pursuit of enjoyable wish-fulfilment against contrasting demands for a degree of plausibility. Those demands came from the erudite preoccupation with ancient theory. They were based firstly on the Aristotelian definition of art as 'imitation'; secondly on the doctrine that works of art should be morally instructive as well as entertaining; then also on an assumption that stories performed in a theatre should be governed by the same rules as were applied to fiction composed for the page.

Poetics and Performance

Greco-Roman literary prescriptions applied, and were seen by their early modern interpreters to apply, as much to narrative poems as to works for the theatre. Aristotle may have been concentrating in his *Poetics* most of all on tragic drama, but this emphasis was not exclusive. The examples he used when discussing how to construct fictional plots were taken from Homer's *Odyssey*, as well as from Sophocles's *Oedipus* and *Antigone*. There are some acknowledgements in his treatise of the fact that tragedies were performed live; but such observations relate to the detailed delivery of words, to how lines of verse can be supported or crafted by rhythm and music. There is little mention, and no analysis, either of an actor's skill or of the effect on those same lines of verse of a performer's delivery.[2] The Latin *Ars poetica* is even more devoid of such references. Horace cannot have been helped in this direction by the fact that Roman law categorized professional actors as *infames*, depriving them of any social rights or status. Their craft did not merit the attention of a gentleman poet and intellectual, an attitude shared by theorists in the sixteenth and seventeenth centuries when faced with professional troupes. We have already remarked (in Chapter 17) that ancient Greek and Roman theories of laughter, when dealing with the comic stage, did not take into account the contribution made by a performer.

As regards prescriptions for drama, therefore, the authority conferred on the ancients related to the content and arrangement of texts: their rules were addressed to writers. Poetics was a discipline for poets. There had been no ancient theories or precepts directed at actors or acting; and so for most of the period covered by this study there were no modern treatises on the subject either. The actor-dramatist Pier Maria Cecchini offered some fragmentary pieces of advice in the early seventeenth century; but his brief treatises did not initiate any tradition of actors' handbooks, and only one of the two was printed.[3] Indeed, the diffidence with which Cecchini formulated his proposals underlines the difficulty of conveying in words instructions which rely on practical demonstration. In the 1770s Denis

---

2   Aristotle's reference in his final chapter to 'unnecessary' bodily movement, which could be taken as a condemnation of bad or exaggerated acting, is directed at flute-players and at members of the Chorus: there is no explicit mention of how a solo actor might perform.
3   Cecchini 1608 and 1628, both transcribed in Marotti & Romei 1991: 67–76, 77–92.

Diderot composed an essay called *Le Paradoxe sur le comédien* [Paradox about the Actor], but it was not published until 1830 and so was not widely known. (Since Diderot was one of the main movers behind the new genre of *drame sérieux*, one wonders how much influence it could have had on specifically comic acting.) In Germany, in his *Hamburgische Dramaturgie* discourses of 1767–69, Gotthold Ephraim Lessing commented that 'we have actors but no art of acting'.[4] He was referring to European theatre in general.

All this meant that comic plays written and staged between 1500 and 1800 were moulded by two different and competing types of influence: ancient dramaturgical doctrine (discussed in Chapters 7, 18, and 20), and insights or habits stemming from customary performance practice (see Chapter 19). The erudite doctrines were clearly formulated and subject to published debates. On the other side, performing formats were all-pervasive in their practical influence, but communicated only by example, like most artisan skills. The two pressures might or might not clash with one another. Playwrights might acknowledge help or resist hindrance, from either side.

Comedy and (In)Coherence

The fact that erudite theoretical prescriptions concerning plots and characters were applied to written narratives, as well as to scripts for performance, meant that developments in the former influenced what was seen as possible, and what might be expected, in the latter. In the eighteenth century in particular, this opened the way to increasing influence on theatre writing from the new genre of the novel. Earlier parts of this study have traced an increase in playwrights' ability, and in their desire, to create recognizable depictions of contemporary society (Chapter 21), and to express the inner feelings of stage characters (Chapter 22). Audience demand for both those tendencies would be supported by the rising popularity of long prose narratives not written for performance.

Nevertheless, there remained inevitable differences between composing for the page and for the stage. In novels there was ample space for reflections or debates about how well or badly society was organizing itself. There was space also for long descriptions, or transcriptions, of the thoughts and feelings of fictional characters, of how they were reacting to events, developing, changing their minds. Theatre allows less room for such leisurely verbal passages. On stage it is required that something should be *happening*: it is a commonplace that the word 'drama' itself comes from a Greek word meaning 'action'. Speeches of reflection and analysis can of course be events in the story, and become a kind of action; but if they are too long and too central, audiences may feel that the play begins to drag. Moreover, for a theatre spectator, what is happening on stage *right now* is paramount. If the text and the performers are forceful enough, then the moment being experienced is all that matters. It can override what in other circumstances, if we were reading from a page, might be elements of jarring incoherence. This is particularly true if the successful moment has been a funny one. Immersion in an instant of laughter can lead us to disregard whether the joke or trick or other amusing event fits plausibly

---

[4] 'Wir haben Schauspieler, aber keine Schauspielkunst' (Lessing 1975: IV, 488).

into the fictional world which the play has established. Comic actors and solo comedians instinctively know this, and they are likely to judge the success of their performance by the number of laughs they have elicited. Whether those laughs fit into a coherent story or train of thought can be less important.

As well as to performers, this applies to writers of comic plays; and this was as true in Italy and France between 1500 and 1800 as in other times and places. In erudite theory, dramatists were expected to compose stories, scenes, and sequences of actions which showed consistency and plausibility, and of which Aristotle would have approved. In practice this requirement stood in a flexible relationship with the simple desire to provoke laughter.[5] Then as now, each laugh was a separate moment, potentially capable of standing alone — a phenomenon of performance not addressed by poetic theory. Some composers of classical comedies were writing to earn a living, and they would want to accumulate an acceptable number of laughs in each script. Those operating less commercially were still aiming to please, and so to entertain, audiences of one kind or another. A minority of scholarly amateurs might state that laughter was not the most important quality of a comedy, some even claiming that the genre could do without it. Most comic dramatists, however, if they did have serious moral or artistic aims to start with, tried to achieve them by means of laughable situations and witty words. The motto *Castigat ridendo mores* stated that it was specifically through laughter (*ridendo*) that customs and behaviour were censured. For those less concerned with castigation, hilarity was the sole point of the exercise. The more laughs — the more *moments* of laughter — the better.

This was especially true when the dramatist was the manager of an improvising troupe, a *capocomico* who needed to find material frequently and quickly. Some scenarios published by Flaminio Scala, who was himself in that position, contain plots which are blatantly cobbled together from disparate sources. An opening story-line, which leads to the Act III denouement, may be padded out for much of Acts I and II with disconnected diversions.[6] All that mattered was that the public should be offered three full acts which engaged their attention from moment to moment, and made them laugh often enough. Linear consistency, in the plot and in the motivations of characters, was not a high priority. This fragmentary approach matched, and indeed was encouraged by, the methods of the *commedia dell'arte* actors themselves, performers whose personal repertoires were lists of separable numbers which they rearranged for each new show (see Chapter 19). Such items might not always be funny — they included the emotional speeches of Lovers, and Isabella Andreini's mad scenes — but they had been devised, and they operated, as moments which stood alone.

By the year 1700, Italian actors as described by Riccoboni relied openly on autonomous *lazzi*, packaged jokes and routines which might be identified by a label, and which were created by performing practice. Artisan comedy, in its search for

---

5 Cecchini, in his unpublished 'Discorso sopra l'arte comica con il modo di ben recitare' (Cecchini 1608), recognized this tension and, despite being an artisan actor-dramatist himself, argued in favour of coherence and against clownish distractions. See Marotti & Romei 1991: 74–75.
6 In Scala 2008, I have categorized as 'third-act scenarios' those which appear as Days 16, 17, 20, 21, and 37.

the maximum number of laughs, produced fragmentary theatre. But the artisans faced a contrasting erudite drive to create in each play a vision, even a thesis, which was not fragmentary. Riccoboni himself wanted to compose comedies and scenarios which went beyond the single performed moment and which confirmed to the principles of *classicisme*. Seeing himself as a poet with a moral message, he sought to impose his own standards and his own voice on each piece of drama, whether fully scripted or improvised. Poetic theory implied a search for coherence; comic performance accepted, and sometimes thrived on, a degree of incoherence.

Consistency of Character

The coherence sought by erudite comedy included consistency in the depiction of character. Artisan performers could be less convinced of its importance.

In Chapter 17, I quoted (from Palaprat's *La Fille de bon sens* of 1692) Colombine's perception that Arlequin had acquired over time two personal qualities which were logically incompatible — he veered between extreme stupidity and extreme cunning. Colombine was acknowledging, metatheatrically, that she and Arlequin existed in a world of stage fiction: they had inhabited dozens of plays by different authors, and could expect to participate in more. In that world, she suggested, the contradictions in Harlequinesque behaviour were perceivable to her (and also, implicitly, to the regular spectators now in the auditorium), but they did not make realistic sense. Her explanation ('I think you've got two souls in your body') belongs to fantasy metaphysics, and was offered as a joke. Alternatively, those contradictions highlight, perhaps still without articulating it, the contrast between a blundering stage persona and his highly skilled performer, each of them enjoyed simultaneously in different ways by the audience.

Sixty years later, in his Preface to *Il servitore di due padroni*, Goldoni was aware that his chosen version of the masked servant Truffaldino was still being shown as 'foolish and clever at the same time'. Writing in the more rationalist climate of the mid-eighteenth century, and following his programmatic desire to dramatize only 'the Truth', the playwright felt that he had to explain the paradox. Truffaldino, he explained, is 'foolish in the things which he does unthinkingly and without preparation, but very smart whenever he is prompted by self-interest and cunning, which is the true character of a peasant'.[7] Goldoni wanted his character to appear plausible and coherent both psychologically and socially, the social explanation being based on an 'essentialist' view of qualities possessed by the lower classes (see Chapter 25). We can add that although he paid tribute in this preface to the skill of Antonio Sacchi in performing Truffaldino, he (like Palaprat in 1692?) was unable or unwilling to state that a spectator might be experiencing a double relationship, with the actor as well as the character. In theoretical discussion at least, the autonomous 'Truth' of the world which Goldoni insisted he was depicting on stage had to be fenced in and guaranteed by Diderot's 'fourth wall' (see Chapter 18).

---

7   'Truffaldino che un Servidore sciocco ed astuto nel medesimo tempo ci rappresenta: sciocco cioè in quelle cose le quali impensatamente e senza studio egli opera, ma accortissimo allora quando l'interesse e la malizia l'addestrano, che è il vero carattere del Villano' (Goldoni 1976: 1, 3).

The principle that characters in fiction should not be self-contradictory is not so obscure as to require elaborate explanation; but it could if necessary be supported by reference to the ancient authorities. In Aristotle's *Poetics* (1454a), we read of 'four qualities to aim at' in constructing a dramatic character, and the fourth of them is consistency — the Greek word used for this quality was *homalón* (ὁμαλόν). Aristotle adds: 'Even if the person who is being represented is inconsistent, and this trait is the basis of his character, he must nevertheless be portrayed as consistently inconsistent' (Chapter 15, Aristotle 1965: 51). In Horace's *Ars poetica*, the same point is made using the Latin word *convenientia* (l. 119), and then the phrase *sibi constet*, 'let it be true to itself' (l. 127, Horace 1989). Early Italian Humanist theorists explicitly put these two quotations side by side, using the perceived agreement between them to reinforce the point they were making; and such observations were comfortably integrated into the doctrine of French *classicisme*.[8] Inconsistency in a created character threatened the principle of verisimilitude on which a large part of that doctrine was based. Aristotle had been writing about epic poetry as well as about drama, and early modern theorists legislated for similarly long narrative poems written in Italian and French. In the seventeenth and eighteenth centuries, they had also to consider the emerging prose novel: there was doubt, initially, whether this was an acceptable form of literature at all, but if it was it had to be subject to pre-existing rules. All categories of fiction, dramatic or not, were open to demands for consistent characterization; and expectations formed in this regard became widely shared. Goldoni's explanation of how Truffaldino could be sometimes stupid and sometimes clever was the answer to a question which he thought a general reader might ask. He was not thinking exclusively of an erudite minority acquainted with the words of Aristotle or Horace.

Nevertheless, theatre audiences still were (and still are) capable of enjoying a spectacle whose characters do not aim very hard at consistency. Spectators in the Théâtre de Bourgogne in 1692 would have been happy with Colombine's indulgent comments about Arlequin's fluctuating levels of intelligence. They would also have enjoyed the implication that she was speaking on their behalf. They appreciated the doctrinally correct dramas of the Comédie-Française, but were equally at home with the more relaxed shows offered by the Italians. Later in Venice, when Goldoni was asking readers to be more discriminating, his spectators were also frequenting traditional *commedia dell'arte* plays mounted by companies like that of Antonio Sacchi. In those shows, Pantalone and Arlecchino (or Truffaldino) were still operating traditionally, without the cultural or moral direction of an erudite dramatist. They were assembling sequences of pre-existing plot lines, speeches, and jokes, and not troubling themselves with inner psychological analysis or coherence.

The fact that we are capable of recognizing and appreciating consistency and plausibility in a fictional construct does not mean that we demand those qualities every time. We accept that comedy is fantasy. Sometimes we enjoy a spectacle which deliberately casts psychological consistency to the winds. This is made easier

---

8   See Weinberg 1961: 130–33 and 159–61, discussing Horatian commentaries by Francesco Lovisini (1554) and Giovanni Battista Pigna (1561).

for us by the fact that we are spectators in the full sense of the word: we watch stage characters, and listen to them, from outside.

Comedy and Interiority

There is a special form of suspension of disbelief which can be achieved in a novel: the illusion, created by the author's text, of perceiving directly and without mediation what is happening in a character's head. In the theatre such knowledge is held at a distance, as indeed it is in our normal social lives. We can observe the speech and action of stage characters, as we can with the people around us; we interpret those people, or those characters, through their words and deeds; we cannot claim to see into their minds. Theatre can thus raise questions about the relationship between people's words (spoken to others, or to themselves) and their feelings or intentions. Some dramatists may be explicitly interested in exploring that relationship. Spectators have to decide whether the words which a playwright has written to be spoken are true indications of a character's inner life or perceivably false. They may occupy a questionable territory between the two. If words are false or unreliable, they may be intended to deceive another character; alternatively the speaker may be deceiving herself or himself.

In some types of drama, especially tragedy, long speeches can have an important function, analysing thoughts and feelings of characters, or the wider implications of events. They can even be experienced as containing the central meaning of the play. Comedy tends to be more behaviouristic than analytical, especially when creating its single moments of laughter. I have argued in Chapter 17 that laughter excludes empathy more often than not, and that the fun sought by classical comedies inclines towards targeting comic victims. Those butts of ridicule are laughed at and judged from outside, on the basis of what spectators see and hear. In plays composed before 1700, it is hard to mount a delicate examination of the inner life or development of comic characters, even of major ones. We do not psychoanalyse Bibbiena's Calandro or Machiavelli's Nicia: it would be like attempting to do the same for Mr Punch, or for his Judy, or indeed for their Crocodile. The same applies to the repeated representations of Pantalone and Arlecchino (of whom I have suggested, quoting A. S. Byatt, that they possess attributes rather than psychology, see Chapter 22). I have argued elsewhere that it is true even of the great comic victims of Molière, meticulously potent though their portrayals can be. Despite the interventions of some modern directors, Harpagon is simply what he says and does, together with the hilarity which he provokes: he was not created as a tortured psyche with a complicated back story, even if modern interpreters may choose to impose such a vision on Molière's text. Young comic heroes and heroines, in the sixteenth and seventeenth centuries, do not express nuanced feelings open to close examination. Lelia, the protagonist of *Gl'ingannati*, undergoes a clear-cut series of emotions, which change in response to developments in the plot, but there is never anything ambiguous about what she feels. The same is true of other Lovers in early Italian comedy. In some of Flaminio Scala's scenarios, Isabella Andreini takes on less farcical roles, of women who adopt a moral stance and assume moral control to resolve emotional tangles; but rather than analysing her own feelings or those of others, she presents sets of exterior obligations which need to be satisfied, and for which she finds almost mathematical solutions (see Chapter 24). Lovers in Molière are portrayed indulgently, but with a degree of distance which often involves mockery.

In the eighteenth century there was a change of direction, with artisan masks appearing alongside attempts at more rounded (more erudite?) characterization. I have discussed this in Chapter 22, with examples from Marivaux and Goldoni. In Marivaux's comedies generally (foreshadowed to some extent by those of Pierre Corneille), the inner lives of the main characters become foregrounded. Dilemmas are primarily emotional, though they are still also comically circumstantial: their resolution depends on understanding and satisfying what characters truly desire. It is significant that Marivaux wrote novels as well as plays: with regard to his theories and explorations of love, at least as much critical ink has been expended on *La Vie de Marianne* as on his comedies. *La Double Inconstance* (see Chapter 22) tells the story of how the desires of Arlequin and Silvie are made to change radically from what they were at the start. Marivaux tries to make their 'inconstancies' plausible; but even here we might choose to see an element of comic fantasy, rather than psychological accuracy, in the way in which the reversals are engineered. The artificial manipulation involved is attributable as much to Marivaux himself as to the Prince and Flaminia.

In Italy, Goldoni's portrayal of comic characters continued to be more behaviourist than interiorizing, aware though he certainly was of Marivaux and other French models. His young Lovers, who in more traditional comedies would be automatically sympathetic, are made to invite scrutiny rather than indulgence: their erotic desires are often viewed externally, from a social or moral angle, and judged from that point of view. Goldoni's blocking characters can be unpleasant, but also individually plausible rather than stereotypical. The eponymous grumbling Sior Todero feels like a figure one has encountered in real life, rather than merely on the stage; but this effect still comes from viewing him and hearing him from outside, not from intimate monologues.

Beaumarchais, especially in *Le Mariage de Figaro*, found his own balance between plain comedy and complex interiority. Our relationship, as spectators, to his individual characters ranges widely between extremes of detachment or intimacy. Bartolo and Basilio in the first two Figaro plays are seen from a derisive comic distance: they are even arguably different from one play to the next. Chérubin in *Le Mariage de Figaro* (as I have suggested in Chapter 26) faces us with a challenge, in which we may or may not choose to recognize instincts of our own. Marceline starts as a comedy duenna, derided simply for being old. She then unexpectedly challenges real social norms, expressing at length her experience of patriarchal exploitation (see Chapter 24); and from then on her maternal feelings for Figaro release her from her initial crude comic template. The four central characters of *Le Mariage de Figaro* — Figaro, Suzanne, the Countess, and the Count — are made to tread a fine line between the externally observed stereotypes of the *arte* tradition and people with serious individual emotions, open both to empathy and to criticism. In this as in other respects, Beaumarchais keeps one foot in the familiar territory of the classical comic tradition, while stepping gently across the border into a new genre.

Arte and *Erudita* in Molière

Molière, standing at a pivotal point in our narrative, is the author who can be seen most clearly as acknowledging two sets of criteria, artisan and erudite, making creative use of the tension between them. In Chapter 17, addressing concepts of high and low comedy, I recalled how the academic theorist Boileau, in his *Art poétique* of 1674, expressed a strong preference in Molière's work for the sophisticated perceptions of *Le Misanthrope*, as opposed to the knockabout farce of *Les Fourberies de Scapin*. These two products of the same author can indeed be seen as representative of the polarity now being proposed, of the two intertwining strands of classical comedy.

The plot of *Les Fourberies de Scapin* is a banal formulaic pretext for a series of comic moments, which rely for their success on performing virtuosity. Originally they exploited the skills of Molière himself, playing the trickster servant Scapin. Two young men, in the city of Naples, want to marry two young women. Indeed, one of the couples is already secretly married. The young men's fathers, who are friends of each other, oppose their son's desires. In particular, they want Octave, son of Argante, to marry Hyacinte, daughter of Géronte. This is exactly what has already happened, in secret, so there should be no conflict at all. The misunderstanding is based on some shaky and incoherent plot details. Just how, and why, has Hyacinte been sent on to Naples from Taranto, ahead of her father? Why is it that her name does not get mentioned in any conversation which could make the matter clear? We never have time to consider such questions. What happens instead, and what we as spectators and customers settle down to enjoy, is a series of elaborately deceptive tricks mounted by Scapin against the two fathers. He recruits another servant, Silvestre, to impersonate an aggressive Capitano-like brother of the unnamed Hyacinte, and to threaten Argante in II.6. For the other father, Géronte, he invents in II.7 a story in which Géronte's son Léandre has been imprisoned on a Turkish galley, and needs large sums of money for a ransom — this cash is really needed by Léandre to buy his beloved Zerbinette from a group of gypsies.[9] Then, as a gratuitous extra treat for the audience, there is inserted into Act III the scene to which Boileau objected. Scapin feels the need to revenge himself on Géronte, for reasons which are only vaguely explained. So he persuades Géronte that a gang of soldiers is out for his blood. Géronte can only escape by hiding in a sack, to be carried home unseen. Once the old man is hidden, Scapin loudly imitates the accents of a series of different thugs, each of whom allegedly beats the sack with Géronte inside it: what Scapin pretends is that he himself was being beaten too, while carrying the sack. The sheer implausibility of this trick needs no underlining; but it worked on stage, and has continued to work in enthusiastic and inventive productions down to the present day. *Les Fourberies de Scapin* is one of Molière's most regularly revived farces, perhaps precisely because it challenges actors and directors to come up each time with new performative inventions: there are far more separate

---

9 See Andrews 2005 for how this *galère* scene relates to a play by Cyrano de Bergerac, and to Italian scenarios.

comic opportunities in the play than I have just listed. No stage solution ever was, or is, likely to satisfy the demands of an Aristotelian theory of poetics, despite the fact that Molière derived his central plot, in a freewheeling manner, from Terence's *Phormio*. Even setting ancient models aside, this play will equally not satisfy a spectator (still less a reader) who seeks from a dramatic text a thoughtful comic exposure of human character and behaviour, such as might be provided by a novel.

It is just such a penetrating exposure, as Boileau and countless others have recognized, which had been supplied by Molière five years earlier in *Le Misanthrope*. To set up a contrast between these 'high' and 'low' aspects of Molière's writing is not exactly a critical innovation; but there is one perception which merits pursuing here. In *Les Fourberies de Scapin*, each scene, each confrontation, each comic moment can be approached and rehearsed by its performers on its own separate terms. How Géronte behaves as a duped victim in III.2 does not need to be influenced by how he behaved in II.7. It is enough that that both scenes involve a ritual of comic humiliation, and that the victim is played by the same actor each time: neither the performer nor the audience have to make careful psychological or behavioural links between one scene and the other. *Le Misanthrope*, on the other hand, draws its story, its subtlety, and indeed its comedy, from the way its characters progressively present themselves from beginning to end. It is impossible for an actor to approach any of its roles without creating a connection or a contrast between earlier and later scenes. Alceste proclaims his own version of moral and social integrity: he then shows that he cannot stick to that principle in practice, and that his besotted love for Célimène undermines it. These contradictions are the very purpose of his role: he is 'consistently inconsistent', as Aristotle recommended. Célimène's self-presentation is equally fragmentary: she veers from benevolent sociability to gleeful mockery of her acquaintances, and then to ruthless self-defence. The actress has to decide how to integrate these scenes into a single role. Without these and other character developments and revelations, there would be no play: they are its subject matter, and they demand of each actor a high level of coherence in presenting and then undermining individual traits. Coherence, psychological and emotional, is a quality which belongs to that erudite category of high comedy in which everyone places *Le Misanthrope*. By contrast, the cheerful artisan incoherence of *Les Fourberies de Scapin* actually contributes to the play's success. The audience wants the drama to be openly implausible and casually incoherent because such explicit game-playing is a source of theatrical pleasure.

Even in *Le Misanthrope*, in fact, we can see one of Molière's feet, or at least a toe, firmly planted in the territory of artisan comic performance. There are a number of scenes and moments which depend on artificial verbal structures of repetition and echoing. I have already cited (in Chapter 19) Alceste's circular elastic reiteration of 'Je ne dis pas cela' in I.2. There are other such word-games at the end of this act, and then more in such scenes as IV.4 ('elastic' delaying repetitions by the servant Du Bois) and V.2–3 (the repetitious, almost stichomythic insistence of Célimène's suitors that she should finally choose between them).[10] I have shown in Chapter 19

---

10   All these repetitive devices were noted and listed long ago by Gustave Rudler, in his edition of *Le Misanthrope*, under the heading of 'Le Comique externe' (Molière 1960: xxvii–xxxii). Rudler

that such devices are rooted in techniques of improvisation. Molière has in a sense copied the Italians; but he also recognized independently that such contrived speech rhythms have an effect and a merit of their own. They are a form of embellishment which helps to make comedy enjoyable, whether it is then categorized as high or low, erudite or artisan. Goldoni would see such devices as the 'Theatre' which he used to express his 'World'.

Conclusions for Erudite Readers

A balance between the erudite and artisan inheritance can be found in all those classically comic plays which are enjoyed by modern readers, and reinterpreted in modern performances. That repertoire includes much of Molière, Marivaux, Goldoni, and Beaumarchais, and single French plays like Corneille's *Le Menteur* and Lesage's *Turcaret*. Italian *commedia erudita* tends to be revived less often, not because it is intellectually abstruse, but because today's audiences find it too distant and too localized in its language and its references. (Modern Italian speech has not been seeded, or infiltrated, by the language of Renaissance theatre, as English has by Shakespeare and his contemporaries.) Italian *commedia dell'arte* scenarios, and the scripts of the Paris Théâtre-Italien, can fascinate theatre historians; but attempts to adapt or transform such artisan products for modern performance have remained a minority taste (though to some of us they still remain vibrant and appealing).

Those classical comedies which are still studied in modern syllabuses, still read by a public interested in theatre, still restaged by modern directors, can only be approached through scripts which have been preserved on a page. However aware we want to be of their performance qualities, it is only imagination and guesswork which can help us to envisage them; and our contemporary notions of what 'performance qualities' consist of may or may not coincide with those of their authors and their first actors. Whether as readers or as practitioners, we are thus in a position not dissimilar to that of the playwrights of the sixteenth and seventeenth centuries who read the comedies of Plautus and Terence, and wanted to resurrect or imitate them. Our perceptions and judgements are inevitably biased towards features which can be perceived in written texts. This remains true even as we are less constrained (or less impressed) than the humanists were by ancient poetics, that is by the precepts or guidelines conveyed to us, also in writing, by Aristotle, Horace, and their later disciples.

In fact, criticism of theatre texts, from the nineteenth century on, has been unavoidably influenced by a search for long-lasting virtues which we also identify in other types of imaginative literature. We admire dramatists who offer us insights into detailed psychology, into how individual humans relate to other individuals, into how they relate to society on a scale both large and small. We admire complexity, qualities which we call 'profundity'. When we lavish praise on Molière and Goldoni for having managed such insights in a comic mode, then those achievements are really there. For readers they are detectable in the scripts;

connects them, no doubt rightly, with French farce: he was not in a position also to make the connection with Italian improvisation.

for actors they are representable on stage. But the more we talk or write about those comedies, then the more we are drawn by the very act of using words into assessing their erudite or literary qualities; and the further we are removed from confronting and enjoying the moments of performance, the moments of laughter, in which the purpose of such scripts also resided. Such moments are by nature ephemeral. They have to be renewed, and have been renewed, in every single performance — in our case from the year 1508 to the present day. Attempts to describe them in words fall short. Words point towards, but can never really convey, the delight in a comic moment which each spectator savours in his or her own way, and which then either lingers or fades in the individual memory. Those epiphanies are contrived by live theatre and its practitioners. The skills deployed are artisan rather than erudite, and like the effects which they produce they are at least partly incommunicable; so they have no written history, and are not acknowledged in pages of written criticism.

Reflections like these can apply to most genres of theatre. In respect of classical comedy, the genre's twin roots and their consequent intertwining strands provide a background for them. We can see and distinguish the erudite and artisan components in authors, plays, scenarios, and theorists. In the seventeenth century in particular, a theatre of *arte* existed in rivalry with the *erudita*, even in conflict with it, though neither of those defining terms was being used at the time. Academicians expressed contempt for professionals; but they imitated them and borrowed from them none the less. Professional actors argued for the authenticity of their own methods; but they had to keep an eye on the formulated *classiciste* precepts, and had to negotiate against accusations of ignorance and vulgarity. Attempts to distinguish respectable comedy from unrespectable farce began with Aristotle himself, and were constant throughout the early modern period. They continue to affect the judgement and preferences of critics, readers, and playgoers today. When we look at *commedia dell'arte* and its offshoots, we may decide that it was characterized by masked stereotypes which were superficial, and by deceits and pretences which were implausible. I have suggested that in *Le Mariage de Figaro* Beaumarchais was consciously trying to move away from those features when he allowed Figaro to recognize the voice of the disguised Suzanne.

'Superficial' and 'implausible' are derogatory words in an erudite critical context. We should step back sometimes, and recognize that in artisan performance they describe elements which can be positive and enjoyable. The irreducible moments of laughter, which most of us seek if we are devotees of comic theatre, sometimes actually depend on superficiality, implausibility, incoherence, and the shattering of literary rules. It is as true now as it was in Paris in the 1690s that theatregoers can feed on, even need, both types of experience. We can appreciate the considered comic drama which probes human behaviour, and offers intellectual satisfaction, but also enjoy the festive game-playing which throws reality to the winds, gives release to the soul, and relaxes inhibitions. In theatre scripts from the past, the former will always be better preserved and communicated than the latter.

★ ★ ★ ★ ★

I conclude with a close-focus reflection on a single comic scene.

In 1.3 of Molière's *L'Avare*, the miser is convinced, for no particular reason, that his servant La Flèche has stolen something from him. 'Show me your hands!', screams Harpagon. La Flèche's hands are empty. '*The other ones!*' On reflection this makes no sense, not even as a depiction of a man obsessed. But it draws a delighted burst of laughter from the auditorium — if the actors are good, if the timing is right, if the audience is in a receptive mood. When we are watching a comedy, things which make no sense can suddenly be the reason why we came.

That theatrical event has been reattempted countless times over more than three centuries. Every interpretation has been and will be more or less successful, more or less entertaining. Each new attempt at raising a laugh, however, is enabled in the first place by the survival of Molière's script. In the first printing of 1669, the words of Harpagon and La Flèche do not look particularly impressive; but the actors cannot do without them.

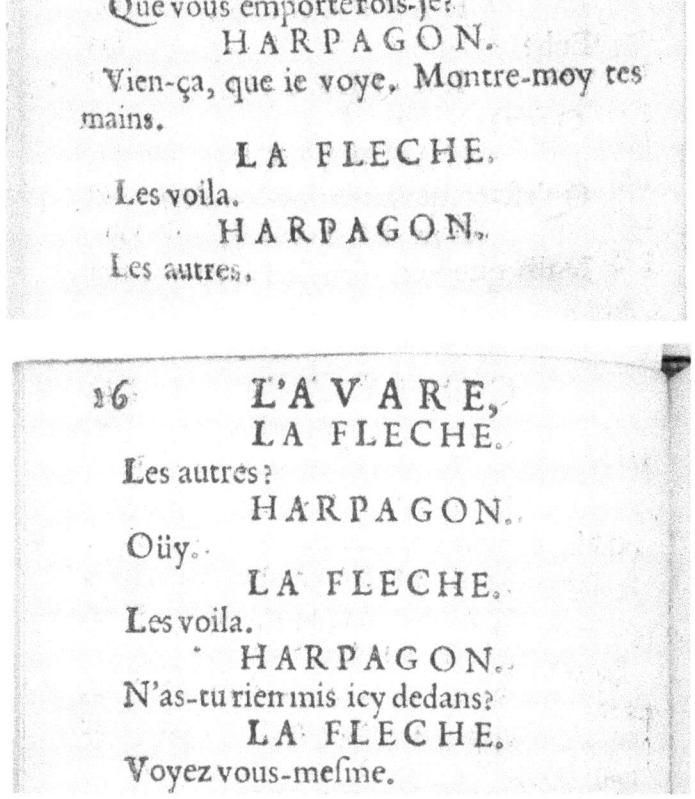

FIG. 27.1. Extracts from pages 15 16 of the first (1669) printing of Molière's *L'Avare*. These simple surviving words on paper are the basis on which actors continue to create a new theatrical moment.

BIBLIOGRAPHY

1. Original Texts (Including Modern Editions, and Translations)

A. Plays, Scenes, and Scenarios

NB. This Bibliography includes an attempt to signal the complex relationships, perhaps still not fully explored, between various different collections entitled *Nouveau Théâtre italien*. It is probable that major bibliographical research is still required in order to distinguish them.

ACCADEMIA DEGLI INTRONATI. 1980 [1537]. *Gl'ingannati*, ed. by Florindo Cerreta (Florence: Olschki)

—— 1984 [1537]. *Il sacrificio degli Intronati; Gl'ingannati*, ed. by Nerida Newbegin (Bologna: Forni) [anastatic reprint of the first printing of 1537]

—— 2018. *All Deceived* [*Gl'ingannati*], trans. by Richard Andrews <http://emothe.uv.es/biblioteca/textosEMOTHE/EMOTHE0427_AllDeceived.php>

ALBERTI, CARMELO. 1996. *Gli scenari Correr: la commedia dell'arte a Venezia* (Rome: Bulzoni)

ANDREINI, GIOVAN BATTISTA. 1986A [1612]. *Lo Schiavetto*, in Laura Falavolti (ed.), *Commedie dei comici dell'arte* (Turin: UTET), pp. 57–213

—— 1986B [1623]. *Le due comedie in comedia*, in Siro Ferrone (ed.), *Commedie dell'arte*, 2 vols (Milan: Mursia), II, 9–105

—— 1997 [1622]. *Amor nello specchio*, ed. by Salvatore Maira and Anna Michela Borracci (Rome: Bulzoni)

—— 2004 [1622]. *La centaura*, ed. by Guido Davico Bonino and Franco Vazzoler (Genoa: Il Melangolo)

—— 2008 [1622]. *La Ferinda*, ed. by Rossella Palmieri (Taranto: Lisi)

—— 2009 [1622]. *Love in the Mirror* [*Amor nello specchio*], ed. and trans. by Jon R. Snyder (Toronto: Iter Press and Centre for Reformation and Renaissance Studies)

ANDREINI, ISABELLA. 1616. *Fragmenti di alcune scritture* (Turin: Tarino)

ARETINO, PIETRO. 1971. *Opere. Vol. II: Teatro*, ed. by G. Petrocchi (Milan: Mondadori)

—— 1978 [1533]. *The Stablemaster* [*Il marescalco*], trans. by George Bull, in Bruce Penman (ed. and trans.), *Five Italian Renaissance Comedies* (Harmondsworth: Penguin), pp. 113–91

—— 1991 [1542]. *Talanta*, trans. by Christopher Cairns, in Christopher Cairns (ed.), *Three Renaissance Comedies* (Lampeter: Edwin Mellen Press), pp. 218–350

ARIOSTO, LUDOVICO. 1974. *Tutte le opere. Vol. IV: Commedie*, ed. by Cesare Segre, with A. Casella, G. Ronchi, and E. Varasi (Milan: Mondadori)

—— 1975. *Comedies*, trans. by Beame and Sbrocchi (Chicago: Chicago University Press)

—— 1991 [1535]. *Lena*, trans. by C. P. Brand, in Christopher Cairns (ed.), *Three Renaissance Comedies* (Lampeter: Edwin Mellen Press), pp. 25–78

BALMAS, ENEA, MICHEL BASSONVILLE, and LUIGIA ZILLI (eds). 1986–97. *Théâtre français de la Renaissance. Première série*, 9 vols (Florence: Olschki; Paris: Presses universitaires de France)

BARGAGLI, GIROLAMO. 1988 [1589]. *The Female Pilgrim* [*La pellegrina*], trans. by Bruno Ferraro (Ottawa: Dovehouse)

BEAUMARCHAIS, PIERRE-AUGUSTIN CARON DE. 1965. *Théâtre de Beaumarchais*, ed. by René Pomeau (Paris: Garnier-Flammarion)
—— 1977. *Parades*, ed. by Pierre Larthomas (Paris: SEDES)
—— 1988. *Œuvres*, ed. by Pierre Larthomas, Bibliothèque de la Pléiade (Paris: Gallimard)
—— 2003. *The Figaro Trilogy*, trans. by David Coward (Oxford: Oxford University Press)
BEECHER, DONALD (trans. and ed.). 2008–09. *Renaissance Comedy: The Italian Masters*, 2 vols (Chicago: Chicago University Press)
BIANCOLELLI, DOMENICO. 1993–97. *Zibaldone* [performance notebooks]. Eighteenth-century French translation, transcribed and edited in Delia Gambelli, *Arlecchino a Parigi* (Rome: Bulzoni)
BIANCOLELLI, PIERRE-FRANÇOIS: see *Nouveau Théâtre italien*, 1712
BIBBIENA (Bernardo Dovizi). 1985 [1521]. *La calandra*, ed. by G. Padoan (Padua: Antenore)
BORSELLINO, NINO (ed.). 1962–67. *Commedie del Cinquecento*, 2 vols (Milan: Feltrinelli)
BRICCIO, GIOVANNI. 1617. *Pantalone imbertonao* (Viterbo: Discepoli)
COLAJANNI, GIULIANA. 1970. *Les Scénarios franco-italiens du ms. 9329 de la B.N. publiés avec une introduction* (Rome: Edizioni di storia e letteratura, Quaderni di cultura francese)
CORNEILLE, PIERRE. 1968. *Théâtre I (Comédies)*, ed. by Jacques Maurens (Paris: Garnier Flammarion; repr. 2006)
—— 1980–87. *Œuvres complètes*, ed. by Georges Couton, 3 vols, Bibliothèque de la Pléiade (Paris: Gallimard)
DANCOURT, FLORENT. 1985–89. *Comédies*, ed. by André Blanc, 2 vols (Paris: Nizet)
DA PONTE, LORENZO. 1956. *Tre libretti per Mozart* (Milan: Rizzoli; repr. 1990)
DAVICO BONINO, GUIDO. (ed.). 1977–78. *Il teatro italiano. Vol. II: La commedia del Cinquecento*, 3 vols (Turin: Einaudi)
DELLA PORTA, GIAMBATTISTA. 1980A. *Teatro, vol. II: Commedie (primo gruppo)*, ed. by Raffaele Sirri (Naples: Istituto Universitario Orientale)
—— 1980B. *Gli duoi fratelli rivali/ The Two Rival Brothers*, bilingual text ed. and trans. by Louise George Clubb (Berkeley: University of California Press)
'Dorimond' (Nicholas Drouin). 1661. *L'Escole des Cocus, ou la precaution inutile* (Paris: Jean Ribou)
—— 1972. [another edition], ed. by H. GASTON HALL, *Australian Journal of French Studies*, 9.2: 117–47
DUFRESNY, CHARLES. 1882. *Théâtre*, ed. by Georges D'Heylli (Paris: E. Hilaire)
DU RYER, ISAAC. 1610. *Le Temps perdu* (Paris: Du Bray)
ESTIENNE, CHARLES. 1540. *Comedie à la maniere des anciens, et de pareille matiere, intitulée Les Abusez* (Paris: Denis Janot for Pierre Roffet)
FALAVOLTI, LAURA (ed.). 1982. *Commedie dei comici dell'arte* (Turin: UTET)
FERRONE, SIRO (ed.). 1986. *Commedie dell'arte*, 2 vols. (Milan: Mursia)
GHERARDI, EVARISTE, and OTHERS (eds). 1701. *Le Théâtre italien de Gherardi, ou Le Recueil General de toutes les Comédies et Scenes Françoises jouées par les Comediens Italiens du Roy*, 6 vols (Amsterdam: Braakman)
—— 1966. *Il 'Théâtre italien' di Gherardi: otto commedie di Fatouville, Regnard et Dufresny*, ed. by Marcello Spaziani (Rome: Ateneo)
—— 1994–96. *Le Théâtre italien*, ed. by Charles Mazouer and Roger Guichemerre, 2 vols (Paris: Société français des textes modernes)
GOLDONI, CARLO. 1935–56. *Tutte le opere*, ed. by Giuseppe Ortolani, 14 vols (Milan: Mondadori)
—— 1976. *Commedie*, ed. by Guido Davico Bonino, 2 vols (Milan: Garzanti)
—— 1983. *Il teatro comico, e Memorie italiane*, ed. by Guido Davico Bonino (Milan: Mondadori; repr. 1995)

GOZZI, CARLO. 1984. *Fiabe teatrali*, ed. by Paolo Bosisio (Rome: Bulzoni)
—— 1994. *Fiabe teatrali*, ed. by Alberto Beniscelli (Milan: Garzanti)
GRASSO, NICOLA. 1978 [1524]. *Eutychia*, ed. by Luigia Stefani (Florence: D'Anna)
LESAGE, ALAIN-RENÉ. 1948. *Théâtre*, ed. by Maurice Bardon (Paris: Garnier)
—— 2000. *Théâtre de la foire*, ed. by Isabelle et Jean-Louis Vissière (Paris: Desjonquières)
LOTTI, GIOVANNI, FRANCESCO BARTALUCCI, and ANON. 1982. *I due gobbi, ovvero la confusione della somiglianza, con Stenterello*, ed. by Enzo Mecacci (San Casciano Val di Pesa: Comune di San Casciano)
MACHIAVELLI, NICCOLÒ. 1964. *Opere letterarie*, ed. by Luigi Blasucci (Milan: Adelphi)
—— 1978 [1521]. *The Mandragola*, in Bruce Penman (ed. and trans.), *Five Italian Renaissance Comedies* (Harmondsworth: Penguin), pp. 11–58
MARIVAUX. 1968. *Théâtre complet*, ed. by Frédéric Deloffre, 2 vols (Paris: Garnier)
MARTINELLI, TRISTANO. [1601]. *Compositions de rhétorique de M. Don Arlequin* (n.p.: 'imprimé de là le bout du monde')
MOLIÈRE. 1949. *L'Avare*, ed. by Ronald A. Wilson (London: Harrap)
—— 1960. *Le Misanthrope*, ed. by Gustave Rudler (Oxford: Blackwell)
—— 1962. *Œuvres complètes*, ed. by R. Jouanny, 2 vols. (Paris: Garnier)
—— 1971. *Œuvres complètes*, ed. by Georges Couton, Bibliothèque de la Pleiade (Paris: Gallimard)
—— 2010. *Œuvres complètes*, ed. by Georges Forestier and others, Bibliothèque de la Pleiade (Paris: Gallimard)
Nouveau Théâtre italien. 1712. *Nouveau Théâtre italien, contenant Le Prince généreux ou le Triomphe de l'amour, La Femme fidèle ou les Apparences trompeuses, Arlequin gentilhomme par hasard, comédies mises au théâtre par M. Dominique Biancolelli*, ed. by Pierre François Biancolelli (Paris: J. Édouard, 1712; expanded edn Antwerp: Huyssens, 1713)
—— 1717. *Nouveau Théâtre italien: ou Recueil général des comédies représentées par les comédiens de S.A.R. le duc d'Orléans, régent du royaume. Tome I*, ed. by Luigi Riccoboni (Paris: Coustellier, 1717; repr. Briasson, 1729)
—— 1733. *Nouveau Théâtre italien, ou Recueil général de toutes les pièces représentées par les Comédiens de S.A.R. Mgr le Duc d'Orléans*, 8 vols (Paris: Briasson 1733; 1753, 10 vols)
PANDOLFI, VITO. 1957–61. *La commedia dell'arte, storia e testo*, 6 vols (Florence: Sansoni)
PICCOLOMINI, ALESSANDRO. 1561. *La sfera del mondo* (Venice: Varisco)
PLAUTUS. 1964. *The Rope, and Other Plays*, trans. by E. F. Watling, Penguin Classics (Harmondsworth: Penguin)
—— 1965. *The Pot of Gold, and Other Plays*, trans. by E. F. Watling, Penguin Classics (Harmondsworth: Penguin)
—— 2011. *Comedies*, ed. and trans. by Wolfgang De Melo, Loeb Classical Library (Cambridge, MA: Harvard University Press)
REGNARD, JEAN-FRANÇOIS. 1875. *Œuvres complètes* ed. by Édouard Fournier (Paris: Laplace, Sanchez)
—— 1920–29. *Chefs-d'œuvre dramatiques*, ed. by Alphonse Séché (Paris: Nelson)
—— 1981. *Comédies du Théâtre Italien*, ed. by Alexandre Calame (Geneva: Droz)
RICCOBONI, LUIGI. 1973 [1721]. *Discorso della commedia all'improvviso e scenari inediti* [ms. 1721–47], ed. by Irène Mamczarcz (Milan: Il Polifilo)
RUSCELLI, GIOVANNI (ed.). 1554. *Delle commedie elette nuovamente raccolte insieme* (Venice: Pietrasanta)
RUZANTE (ANGELO BEOLCO). 1967. *Teatro*, ed. by Ludovico Zorzi (Turin: Einaudi)
—— 1991 [1529]. *Posh Talk* [*La moscheta*], trans. by Ronnie Ferguson, in Christopher Cairns (ed.), *Three Renaissance Comedies* (Lampeter: Edwin Mellen Press), pp. 137–202
—— 1995 [1528]. *The Veteran* [*Parlamento de Ruzante*] and *Weasel* [*Bilora*], trans. by Ronnie Ferguson (New York, Frankfurt am Main & Paris: Lang)

SCALA, FLAMINIO. 1976 [1611]. *Il teatro delle favole rappresentative*, ed. by Ferruccio Marotti, 2 vols (Milan: Il Polifilo)
—— 2008 [1611]. *The Commedia dell'Arte of Flaminio Scala: A Translation and Analysis of 30 Scenarios*, trans. and ed. by Richard Andrews (Lanham, MD: Scarecrow Press)
—— 2018 [1611]. *Il teatro delle favole rappresentative* [full photographic reproduction of the 1611 printing issued in hard copy] (London: Forgotten Books)
TESTAVERDE, ANNA MARIA (ed.). 2007. *I canovacci della commedia dell'arte* (Turin: Einaudi)
TERENCE. 1976. *The Comedies*, trans. by Betty Radice, Penguin Classics (Harmondsworth: Penguin)
—— 2001. *Comedies*, ed. and trans. by John Barsby, Loeb Classical Library (Cambridge, MA: Harvard University Press)

B. Theoretical Background (Including Modern Anthologized Collections)

ARISTOTLE. 1965. *Poetics*, trans. by T. S. Dorsch, in *Aristotle; Horace; Longinus*, Classical Literary Criticism (Harmondsworth: Penguin)
BARBIERI, NICCOLÒ. 1971 [1634]. *La Supplica. Discorso famigliare a quelli che trattano de' comici*, ed. by Ferdinando Taviani (Milan: Il Polifilo)
BARTOLOMMEI SMEDUCCI, GIROLAMO. 1658. *Didascalia, cioè Dottrina comica* (Florence: Stamperia Nuova)
BEAUMARCHAIS, PIERRE-AUGUSTIN CARON DE. 1768. *Essai sur le drame sérieux*; in *Eugénie* [...] *avec un Essai sur le drame sérieux* (Paris & Lausanne: Grasset)
BOILEAU, NICOLAS. 1985 [1674]. *Art poétique*, in *Satires; Épîtres; Art poétique*, ed. by Jean-Pierre Collinet (Paris: Gallimard)
BRANTÔME, PIERRE BOURDEILLE, SEIGNEUR DE. 1867. *Œuvres de Brantôme*, ed. by L. Lalanne (Paris: Renouard)
CARLSON, MARVIN. 1993. *Theories of the Theatre* (Ithaca, NY, & London: Cornell University Press)
CASTELVETRO, LODOVICO. 1979 [1570]. *Poetica d'Aristotile vulgarizzata e sposta*, ed. by Werther Romani (Rome: Laterza)
—— 1984 [1570]. *Castelvetro on the Art of Poetry*, trans. by Andrew Bongiorno (Binghamton, NY: Medieval and Renaissance Texts and Studies)
CECCHINI, PIER MARIA. 1608. 'Discorso sopra l'arte comica con il modo di ben recitare' (unpublished)
—— 1614. *Discorsi intorno alle comedie*. (Vicenza: Amadio)
—— 1628. *Frutti delle moderne comedie et avisi a chi le recita* (Padua: Guareschi)
CICERO, MARCUS TULLIUS. 2014. *De oratore*, ed. by H. Rackham, trans. by E. Sutton, Loeb Classical Library (Cambridge, MA: Harvard University Press)
CHESTERFIELD, EARL OF (Philip Dormer Stanhope). 1890. *Letters Written by Lord Chesterfield to his Son*, ed. by Charles Sayle (London: Walter Scott)
DI BELLA, SARAH. 2009. *L'Expérience théâtral dans l'œuvre théorique de Luigi Riccoboni: contribution à l'histoire du théâtre au XVIIIe siècle, suivie de la traduction et l'édition critique de 'Dell'arte rappresentativa', de Luigi Riccoboni* (Paris: Honoré Champion)
DONATUS [AND EVANTHIUS]. 1902–08. *Aeli Donati quod fertur commentum Terenti*, ed. by Paul Wessner, 3 vols (Leipzig: Teubner)
GILBERT, ALLEN H. 1962. *Literary Criticism: Plato to Dryden* (Detroit: Wayne State University Press)
GOZZI, CARLO. 1797. *Memorie inutili della vita*, 3 vols (Venice: Palese)
HOBBES, THOMAS. 1998 [1651]. *Leviathan*, ed. by J. C. A. Gaskin (Oxford & New York: Oxford University Press)

HORACE (Quintus Horatius Flaccus). 1965. *Ars poetica*, trans. by T. S. Dorsch, in *Aristotle; Horace; Longinus*, Classical Literary Criticism (Harmondsworth: Penguin)
—— 1989. *Ars poetica*, trans. by D. A. Russell, in *Classical Literary Criticism*, World's Classics (Oxford: Oxford University Press)
INGEGNERI, ANGELO. 1989 [1598]. *Della poesia rappresentiva e del modo di rappresentare le favole sceniche*, ed. by Maria Luisa Doglio (Modena: Panini)
LAWTON, H. W. 1949. *Handbook of French Renaissance Dramatic Theory* (Westport, CT: Greenwood Press; repr. 1972–74)
LESSING, GOTTHOLD EPHRAIM. 1975 [1767–68]. *Werke*, 5 vols, Bibliothek Deutscher Klassiker (Berlin & Weimar: Aufbau-Verlag)
OTTONELLI, GIAN DOMENICO. 1655. *Della christiana moderatione del theatro* (Florence: Bonardi)
PAVONI, GIUSEPPE. 1589. *Diario [...] delle feste celebrate nelle solennissime Nozze* (Bologna: Rossi)
PREMINGER, ALEX, and OTHERS (eds). 1974. *Classical and Medieval Literary Criticism: Translations and Interpretations* (New York: Frederick Ungar)
RICCOBONI, LUIGI. 1973 [1721]. *Discorso della commedia all'improvviso e scenari inediti* [ms. 1721–47], ed. by Irène Mamczarcz (Milan: Il Polifilo)
—— 1979 [1728]. *Dell'Arte Rappresentativa* (Bologna: Forni)
—— 1728. *Histoire du théâtre italien* (Paris: André Caillot)
—— 1743. *De la réformation du théâtre* (Paris: n.pr.)
ROMANSKA, MAGDA, and ALAN ACKERMAN (eds). 2017. *Reader in Comedy: An Anthology of Theory and Criticism* (London: Bloomsbury)
SCALIGER, IULIUS CAESAR (Giulio Bordon). 1561. *Poetices* (Lyon: n.pr.)
SERLIO, SEBASTIANO. 1978 [1584]. *I sette libri dell'architettura* (Bologna: Forni) [anastatic reprint]
SIDNELL, MICHAEL J., and OTHERS (eds). 1994. *Sources of Dramatic Theory. Vol. 2: Voltaire to Hugo* (Cambridge: Cambridge University Press)
SIDNEY, PHILIP. 2002 [1595]. *An Apology for Poetry, or The Defence of Poesy*, ed. by G. Shepherd, rev. by R. W. Maslen (Manchester & New York: Manchester University Press)
VANBRUGH, JOHN. 1927. *The Complete Works of Sir John Vanbrugh*, ed. by Bonamy Dobrée, 4 vols (London: Nonesuch Press)
WEINBERG, BERNARD. 1970–74. *Trattati di poetica e retorica del Cinquecento*, 4 vols (Bari: Laterza)

2. Secondary Studies

ADAM, ANTOINE. 1997. *Histoire de la littérature française au XVIIe siècle* (Paris: Albin Michel)
ALLANBROOK, WYE J. 1982. 'Pro Marcellina: The Shape of *Figaro*, Act IV', *Music & Letters*, 73: 69–84
ANDREWS, RICHARD. 1982. '*Gli Ingannati* as a text for performance', *Italian Studies*, 37: 26–48
—— 1988. 'Rhetoric and Drama: Monologues and Set Speeches in Aretino's Comedies', in Peter Hainsworth and others (eds), *The Languages of Literature in Renaissance Italy* (Oxford: Clarendon Press), pp. 152–68
—— 1989. '*Arte* dialogue structures in the comedies of Molière', in Christopher Cairns (ed.), *The Commedia dell'Arte from the Renaissance to Dario Fo* (Lampeter & Newiston: Edwin Mellen Press), pp. 141–76
—— 1991A. 'Written Texts and Performed Texts in Italian Renaissance Comedy', in J. R. Dashwood and J. E. Everson (eds), *Writers and Performers in Italian Drama from the Time of Dante to Pirandello* (Lampeter & Newiston: Edwin Mellen Press), pp. 75–94
—— 1991B. 'Scripted Theatre and the Commedia dell'Arte', in J. R. Mulryne and M. Shewring (ed.), *Theatre of the English and Italian Renaissance* (London: Macmillan), pp. 21–54

—— 1993. *Scripts and Scenarios: The Performance of Comedy in Renaissance Italy* (Cambridge: Cambridge University Press)
—— 1997A. 'Anti-feminism in *commedia erudita*', in Janet Clare and Roy Eriksen (eds), *Contexts of Renaissance Comedy* (Oslo: Novus Forlag), pp. 11–31
—— 1997B. 'Goldoni's *Venetian Twins*: Whose Side is the Audience on?', in Joseph Farrell (ed.), *Carlo Goldoni and Eighteenth-Century Theatre* (Lampeter: Edward Mellen Press), pp. 173–92
—— 1998. 'Shakespeare, Molière, et la Commedia dell'Arte', in Irène Mamczarz (ed.), *La Commedia dell'Arte, le Théâtre Forain, et les spectacles de plein air en Europe: XVIe–XVIIIe siècles* (Paris: Klincksieck), pp. 15–27
—— 2000. 'Isabella Andreini and Others: Women on Stage in the Late Cinquecento', in Letizia Panizza (ed.) *Women in Italian Renaissance Culture and Society* (Oxford: European Humanities Research Centre), pp. 316–33
—— 2001. 'From Beaumarchais to Da Ponte: A New View of the Sexual Politics of *Figaro*', *Music & Letters*, 82.2: 214–33
—— 2005. 'Molière, Commedia dell'Arte, and the Question of Influence in Early Modern European Theatre', *Modern Language Review*, 100.2: 444–63
—— 2006. 'Molière's *L'Avare* as translated *commedia dell'arte*', in Cormac Ó Cuilleanáin, Corinna Salvadori, and John Scattergood (eds), *Italian Culture. Interactions, Transpositions, Translations* (Dublin: Four Courts Press), pp. 121–39
—— 2008. *The Commedia dell'Arte of Flaminio Scala: A Translation and Analysis of 30 Scenarios*, trans. and ed. by Richard Andrews (Lanham MD: Scarecrow Press)
—— 2010. 'Il contributo senese al teatro europeo', *Bullettino Senese di Storia Patria*, 117: 493–523
—— 2013. 'Isabella Andreini's Stage Repertoire: the *Lettere* and *Fragmenti*', in Donatella Fischer (ed.), *The Tradition of the Actor-author in Italian Theatre* (Oxford: Legenda), pp. 30–40
—— 2016. 'Levels of Orality in the Published Scenarios of Flaminio Scala', in Luca Degl'Innocenti, Brian Richardson, and Chiara Sbordoni (eds), *Interactions between Orality and Writing in Early Modern Italian Culture* (London & New York: Routledge), pp. 99–112
ANGELINI, FRANCA. 1993. *Vita di Goldoni* (Bari: Laterza)
ATTOLINI, GIOVANNI. 1997. *Teatro e spettacolo nel Rinascimento* (Bari: Laterza)
BALME, CHRISTOPHER B., PIERMARIO VESCOVO, and DANIELE VIANELLO (eds). 2018. *Commedia dell'Arte in Context* (Cambridge: Cambridge University Press)
BALSAMO, JEAN. 1992. *Les Rencontres des muses: italianisme et anti-italianisme dans les lettres françaises de la fin du XVIe siècle* (Geneva: Slatkine)
BEARD, MARY. 2014. *Laughter in Ancient Rome: On Joking, Tickling, and Cracking Up* (Berkeley: University of California Press)
BEACHAM, R. C. 1991. *The Roman Theatre and its Audience* (London: Routledge)
BISHOP, TOM, and ROBERT HENKE. 2017. 'Institutional Frameworks for Theatre, 1440–1650: Mapping Theatrical Resouces', in Robert Henke (ed.), *A Cultural History of Theatre in the Early Modern Age. Volume 3* (London: Bloomsbury), pp. 15–34
BORSELLINO, NINO. 1974. *Rozzi e Intronati: esperienze e forme di teatro dal 'Decameron' al 'Candelaio'* (Rome: Bulzoni)
BOURQUI, CLAUDE. 1999. *Les Sources de Molière* (Paris: SEDES)
BRADBY, DAVID, and ANDREW CALDER (eds). 2006. *The Cambridge Companion to Molière* (Cambridge: Cambridge University Press)
BRAND, C. P. (Peter). 1988. 'Disguise, Deception and Concealment of Identity in Ariosto's Theatre', in Eileen A. Millar (ed.), *Renaissance and Other Studies: Essays Presented to Peter M. Brown* (Glasgow: University of Glasgow), pp. 129–43

—— 1991. 'Disguise and Recognition in Renaissance Comedy', *Journal of Anglo-Italian Studies*, 1.1: 16–32
—— 1993. 'Discovering Disguise: The Progress of a Dramatic Device in the Renaissance', *Journal of the Institute of Romance Studies*, 2: 191–201
—— 1994. '*Enamoradas* and *Varoniles*: Female Cross-dressing in Italian and Spanish Theatre in the Renaissance', *Journal of the Institute of Romance Studies*, 3: 97–109
BRAY, RENÉ. 1931. *La Formation de la doctrine classique en France* (Lausanne: Payot)
BRERETON, GEOFFREY. 1977. *French Comic Drama from the Sixteenth to the Eighteenth Century* (London: Methuen)
BROWN, PAMELA ALLEN. 2021. *The Diva's Gift to the Shakespearean Stage: Agency, Theatricality, and the Innamorata* (Oxford: Oxford University Press)
BROWN, PETER M. 1973. 'Prose or Verse in the Comedy: A Florentine Treatment of a Sixteenth-Century Controversy' (inaugural lecture, University of Hull)
BURN, A. R. 1966. *The Pelican History of Greece* (Harmondsworth: Penguin)
BYATT, A. S. 2011. [REVIEW], *Guardian*, 6 August
CAIRNS, DAVID. 2007. *Mozart and his Operas*, 2nd edn (Harmondsworth: Penguin)
CARTER, TIM. 2004. '*Che cosa è amor?* Music and Love in Mozart's *Così fan tutte*', in Brian Richardson, Simon Gilson, and Catherine Keen (eds), *Theatre, Opera, and Performance in Italy from the Fifteenth Century to the Present.* (Leeds: Maney/ Society for Italian Studies), pp. 155–72
CARTER, TIM (ed.). 1987. *Cambridge Opera Handbook to 'Le nozze di Figaro'* (Cambridge: Cambridge University Press)
CLARKE, JAN. 2006. 'The Material Conditions of Molière's Stage', in David Bradby and Andrew Calder (eds), *The Cambridge Companion to Molière* (Cambridge: Cambridge University Press), pp. 15–36
CLUBB, LOUISE GEORGE. 1965. *Giambattista Della Porta, Dramatist* (Princeton, NJ: Princeton University Press)
—— 1989. *Italian Drama in Shakespeare's Time* (New Haven, CT, & London: Yale University Press)
—— 2019. '*Commedia erudita*: Birth and Transfiguration', in Michele Marrapodi (ed.), *Anglo-Italian Renaissance Literature and Culture* (London & New York: Routledge), pp. 101–18
COUTON, GEORGES. 1986. *Richelieu et le théâtre* (Lyon: Presses universitaires de Lyon)
D'AMICO, SILVIO (ed.) 1954–68. *Enciclopedia dello Spettacolo*, 10 vols (Rome: Le Maschere)
DANE, J. 1999. 'On Metrical Confusion and Consensus in Early Editions of Terence', *Humanistica Lovaniensia*, 48: 103–31
DESCOTES, MAURICE. 1974. *Les Grands Rôles du théâtre de Beaumarchais* (Paris: Presses universitaires de France)
DUCHARTRE, PIERRE LOUIS. 1929. *The Italian Comedy*, trans. by R. T. Weaver (London: Harrap; repr. New York: Dover, 1966)
DUCKWORTH, G. E. 1952. *The Nature of Roman Comedy: A Study in Popular Entertainment* (Princeton, NJ: Princeton University Press)
EGGINTON, WILLIAM. 2016. *The Man Who Invented Fiction: How Cervantes Ushered in the Modern World* (London & New York: Bloomsbury)
EINSTEIN, ALFRED. 1969. *Mozart: His Character, his Work*, trans. by Arthur Mendel and Nathan Broder (London: Panther Books)
ELLIS, ANTHONY. 2009. *Old Age, Masculinity, and Early Modern Drama* (Farnham: Ashgate)
FARRELL, JOSEPH (ed.). 1997. *Carlo Goldoni and Eighteenth-Century Theatre* (Lampeter: Edward Mellen Press)
FARRELL, JOSEPH, and PAOLO PUPPA (eds). 2006. *The Cambridge History of Italian Theatre* (Cambridge: Cambridge University Press)
FERGUSON, RONNIE. 2000. *The Theatre of Angelo Beolco (Ruzante)* (Ravenna: Longo)

FERRONE, SIRO. 1993. *Attori mercanti corsari: la commedia dell'arte in Europa tra Cinque e Seicento* (Turin: Einaudi)
—— 2006. *Arlecchino: vita e avventure di Tristano Martinelli* (Rome: Laterza)
—— 2014. *La Commedia dell'Arte: attrici e attori italiani in Europa (XVI–XVIII secolo)* (Turin: Einaudi)
FIASCHINI, FABRIZIO. 2007. *L'"inaccessibile agitazione": Giovan Battista Andreini tra professione teatrale, cultura letteraria e religione* (Pisa: Giardini)
FIDO, FRANCO. 1997. *Guida a Goldoni* (Turin: Eninaudi)
FITZPATRICK, TIM. 1995. *The Relationship of Oral and Literate Performance Processes in the Commedia dell'Arte: Beyond the Improvisation/ Memorisation Divide* (Lewiston, Queenston, & Lampeter: Edwin Mellen Press)
FORESTIER, GEORGES. 1988. *Esthétique de l'identité dans le théâtre français (1550–1680): le déguisement et ses avatars* (Geneva: Droz)
GAMBELLI, DELIA. 1993–97. *Arlecchino a Parigi*, 3 vols (Rome: Bulzoni)
GLOVER, JANE. 2018. *Handel in London* (London: Macmillan)
GOLDBERG, SANDER M. 2007. 'Comedy and Society from Menander to Terence', in Marianne McDonald and J. Michael Walton (eds), *The Cambridge Companion to Greek and Roman Theatre* (Cambridge: Cambridge University Press), pp. 124–37
GORDON, MEL. 1983. *Lazzi: The Comic Routines of the Commedia dell'Arte* (New York: Performing Arts Journal Publications)
GOULBOURNE, RUSSELL. 2006. *Voltaire, Comic Dramatist* (Oxford: Voltaire Foundation)
—— 2007. 'Satire in Seventeenth- and Eighteenth-Century France' in Ruben Quintero (ed.), *A Companion to Satire: Ancient and Modern* (Oxford: Blackwell), pp. 139–59
GRANTHAM, BARRY. 2000. *Playing Commedia: A Teaching Guide to 'commedia' Techniques* (London: Nick Hern Books)
GRENDEL, FRÉDÉRIC. 1973. *Beaumarchais ou la calomnie* (Paris: Flammarion)
—— 1977. *The Man Who was Figaro*, trans. by R. Greaves (London: Macdonald & Jane's)
GRENE, NICHOLAS. 1980. *Shakespeare, Jonson, Molière: The Comic Contract* (London: Macmillan)
GÜNSBERG, MAGGIE. 1997. *Gender and the Italian Stage* (Cambridge: Cambridge University Press)
—— 2001. *Playing with Gender: The Comedies of Goldoni* (Leeds: Northern Universities Press)
HELLER, HENRY. 2003. *Anti-Italianism in Sixteenth-Century France* (Toronto: University of Toronto Press)
HENKE, ROBERT. 2002. *Performance and Literature in the Commedia dell'Arte* (Cambridge: Cambridge University Press)
HENKE, ROBERT (ed.). 2017. *A Cultural History of Theatre in the Early Modern Age* (London: Bloomsbury)
HERZEL, ROGER. 1978. 'The Décor of Molière's Stage: The Testimony of Brissart and Chaveau', *PMLA*, 93.4 (1978): 925–54
HILGER, MICHAEL JOHN. 2007. *The Rhetoric of Comedy: Comic Theory in the Terentian Commentary of Aelius Donatus* (Ann Arbor: University of Michigan)
HOLME, TIMOTHY. 1976. *A Servant of Many Masters: The Life and Times of Carlo Goldoni* (London: Jupiter)
HOWARTH, W. D. 1973. 'La Notion de la catharsis dans la comédie française classique', *Revue des Sciences Humaines*, 152: 521–39
—— 1978. *Comic Drama: the European Heritage* (London: Methuen)
—— 1982. *Molière: A Playwright and his Audience* (Cambridge: Cambridge University Press)
—— 1995. *Beaumarchais and the Theatre* (London: Routledge)
—— (ed.). 1997. *French Theatre in the Neo-classical Era, 1550–1789* (Cambridge: Cambridge University Press)

HOWE, ELIZABETH. 1992. *The First English Actresses: Women and Drama, 1660–1700* (Cambridge: Cambridge University Press)

HOXBY, BLAIR. 2017. 'Technologies of Performance', in Robert Henke (ed.), *A Cultural History of Theatre in the Early Modern Age* (London: Bloomsbury), pp. 161–82

HULFIELD, STEFAN. 2018. 'Notebooks, Prologues and Scenarios', in Christopher B. Balme, Piermario Vescovo, and Daniele Vianello (eds), *Commedia dell'Arte in Context* (Cambridge: Cambridge University Press), pp. 34–55

JEFFERY, BRIAN. 1969. *French Renaissance Comedy* (Oxford: Clarendon Press)

JONES, SUZANNE. 2020. *The First English Translations of Molière: Drama in Flux, 1663–1732* (Oxford: Legenda)

JORDAN, PETER. 2014. *The Venetian Origins of the Commedia dell'Arte* (London & New York: Routledge)

KATRITZKY, M. A. 1989. 'The Recueil Fossard 1928–88: A Review and Three Reconstructions', in Christopher Cairns (ed.), *The Commedia dell'Arte from the Renaissance to Dario Fo* (Lampeter & Newiston: Edwin Mellen Press), pp. 99–116

—— 2006. *The Art of Commedia* (Amsterdam & New York: Rodopi)

LACOUR, LÉOPOLD. 1921. *Les Premières Actrices françaises* (Paris: Librairie Française)

LAIENA, SERENA. 2021. '*Meretrices* ergo Dive: Academic Encomia and the Metamorphosis of Early Modern Actresses', *The Italianist*, 41.1, DOI: 10.1080/02614340.2021.1983981

LANCASTER, HENRY CARRINGTON. 1929–42. *A History of French Dramatic Literature in the Seventeenth Century*, 9 vols (Baltimore, MD: Johns Hopkins Press; Paris: Les Presses universitaires de France)

LAZARD, MADELEINE. 1960. *Le Théâtre en France au XVIe siècle* (Paris: Presses universitaires de France)

LEA, KATHLEEN M. 1934. *Italian Popular Comedy*, 2 vols (Oxford: Clarendon Press)

LOUGH, JOHN. 1979. *Seventeenth-Century French Drama: The Background* (Oxford: Clarendon Press)

MAJORANA, BERNADETTE. 2018. 'Commedia dell'Arte and the Church', in Christopher B. Balme, Piermario Vescovo, and Daniele Vianello (eds), *Commedia dell'Arte in Context* (Cambridge: Cambridge University Press), pp. 133–48

MALLINSON, G. J. 1984. *The Comedies of Corneille: Experiments in the Comic* (Manchester: Manchester University Press)

MAMCZARZ, IRÈNE (ed.). 1998. *La Commedia dell'Arte, le Théâtre Forain, et les spectacles de plein air en Europe: XVIe–XVIIIe siècles* (Paris: Klincksieck)

MANES, YAEL. 2011. *Motherhood and Patriarchal Masculinities in Sixteenth-Century Italian Comedy: Studies in Performance and Early Modern Drama* (Farnham: Ashgate)

MANGO, ACHILLE. 1966. *La commedia in lingua nel Cinquecento* (Milan: Lerici)

MARITI, LUCIANO. 1978. *Commedia Ridicolosa [...] storia e testi* (Rome: Bulzoni)

MAROTTI, FERRUCCIO, and GIOVANNA ROMEI. 1991. *La commedia dell'arte e la società barocca: la professione del teatro* (Rome: Bulzoni)

MAZOUER, CHARLES. 2002A. *Le Théâtre d'Arlequin: comédies et comédiens italiens en France au XVIIe siècle* (Fasano: Schena; Paris: Université de Paris-Sorbonne)

—— 2002B. *Le Théâtre français de la Renaissance* (Paris: Champion)

MCDONALD, MARIANNE, and J. MICHAEL WALTON (eds). 2007. *The Cambridge Companion to Greek and Roman Theatre* (Cambridge: Cambridge University Press)

MCKEE, KENNETH. 1958. *The Theater of Marivaux* (London: Peter Owen)

MCLAUGHLIN, MARTIN. 2015. 'The Recovery of Terence in Renaissance Italy: From Alberti to Machiavelli', in T. F. Earle and Catarina Fouto (eds), *The Reinvention of Theatre in Sixteenth-Century Europe. Traditions, Texts and Performance* (Oxford: Legenda), pp. 115–39

MEREDITH, GEORGE, and HENRI BERGSON. 1956. *Comedy*, ed. by Wylie Sypher (New York: Doubleday)

MOLINARI, CESARE. 1985. *La commedia dell'arte* (Milan: Mondadori)
MOORE, W. G. 1964. *Molière, A New Criticism*, 2nd edn (Oxford: Clarendon Press)
—— 1969. *French Achievement in Literature* (London: G. Bell & Sons)
—— 1971. *The Classical Drama of France* (London: Oxford University Press)
NICHOLSON, ERIC. 1999. 'Romance as Role Model: Early Female Performances of *Orlando furioso* and *Gerusalemme liberata*', in Valeria Finucci (ed.), *Renaissance Transactions: Ariosto and Tasso* (Durham, NC, & London: Duke University Press), pp. 246–69
NICOLL, ALLARDYCE. 1963. *The World of Harlequin* (Cambridge: Cambridge University Press)
OJEDA CALVO, MARIA DEL VALLE. 2007. *Stefanelo Botarga e Zan Ganassa: scenari e zibaldoni di comici italiani nella Spagna del Cinquecento* (Rome: Bulzoni)
ORSINO, MARGHERITA. 1993. 'Pierre-François Biancolelli dit Dominique-le-Fils (1680–1734)' (unpublished doctoral thesis, Università Degli Studi di Genova)
—— 1998. 'Errances d'Arlequin: Pierre-François Biancolelli aux Théâtres de la Foire entre 1708 et 1717', in Mamczarz, Irène (ed.), *La Commedia dell'Arte, le Théâtre Forain, et les spectacles de plein air en Europe: XVIe–XVIIIe siècles* (Paris: Klincksieck), pp. 115–27
PADOAN, GIORGIO. 1996. *L'avventura della commedia rinascimentale* (Padua: Piccin Nuova Libreria)
PARISH, RICHARD. 2006. 'How (and Why) Not to Take Molière Too Seriously', in David Bradby and Andrew Calder (eds), *The Cambridge Companion to Molière* (Cambridge: Cambridge University Press), pp, 71–82
PAPADOPOULOU BRADY, VALENTINI. 1970. *Love in the Theatre of Marivaux: A Study of the Factors Influencing its Birth, Development and Expression* (Geneva: Droz)
PEYRONNET, PIERRE. 1978. 'Voltaire "metteur en scène" des ses propres œuvres', *Revue d'histoire du théâtre*, 30 (1978): 38–54
PIERI, MARZIA. 1989. *La nascita del teatro moderno in Italia tra XV e XVI secolo* (Turin: Bollati Boringhieri)
PIPERNO, FRANCO. 1991. Sleeve note to the Philips Complete Mozart edition of *La finta semplice* (Philips discs 422 528-2)
QUINTERO, RUBEN (ed.). 2007. *A Companion to Satire: Ancient and Modern* (Oxford: Blackwell)
RAYFIELD, LUCY. 2021A. 'The Poetics of Comedy in Jacques Peletier Du Mans's *Art poëtique* (1555)', in *Classical Receptions Journal*, 13.1: 31–48
—— 2021B. *Poetics, Performance and Politics in French and Italian Renaissance Comedy* (Oxford: Legenda)
REBAUDENGO, MAURIZIO. 1994. *Giovan Battista Andreini tra poetica e drammaturgia* (Turin: Rosenberg & Sellier)
REVERMANN, MARTIN (ed.). 2014. *The Cambridge Companion to Greek Comedy* (Cambridge: Cambridge University Press)
REYNOLDS, LEIGHTON D. (ed.). 1986. *Texts and Transmission: A Survey of the Latin Classics* (Oxford: Clarendon Press)
RICHARDS, KENNETH, and LAURA RICHARDS. 1990. *The Commedia dell'Arte: A Documentary History* (Oxford: Blackwell)
ROBBINS DUDECK, TERESA, and CAITLIN MCCLURE. 2018. *Applied Improvisation* (London: Bloomsbury)
ROBINSON, MICHAEL F. 1978. *Opera Before Mozart*, 3rd edn (London: Hutchinson)
RUGGIERO, GUIDO. 1985. *The Boundaries of Eros: Sex, Crime and Sexuality in Renaissance Venice* (Oxford: Oxford University Press)
RUSTEN, JEFFREY (ed.). 2011. *The Birth of Comedy* (Baltimore, MD: Johns Hopkins University Press)

SADIE, STANLEY (ed.). 2001. *The New Grove Dictionary of Music and Musicians*, 2nd edn, 29 vols (London: Macmillan)

SAND, MAURICE. 1860. *Masques et bouffons (comédie italienne)* (Paris: Michel Lévy frères)

SAULINI, MIRELLA. 1995. *Indagine sulla donna in Goldoni e Gozzi* (Rome: Bulzoni)

SAVOIA, FRANCESCA, and TED EMERY. 1993. 'Goldoni as Librettist: Theatrical Reform and the "Drammi Giocosi per Musica"', *Italica*, 70.2: 231

SCHERER, JACQUES. 1954. *La Dramaturgie de Beaumarchais* (Paris: Nizet; repr. 1980)

SCÈVE, MAURICE. 1997. *The Entry of Henri II into Lyon: September 1548*, ed. by Richard Cooper (Tempe: Medieval and Renaissance Texts and Studies)

SCHIRONI, FRANCESCA. 2013. 'The Trickster on the Stage: The Cunning Slave from Plautus to *commedia dell'arte*', in S. Douglas Olson (ed.), *Ancient Comedy and Reception. Essays in Honour of Jeffrey Henderson* (Berlin: De Gruyter), pp. 447–78

SCHMITT, NATALIE CROHN. 2020. *Performing Commedia dell'Arte, 1570–1630* (Abingdon & New York: Routledge)

SCOTT, VIRGINIA. 1990. *The Commedia dell'Arte in Paris* (London: University Press of Virginia)

—— 2000. *Molière: A Theatrical Life* (Cambridge: Cambridge University Press)

—— 2010. *Women on the Stage in Early Modern France* (Cambridge: Cambridge University Press)

SERAGNOLI, DANIELE. 1980. *Il teatro a Siena nel Cinquecento* (Rome: Bulzoni)

SHAPIRO, JAMES. 2005. *1599. A Year in the Life of William Shakespeare* (London: Faber & Faber)

SMITH, PATRICK J. 1971. *The Tenth Muse* (London: Gollancz)

STEELE, E. 1981. *Carlo Goldoni: Life, Work and Times* (Ravenna: Longo)

TAVIANI, FERDINANDO. 1970. *La commedia dell'arte e la società barocca: la fascinazione del teatro* (Rome: Bulzoni)

—— 2018. 'Knots and Doubleness: The Engine of the Commedia dell'Arte', in Christopher B. Balme, Piermario Vescovo, and Daniele Vianello (eds), *Commedia dell'Arte in Context* (Cambridge: Cambridge University Press), pp. 17–33

TAVIANI, FERDINAND, and MIRELLA SCHINO. 1982. *Il segreto della commedia dell'arte* (Florence: Usher)

TESSARI, ROBERTO. 1969. *La commedia dell'arte nel Seicento: industria e arte giocosa nella società barocca* (Florence: Olschki)

—— 1981. *Commedia dell'arte: la maschera e l'ombra* (Milan: Mursia)

THOMAS, KEITH. 1977. 'The Place of Laughter in Tudor and Stuart England', *Times Literary Supplement*, 21 January, pp. 77–81

TURNER, VICTOR. 1982. *From Ritual to Theatre: The Human Seriousness of Play* (New York: PAJ)

VESCOVO, PIERMARIO. 2018. 'Between Improvisation and Book', in Christopher B. Balme, Piermario Vescovo, and Daniele Vianello (eds), *Commedia dell'Arte in Context* (Cambridge: Cambridge University Press), pp. 56–63

VUILLERMOZ, MARC (ed.). 1998. *Dictionnaire analytique des œuvres théâtrales françaises du XVIIe siècle* (Paris: Champion)

WEINBERG, BERNARD. 1961. *A History of Literary Criticism in the Italian Renaissance* (Chicago: University of Chicago Press)

INDEX

Works by early modern Italian and French writers are listed in chronological order, under their authors' names. Where two dates are given for a play, the first denotes its (probable) first staging, and the second its first printing. A single date shows the first known staging; if only the first printing date is known, then this is indicated by 'pub.'.

Académie Française 45, 51, 144, 221
Academies, Italian 18, 23, 33–34, 104, 211, 236
Accademia degli Intronati 19, 20, 23, 27, 68, 104, 118 n. 3, 124, 140, 151–52, 156, 162–63, 165, 181–84, 188, 202, 204, 211, 213, 214, 218, 221, 228 n. 1, 229, 231, 237–38, 244–45, 246, 250, 255, 263
    Gl'ingannati (1532/1537) 19, 20, 27, 68, 104, 124, 140, 156, 162, 181–84, 188, 202, 204, 213, 218, 221, 228 n. 1, 229, 231, 237–38, 244–45, 246, 250, 263
    L'amor costante (pub. 1540) [attributed to Alessandro Piccolomini] 162–63, 182, 202
    Alessandro (1544/1545) [attributed to Alessandro Piccolomini] 162–63, 182
    La Pellegrina (1565/1589) [attributed to Girolamo Bargagli] 151–52, 162–63, 165, 202, 211, 214, 218
Accesi (troupe) 29, 30
act divisions and numbering 25, 118–21, 144
actresses 23–24, 27, 207–12, 214, 217, 218
adultery plots 20, 224–25, 239
Aeschylus (c. 525–c. 455 BCE) 148
Alamanni, Luigi (1495–1556) 27
    La Flora (1549/1556) 27
Amsterdam 54
Andreini, Francesco ('Capitano Spavento' on stage, 1548–1624) 24, 29, 30–32, 132, 243, 245
Andreini, Giovan Battista ('Lelio' on stage, 1576–1654) 33–39, 74, 107–09, 121, 142, 152, 186, 209, 211, 244–45
    Lo Schiavetto (pub. 1612) 108–09
    Prologo in dialogo fra Momo e Verità (treatise, pub. 1612) 107–09
    Amor nello specchio (pub. 1622) 142
    Li duo Leli simili (pub. 1622) 244–45
    La Ferinda (libretto, pub. 1622) 33 152
    La Centaura (pub. 1622) 39
    Le due comedie in comedia (pub. 1623) 109, 121
Andreini, Isabella ('Isabella' on stage; 1562–1604) 24, 29, 30–32, 40, 41, 61, 113, 131–32, 135, 151, 185, 186, 207, 209–10, 211, 214, 250, 260, 263
    Lettere e Fragmenti (pub. 1607–17) 132
    Mirtilla (pub. 1588) 24
    Rime (lyric poems, pub. 1601) 250 n. 18

Anne of Austria (Queen of France) 53
Aretino, Pietro (1492–1556) 19, 137–38, 144–45, 162 n. 9, 247, 248, 255
    La cortigiana (1525/1534) 145, 162 n. 9, 247
    Il marescalco (pub. 1533) 162 n. 9
    La Talanta (1542/1542) 137
    Lo hipocrito (pub. 1542) 248
Ariosto, Ludovico (1474–1533) 11, 16–19, 37, 41–42, 45, 47, 94–95, 113, 118, 122, 145, 149–51, 161–62, 177–78, 199, 213, 221, 229, 231, 232–33, 241, 243 n. 4, 247, 251, 255
    La cassaria (1508/1510) 1, 11, 16, 17, 19, 113, 118, 122, 145, 149–51, 161, 199, 232, 241
    I suppositi (1509/1510) 16, 19, 27, 30, 45, 69, 113, 118, 161, 199, 221, 231, 232, 241, 247
    Il negromante (1528/1535) 161, 233, 243 n. 4
    La Lena (1529/1535) 161–62, 199, 213, 229, 251
    I studenti/La scolastica (pub. 1547) 37, 94
Aristophanes (c.446–c.386 BCE) 14, 102, 160, 195
    The Clouds 160
Aristotle (384–322 BCE) 14–15, 21, 44, 45, 94, 101–02, 103, 111–14, 241, 258–59, 262, 266, 267–68
    Nicomachean Ethics 101, 103
    Poetics 14–15, 21, 111, 241, 258, 262, 266
Arlecchino/Arlequin, see Harlequin
Armani, Vincenza (actress, 1530–69) 208–09
asides on stage 82, 125–26

'bad disguise trick' 247–48
Baïf, Jean-Antoine de (1532–89) 28
Balletti, Zanetta ('Silvia' on stage, 1701–58) 52, 61, 67
Barbara Flaminia (actress) 208
Barbieri, Niccolò ('Beltrame' on stage; 1576–1641):
    La Supplica (treatise, pub. 1634) 104–05, 130
Bargagli, Girolamo (1537–86), see Accademia degli Intronati
Barnett, Samuel (actor) 252 n. 22
Barrault, Jean-Louis (1910–94) 98
Bartolommei Smeducci, Girolamo (1584–1662):
    Didascalia, ovvero Dottrina comica (treatise, with original scenarios, pub. 1658) 57
Basel 21
Beard, Mary 111 n. 30, 256 n. 1

Beaumarchais (Pierre-Augustin Caron, 1732–99) 1, 6, 7, 41, 70, 71, 84–90, 91–92, 97–98, 106, 110, 111, 120, 124–25, 127, 134, 139, 147, 155, 158, 161, 172–74, 180, 184, 204, 206, 217–19, 222, 225, 229, 235, 238, 240–41, 243–44, 247, 253–54, 257, 264–65, 267, 268
  Parades (early 1760s, pub. 1977) 71, 85, 106
  Eugénie (1767) 70, 84, 85
  Essai sur le drame sérieux (treatise, pub. 1768) 85, 110
  Les Deux amis (1770) 85
  Le Barbier de Séville, ou la Précaution inutile (1775) 1, 8, 84, 85–86, 87, 92, 97, 105, 120, 127, 134, 139, 155, 158, 161, 174, 204, 217–19, 229, 235, 241, 253–54, 264–65
  La Folle journée, ou le Mariage de Figaro (1784) 1, 8, 84, 86–89, 106, 120, 124–25, 127, 134, 147, 155, 158, 161, 174, 206, 217–19, 222, 225, 235, 243–44, 247, 252–54, 257, 268
  La Mère coupable (1797) 84, 87, 92, 96, 120, 174
'bed trick' 221, 247
Beolco: see Ruzante
Bergamo 24, 63, 66, 105, 114, 136, 140
  dialect 24, 66, 105, 136, 140
Biancolelli, Caterina/Catherine ('Colombine' on stage, 1665–1716) 61
Biancolelli, Domenico ('Arlecchino' on stage; 1636–88) 53–54, 63, 106, 108, 113–14, 169, 231
  scenario notes (covering 1667–1680) 53, 63, 106, 113–14, 169, 231
Biancolelli, Francesca/Françoise ('Isabelle' on stage, dates unknown) 61
Biancolelli, Louis (1666–1729):
  Arlequin misantrope [attrib.] (1692) 171 n. 22
Biancolelli, Pierre-François ('Arlequin' and 'Trivelin' on stage; 1680–1734) 57, 63, 67, 234
  plays and sketches (1704–1733) 57, 63
  Le Nouveau Théâtre Italien (anthology, pub. 1712) 57
  Le Procès des comédiens Français et Italiens, ou l'ombre de Dominique (pub. 1713) 63
'Bibbiena' (Bernardo Dovizi, 1470–1520):
  La Calandra (1513/1521) 19, 20, 27, 104, 118 n. 3, 145, 208, 213, 225, 228, 232, 244–45, 255, 263
bienséance, see classiciste rules
Bizet, Georges (1838–75):
  Carmen (opera, 1875) 73
Boccaccio, Giovanni (1313–75) 20, 48, 164, 213, 222, 225, 247
Boileau, Nicolas (1636–1711):
  Art poétique (verse treatise, 1674) 103, 229, 265–66
Boisfranc (possibly Germain Boffrand, 1667–1754):
  Les Bains de la Porte St-Bernard (1696) 249
Bologna 24, 37, 165 n. 13, 189
  dialect 24, 189
Bonaparte, Napoléon 87, 96, 174
Boso, Carlo 188 n. 13

Bourgeois, Jacques (dates unknown):
  Comédie tres elegante ... [from Ariosto: *Suppositi*] (pub. 1545) 27–28, 30, 45
Brand, Peter 246 n. 10
Brantôme, Seigneur de (Pierre Bourdeille, c.1540–1614) 208
Bray, René 45, 148, 156
Briasson (printer):
  Nouveau Théâtre Italien (1729) 67
Briccio, Giovanni (1579–1645) 34–35, 137–38, 195–97
  Pantalon imbertonao (pub. 1620) 137–38, 195–97
Brighella (mask) 24, 79, 93, 139, 180, 233
Brown, Pamela Allen 209
Bruni, Domenico (c. 1660–66) 130
Burn, A.R. 195
Byatt, A.S. 185 n. 11, 263

Calmo, Andrea (1510–71) 50, 128, 198
  La Rhodiana (1540/1553) 50
canovacci: see scenarios
Capitano (mask) 24–25, 34, 74, 112, 131–34, 135–36, 157, 179, 185, 200, 245, 248, 265
Carné, Marcel (1906–96):
  Les Enfants du paradis (film, 1945) 98
Carnival 57, 76
cartoon characters, modern 185–86
Castelvetro, Lodovico (c. 1505–71) 21, 45, 94, 146
'castigat ridendo mores' (motto) 108, 159, 255, 260
Castiglione, Baldassarre (1478–1529):
  Il libro del cortegiano (pub. 1528) 111 n. 29
Cavalli, Francesco (1602–76):
  Calisto (opera, 1651) 36, 74
Cecchi, Giovan Maria (1518–87):
  L'assiuolo (1549/1550) 147, 225
Cecchini, Pier Maria ('Fritellino' on stage; 1563–1645) 33–34, 211, 260 n. 5
  Discorso sopra l'arte comica (treatise, c. 1608) 33–34, 260 n. 5
  Discorsi intorno alle commedie (treatise, pub. 1614) 211
  Frutti delle moderne commedie (treatise, pub. 1628) 33–34
censorship 21, 38–39, 84, 103, 106, 107, 164–65
Chapelain, Jean (1595–1674) 45, 47
Chaplin, Charlie ('tramp' mask) 185, 189
Charpentier, Marc-Antoine (composer, 1643–1704) 50
Chekhov, Anton (1860–1904) 126
Chesterfield, Lord (Philip Stanhope, 1694–1773) 108 n. 5
Chiari, Pietro (1712–85) 180
Christine de Lorraine (French princess) 131
Cibber, Colley (1671–1757) 70
Cicero, Marcus Tullius (106–43 BCE) 108, 110
Cicognini, Giacinto Andrea (1606–51) 36
  Le Gelosie fortunate del principe Rodrigo (pub. 1654) 36
  Il convitato di pietra (pub. 1691) 36

Cicognini, Jacopo (1577–1631) 36
  Il Trionfo di David (1628/1633) 36
classiciste rules 3, 21, 43–47, 74, 61, 81, 103, 106, 127,
  144–58, 170, 183–84, 216, 221–22, 253, 261–62
  bienséance 44, 46, 61, 81, 103, 106, 221–22
  decorum 44, 183–84
  Unity of Action 21, 44, 156–58
  Unity of Place 21, 44, 148–55, 216
  Unity of Time 21, 44, 144–45, 146–48
  vraisemblance 43–44, 61, 81, 152, 170, 183–84, 253, 262
clergy on stage 164–65, 168
Clubb, Louise George 183
Cochin, Charles-Nicolas *fils* (1715–90) 59
collusion, comic 105, 109–10, 111–16, 164, 231,
  235–40, 248–49
Colombine (French mask) 62–63, 79, 98, 114–15, 203,
  225, 238, 249, 251, 261–62
Comédie-Française 51, 53–66, 68, 71, 73, 84, 119, 155,
  158, 170–74, 180, 181, 184, 212, 219, 229, 238, 262
comédie larmoyante 2, 70–71, 75–76, 78, 128, 155, 174,
  191, 256
comedy of character 51, 60
commedia erudita 18–21, 23. 25, 34, 37, 104, 120, 122,
  133, 145, 156, 161–65, 178 187, 188, 189–90,
  199–200, 202, 205, 208, 211, 213–14, 216, 221,
  229, 232, 236, 242–43, 244–45, 248, 251, 255, 267
commedia grave 21, 46, 164, 211, 214, 222, 229, 248
'*commedia ridicolosa*' 34–35, 105, 133–34, 137–38, 195–97,
  211
concert arias 135
Confidenti (troupe) 30
Congreve, William (1670–1729) 2
contaminatio (borrowing of material) 145, 181
Corneille, Pierre (1606–84) 40–41, 43, 51, 68, 106, 119,
  122–23, 146–47, 148–49, 152, 155, 156–57, 167,
  181, 187, 190, 200, 203, 206, 211, 217, 219, 221,
  223, 229, 234, 243, 248, 267
  Mélite (1631) 40, 167, 181
  La Galerie du Palais (1631–32) 41, 147, 167, 223
  La Veuve (1631–32) 146, 152, 167, 223
  La Place Royale (1634) 41, 167, 223
  La Suivante (1634) 152, 167
  L'Illusion comique (1636/1639) 40
  Le Cid (1637) 43
  Le Menteur (1643) 167, 190, 248, 267
  La Suite du Menteur (1644–45) 40, 167 n. 16, 223, 248
  Discours des trois unités (treatise, pub. 1660) 146, 148,
  156
Costantini, Angelo ('Mezzettino' on stage, 1654–1729)
  62
courts, Italian (as theatre venues) 16–18, 104, 113, 236,
  237, 239
Crispin (French mask) 60, 86, 187
cross-dressing on stage 124, 211, 214–16, 244, 246,
  241–53

Dalmatia 162
Danton, Georges Jacques (1759–94) 87, 174
d'Arbes, Cesare (actor, c. 1710–1778) 246
Da Ponte, Lorenzo (1749–1838) 1, 8, 77, 88–89, 91–92,
  124–25, 158, 206, 219, 222, 225, 235–36, 238–40,
  243–44, 252–53, 257
  Le nozze di Figaro (libretto, 1786) 1, 8, 88–89,
  91–92, 124–25, 158, 206, 219, 222, 225, 238–40,
  243–44, 252–53, 257
  Don Giovanni (libretto, 1787) 91, 235–36
  Così fan tutte (libretto, 1790) 91–92
de Baïf, Jean-Antoine (1532–1589) 28
Debureau, Jean-Gaspard (1796–1846) 98
deceit in stage plots 5, 6–7, 19, 25, 71, 233, 241–54
decorum in drama (*see classiciste* rules)
de la Taille, Jean (c.1540–c.1607) 28
Del Buono, Luigi (1751–1832) 98
Delisle de la Drevetière, Louis François (1682–1756):
  Arlequin Sauvage (1721/1733?) 194 n. 19
  Timon le misanthrope (1722/1733?) 194 n. 19
Della Porta, Giovanni Battista (1535?–1615) 21, 222, 251
  La fantesca (pub. 1592) 251 n. 20
  La Cinzia (pub. 1601) 251 n. 20
del Monaco, Francesco Maria (1593–1651) 211
Deloffre, Frédéric 70
derision, comic 4, 20, 68, 159, 164, 229, 231, 235–40,
  241, 248–49, 263–64
Diderot, Denis (1713–1784) 92, 98, 128, 259, 261
  Discours sur la poésie dramatique (treatise, 1758) 92,
  128
  Paradoxe sur le comédien (treatise, c. 1770, pub. 1830)
  259
disguise/false identity 1, 6, 7, 19, 25, 62, 69–70, 76, 86,
  89, 91, 241–54
Docteur/Dottor Graziano (mask) 24–26, 34, 79, 131,
  133–34, 135, 142, 185–87, 189, 193–94, 200, 203,
  204–05, 229, 232, 249
Donatus, Aelius (4th century CE) 13–14, 21, 102,
  119 n. 6, 123, 127–28, 144–45, 160, 198
Donizetti, Gaetano (1797–1848) 97
Don Juan, *see* Tirso de Molina
Dovizi: *see* Bibbiena
drame bourgeois/sérieux 2, 70–71, 75–76, 85, 87, 91–94,
  98, 128, 191, 190, 253–54, 256, 259
Dufresny, Charles (1648?–1724) 60–61, 155, 190
  Le Double veuvage (1702) 61
  La Joueuse (1709) 190

eavesdropping on stage 123–25, 126–27,
'Echo' scenes 139
'elastic' dialogue routines 34, 135–39, 266–67
Ellis, Anthony 198
empathy 185, 191–94, 244, 246, 253–54, 259, 263–65
emplois (French role categories) 60, 184, 187, 217
Enlightenment philosophy 69, 71, 174–75, 224, 238

essentialism 212, 229–32, 236–40, 261
Este dynasty (Dukes of Ferrara) 16–19, 162
Estienne, Charles (1504–64) 19, 27, 157
    Comédie du sacrifice, later *Les Abusez* [from
        Gl'ingannati] (pub. 1540) 19, 27, 157
    Andria [translated from Terence] (pub. 1542) 27
Euripides (c. 480–c. 406 BCE) 148
Evanthius (4th century CE) 13–14, 128 n. 35

Fabri, Giovan Paolo (actor, 1567–1627) 109
'false' in play titles 248, 253
families divided, on stage 51, 163, 242–46
fantasy (essential component of comedy) 6, 197, 228,
    232, 238, 253–54, 256–58, 261
farce (as a definition) 102, 103 n. 2, 174, 210, 234
farce, French 25, 40, 105
Fatouville, Anne Maudit de (d. 1715) 60, 62, 63, 170–71
    La Matrone d'Éphèse (1682) 170
    Arlequin Protée (1683) 63, 65
    Arlequin Empereur dans la lune (1684) 56, 64, 231
    Arlequin Jason, ou la Toison d'Or comique (1684) 62,
        170–71
Federico, Gennaro Antonio (d. 1744):
    La serva padrona (libretto, 1733) 75
Ferguson, Ronnie 236 n. 15
Ferrara 16–19, 41, 113, 149–51, 161–62, 213
Ferrone, Siro 108, 132, 209 n. 7
Fêtes galantes 59
Feydeau, Georges (1862–1921) 98
'finto', *see* 'false'
Fiorillo, Silvio ('Pulcinella' and 'Capitan Mattamoros'
    on stage; fl. 1570–1632) 34
Fiorilli, Tiberio ('Scaramouche' on stage; 1608–94) 34,
    48–49, 179–80
Firenzuola, Agnolo (1493–1543):
    I Lucidi (1542/1549) 27
Florence 29, 35, 80, 117, 131–32, 151–52, 162,
    165 n. 13, 196, 197, 211, 213, 237
    dialect 97–98
Fo, Dario 132
Forestier, Georges 242 n. 1, 243
Fornaris, Fabrizio ('Capitan Coccodrillo' on stage; d.
    1637):
    L'Angelica (pub. 1585) 30
Fortune (in comic plots) 233, 241
Fossard, Receuil (collection of illustrations) 186
'fourth wall' 125–28, 145, 261
Franceschina (mask) 34, 131, 142, 186, 225, 235, 238
François I, King of France 27–28
French Revolution 1, 76, 82, 96, 119, 198
friendship (between stage characters) 175, 222–24
Funambules, Théâtre des 98

Gascoigne, George (1535–77):
    Supposes [from Ariosto's *Suppositi*] (1566/1573) 19, 231

Gaultier-Gargouille (Huges Guéru, d. 1633) 42
Gay, John (1685–1732):
    The Beggar's Opera, 1728: 73
Gelli, Giambattista (1498–1563):
    La sporta (1543) 205
Gelosi (troupe) 29, 30–32, 105, 131–32, 151–52, 165,
    211
Genoa 165 n. 13
Geratoni, Giuseppe ('Pierrot' on stage, fl. 1639–97) 186
Germany 94, 162
Gherardi, Evaristo ('Arlecchino' on stage; 1663–1700)
    54–57, 63, 67, 73, 85, 114, 169–71, 241
    Le Théâtre Italien (anthology, pub. 1694/1700) 54,
        59, 67, 73, 85, 114, 169–71
Giancarli, Gigio Artemio (d. 1561?) 128, 132
    La Zingana (pub. 1545) 132
Giannotti, Donato (1492–1573) 197, 225
    Il vecchio amoroso (c. 1533/1850) 197, 225
Gilles (mask) 186
Giraldi Cinthio, Giambattista (1504–1573) 128 n. 35
Gluck, Christoph Willibald (1714–87):
    Iphigénie en Aulide (opera, 1774) 75
Goethe, Johann Wolfgang von (1739–1832) 1, 94
Goldberg, Sander M. 159
Goldoni, Carlo (1707–93) 5, 7, 57, 63, 71, 76, 78–83,
    86, 88, 92–95, 102, 106–07, 115–16, 120, 123, 125,
    134–35, 139, 140–42, 143, 147, 155, 158, 166, 175–
    76, 180, 184, 187, 190, 193–94, 195, 198, 201, 204,
    206, 212, 220, 215–17, 221–24, 225, 228, 229–30,
    233–34, 246, 247, 248, 251–52, 257, 261–62, 264,
    267
    'Mondo' & 'Teatro' 81–82, 123, 261, 267
    L'Arcadia in Brenta (libretto, 1741) 102
    Momolo cortesan/L'uomo di mondo (1738/1757) 175
    Momolo sulla Brenta/Il prodigo (1739/1757) 175
    Il mercante fallito/La bancarotta (1741/1757) 139
    La donna di garbo (1743) 187, 216
    Il servitore di due padroni (1745/1753) 78–79, 107,
        140–42, 143, 155, 216, 228, 234, 247, 261–62
    Il frappatore (1745) 216
    I due gemelli Veneziani (1747) 139, 175, 187, 224, 246
    L'uomo prudente (1748) 190
    La vedova scaltra (1748) 187, 190
    Il teatro comico (1750) 78–79, 134, 166, 193–94, 195
    Il giuocatore (1751) 190
    Il vero amico (1751) 190
    La locandiera (1753) 80, 81, 115–16, 176, 217, 228
    La madre amorosa (1754) 206, 212
    La pupilla (1757) 95
    Gli innamorati (1759) 80, 175–76, 220
    La casa nova (1760) 80
    I rusteghi (1760) 80–81, 190, 201, 251–52
    'Villeggiatura' trilogy (1761) 80–82, 86, 125, 155, 204,
        215, 257
    La buona madre (1761) 206

Sior Todero brontolon (1762) 80–81, 190, 201, 264
Le baruffe chiozzotte (1762) 71, 80
L'amore paterno (1763) 192
Le Bourru bienfaisant (1771) 82, 190
L'Avare fastueux (1776) 82, 190
Mémoires (pub. 1787) 78, 82–84, 94
Goldsmith, Oliver (1728–1774) 2, 6, 218
    She Stoops to Conquer (1773) 6, 218
Gonzaga dynasty (Dukes of Mantua) 19, 35
Goulbourne, Russell 174
Gozzi, Carlo (1720–1806) 26, 82, 92–94, 134, 175, 180
    L'amore delle tre melarance (1761) 93
    Il corvo (1761) 93
    Turandot (1762) 93
    Memorie inutili (pub. 1797) 134
Grasso, Nicola (dates unknown):
    Eutychia (1513/1524) 178
Greece 162
Grene, Nicholas 123
Grévin, Jacques (1539–1570) 28
Gros-Guillaume (Robert Guérin, d. 1634) 42
Guez de Balzac, Jean-Louis 45, 47
Günsberg, Maggie 206, 216 n. 24, 233

Handel, Georg Frideric (1685–1759) 76, 89, 135
    Radamisto (opera, 1720) 89
happy ending 3–4, 6, 81–82, 109, 232–33
Harlequin (Arlecchino, Arlequin, mask) 8, 24, 29–30, 34, 36, 41, 61, 63–66, 67–70, 79, 81, 93, 96, 106, 108, 112, 113–15, 132, 139, 142, 165, 169–70, 172–73, 180, 185–87, 189, 191, 225, 229, 232–33, 234, 235, 238, 249, 251, 261–62, 263
    see also: Biancolelli; Gherardi; Martinelli; Soleri; Visentini
Haydn, Joseph (1732–1809) 76
Henke, Robert 133, 179
Henri II, King of France 27, 207–08
Henri IV, King of France 30, 31
'high' and 'low' comedy 14–15, 101–07, 119, 180, 253, 255–69
Hobbes, Thomas (1588–1679) 111 n. 30
Homer 258
Horace (Quintus Horatius Flaccus, 65–8 BCE) 14–15, 18, 21, 43, 44, 45, 94, 108, 111, 118–19, 144–58, 183, 198, 258, 262, 267
Houdar de la Motte, Antoine (1672–1731):
    Les Originaux, ou l'Italien (1693) 217 n. 25
Howarth, W.D. 3, 4–5, 102 n. 5, 252 n. 22
Hugo, Victor (1802–85) 96–97
Hytner, Nicholas (stage director) 253 n. 23

improvisation 25, 62, 68–69, 125, 129–43,
indoor settings 18, 151–55, 216–17
Ingegneri, Angelo (1550–1613) 104, 119, 121, 152, 177, 180, 214

innamorati (Lovers; stage role category) 4–5, 7, 24–25, 34, 50, 60, 61, 68, 74, 112, 114, 131, 132, 135–36, 157–58, 164, 170, 179, 184, 186, 190, 195–206, 249, 260, 263–64
inner emotions, *see* empathy
interludes/*intermezzi* (performed, between acts) 119, 152–52, 208
Intronati, *see* Accademia
Isabelle (French mask) 61 203

Jones, Suzanne 121, 242
Jonson, Ben (1572–1637) 2, 7, 118
Jodelet (Julien Bedeau, 1591–1660) 42, 186
Jodelle, Étienne (1532–73) 27
    Eugène (1552/1574) 27
Jordan, Peter 198
Joseph II, Holy Roman Emperor 88, 239
Juvenal (Decimus Junius Juvenalis, 1st century CE) 159

Katritzky, M.A. 186 n. 12
Kaut-Howson, Helena (theatre director) 252 n. 22

L'Angelier, Abel (printer) 30
La Bruyère, Jean de (1645–96) 181
Laiena, Serena 209 n. 10, 211 n. 13
Larivey, Pierre (1549–1619) 29
    Six Premières Comédies (anthology, pub. 1579) 29
    Trois Comédies (anthology, pub. 1611) 29
laughter, analysis of 107–16, 256–59
lazzi (inserted jokes and routines) 260–61
Lecoq, Jacques (1921–99) 188
legal systems satirized 169–71, 238
Leoncavallo, Ruggero (1857–1919):
    I pagliacci (opera, 1892) 98, 226
Lesage, Alain-René (1668–1747):
    Turcaret (1709) 60, 172, 267
Lessing, Gotthold Ephraim (1729–81) 259
    Hamburgische Dramaturgie (essays, 1767–69) 259
Leszczynska, Marie, Queen of France 75
libri generici, *see* actors' repertoire
Livorno 81
Locatelli, Basilio (c.1591-before 1654):
    Della scena de' soggetti comici (scenario collection, mss dated 1628 and 1632) 34, 248
Lope de Vega (1562–1635):
    Arte nuevo de hacer comedias (treatise, pub. 1609) 40, 145
Louis XIII, King of France 38, 44, 45, 105, 106
Louis XIV, King of France 38–39, 48–51, 53–54, 57, 58, 62, 168, 171, 172
Louis XV, King of France 57, 75
Louis XVI, King of France 84, 174
love (expressed on stage) 219–22, 250
Lully, Jean-Baptiste (1632–87) 50, 73, 76
Lyon 27, 29, 207–08, 209, 213

Machiavelli, Niccolò (1469–1527) 19, 20, 118 n. 3,
    144, 147–48, 196, 197–98, 212–13, 220, 232, 255,
    256–57, 263
  La mandragola (c. 1518/1521) 19, 20, 118 n. 3, 144,
    147, 197–98, 220, 256–57, 263
  Clizia (1525/1537) 19, 196, 212–13
'mad scenes' 113, 132, 214, 260
madrigal opera 74
Maggi, Carlo Maria (1630–1699) 35
Magnifico (mask) *see* Pantalone
Maintenon, Madame de 39, 54
Manes, Yael 205 n. 12
Mango, Achille 183 n. 8, 251
Mantua 16, 19, 35 165 n. 13, 208
Manzoni, Alessandro (1785–1873) 97
Marie Antoinette, Queen of France 87–88
Marivaux (Pierre Carlet de Chamblain, 1688–1763) 2,
    5, 7, 41–42, 60, 67–72, 98, 106, 120, 123, 125, 134,
    139, 147, 155, 158, 173, 180, 184, 187, 191–93, 200,
    203, 206, 216, 217, 219, 221–22, 223, 225, 229,
    231–32, 238, 243, 257, 264, 267
  Arlequin poli par l'amour (1720) 67, 69
  La Double inconstance (1723) 69, 173, 191–93, 229,
    238, 264
  La Fausse Suivante (1724 5) 5, 68, 216
  Le Prince travesti (1724) 173 n. 27
  L'Île des esclaves (1725) 173, 238
  L'Île de la raison (1727) 173
  La Colonie (1729/1750) 173
  Le Jeu de l'amour et du hasard (1730) 69–70, 173,
    231–32, 238, 264
  Les Serments indiscrets (1732) 120 n. 10
  Les Fausses confidences (1737) 71
marriage in stage plots 19–20, 25, 60–61, 157–58, 164,
    199, 218, 224–26
Martinelli, Tristano ('Arlecchino' on stage, c.1555–1630)
    29–30, 31, 35
masks (facial) 177–80, 245
masks (fixed characters) 177–94
Mazarin, Cardinal (Giulio Raimondo Mazzarino,
    1602–61) 39, 53, 211
Mazouer, Charles 242
Medebach, Teodora ('Rosaura' on stage, 18th century,
    dates unknown) 187
Medici, Alessandro de', Duke of Florence 165, 197–98
Medici, Caterina de', Queen of France 27, 29, 207–08
Medici, Cosimo I de', Grand Duke of Tuscany 197
Medici dynasty (Florence) 197–98
Medici, Ferdinando I de', Grand Duke of Tuscany
    131–32, 165, 237
Medici, Lorenzino de' (1514–48) 145 n. 5, 197–98,
    201, 221
  Aridosia (1536/1548) 145 n. 5, 197–98, 201, 221
Medici, Maria de', Queen of France 30, 31
Menander (c.342-c. 290 BCE) frontispiece; 14, 102, 145,
    159–60, 181

Meneghino (mask) 35
Mercier, Louis-Sébastien (1740–1814) 96
Meredith, George (1828–1909) 119 n. 6
Mesnadière, Hippolyte-Jules de la 45
Metastasio, Pietro (1698–1782) 74, 76, 135
Mezzettino (mask) 62
Milan 35, 80, 141 n. 25, 165 n. 13, 175
  dialect 35
mirroring of scenes 139–43
Modena 21, 162
modular dramaturgy 131–57, 183
Molière (Jean-Baptiste Poquelin, 1622–73) 7, 19, 35,
    36, 41, 42, 48–52, 53, 58, 60, 68, 78, 98, 102–03,
    106, 113, 119, 123, 124, 125, 127, 133–34, 138–39,
    147, 152–53, 160, 167–69, 170–71, 179–81, 184, 187,
    188, 190–91, 200–01, 203, 204, 205, 206, 211–12,
    217–18, 220, 221, 223, 225, 228, 229, 233–34, 238,
    243, 247, 248, 257, 263, 264, 265–69
  Le Médecin volant (1645/1819) 48–50
  La Jalousie du Barbouillé (c. 1650/1819) 48–50,
    133–34
  Le Dépit amoureux (1656) 220
  Les Précieuses ridicules (1659) 42
  Dom Garcie de Navarre (1661) 36
  L'École des maris (1661) 201, 204
  L'École des femmes (1662) 86, 106, 167, 201, 204
  La Critique de l'École des femmes (1663) 102, 106, 168
  L'Impromptu de Versailles (1663) 168
  Le Tartuffe (1664/1669) 50, 124, 138, 152, 160, 168,
    201, 203, 206, 217, 225, 233–34, 248
  Dom Juan (1665) 168
  Le Misanthrope (1666) 2, 5, 51, 68, 103, 152, 217,
    265–67
  Le Médecin malgré lui (1666) 50, 103, 138
  Amphitryon (1668) 51, 247
  George Dandin (1668) 50, 188
  L'Avare (1668) 51, 127, 132, 134, 138, 154, 191, 201,
    205, 206, 228, 233, 243, 247, 263, 269
  Le Bourgeois gentilhomme (1670) 201, 206, 220,
    233–34, 257
  Les Fourberies de Scapin (1671) 51, 103, 170, 229,
    265–67
  Les Femmes savantes (1672) 50, 152, 168, 206,
    217–18, 225
  Le Malade imaginaire (1673) 153, 169, 190, 201, 206,
    233
Momus (Roman god of mockery) 63
monologues: *see* soliloquies
Monteverdi, Claudio (1567–1643) 36, 74
  L'incoronazione di Poppea (opera, 1643) 74
Moore, W.G. xvi, 112, 167 n. 17
moral purpose of comedy 107–16, 232, 248, 255–56,
    260–61
Mozart, Wolfgang Amadeus (1756–1791) 1, 8, 72, 76,
    77, 88–89, 91–92, 97, 124–25, 135, 206, 219, 222,
    225, 235–36, 238–40, 243–44, 248, 252–53

La finta semplice (1768) 248
Die Entführung aus dem Serail (1782) 97, 243
Le nozze di Figaro (1786) 1, 8, 88–89, 91, 124–25, 206, 219, 222, 225, 238–40, 243–44, 252–53
Don Giovanni (1787) 91, 235–36
Cosí fan tutte (1790) 91–92
Musset, Alfred de (1810–57) 97
Myra, Turkey 178

Naples 75–76 165, 189, 265
dialect 24, 50
New Comedy, Athenian 14, 101–02, 145, 160, 181
New Orleans 88
Nolfi, Ludovico 188 n. 13

Oddi, Sforza (1540–1611):
Erofilomachia (1572) 157, 222
Offenbach, Jacques (1819–80) 98
Opéra (Paris) 62–63, 73–74, 75
opera, comic (*opera buffa; opéra comique*, etc.) 73–77, 91–92, 139, 157, 174, 248, 253
opera seria 73, 74, 76–77, 87, 97, 123, 152, 241
Ottoman empire 163, 243
Ottonelli, Gian Domenico (1584–1670) 211

Padua 162, 165 n. 13
dialect 162
Paisiello, Giovanni (1740–1816):
Il barbiere di Siviglia (opera, 1782) 88
Palaprat, Jean de (1650–1721):
La Fille de bon sens (1692) 63, 114–15, 261
Pantalone (mask) 7, 29, 34, 41, 74, 77–80, 86, 93, 103 n. 7, 124, 131, 132–33, 135–37, 141–42, 175, 179, 184–87, 189, 193–94, 195–97, 198, 203, 204, 205, 229, 232, 248, 262, 263
parades 71, 106
Parma 165 n. 13
parasites (characters in comedy) 112
Paris 29, 35, 37, 38–42, 48–66, 74, 75–76, 82–83, 93, 98, 105, 113, 119, 167–74, 180, 189, 211–12, 238, 245, 249, 268
see also Comédie-Française; Théâtre-Italien
Paris Fairs 54–57, 60, 71, 77, 172
pastoral drama 20–21, 24–25, 35, 61–62, 139, 151–52, 214
Paul Scarron, Paul (1610–60) 42, 85
Jodelet, ou Le Maître Valet (1643) 42
La Précaution inutile (short story, pub. 1655) 85
Pavoni, Giuseppe (chronicler, c. 1551–1641) 131–32
Pedrolino (mask) 74, 113, 124, 142, 165, 185–86, 189, 225, 232
Peletier, Jacques (1517–1582) 27, 44
Pellegrino da Udine (1467–1547) 149–51
Pellesini, Giovanni ('Pedrolino' on stage, 1526-c. 1615) 186
performer, audience response to 112–16, 122, 128, 202, 242, 258–60, 262, 265–67

Pergolesi, Giovanni Battista (1710–36):
La serva padrona (opera, 1733) 75
Perugia 165 n. 13
Pesaro 165 n. 13
Philippe of Orléans (Regent of France) 57–58, 62 171
Piccolomini, Alessandro (1508–78) 181–84
La sfera del mondo [treatise] (1561–64) 181–84
see also Accademia degli Intronati
Pierrot (mask) 62, 98, 179, 186, 249
Piissimi, Vittoria (actress, fl. 1573–95) 131–32, 211
Pino da Cagli, Bernardino (c. 1525–1601) 109–10, 112, 200
Breve considerazione… (treatise, pub. 1553) 109–10, 112
Piperno, Franco 248
Pisa 152, 162–63
Plautus (c. 254–c. 184 BCE) 3, 7, 10, 13–15, 16–21, 27, 41, 42, 43, 47, 48, 51, 69, 86, 102, 117–28, 144–58, 160–62, 173, 181, 196, 197, 199, 205, 213, 227, 229, 231, 232, 234, 243, 244–45, 246, 247, 252, 255, 267
Amphitruo 20, 51, 247
Aulularia 126–27, 205
Bacchides 244
Captivi 42, 69, 243
Casina 196, 213, 243
Epidicus 243
Menaechmi 7, 47, 121–22, 125, 244–45
Mercator 196
Miles gloriosus 124, 213
Pseudolus 126, 197 n. 5, 229, 246, 252
poissades 71
Poisson, Raymond & Paul ('Crispin' on stage) 60, 187
Pomeau, René 60, 88
prologues 61, 121–22, 144–45, 231
prose, as medium for comedies 18–19, 28, 51, 68
Proteus (marine god) 63, 65, 249
'Publio Philippo Mantovano' (pseudonym of anonymous playwright):
Formicone (1503/1524) 16
Punch (English puppet character) 34, 35, 263

Querelle des bouffons 75

Racine, Jean (1639–99) 123, 211, 242
Rapin, Père René 45
Receuil Fossard (collection of illustrations) 186
Regnard, Jean-François (1655–1709) 60, 61, 86, 155, 190, 204, 234, 245
Le Divorce (1688) 61
Le Joueur (1696) 190
Les Folies amoureuses (1704) 86, 204, 234
Les Ménechmes (1705) 245
repertoire speeches, recyclable 129–36, 183, 205, 220, 260
repetitions on stage 139–43
Restoration Comedy, English 188, 219
Ricciolina (mask) 130–31

Riccoboni, Luigi ('Lelio' on stage; 1676–1753) 36–37, 57, 63, 67, 78, 94–95, 106–07, 120, 155, 203–04, 216, 223–24, 229, 234, 260–61
   Six manuscript scenarios 36, 107, 120 n. 11, 203, 216, 223–24, 234
   Nouveau Théâtre Italien (1716) 67
Richardson, Samuel (1689–1761) 2
Richelieu, Cardinal de (Armand Jean du Plessis, 1585–1642) 39, 45–46, 106, 167, 200
Romanticism 1, 96–98
Rome 16, 34, 105, 145, 163, 165
Rossi, Bartolommeo (dates unknown):
   La Fiammella (pub. 1584) 30
Rossini, Gioacchino (1792–1868) 8, 86, 97, 218
   L'italiana in Algeri (opera, 1813) 243
   Il barbiere di Siviglia (opera, 1816) 8, 86, 97, 218
   La Cenerentola (opera, 1817) 8, 97
   Guillaume Tell (opera, 1829) 97
Rotrou, Jean de (1609–50):
   Les Ménechmes (1632/1636) 245
Rousseau, Jean-Jacques (1712–78) 75
Rushton, Julian 77
Ruzante (Angelo Beolco; c. 1502–1542) 128, 145 n. 5, 147, 236–37, 238, 247, 255
   La moscheta (1529/1551) 147, 247
   La vaccaria (1533/1551) 145 n. 5, 236–37

Sacchi, Antonio, (actor, 1708–88) 92–93, 180, 261–62
sacre rappresentazioni 122
Salieri, Antonio (composer, 1750–1825) 91
Sand, Maurice 188
Santeul, Jean-Baptiste de (1630–97) 108
Saturnalia 6, 112
Saulini, Mirella 217–18
Scala, Flaminio ('Flavio' on stage; 1547–1624)
   Il teatro delle favole rappresentative (scenario collection, pub. 1611) 33–34, 93, 127, 141–42, 147, 157, 165–66, 185, 186, 189, 214, 216, 217, 223, 245–46, 248, 250, 260, 263–64
   Day 1: *Li duo vecchi gemelli* 245
   Day 16: *Lo specchio* 142
   Day 17: *Li duo Capitani simili* 245
   Day 18: *Li tragici successi* 189
   Day 25: *La gelosa Isabella* 245
   Day 29: *Il fido amico* 124
   Day 31: *Il pedante* 124
   Day 34 *Il finto cieco* 223
   Day 37: *La caccia* 141
   Day 38: *La pazzia di Isabella* 132, 214 n. 21
   Day 41: *La forsennata principessa* 214 n. 21
Scaliger, Julius Caesare (Giulio Cesare della Scala, 1484–1558) 21, 45, 148
Scaramouche/Scaramuccia (mask) 24, 34, 48–49, 179–80, 249
Scarron, Paul (1610–60) 42, 85
   Jodelet, ou Le Maître valet (1643) 42
   La Précaution inutile (short story, pub. 1655) 85

scenarios/*canovacci* 8–9, 25–26, 50, 118 n. 4, 119, 133, 165–66, 201, 216, 220–21, 222, 233, 238, 244–45, 246–47, 251, 253, 267
scene divisions and numbering 118–21
scenography 18, 121, 148–55
Schiller, Friedrich (1759–1805) 94
Schmitt, Natalie Crohn 188 n. 15
Scott, Virginia 171
Sébillet, Thomas (1512–1589) 27
Seneca, Lucius Annaeus (4 BCE–65 CE) 118–19, 122–23
sensibilité 70–71, 223, 234
Seragnoli, Daniele 182
Serlio, Sebastiano (1475–1554) 150–51
servi (Servants; stage role category) 4–5, 40, 46, 50, 60, 61, 86, 93, 112, 132–33, 135–38, 164, 179, 184, 190, 227–40
sexual activity (explicit allusions to) 103–04, 204, 221–22, 225, 229, 251–52
Sganarelle (mask of Molière) 187, 234, 247
Shakespeare, William (1564–1616) 7, 18, 21, 44, 133, 135, 139, 146, 163, 164, 176, 189, 202, 213, 219–20, 229–30, 231, 244–46, 247–48, 249–50, 256, 267
   As You Like It 7, 249–50
   Comedy of Errors 7, 139, 244–46, 247
   Hamlet 176, 256
   Henry IV, Part 1 133
   Merchant of Venice 7, 135
   Merry Wives of Windsor 7, 133, 247–48
   Midsummer Night's Dream 7
   Much Ado About Nothing 21, 163, 202
   Pericles 146
   Romeo and Juliet 18, 164, 189, 219–20, 229–30
   Taming of the Shrew 231, 247
   Twelfth Night 20, 213, 244–46, 250
   Winter's Tale 44, 146, 230
Shapiro, James 191 n. 17
Sheridan, Richard Brinsley (1751–1816) 2, 6, 218
   The Rivals (1775) 6, 218
Sidney, Sir Philip (1554–1586) 111 n. 30
Siena (*see also* Accademia degli Intronati) 119 n. 6, 181–84
Silvia (mask) *see* Balletti
slapstick violence on stage 103, 228
Smeraldina (mask) 93
Soleri, Ferruccio ('Arlecchino' on stage, b. 1929) 188 n. 14
soliloquies 25, 126–28, 131–35, 141, 259
Sophocles (c. 497–c. 406 BCE) 117, 119, 149. 178, 241, 258
   Antigone 258
   Oedipus at Colonus 149
   Oedipus tyrannus 178, 241, 258
soubrette role 46, 61, 179, 217, 253
Spanish language on Italian stage 24
Spanish theatre, influences of 2, 36, 40–41, 119 n. 6
Speroni, Sperone (1500–1588) 128 n. 35
stage directions 121–22

Steele, Richard (1672–1729) 70, 108 n. 5
Stenterello (mask) 35, 98
Sterbini, Cesare (1784–1831) 86
    Il barbiere di Siviglia (libretto, 1816) 86
Strehler, Giorgio (theatre director, 1921–1997) 141 n. 25

Taille, Jean de la 28
Tartaglia (mask) 93
Tasso, Torquato (1544–95):
    Aminta (1573/1580; French version 1584) 30
Terence (Terentius; c. 195-c. 159 BCE) 3, 10, 12, 13–15, 16–21, 27, 45, 47, 48, 51, 92, 102, 108 n. 5, 117–28, 144–58, 160–61, 181, 197 n. 5, 199, 201, 205, 221, 229, 243, 251, 266, 267
    Adelphoe 201, 205
    Andria 12, 92, 221, 243
    Eunuchus 120, 128, 243, 251
    Heautontimorumenos 108 n. 5
    Hecyra 243
    Phormio 51, 125, 197 n. 5, 266
Tertullian (Quintus Septimus Florens Tertullianus, c. 155–c. 220 CE) 117
Théâtre-Italien 2, 39, 53–66, 69–70, 75, 82, 108, 119, 122, 134, 155, 169–71, 173, 180, 186, 187, 188, 191, 198, 203, 212, 221, 225–26, 231, 233, 238, 242, 251, 255, 267
Theophrastus (c. 371–287 BCE) 180–81, 184
Thomas, Keith 111 n. 30
Tirso de Molina (1579–1648):
    El burlador de Sevilla y convidado de piedra (c. 1620/c. 1630) 91, 235
tragedy 1, 13, 24, 35–36, 61–62, 92, 119, 122–23, 126, 145–46, 148–49, 151–52, 156, 203, 214, 241, 263
tragicomedy 4, 20–21, 241
Trissino, Giangiorgio (1478–1550):
    Sofonisba (1515) 178
Trivelin (mask) 67, 106, 234
Truffaldino (mask) 66, 93, 107, 141–42, 180, 234, 261–62
Turlupin (Belleville, dates uncertain) 42
Turner, Victor 199 n. 7
Turnèbe, Odet de (1552–81) 28, 29
    Les Contens (pub. 1584) 29
twins on stage 139, 244–46

Uniti (troupe) 30
Unities, see classiciste rules
Urbino 145

Vadé, Jean-Joseph (1720–57) 71
Vanbrugh, John (1664–1726) 109, 115, 159
vaudevilles 73, 85
vecchi (Elders, stage role category) 4–5, 7, 50–51, 61, 68, 80, 112, 135–38, 157, 164, 179, 284, 195–206, 227–40
Vecchi, Orazio (1550–1605):
    Anfiparnaso ('madrigal comedy', pub. 1597) 74
Venice 23, 35, 36–37, 76, 78–83, 92–94, 96, 128, 133, 136, 137, 140, 162–63, 165 n. 13, 175–76, 189, 198, 229, 248, 262
    dialect 24, 80–81, 136, 140, 162, 174–76, 189, 198
Verdi, Giuseppe (1813–1901) 97, 222
    Aïda (opera, 1871) 222
verisimilitude/vraisemblance, see classiciste rules
verse, as medium for comedies 16, 19, 41, 51, 68, 95, 118, 123, 223, 245
Verucci, Virgilio (c. 1585-c. 1650) 34–35, 138
    Li diversi linguaggi (pub. 1609) 34, 138
Vicenza 178
Vilar, Jean 203 n. 10
virtuosity of performers 112–16, 122, 128, 242, 258
Visentini, Tommaso ('Arlequin' on stage, 1682–1739) 57, 63–66, 67, 69–70, 71, 191–92, 234
Vitruvius 151
Voltaire (François-Marie Arouet; 1694–1778) 71, 92, 94, 122, 155, 171–72, 190
    L'Envieux (1738) 122
    L'Indiscret (1725) 190
    La Prude (1739) 2, 190
    Socrate (pub. 1759) 171
    Le Droit du Seigneur (1760) 171
    Saül (pub. 1762) 171
vulgarity on stage 102–07, 255–56

Watteau, Jean-Antoine (1684–1721) 54–55, 59, 186
Wilson, Ronald A. 203 n. 10
West, Timothy (actor) 126 n. 28
Wycherley, William (1641–1716) 2
    The Plain Dealer (1676) 2
women performers, see actresses

Zan Ganassa (Alberto Naseli, actor, 1540?-1584) 29
Zani (mask) 24, 29, 34, 63, 105, 113, 131, 133, 136–38, 165, 184, 186, 229, 235, 238
Zeno, Apostolo (1669–1750) 74
zibaldoni, see repertoire speeches

www.ingramcontent.com/pod-product-compliance
Lightning Source LLC
Chambersburg PA
CBHW080439170426
43195CB00017B/2819